DISABILITIES OF THE COLOR LINE

Disabilities of the Color Line

Redressing Antiblackness from Slavery to the Present

Dennis Tyler

NEW YORK UNIVERSITY PRESS
New York

NEW YORK UNIVERSITY PRESS
New York
www.nyupress.org

References to Internet websites (URLs) were accurate at the time of writing. Neither the author nor New York University Press is responsible for URLs that may have expired or changed since the manuscript was prepared.

Library of Congress Cataloging-in-Publication Data
Names: Tyler, Dennis, author.
Title: Disabilities of the color line : redressing antiblackness from slavery to the present / Dennis Tyler.
Description: New York : New York University Press, [2022] | Includes bibliographical references.
Identifiers: LCCN 2021013994 | ISBN 9781479805846 (hardback ; alk. paper) | ISBN 9781479831128 (paperback ; alk. paper) | ISBN 9781479821853 (ebook) | ISBN 9781479817344 (ebook other)
Subjects: LCSH: African Americans—History. | Racism—United States—History. | Slavery—United States—History. | Disabilities—United States—History. | Sociology of disability—United States—History.
Classification: LCC E185 .T95 2021 | DDC 973/.0496073—dc23
LC record available at https://lccn.loc.gov/2021013994

New York University Press books are printed on acid-free paper, and their binding materials are chosen for strength and durability. We strive to use environmentally responsible suppliers and materials to the greatest extent possible in publishing our books.

Manufactured in the United States of America

10 9 8 7 6 5 4 3 2 1

Also available as an ebook

To my parents,

who taught me the importance of perseverance

CONTENTS

PROLOGUE

The color line was a problem of the nineteenth century, a disabling one that would persist into the twenty-first century.[1]

You could read about the disabilities of the color line in antebellum slave narratives, which reveal how fugitives from slavery were punished with disablement or disfigurement, including amputations, severed hamstrings, or brands on the flesh. You could find them in the testimonies of the formerly enslaved, who detailed how the purported crime of attempted literacy could result in a dismembered forefinger or a lacerated back. They are evident in the bodily assaults against Black people who had ventured to cross (or were presumed to have crossed) the color line during Jim Crow. This list included those who moved into spaces marked "For Whites Only"; who, during interstate travel, sat resolutely in the first-class train seats that they had purchased; who consorted, married, or had consensual sex with white people (especially white women); who refused to move to the back of the bus; or who merely took up more space than the law allowed. In the age of color blindness, a period that spans from the nineteenth century to the present, you can observe the disabilities of the color line in the ongoing racial injuries inflicted on Black people—in particular, anti-Black vigilantism, police brutality, and insufficient health care—that often go disregarded due to an ableist performance of disability, a feigned inability of many Americans to recognize or perceive racial differences and racism. Such disabilities can be found in texts that depict all Black bodies, minds, and blood as inherently defective or diseased. They reside in narratives that dispute a Black person's capacity for citizenship, suffrage, and other essential rights. You can locate them almost anywhere that Black lives have been disprized and oppressed, almost any place that Black lives have been determined not to matter. You need to know only where to search, what to examine, and how to interpret the findings once you dare to look.

A political abolitionist, author, and orator par excellence, Frederick Douglass was among the first who dared to describe the color line's continuity between the antebellum and postbellum periods in terms of its varied disabilities. In June 1881, almost sixteen years after the ratification of the Thirteenth Amendment that formally abolished slavery and nearly fifteen years before the US Supreme Court's decision of *Plessy v. Ferguson* (1896) upheld the separate-but-equal doctrine, Douglass fashioned a deft account of such continuity in his essay "The Color Line," published in the *North American Review*. "To explain all the malign influences which assail the newly emancipated millions to-day," Douglass returned to the recent past. He wrote, "Out of the depths of slavery has come this prejudice and this color line. . . . Slavery is indeed gone, but its shadow still lingers over the country and poisons more or less the moral atmosphere of all sections of the republic."[2] The way Douglass saw it, slavery cast a mulish shadow, for it also poisoned the nation with the prejudicial color line during the initial period of emancipation.

Douglass primed his descriptions of color prejudice and the color line with metaphors related to disability and ethics, figuring white Americans as the primary agents of both forms of discrimination. He depicted color prejudice as "a moral disorder," described the color line as "a moral disease" contaminating "an infected country," and portrayed white people's general character as ingrained with color prejudice that regulates the color line. "It is claimed," he noted, "that this wonder-working prejudice . . . is a natural, instinctive, and invincible attribute of the white race, and one that cannot be eradicated; that even evolution itself cannot carry us beyond or above it." Douglass's passive voice obscures the author of this claim, but his criticism was an attack on white Americans nevertheless. It ascribed their prejudice to their essence, and it rendered their essence as symbolic of a disorder. For a man with a reputation for placating the white abolitionists who supported him, Douglass's blanket assault on white people was a risky, calculated move. It was a scathing indictment of white folks' "color-line feeling," a "diseased imagination" that acted as "judge, jury, and prosecutor" of nonwhite people.[3]

This assessment was also highly rhetorical. Douglass spent the better part of his essay disputing the notion that color prejudice was an endemic trait of white people. While he maintained that white supremacy was a disorder and as pernicious to white Americans who upheld the color line as it was to Black folks who were disciplined by it, he contested the idea of racial prejudice as born of something natural.[4] In fact, he sketched a seven-point proposal on the subject, and each time he raised the possibility of racism as an intrinsic attribute of white people, he later dismissed that point as fundamentally unsound. Ultimately, he concluded that there was no merit to the claim.

Douglass's rhetorical gesture, however, served an ulterior motive: if the portrayals of white people's innate moral disease were determined to be summarily false, then, by extension, so too were the depictions of *all* Black people as inherently disabled. In his essay, Douglass accounted for the long-standing fictions regarding the innate defects of all Black folks during the periods of slavery, Reconstruction, and Jim Crow in the United States. He did not definitively name the numerous statesmen, laws, and laypeople that publicized these fictions because he did not have to. They were ubiquitous. Such claims could be found in, say, the US Supreme Court majority opinion of *Dred Scott v. Sandford* (1857), which stated that Black people are not "entitled to all the rights, and privileges, and immunities, guarantied by [the Constitution] to the citizen" because a presumed lifelong "stigma, of the deepest degradation, was fixed upon the whole race."[5] What Douglass did provide in his essay was an overview of how Black people have been variously depicted as "fit only for slavery," "weak in intellect," "incapable of learning," "destitute of manhood," "companion of horses and mules," "too ignorant and stupid properly to exercise the elective franchise," "originally and permanently inferior to the white race," and contagious given how white Americans "[shrank] back in horror from contact with the negro as a man."[6]

These fictions of Black people were a litany of complaints broadcast on a repetitive loop; each claim compounded the others. Their purpose was to maintain white supremacy and dominion by stigmatizing Black people as unfit for freedom, intellectually stunted, and highly communicable, and there was hardly any place in the United States where Black folks could turn without encountering this stigma head-on. Douglass declared, "In nearly every department of American life they [Black people] are confronted by this insidious influence. It fills the air. It meets them at the workshop and factory, when they apply for work. It meets them at the church, at the hotel, at the ballot-box, and worst of all, it meets them in the jury-box."[7] In all of these spaces, the most treasured, prized possessions—the right to health, to work, to worship, to shelter, to vote, to have a speedy and fair trial—were either denied or regulated by the perilous color line. It restricted where Black people could go, how they could move, what they could do, and whom they could mingle with, and its toxicity and pervasiveness produced a suffocating effect. As Douglass observed, the color line reconfigured both space and weather—poisoning the atmosphere and polluting the air that Black folks breathed.[8]

To misconstrue Douglass's remarks about the color line as merely a rejection of disability or of disabled people would be a mistake. Such an error would miss how his work (and that of other Black writers and activists) affirms disability as a part of Black social life—despite how the discourse and production of disability historically have been used against Black people to implement pain and punishment, disdain and discrimination. Even as Douglass renounced the idea that all Black people are innately disabled, he did not deny their physical and psychological disabilities. He took care to make a distinction between inflicted and congenital disabilities. "The greatest injury this side of death, which one human being can inflict on another, is to enslave him, to blot out his personality, degrade his manhood, and sink him to the condition of a beast of burden; and just this has been done here during more than two centuries," Douglass wrote. Moreover, he recorded "the long years of wrong and injury inflicted upon the colored race in this country, and the effect of these wrongs upon that race, morally, intellectually, and physically."[9] Here was evidence of Douglass's primary aim: to forge an affinity between disability and disablement in Black life—between a condition, injury, or restriction and between the process by which Black people are rendered disabled or injured through acts of violence perpetrated by anti-Black regimes. Douglass, who was born in February 1818 and died the same month in 1895, had a particular vantage point of such disabilities across slavery, Reconstruction, and Jim Crow, for both his life and body of work, which spanned from the 1840s to the 1890s, overlapped with each of these eras.[10] Throughout the long arc of his life and career, his view of ability and disability shifted dramatically. While the younger Douglass, in 1848, misguidedly thought it was necessary for individuals to prove their capacity for rights, the older Douglass, in 1881, reframed disablement as proof of rights denied, owning disability in a way that gestures toward the kind of cross-movement work that could beget liberation.[11]

With Douglass's focus on the metaphorical and material properties of the pre- and post–Civil War color line as well as his distinction between inherent and imposed disabilities, he captures the chief concerns of this book. *Disabilities of the Color Line* explores how Black people from the antebellum period to the present have been cast as disabled—as unfit for freedom, incapable of self-governance, or contagious within the national body politic. Such casting has been frequently resisted within the Black literary tradition through metaphorical reversals like Douglass's, where the color line (or racism and antiblackness) is instead the disability, disorder, or disease that demands careful scrutiny. Yet the key contribution of *Disabilities of the Color Line* lies in an important observation that is overlooked in Black studies and disability studies. Rather than simply engaging in a prevailing narrative of overcoming, in which both disability and disablement are shunned alike, Black authors and activists have consistently avowed disability in varied, complex, and contradictory ways.[12] Sometimes their affirmation of disability serves to clarify their own experience of racial injury, to represent how the bodies, minds, and health of Black people have been made vulnerable to harm and impairment by the state and anti-Black vigilantes. Sometimes their assertion of disability symbolizes a sense of community and commonality that comes not only from a recognition of the shared subjection of blackness and disability but also from a willingness to imagine and engender a world distinct from the dominant social order that devalues certain bodies and minds over others. Theirs, then, could be understood as an expression of *interability compassion*: a compassion of people with mixed abilities that is rooted in a practice of care and the twin pursuit of racial and disability justice.[13] Douglass's writing represents an early example of this public avowal of disability—though the import and influence of his take on the color line are often neglected, given that most scholars cite W. E. B. Du Bois, not Douglass, in their examinations of the color line.

Nevertheless, Douglass's words have resounded beyond the nineteenth century. If we listen closely to the commentary of Black activists in the twenty-first century, we hear echoes of Douglass's words within their remarks about the injuriousness of slavery, systemic racism, police brutality, and inequitable access to health care and education—all examples of what I call the *disabilities of the color line.* By that phrase, which I develop throughout this book, I mean to capture the historical and ongoing anti-Black systems of division that maim, immobilize, stigmatize, and traumatize Black people in a manner that advances or sustains white supremacy and white privilege.

Take, for instance, the comments of the activist and educator Brittany Packnett Cunningham, formerly an appointed member of President Obama's Task Force on 21st Century Policing and of the Ferguson Commission, an independent group appointed by Missouri governor Jay Nixon to address the social and economic conditions in St. Louis that propelled the protests in the aftermath of Michael Brown Jr.'s death. Cunningham, in 2020, cautioned viewers of *AM Joy*, a political weekend show that aired on MSNBC, not to allow the looters or the anarchy of white-supremacist groups who infiltrated the protests in Minneapolis, Minnesota, to derail a vital conversation about defunding law enforcement in the wake of George Floyd's death:

> This country sits on looted land and was built with looted labor, and it loots Black life every day. Now that is not to excuse the white supremacists and the other forces that are coming in to take advantage of protests that are all about . . . systemic racism and ending systemic racism. But what is true is that what would set all of this to calm and actually to peace is to deal with the conditions that caused people to react in the first place instead of spending all of this time on the symptoms. People are frankly tired of America dealing with the symptoms and not the virus.[14]

Cunningham's double entendre is purposeful here, for her reference to "the virus" effectively demonstrates the entanglement of COVID-19 and systemic racism for Black people. In particular, her comparison of systemic racism to a virus is similar to Douglass's comparison of color prejudice to a disease. The starkest difference between their two statements is the nearly 139-year gap that separates them. Moreover, what makes Cunningham's commentary so noteworthy is her acknowledgment of disability. Similarly to Douglass, she distinguishes the "symptoms" from the "virus" that produces said symptoms without eschewing disability in the process. The circumstances that contributed to George Floyd's premature death are Cunningham's central concern, and her allusions to settler colonialism, enslavement, and police brutality implicitly outline the underlying conditions that led to Floyd's stolen Black life.

Rev. Al Sharpton, the civil rights activist and founder of the National Action Network, also figured racism as a public health crisis in his eulogy at George Floyd's memorial service:

> The reason we could never be who we wanted and dreamed of being is you kept your knee on our neck. We were smarter than the underfunded schools you put us in, but you had your knee on our neck. We could run corporations and not hustle in the street, but you had your knee on our neck. . . . What happened to Floyd happens every day in this country, in education, in health services, and in every area of American life; it's time for us to stand up in George's name and say get your knee off our necks. . . . The reason why we are marching all over the world is we were like George, we couldn't breathe.[15]

This section of Sharpton's eulogy earned him a standing ovation; nearly everyone attending the memorial held at North Central University stood and clapped for almost a minute. Sharpton's eulogy captured the fact that officer Derek Chauvin was filmed kneeling on Floyd's neck for more than eight minutes in addition to the disabling and deadly pressure that racism exerts on the lives of Black people writ large. His eulogy recalled not only Eric Garner's and George Floyd's dying declarations, "I can't breathe," but also the suffocation that Black folks experience due to daily racial violence. And given that Floyd tested positive for COVID-19, an infectious disease that primarily affects the lungs and has a greater effect on individuals with comorbidities such as hypertension and diabetes (two underlying conditions that disproportionately impact Black communities), Sharpton's references to obstructed breathing and systemic racism would have landed bitterly with Black listeners living during a global pandemic. George Floyd's "I can't breathe" reverberated as an utterance of respiratory distress because of police brutality and the coronavirus, dual forces of destruction deadly enough to level his life. But Sharpton's empathetic pronouncement—"we were like George, we couldn't breathe"—transforms Floyd's singular plea into a matter of communal and collective Black suffering.[16] Such declarations represent assertions of disability along with calls for mercy and justice. They are powerful reminders of the manifold ways Black lives are at risk for and on guard against state violence and terror, and they are demands to redress the terror that endangers Black lives. All of this probably resonated with Sharpton's audience.

Listening to Sharpton, I also heard resonances of Frederick Douglass, whose words have proven just as relevant in the twenty-first century as they were in the nineteenth. Perhaps Douglass, who once boldly pronounced himself "a prophet" of Black people, was one indeed.[17] He certainly made several prophetic statements about the disabilities of the color line, statements that many Black writers would amplify. But what I know for sure is that Douglass was, above all, a perceptive historian. His uncanny ability to imagine and produce a new world was matched by his unique capacity to remember and reconcile hard-earned lessons from old ones. Douglass's links between the disabilities of the antebellum color line and the disabilities of the postbellum one are significant for this book. Equally important, though, is the way his work both harks back to and foreshadows that of other Black authors, abolitionists, and activists who are explored in this book, including David Walker, Henry Box Brown, William and Ellen Craft, W. E. B. Du Bois, Charles Waddell Chesnutt, Frances Ellen Watkins Harper, James Weldon Johnson, and Mamie Till-Mobley. Douglass's affirmation of disability might strike some readers as surprising or unexpected, as an unpromising path toward combating the pernicious color line. But it is not. This approach is shared by many Black folks aiming for collective liberation and yearning for another world "where no body/mind is left behind."[18]

Their approaches are part of the larger traditions of Black radicalism and disability justice, and the Black writers and activists in this book employ the methods that make those traditions so formidable: the relentless pursuit for "an elsewhere," the steady movement toward "an elsewhen," and the exceptional aptitude to envision and occasion "otherwise."[19] Altogether, they represent an impressive force, imagining and creating another place, another time, and another possibility in the present and in the future. May their words and deeds welcome you into the fold.

Introduction

At the Threshold of the Color Line

The color line has been shaped as much by disability as it has by race, sexuality, gender, geography, photography, and sound.[1] It has been, in no uncertain terms, a serious delimitation on the health and life of Black folks in the United States, stigmatizing their bodies, minds, and blood. Through law and custom, it defined the blood of Black people as diseased and tainted and the blood of white people as unsullied and pure. It named people by proportions of blood: *full-blood, half-breed, mulatto, mestizo, quadroon, octoroon, mixed-blood,* or merely *mixed*— words that attempted to make descent legible mainly to maintain the lie of white racial purity and to separate, immobilize, and contain non-white people along lines of color and race. It is why, in some states, Black blood quantum amounted to a sociolegal disability: a prohibition of or disqualification from citizenship, literacy, and franchise; in others, any quantity of Black blood—even if only a drop—was enough to deny a Black person rights, privileges, access, and mobility. For fugitives from enslavement, the cost of being caught was a loss of limb or a brand on the body. For those living during Jim Crow, lynching and racial terror loomed large. And for those of us living in the present, the disabling systemic violence inflicted on Black communities stands as a dire reminder of the color's line continuity. The contours of the color line have a discursive-material life. They live in language, and they have been exacted on the body and mind too.

Yet these examples represent only part of the story this book details. Parallel to these disabilities of the color line reside an *aesthetics of redress*: modes of resistance that variously show how Black communities have rigorously engaged disability as both a response to forms of oppression and a quest for social justice and compassion. One common method of redress involves reframing racism as a disability or disorder.

But an exclusive focus on that method obscures a more vital and inter-sectional one that this book brings to light. *Disabilities of the Color Line* exhibits how Black writers and activists live through, recount, and avow such discursive and material disablement without unequivocally dis-claiming disability or the lived experiences of disabled people. In doing so, they conceive or create dynamic new worlds that account for people of all abilities through a variety of ways: their acts of writing, accessible book design, radical traditions and performances, activism and defiance against ableism and racism, or strategic uses of technology that incite the world to perceive Black folks otherwise. The historian Vincent Hard-ing asserts "that part of the responsibility of black scholars is to help remind themselves and the community that they have constantly moved through darkness to light, constantly moved through pain to healing."[2] Attending to an aesthetics of redress in Black literature and culture is my way of heeding Harding's call. To focus only on pain and darkness at the expense of healing and light would, says the Black cultural theo-rist Roderick A. Ferguson, "reduce black life to its social repressions."[3] This book foregrounds social upheaval and social unrest to capture the "brokenbeautiful" aspects of Black life—the resilience, the resistance, the survival, and the care.[4]

My engagement with disability is incredibly heterogeneous, as this book relies primarily on the historical definition of the term *disability*, which possesses a potent but flexible etymology that refers to both the condition of an individual and the restrictions of a system. The capa-cious meaning of *disability*, however, is often overlooked largely due to the passage and the perception of the Americans with Disabilities Act of 1990 (ADA), which effectively narrowed the definition of the word by focusing only on the individual. The ADA defines disability "as a physi-cal and mental impairment that substantially limits one or more major life activities of [an] individual," and it requires either "a record of such an impairment" or "being regarded as having such an impairment."[5] Yet this definition is only one of at least three operational uses of the word. *Disability* is also defined as an "incapacity in the eye of the law, or cre-ated by the law; a restriction framed to prevent any person or class of persons from sharing in duties or privileges which would otherwise be open to them; a legal disqualification"; and, more generally, as a "lack of ability (*to* discharge any office or function)."[6] Disability is often the

sequela of a disease, deformity, illness, injury, or a legal restriction. The terms in this lexicon are not the same, but they are related.

As these various meanings attest, the import of disability is more dynamic and prolific than the ADA allows. We have historically used the same word for a bodily condition and a system—for an impairment that restricts the movements, functions, and activities of a person and for a legal or structural system that creates a restriction. Defining disability only in terms of the individual (as the ADA does) fails to reference disabling systems and structures, suppressing a key aspect of the term's meaning that would have been familiar to writers of an earlier period.

My take on how the ADA definition narrows our understanding of disability is at odds with accounts of the breadth of that definition. The disability studies scholar Emily Russell, for instance, describes the ADA as "a broad legislative statement," explaining that in "the ADA definition, 'impairment' (the body), 'record' (the text), and 'regard' (the social) act in concert to trace out the contours of disability in the discourse of American individualism."[7] While I agree with Russell's reading of the ADA's language, it does not change the fact that its definition focuses only on individual identity and behavior to the exclusion of systemic disablement.[8] Looking to this law for a comprehensive definition of disability is futile, for the ADA does not implicate itself. Accordingly, in this book, *disability* refers to a restrictive system as well as an individual condition; *disablement* refers to the action of disabling Black subjects via systemic or physical acts of violence; and *racial injury* (or *racial injuries*) refers to the sometimes deadly and often disabling consequences—social, corporeal, and psychiatric—of racism. The elasticity and interrelatedness of these terms did not escape the attention of Black authors and activists, who sometimes deployed disability to reverse a negative metaphor levied against them and sometimes crucially acknowledged disability and disablement as an expression of their personal experience of racism or an awareness of the mutual subjugation of blackness and disability. Unfortunately, their work has been either misunderstood or elided within the criticism of certain disability studies scholars and Black literary studies scholars.

Indeed, this book challenges a notion within the fields of disability studies and Black studies that has been readily taken for granted and is starting to become commonplace: the assumption that Black folks felt

compelled to repudiate disability. For example, the disability historian Douglas C. Baynton argues, "The attribution of disease or disability to racial minorities has a long history. Yet, while many have pointed out the injustice and perniciousness of attributing these qualities to a racial or ethnic group, little has been written about why these attributions are such powerful weapons for inequality, why they were so furiously denied and condemned by their targets, and what this tells us about our attitudes toward disability."[9] Baynton rightly points out that critics have not sufficiently examined why attributions of disability serve as potent tools for engendering inequality. However, his claim that targeted racial groups have vigorously denied attributions of disability not only overstates matters but also overlooks how Black folks harness the concept of disability in multivalent ways to explain and resist their unique racial and social oppression.

It is true that connecting blackness and disability was a dangerous and risky maneuver for Black people, for it could have been easily perceived as trafficking too closely in the language of scientific racism. As the African American literary studies scholar Jennifer C. James argues, "In post–Civil War African American literature particularly, it was imperative that the black body and the black 'mind' be portrayed as uninjured by the injuring institution of slavery in order to disprove one of the main antiblack arguments that surfaced after emancipation—that slavery had made blacks 'unfit' for citizenship, 'unfit' carrying a dual psychological and physical meaning."[10] Yet it is also true that several prominent Black writers made such connections despite these anti-Black arguments. The imperative insight, it turns out, was to think about the relationship between blackness and disability as constructed and imposed, not as innate or inherent. Black people asserting that they are not inherently disabled because of their race is a disavowal of a particular kind of racist discourse. But the expressions of Black authors and activists regarding how they have been socially, physically, or psychologically disabled by the institutions of slavery, Jim Crow, or the doctrine and practice of color blindness reflect a keen awareness of the significance of disability rather than a repudiation of it or, as Baynton puts it, a furious denial. There were even some Black writers who used disability to enact their escapes from slavery. Henry Box Brown, for example, burned his finger with sulfuric acid so he could get a day off from work and fulfill his plot

of mailing himself in a wooden box to Philadelphia and escaping to the North. Additionally, Ellen Craft disguised herself as a disabled, white male planter, and her husband played the role of the planter's slave in their pursuit of freedom. These Black abolitionists employed disability as a technique of liberation rather than an expression of condemnation.

Disabilities of the Color Line examines how disablement as both experience and discourse has shaped the racial subjecthood of Black people since the antebellum period, and in this book, I make two principal arguments that have been underexplored in studies of US history, literature, and law. First, I argue that disability is central, not peripheral, to racial formation during the antebellum and postbellum periods in the United States and that the color line—which functions both as a metaphorical, legal barrier and as a material, literal boundary of separation and division—is as informed by disability as it is by race and other categories. This first argument is significant because it unsettles the way scholars have typically framed the color line as pertaining to race, not disability, and as historically situated during the postbellum period, not before.[11] Frederick Douglass's description of the color line (in addition to the descriptions of other Black writers) as a disabling phenomenon that existed in and extended beyond slavery portrays the color line as a continuum of, not a rupture from, the antebellum period that preceded the Civil War, Reconstruction, and Jim Crow. Second, instead of denying attributions of disability, I argue, a notable cohort of Black writers and thinkers interrogate how disability intersects with blackness not only to understand the complexities of racial injury and subjection but also to acknowledge the open-ended possibilities of disability. Moving from a consideration of slave codes that mandated illiteracy for enslaved people and prescribed dismemberment and disfigurement as punishments for fugitives from slavery to an examination of the physical and psychological injuries wrought by the regime of Jim Crow and the custom and performance of color blindness, this book explores the fraught and deeply intertwined relationship of blackness and disability in US law, literature, and culture.

Disabilities of the Color Line tells two stories. The first and more central story is about how the work of a distinct group of Black abolitionists, authors, and activists—including David Walker, Henry Box Brown, William and Ellen Craft, Frederick Douglass, Frances E. W. Harper, Charles

W. Chesnutt, W. E. B. Du Bois, James Weldon Johnson, Mamie Till-Mobley, and Patricia J. Williams—challenge dominant narratives of disability and practices of disablement in the pre– and post–Civil War eras. By investigating the ways that Black people engage in an aesthetics of redress regarding claims about their presumed innate racial defects, this narrative clarifies what disability meant, whom it was meant to target, and how it could be used to subvert racial oppression and corporeal subjugation. It also invites a critical reevaluation of how Black folks understood and affirmed the radical promise of disability, highlighting how they bridged a chasm between blackness and disability in their work despite the potential pitfalls of such a maneuver. In so doing, they exhibit a familiarity with history, law, science, and culture, and they often explicitly invoke and respond to a variety of historical texts, materials, and personages in their work.

The second story concerns the historical formation of blackness and disability. It focuses on the dominant customs circulating in the antebellum and postbellum periods that either characterized Black people as innately disabled or engendered their disablement. This story offers insights about some familiar literary and legal texts—Thomas Jefferson's *Notes on the State of Virginia*, the US Constitution, the Declaration of Independence, *Dred Scott v. Sandford*, *Plessy v. Ferguson*, and *Brown v. Board of Education*—in addition to a number of other significant though lesser-known sources like, for example, the *Code Noir* and state slave laws of Georgia, Virginia, North Carolina, and South Carolina. I turn to these sources in large part because of their profound literariness: the way these texts refer to and outline the political terms of Black writing, life, and literacy as well as how they rely heavily on literary devices like metaphor. The use of metaphor adds a conceptual weight and gravitas to these documents, which include arguments that attach stigma to Black folks by framing them as threats to national health and safety. It is no wonder that so many Black writers relied heavily on metaphor to depict the disabilities of the color line.

Black writers, abolitionists, and activists were acutely aware of this stigmatization and the ways it connected to racial health, corporeality, citizenship, and notions of fitness. Indeed, their attunement to the complicated history of blackness and disability put them in the unique position of transforming the narrative about race and disability. To challenge the various forms of bodily, linguistic, and social violence that marked Black folks as disabled, they did something inventive—they used the language and strategies of their oppressors against them. In addition to Douglass's writing, the works of W. E. B. Du Bois, Charles W. Chesnutt, and Frances E. W. Harper demonstrate this ingenuity.

Disabilities of the Color Line and Racial Injury

Frederick Douglass was one of the earliest writers to describe the disabilities of the color line and its racial injuries. In a speech delivered to the Convention of Colored Men in Louisville, Kentucky, in September 1883, he described the color line as "color madness," which he saw pervading the entire nation:

> Thus in all the relations of life and death we are met by the color line. We cannot ignore it if we would, and ought not if we could. It hunts us at midnight, it denies us accommodation in hotels and justice in the courts; excludes our children from schools, refuses our sons the chance to learn trades, and compels us to pursue only such labor as will bring the least reward. While we recognize the color line as a hurtful force, a mountain barrier to our progress, wounding our bleeding feet with its flinty rocks at every step, we do not despair. We are a hopeful people.[12]

In the two years between the publication of his seminal essay "The Color Line" and his address at this convention, Douglass's take on the color line had become more refined. Here, he acknowledged the scope of the color line's injuriousness, spotlighting its predatory and discriminatory qualities and making it clear that those Americans who ignore its harmfulness do so at their peril. Yet Douglass was not the only Black writer to characterize the color line in this fashion. A subsequent collective of Black writers, especially Du Bois, Chesnutt, and Harper, echoes and expands Douglass's take by focusing closely on the historical, psychological, and legal aspects of the color line.

In fact, Douglass is not usually the historical figure that most critics refer to when examining the color line. That recognition typically goes to Du Bois, who memorably declared in *The Souls of Black Folk* (1903), "The problem of the twentieth century is the problem of the color-line,—the relation of the darker to the lighter races of men in Asia and Africa, in America and the islands of the sea."[13] While Du Bois's definition of the color line is more global in scope (given its explicit reference to continents other than North America and Europe), he was clearly a student of Douglass, whose words inform various parts of *Souls* and whose considerations of the color line are evident in Du Bois's description. In particular, Du Bois also linked the problem of the color line to the antebellum period. "It was a phase of this problem," Du Bois wrote, "that caused the Civil War; and however much they who marched South and North in 1861 may have fixed on the technical points of union and local autonomy as a shibboleth, all nevertheless knew, as we know, that the question of Negro slavery was the real cause of the conflict."[14] Although known for historically locating the color line in the twentieth century, Du Bois observed that the color line was also a pressing problem of slavery.

Souls was not the first source where Du Bois mentioned the concept of the color line. He did so in his 1901 essay "The Freedmen's Bureau," which was published in the *Atlantic Monthly* and was later revised and published in *Souls* as the second chapter, "Of the Dawn of Freedom." He also cited the color line in *The Georgia Negro: A Social Study*, the first of two sets of infographics exhibited in Paris at the 1900 *Exposition des Nègres d'Amerique*, which offered a visual representation of the continuity between the color line and slavery. And he introduced the concept in his 1899 book *Philadelphia Negro: A Social Study*, where he wrote, "In all walks of life the Negro is liable to meet some objection to his presence or some discourteous treatment; and the ties of friendship or memory seldom are strong enough to hold across the color line." Here, the color line is linked explicitly to color prejudice, which, in the city of Philadelphia, Du Bois argued, "is something between [the] two extreme views [of Black and white people]: it is not to-day responsible for all, or perhaps the greater part of the Negro problems, or of the disabilities under which the race labors; on the other hand it is a far more powerful social force than most Philadelphians realize."[15] Even in his earlier work on color prejudice and the color line, Du Bois acknowledged the presence of disability. But it was in his description of double consciousness, which he depicted as a disorienting experience, where he expressed more fully the disabling aspects of the color line.

In Du Bois's 1897 *Atlantic Monthly* article "Strivings of the Negro People," where he first articulated his famous dictum about American racial doubleness and which served as an early version of the first chapter in *Souls*, perhaps nothing is more striking than his rhetorical association of blackness and disability. Focusing on the marginality of African Americans in the nation, Du Bois stated, "A people thus handicapped ought not to be asked to race with the world, but rather allowed to give all its time and thought to its own social problems."[16] At first glance, Du Bois's remark appears peculiar. He, like others writing against the racist discourses of Black degeneracy, showed an investment in emphasizing the extraordinary ability and capacity of African Americans, and he argued in his landmark address "The Conservation of the Races," delivered at the American Negro Academy the same year "Strivings" was published, that Black folks have a monumental and unique "contribution to make to civilization and humanity, which no other race can make."[17] But as a post–Civil War response to the wounds of slavery, the failures of the Freedmen's Bureau, the disintegration of Reconstruction, the terrorism and violence of the Ku Klux Klan, and the futility of the legal system, Du Bois's observation makes more sense.

Du Bois's characterization of Black people as "handicapped" crafts a curious relationship between the racialized construction of blackness and the specular representation of disability through the metaphors of racial competition and rehabilitation. Du Bois's allusion to competition was certainly a nod to nineteenth-century social Darwinists, who applied theories of natural selection and survival of the fittest to race and politics and attempted to diagnose the disparities in economic and social well-being among racial groups as a symptom of a group's innate fitness or defects. Du Bois, however, turned that theory on its head. His strategic use of the word *handicapped*, which refers both to a mental and physical disability as well as to an artificial advantage given to or a disadvantage imposed on a competitor in a race or contest, offered him tremendous narrative flexibility. This "race with the world" metaphor is a recurrent theme in the writings of Black authors, and it exemplifies how Du Bois again echoed Douglass, who insisted in "The Color Line" "that all arbitrary barriers against his [the Negro's] manhood, intelligence, and elevation shall be removed, and a fair chance in the race of life be given to him."[18] A natural wordsmith with a keen-eyed, vibrant, and meticulous care for language, Du Bois intuitively understood the vitality of a finely tuned narration. In his story, it is not that the Black body is innately disabled but that the US institutions of slavery, Jim Crow, and corporal punishment are disabling. In other words, Du Bois described disability as a social and legal phenomenon, where the movement and mobility of Black people are directly related to their environment and surroundings. Without these regimes of torture that injure, deform, and disable African Americans, the strivings "in the souls of black folk" would prevail over the debilitating tyranny of the color line.[19]

Black folks have the best vantage point from which to view the tyranny of the nation, for, as Du Bois wrote in *Souls*, they are "gifted with second-sight."[20] This kind of clairvoyance is a double-edged sword. In the high drama of US life, it casts Black people as spiritual soothsayers, tenacious voyagers, and valiant time travelers, as a people capable of transcending the rules of time and space to pilgrimage into the past, foretell the future, and spellbind the present. Such a sixth sense yields unparalleled visual and perceptual power, seemingly boundless in its ability to detect people and objects unnoticed by the five senses. They could commune with the dead, the supernatural, and the Almighty. They could even see themselves through another's eyes. Yet like most extraordinary beings bestowed with enchanted powers, their gift is a blessing and a curse. They are fortunate to see things that others cannot but are unfortunate in that they cannot unsee the terrible, traumatic things that they witness. While wondrous and sublime in many ways, possessing second sight, Du Bois suggested, can be quite perilous as well.

Du Bois called this exceptional sensibility "double-consciousness," and his description of its disfiguring and deforming qualities hinted at how it is both a birthright and a burden.[21] He wrote, "It is a peculiar sensation, this double-consciousness, this sense of always looking at one's self through the eyes of others, of measuring one's soul by the tape of a world that looks on in amused contempt and pity. One ever feels his two-ness,—an American, a Negro; two souls, two thoughts, two unreconciled strivings; two warring ideals in one dark body, whose dogged strength alone keeps it from being torn asunder."[22] Although Du Bois framed double consciousness as a dual sensation, his lengthy catalogue of the way a Black person "feels his two-ness" suggested that more than two identities exist; national, racial, spiritual, and psychological identities are implicated. Moreover, these manifold identities are in conflict with one another—so much so that, were it not for the resilience of African Americans, the "two unreconciled strivings" and "two warring ideals" would rend the Black body into parts. Framed in extraordinarily violent terms, Du Bois's "double-consciousness" registers as what the literary critic Robert B. Stepto refers to as "an imposed schizophrenia" or, as the Black cultural and literary studies scholar Kevin Quashie puts it, as "a fractured consciousness that is overdetermined by the public language of black inferiority."[23] It produces not only psychological trauma but also corporeal and sensory disturbance, and it offers no easy resolution to these conflicting feelings. The clash between nation and race—between "American" and "Negro"—is a serious point of contention with significant consequences, since it is the exclusion of Black people from the nation that engenders this bodily rupture. It also produces a distortion in the visual field, for the unworldly "looks" of "amused contempt and pity" misalign with Du Bois's racial vision of an alternate future.

Charles W. Chesnutt, one of Du Bois's contemporaries, was equally enthralled by the entanglements of blackness, disability, and distortion. He made a link between sight and the disabilities of the color line by looking through the lens of turn-of-the-century Jim Crow. In his 1901 novel *The Marrow of Tradition*, which explicitly engages the 1896 legal case of *Plessy v. Ferguson* while providing a fictional account of the 1898 riot in Wilmington, North Carolina, Chesnutt echoed Du Bois's sentiments about the corporeal dangers of the harsh, volatile color line in his description of the Jim Crow train car. He wrote, "Surely, if a classification of passengers on trains was at all desirable, it might be made upon some more logical and considerate basis than a mere arbitrary, tactless, and, by the very nature of things, brutal drawing of a color line. It was a veritable bed of Procrustes, this standard which the whites had set for the negroes."[24] To convey the disablement of Jim Crow, Chesnutt compared the color line to Procrustes's bed. Procrustes is a Greek mythological figure infamous for forcing strangers to lie on his iron bed and violently reshaping their bodies to adhere to the dimensions of that bed. By employing the Procrustean metaphor, Chesnutt exposes how the execution of racial oppression and subjection is tied to the literal and figurative dismemberment and deformation of the human body. "Those who grew above it [the standard of the color line] must have their heads cut off, figuratively speaking," Chesnutt wrote, "must be forced back to the level assigned to their race; those who fell beneath the standard set had their necks stretched, literally enough, as the ghastly record in the daily papers gave conclusive evidence."[25] *Marrow* illuminates the manner in which Chesnutt's work links bodily disintegration to visuality, mythology, and judicial and extrajudicial matters, which all coalesce in the grim images of deformity, amputation, and lynching. These violent practices allude to what Chesnutt referred to in his 1889 essay "What Is a White Man?" as the "disability of color," a phrase that represents how the white supremacy of the republic is sustained by the state-sanctioned terror and injury of Black people as well as their isolation and containment.[26]

A key corollary to Chesnutt's "disability of color" appears in Frances E. W. Harper's novel *Iola Leroy, or Shadows Uplifted*. Published in 1892, Harper's book expands the meaning of the phrase in one of its crucial scenes, where the former slave Iola Leroy explains to the white Dr. Gresham why their interracial marriage would inevitably fail in the aftermath of the Civil War. Dr. Gresham, operating under the false assumption that "the color line is slowly fading out in our public institutions," asks Iola, for the second time, to be his wife: "Iola, will you not grant me the privilege of holding this hand as mine all through the future of our lives?" Rejecting Gresham's theory that the color line is fading as well as rejecting his second proposal, which he couples with a thinly veiled request for her Black racial disavowal, the eponymous heroine responds to his plea with a proverbial slap in the face. "No, Doctor," she asserts, "I am not willing to live under a shadow of concealment which I thoroughly hate as if the blood in my veins were an undetected crime of my soul." In her view, "it is easier to outgrow the dishonor of crime than the disabilities of color." Despite her distinction between "dishonor of crime" and "disabilities of color," Iola's reference to the "disabilities of color" is flush with ambiguity, rendering differences between the social and the physical, the legal and the corporeal, and the illicit and the injurious hard to delineate.[27]

Part of the challenge in deciphering Iola's precise meaning stems from the way Harper framed her dialogue with Dr. Gresham. Based on the sequence of events in the novel, Harper connected Iola's response to at least three key moments. First, Iola's lines follow a protracted series of flashbacks about her familial and racial background, which suggest that her parents' interracial marriage, the subsequent nullification of their matrimony, and their ill-advised decision to conceal the Black racial identity of Iola's mother (who is strikingly fair-skinned) have a significant bearing on her rejection of Gresham. Second, since her remark comes on the heels of a memory regarding the differential treatments meted out to "an outcast colored girl" and "an outcast white girl" at an "asylum for fallen women," it hints at Iola's irrepressible fear of the persistent dangers of racism and sexism. Third, Iola's parallel between her romantic dispute with Dr. Gresham and the "fratricidal strife" brewing between the North and the South as well as the disabilities of white and Black male soldiers mixes the personal with the political—thereby connecting the drawbacks of interracial marriage to the injurious repercussions of the Civil War.[28]

Each of these plot details is a clear example of what I identify as the Black literary tradition's underrecognized and long-standing avowal of disability. These details push the reader to consider the entanglement of blackness and disability in more expansive ways—connecting disability to slavery, the color line, the nullification of interracial marital and sexual unions, exclusionary institutional asylums, and the ravages of war. *Iola* is not merely a novel preoccupied with conventional marriage plots and romantic couplings. It is also a political text of nineteenth-century Black feminist activism and dissent. It is a literary work in which anti-slavery, antiracism, antiwar, and antiableism sentiments swirl in abrupt and purposeful ways—but usually to dispel notions of inherent racial inferiority. In Harper's hands, the intersections of blackness and disability are voluminous and wide.

Clearly, Harper, Douglass, Du Bois, and Chesnutt produce a panoply of meanings regarding the disabilities of the color line. The messiness and perilousness of racism require a multipronged response. Put differently, the capaciousness of these writers' approaches is proportionate to the magnitude of onslaughts with which they had to contend. The breadth of their coverage is crucial, because the dominant narratives and actions they were responding to are far-reaching in both range and influence. What they were fighting against is a long and elaborate racialism that has for centuries portrayed all Black folks as immanently disabled; that has measured the state of Black health and well-being on the scales of racial injustice and corporeal degradation; and that has attempted, in numerous ways, to maim, stigmatize, and traumatize Black people. An uncomplicated approach to this barrage of assaults would have been unconscientious and, gratefully, unlike anything Douglass, Du Bois, Chesnutt, and Harper have ever done.

Their meticulous work inspired the title of this book, which is an ode to their nuanced examinations of the color line's material and metaphorical characteristics. Through their writing, I have come to understand how blackness becomes deeply intertwined with disability and disablement, particularly at the threshold of the color line: the point at which the color line is either encountered or breached (deliberately or unknowingly) and a physiological or psychological effect ensues. For Black people, a host of seemingly minor activities have affected the color line, which, while disabling and sometimes deadly, is a fragile thing. An enslaved person in possession of a book, a Black person traveling on a southbound first-class train car in the mid-twentieth century, and a Black teenage boy falsely accused of wolf-whistling at a white woman are just a few examples of when racial injury is meted out to those who cross the color line—a metaphorical construction, yes, but also one with serious material consequences. This book focuses on the material and metaphorical aspects of the color line in a way that does not hierarchize one over the other but instead considers them in tandem and thus as difficult to disentangle because of how they mutually conspire to stigmatize Black bodies and minds. While my larger point is to argue that the generative relationship between disability and blackness has never been reducible to a mere reversal of stigmatization, the stigmatization of blackness is a matter of significant importance that must be examined, particularly within the context of the body politic. This context explains how stigma is materialized for Black folks and why it is such a luring though harmful form of discrimination. Accordingly, I address a crucial matter that, as Douglas Baynton observes, is barely acknowledged: why attributions of disability function as powerful instruments for discrimination and how they are weaponized to perfect inequality.

Stickiness, Stigma, and the Persuasion of the Body Politic

What makes the metaphor regarding the innate incapacity of Black people a powerful form of racial subjection is its "stickiness" factor, what the journalist Malcolm Gladwell describes as a message (or an idea, product, or behavior) conveyed in such a memorable way that it becomes a social epidemic and begins to "spread just like viruses do."[29] Of all the literary devices in our repertoire, metaphors are especially good at making messages stick. They can deliver an idea in such arresting language that it holds you in its grasp and impresses your mind, and they have an extraordinary knack for turning the foreign into the familiar and for translating abstract concepts into a common language that the masses can understand.

In 1963, the sociologist Erving Goffman had another name for this stickiness factor. He called it "stigma." *Stigma*, as Goffman observed, refers to "various physical deformities" of the body, such as scars, brands, leprosy, and physical disability; to "blemishes of individual character," such as "mental disorder, imprisonment, addiction, alcoholism, homosexuality, unemployment, suicidal attempts, and radical political behavior"; and to "the tribal stigma of race, nation, and religion . . . that can be transmitted through lineages and equally contaminate all members of a family." Goffman insisted that stigmatization should be considered as a social, relational, and situational process. In addition to being social and relational, stigma is also exceedingly metaphorical, and, like stickiness, it often relies on the metaphor of the body. The language of disability, disease, deformity, and contamination rules the etymology of *stigma*, which relies significantly on bodily metaphors to make its meaning stick.[30]

The human body and mind, of course, have inspired a wellspring of metaphors. Consider for a moment that we have anatomized a number of inanimate objects: tables have feet, beds have legs, sofas have arms, chairs have backs, books have spines, bottles have necks, cups have lips, shoes have tongues, and mattresses have memory.[31] Or pause to reflect on how often our technologies represent extensions of the human self, how astonishing and solipsistic it is that we adorn our most prized innovations with the names of our sensorial attributes like the hands of clocks, the noses of planes, the sockets of electricity, and the brains of computers. Comparing the seductive and incandescent kiss of a woman to the labyrinth of electrical lines that transmit messages throughout our world, the poet and novelist Jean Toomer even likens human "lips," "tongue," and "breath" to the live, kinetic "Copper Wire" of our technological systems.[32] The point is that we source our language through our bodies, and we do it so often and with such ease and dexterity that we barely notice how deeply it affects our lives. In a book on the secret, shape-shifting power of metaphor, James Geary says it best: "Our bodies prime our metaphors, and our metaphors prime how we think and act."[33]

With regard to politics, the collective body, not merely its parts, serves as "one of the most pervasive political metaphors," according to Geary.[34] It is the idea that the nation itself is a body, often referred to as the "body politic." The phrase *body politic* has been in circulation since the fifteenth century, even before Elizabeth I, on her ascension to the throne in 1558, proclaimed that she possessed two bodies. "I am but one body naturally considered," she said, "though by His permission a body politic to govern."[35] It gained greater currency with the publication of Thomas Hobbes's 1651 *Leviathan* and its fantastic frontispiece, which features an empowered king emerging from the landscape clutching a sword in his right hand and a crosier in his left, with his torso and arms tattooed with the bodies of a deferential populace. *Leviathan*'s frontispiece offered a visual imprint of an abstract idea. It illustrated one of Hobbes's key theories that "a multitude of men are made 'one' person, when they are by one man or one person represented; so that it be done with the consent of every one of that multitude in particular."[36] The movement from the multitude to the one and the one to the multitude has been productive also for democracies like the United States, always fond of invoking "the people" to mobilize the governance of a single authority. The first words of the preamble to the Constitution ("We, the people of the United States") pledges a commitment to a democratic creed that most Americans hold dear, and the memorable phrasing from Abraham Lincoln's "Gettysburg Address" ("government of the people, by the people, for the people") reinforces the purpose of that creed during the crisis of the Civil War.

Clearly, the body politic has been an enduring metaphor—situated at the center of debates around legitimacy, nationalism, excommunication, immigration, exclusion, constitutional rights, and citizenship for centuries. It is also clear that it has been a primer for inciting racial animus and racial injuries. The metaphor of the body politic has significant import, particularly in reference to Black people and disability metaphors. As the literary and disability studies scholar Sami Schalk asserts, "Reading for both the metaphorical and material significance of disability in a text allows us to trace the ways discourses of (dis)ability, race, and gender do not merely intersect at the site of multiply marginalized people, but also how these systems [ableism and racism] collude or work in place of one another." Schalk is responding to a position in disability studies that univocally dismisses metaphorical uses of disability and thus, as she states, "ignores the mutual constitution of (dis)ability, race, and gender as social categories and cultural discourses which have material effects on people's lives."[37] Simply put, Black folks cannot afford the luxury of being dismissive about metaphors of disability, for the cost is prohibitive. We know all too well the way such metaphors attach to the body and mind and spread within a population or nation like an ever-mutating virus.

The metaphor of the body politic is effective at producing racial discord in part because it frames the nation as vulnerable to contamination—imbuing it with the fragility of the human body and charging its citizens with the task of protecting its health even if it means causing harm to others. If the US nation is a body, then it, like us all, is susceptible to disease and disability. Our national body parallels our former de facto national motto: as a collective group united by the government, we embody *e pluribus unum* (out of many, one). Being a part of this synthesized political body, we bear tremendous responsibility, not only to ourselves but also to each other. We, as a political body, are deeply dependent on one another. We, as Eula Biss writes in her treatise on immunity, "owe each other our bodies."[38] As much as independence and individualism suffuse our US sensibilities and founding documents, our health and safety have always been contingent on the health and safety of our fellow Americans. With regard to health, we are an interdependent bunch. At times—such as when we are caring for family members, friends, and loved ones—this responsibility for each other's health can unite us. At others—such as, say, during slavery, Jim Crow, or a global pandemic—it can divide us. In a world where our bodies prime metaphors such as the body politic, racist notions of all Black people as inherently defective or of Black blood as diseased function as a formidable form of racial discipline and restraint because they conjure up the image of corporeal illness and contagion—capable of affecting the health of many, not just one. And any persons who pose or are perceived as a threat to the nation's collective health could be contained, injured, or even destroyed, which demonstrates how metaphors of disability are made material on Black bodies and minds. This enforcement of racial discipline and the manufacturing of disability in the name of protecting nationalism are examples of what the theorist Jasbir K. Puar calls "the biopolitics of debilitation," systemic processes "that render some populations as definitively unworthy of health and targeted for injury."[39]

Black folks are intimately familiar with the metaphorical-material burden of biopolitics, and Black literature serves as an archive of both the manifestation and operation of that burden. In "The Literature of the Negro in the United States," an essay in the author's 1957 collection *White Man, Listen!*, Richard Wright captured this point, declaring, "The Negro is America's metaphor." He wrote, "The history of the Negro in America is the history of America written in vivid and bloody terms. . . . We black folk, our history and our present being, are a mirror of all the manifold experiences of America. What we want, what we represent, what we endure, is what America *is*. If we black folk perish, America will perish. If America has forgotten her past, then let her look into the mirror of our consciousness and she will see the *living* past living in the present." To uncover this living history, Wright mapped Black literature on an imaginary culture line, instead of a color line, with "entity" (described as a group "integrated with their culture") and "identity" (described as a group "at odds with their culture, striving for personal identification") occupying opposite ends of the spectrum. What Wright found as he sifted through Black literature on the identity side of the culture line was a relatively consistent articulation of racial terror and disablement, a historical record of the racial injuries brought forth by enslavement, lynching, Jim Crowism, and sexual and economic exploitation. Wright was careful to note that "despair is not the entire picture" depicted in Black literature. In addition to indexing pain and trauma, Black literature has generally always included expressions of "shared hopes and aspirations," visions and testimonies of freedom and beauty that function as a beacon of light for the United States and the rest of the world. Nevertheless, his essay acknowledged how the disabling metaphors of the nation are made material for Black people, and it emphasized that those metaphors are as informative about perpetrators of racial violence as they are about the people who are made vulnerable by them.[40]

Aesthetics of Redress and Chapter Overview

Using diverse interdisciplinary methods, *Disabilities of the Color Line* pairs disability studies and Black literary and cultural studies alongside critical race studies and performance studies, and it contributes to the conversations of scholarly texts that have provided varied accounts of racial formation in the United States.[41] My methodology follows the lead of Black literary and cultural studies scholars such as Saidiya Hartman, Daphne Brooks, and Hortense Spillers. These scholars have acknowledged that the elisions and gaps in the archive of the enslaved and emancipated demand piecing together disparate forms of evidence to illuminate the various strategies of resistance and modes of redress central to Black subjectivity.

What makes the approaches that Hartman and Brooks take particularly compelling is the way that each scholar describes her respective methodology and framework as informed by disfiguration, deformation, trauma, or self-fragmentation. Hartman explains that her "attempt to read against the grain is perhaps best understood as a combination of foraging and disfiguration—raiding for fragments upon which other narratives can be spun and misshaping and deforming the testimony through selective quotation and the amplification of issues germane to this study."[42] The archive of slavery and emancipation demands such scrutiny because the legacy of postbellum emancipation is apocryphal, making it difficult to form bright-line distinctions between slavery and freedom. "The abolition of chattel slavery," she continues, "however laudable, long awaited, and cherished, fail to yield such absolute distinctions; instead fleeting, disabled, and short-lived practices stand for freedom and its failure."[43] Brooks highlights her approach to nineteenth- and early-twentieth-century Black performers through a strategy she describes as "Afro-alienation acts," which refers to how "the condition of alterity converts into cultural expressiveness and a specific strategy of cultural performance."[44] Drawing from what Hortense Spillers refers to as "the 'dehumanizing, ungendering, and defacing' conditions that African peoples encountered in the New World" and utilizing Spillers's framing of the mythical Black body as possessing a "powerful stillness" and "no movement in the field of signification," Brooks states that an act of

"Afro-alienation is thus encoded with the traumas of self-fragmentation resulting from centuries of captivity and subjugation."[45]

Both Hartman and Brooks model productive ways of developing a methodology or framework that rely on disfiguration and deformation in order to interrogate the social conditions of Black life. For Hartman, a pointed question motivates her method: "In short, how does one adequately render the double bind of emancipation—that is, acknowledge the illusory freedom and travestied liberation that succeeded chattel slavery without gainsaying the small triumphs of Jubilee?"[46] Brooks describes her approach in a slightly different way. Her goal, she states, "is not to suggest a totalizing narrative of nineteenth-century black performance, but rather to continuously ask 'what do we know about these performances?' and 'how do we know what we know?'"[47] Their questions suggest that they allow neither official archives nor dominant narratives to dictate the sole trajectory of their research. They also closely observe the practices, performances, behaviors, and tactics of Black people in the antebellum and postbellum periods. Their methods are infused by the lived bodily experiences and testimonies of their subjects, by not only their flawed emancipation, elusive freedom, and traumatic subjugation but also their innovative responses, some of which may not be present in "dominant paradigms" or "official history" given "the provisionality of the archive as well as the interests that shape it and thereby determine the emplotment of history."[48]

Mindful simultaneously of the dominant narratives and practices of disability as well as of Black strategic modes of resistance to them, *Disabilities of the Color Line* employs this kind of dynamic methodology of deformation to consider matters of redress.[49] At the heart of my method lie two central questions: If the labor-intensive work of slavery led to the sensational representations of the Black body as a paragon of physicality and vigor, then how and why did the experience of disablement and discourse of disability become so frequently inflicted on Black bodies in the antebellum and postbellum periods? Moreover, how have Black writers and activists wrestled with these concerns in their work to demonstrate the radical potential of disability and to exhibit an ethics of interability compassion? This book engages these questions by examining a plethora of sources: nonfiction, fiction, poetry, legal documents, scientific texts, material culture, epistolary exchanges, and lynching photographs—all to uncover the significant role disability has played in racial formation. Each individual source, however, tells a sliver of the story. The elaborate interplay among these sources, in addition to the defiant tactics of Black people, matters as well. My engagement in an aesthetics of redress involves an attentiveness to both the history of domination and practices of disability and disablement as well as the strategies for survival, the modes of self-fashioning, and the cultivation of care and community. Redress, of course, can be limited, for, as Hartman argues, "it is impossible to fully redress th[e] pained condition without the occurrence of an event of epic and revolutionary proportions—the abolition of slavery, the destruction of a racist social order, and the actualization of equality."[50] Still, the promise of redress makes it an ever-worthwhile pursuit for those who have been assaulted by anti-Black regimes, since redress opens up the possibility of an exit from oppressive systems that are so unyielding.[51] In this book, I frame the writing and activism of Black folks as redress, as relief from or a means of seeking a remedy for the routinized and ongoing disabilities of the color line. Such forms of redress, again, have often affirmed disability in ways that are geared toward coalitional work and that articulate the mutual subjection of blackness and disability while contesting a discriminatory social order that hierarchizes certain bodies and minds above others.

This work toward racial and disability justice, however, is hardly ever recognized—largely because of a persistent refrain in Black studies and disability studies: an assertion that the Black community's investment in narratives of ability and capacity inevitably necessitates a fierce disavowal of disability.[52] This assumption has posed challenges to scholars such as me working on the intersections of blackness and disability. In fact, one of the principal critiques of Black studies has been that either the field does not give enough attention to the subject of disability or it distances itself from disability entirely; and one of the critiques levied against the field of disability studies has been that it does not offer a substantial consideration of race. Providing an intersectional analysis of blackness and disability has often entailed putting the fields of disability studies and Black studies in conversation with each other. Yet the two have been at odds. As a scholar of both fields, I have found reconciling the two a demanding affair for three main reasons.

First, disability studies, for a significant length of time, had a race problem. The field failed to adequately address concerns about race, intersectionality, or people of color. As the disability studies scholar Chris Bell has put it, early work in disability studies, "while not wholeheartedly excluding people of color from its critique, by and large focuses on the work of white individuals and is itself largely produced by a corps of white scholars and activists."[53] There are, of course, notable exceptions. Rosemarie Garland-Thomson's foundational *Extraordinary Bodies* immediately comes to mind. But, to a large degree, the field's early emphasis on whiteness and white people minus a sustained engagement with race and race theory has marginalized the experiences of people of color with disabilities and given short shrift to the central role of disability in racial formation. "The epistemic whiteness of the field is no dirty secret," argues Puar. "Part of how white centrality is maintained is through the policing of disability itself: what it is, who or what is responsible for it, how one lives it, whether it melds into an overarching condition of precarity of a population or is significant as an exceptional attribute of an otherwise fortunate life," she states.[54] Since one of the aims of this book is to put blackness and disability in productive conversation, the absence of a deep examination of race and the various ways disability is policed within disability studies are two considerations that I have had to confront.

Second, the relationship between the fields has been "discomforting," as the disability studies scholars David T. Mitchell and Sharon L. Snyder describe it, largely because, as some writers of "feminist, race, and sexuality studies sought to unmoor their identities from debilitating physical and cognitive associations, they inevitably positioned disability as the 'real' limitation from which they must escape."[55] Mitchell and Snyder, highlighting the distancing of other fields from disability, call our attention to a common misstep among those who suffer from oppression and discrimination. To protect themselves from harm and to deflect persecution, some disadvantaged groups might participate in a strategy of disavowal that has the potential to position them atop another such group in a manner that reinforces the oppression of others usually for the sake of their own security. This strategy is a significant historical issue with social, political, and material consequences. The disability studies scholar Michelle Jarman articulates this point when she states that the "very real need to challenge fallacious biological attitudes linked to race, gender, sexuality, and poverty—such as physical anomaly, psychological instability, or intellectual inferiority—has often left stigma around disability unchallenged—except by those specifically engaged in activism and in disability studies."[56] In light of these concerns about the fraught relationship between race and disability, I pay close attention to the moments when a disassociation between the two occurs in addition to the moments when such separation does not occur. My approach has involved pointing out fine distinctions that could be easily overlooked. For example, some of the Black writers in my project proclaim that they are not innately disabled because of their race, but they simultaneously claim to be disabled by structural systems of oppression—which is to say that they recognize that disability is inflicted on them. The distinction between innate and imposed disability is crucial in this book.

A third (but not final) reason that this kind of interdisciplinary work has been challenging emerges from how some scholars in disability studies have redefined the word *disability* in ways that are noninclusive and that do not align with historical definitions of the term. As the literary and disability studies scholar Tom Couser states, "Fundamental to the formation and the focus of the field has been a conceptual distinction between impairment and disability, in which the latter term is defined in a counterintuitive way, as a social construct. Thus, whereas 'impairment' denotes a defect, dysfunction, or other anomaly in the body itself, 'disability' refers to features of the environment which disfavor, exclude, or somehow limit those with bodily impairments."[57] Such conceptual distinctions function as a way to distinguish the social model of disability from the medical model; it is an attempt to move away from the body and focus on the physical and social barriers that limit the body. However, this reformulation puts the two models in competition, and the social model, while crucially exposing the significant barriers facing people with disabilities, also suppresses corporeal testimony, silencing expressions of lived bodily experiences. This redefinition shrouds a significant part of the term's genealogy, limiting the word's vast meanings and the ways it has been used to enact racial oppression.[58]

If scholars ignore the historical definitions of *disability*, we rob the word of its ability to capture the full range of human embodiment and redefine it in ways that would not have been apparent to writers in earlier periods. This redefinition has also encouraged scholars to consider debility as a supplement to disability. For example, in *The Right to Maim*, Puar "mobilize[s] the term 'debility' as a needed disruption (but also expose[s] it as a collaborator) of the category of disability" and "contend[s] that the term 'debilitation' is distinct from the term 'disablement' because it foregrounds the slow wearing down of populations instead of the event of becoming disabled."[59] The disruption and distinction that Puar makes between disability and debility and between disablement and debilitation are necessary only if disability is narrowly understood as a social construct apart from lived bodily experiences or as an individual identity separate from systemic oppression and if disablement is construed as a singular event rather than as a historical and ongoing process like the color line. One danger of Puar's configuration of biopolitical debilitation is the possibility that disability will become "articulated solely through the lens of pathology," which the prison abolition and disability studies scholar Liat Ben-Moshe insists should not happen: "The potential peril of discussing disability solely on the level of the biopolitics of debilitation is that we are left with prevention and assimilation discourses as the only available frameworks that can account for ways of effectively living with disability."[60] In this book, I offer an extensive and nuanced understanding of disability and disablement so that the particular perspectives in the work of Black authors and activists can be understood more fully as connecting lived bodily experiences to systemic racism without framing disability exclusively through the perspective of pathology.

Notwithstanding these challenges, research on the intersections of race, disability, or other identity categories is burgeoning, and an increasing number of scholars understand the significance and necessity of examining the relationships among these subjects. For instance, Black disability studies, a field that did not exist (at least in name) when I began working on this project as a doctoral student, can no longer quite be described as emerging. You could trace the development of the field from Chris Bell's posthumously published edited collection of essays *Blackness and Disability* (2011) and the fiftieth-anniversary special issue of *African*

American Review on blackness and disability, published in 2017, to the monographs of Sami Schalk (2018) and Therí Pickens (2019) that examine disability within Black speculative fiction. Crip theory as well as its persistent promise to "comprehend disability otherwise" and "somehow access other worlds and futures," as the queer and crip cultural studies scholar Robert McRuer puts it, has been a balm as I have navigated the terrain of interdisciplinary work on blackness and disability.[61] According to the feminist-queer-crip scholar Alison Kafer, "Crip theory is more contestatory than disability studies, more willing to explore the potential risks and exclusions of identity politics" by "arguing for the necessity of including within disability communities those who lack a 'proper' (read: medically acceptable, doctor-provided, and insurer-approved) diagnosis for their symptoms." This kind of imaginative cross-movement work, Kafer argues, opens up the "possibility for thinking disability differently" and makes space for a project like mine to emerge.[62] Additionally, the scholarship on the color line—from Siobhan B. Somerville's *Queering the Color Line* (which examines the parallel formations of sexuality and racialization) to Jennifer Stoever's *Sonic Color Line* (which examines the process of racializing sound and listening)—has been attentive to the intersections of blackness and embodiment, expanding our understanding of the color line in terms of sexuality and sound. In conversation with these scholars, this book makes key contributions to disability studies, Black studies, critical race studies, and performance studies by engaging in a critical and dynamic exploration of blackness and disability both to enhance our knowledge of the racialized embodiment and disablement of Black people and to uncover the promise and possibilities of disability in a world constrained by the color line.

Disabilities of the Color Line is divided into three parts. Part 1 includes two chapters. Chapter 1 argues that the purposeful design of David Walker's *Appeal*—its punctuation, typography, emphasis on recitation and performance, and citations of US founding documents and Thomas Jefferson's *Notes on the State of Virginia*—accounts for the history of blackness and disability during slavery to create an accessible work for multiple audiences: free and enslaved people; literate, semiliterate, and illiterate folks; and impaired and nondisabled communities. Walker's instruction for his *Appeal* to be read aloud and heard serves as an example of interability compassion, for he writes the *Appeal* in a way that priori-

tizes illiterate and literate audiences alike and intimates that illiterate auditors, after they have listened to the *Appeal*, could enhance the ideas in
the pamphlet via their delivery and recitation because of their instinctive
speaking skills. Chapter 2 examines the intersections of blackness and
disability in the slave narratives of Henry Box Brown and William and
Ellen Craft, focusing specifically on how these narratives imagine and
enact disability as a possibility for freedom—an egress outside of a social
world order that offers enslaved Black folks limited opportunities for escape. Brown and the Crafts artfully manipulated their bodies primarily
to challenge the proslavery argument that Black enslaved folks would be
disabled by freedom. Their bodily transformations reveal the centrality
of disability to concepts of personhood and citizenship, allowing Brown
and the Crafts to partake in the bold and *"beautiful experiment"* of Black
fugitivity and freedom.[63]

Part 2 includes three chapters. Transitional to the postbellum period,
chapter 3 examines how the etymology of the term *Jim Crow* and the US
Supreme Court decision in *Plessy v. Ferguson* are suffused with notions
of disability. In particular, *Plessy* represents an example of how disablement is sutured to the social and political world of the body politic, and
Homer Plessy's plot to violate Louisiana's Separate Car Act of 1890 serves
as an attempt to contest racial classifications within the law. Chapter 4
explores the particular ways that disability functions as an integral element of the post–Civil War United States. This chapter focuses especially
on the work of Charles W. Chesnutt, whose essays outline how legal
definitions of race impose "the disability of color"; whose *Conjure Stories* highlights disability through its focus on bodily dispossession and
literal and figurative dismemberment; and whose 1901 historical novel
The Marrow of Tradition offers not only a fictionalized account of the
violent riots in Wilmington, North Carolina, but also a critical investigation of how the separate-but-equal doctrine espoused in *Plessy v. Ferguson* relied on the trope of disability. Chesnutt's emphasis on blackness
and disability, however, does not prevent him from framing the toxicity
of US racism as a national health crisis, one that affects the health and
well-being of Black *and* white Americans and that disrupts dominant
narratives of wholeness and normalcy. Chapter 5, which focuses primarily on scenes of racial exclusion and violence in James Weldon Johnson's
autobiography *Along This Way* and his novel *The Autobiography of an*

Ex-Colored Man, exposes how disability is one of the Jim Crow caste system's most effective tools of racial oppression. Instead of exclusively framing Jim Crow as a social system that separated white people from Black people, this chapter maps out in more detail the disabilities of Jim Crow—the way the system inflicted physical and psychological injuries on Black folks, disciplined their bodies, stigmatized them, and restricted their movement in public spaces. This chapter also argues for the necessity of considering Johnson's autobiography alongside his novel—for his autobiography presents an alternative path for the Black artist, one other than racial passing, and thus counters the cowardice of the novel's protagonist.

Chapter 6, in part 3, investigates the irony of racial color blindness—how performances of color blindness seemingly embrace disability and frequently profess racial equality but nevertheless perpetuate both racism and ableism. This chapter demonstrates how the doctrine and practice of color blindness—ableist performances of disability that have been injurious to Black people from the nineteenth century to the present—allow the disabilities of the color line to thrive. To demonstrate this phenomenon, I examine the deployment of color-blind constitutionalism within the law by focusing on Justice Marshall Harlan's dissent in *Plessy v. Ferguson* as well as the cultivation of color blindness within national culture by focusing on the disabling and deadly consequences of color blindness in the cases of Emmett Till and Eric Garner—two disabled, Black males whose intersectional identities made them vulnerable to state and anti-Black vigilante violence. I conclude this chapter by focusing on the intersectional and inclusive care work of contemporary Black activists. The epilogue considers the emergence of the "racial pandemic" within the viral pandemic by positing the color line as an ongoing problem that persists in the age of COVID-19.[64] The racist discourses surrounding the virus repeat a familiar narrative in which Black people are once again cast as disabled and held responsible for health conditions they have been exposed to.

The actions of the Black authors and activists in this book were both radical and resourceful. They enacted and created innovative responses to an oppressive and injurious legal, national, and social system that was designed to stigmatize and disable them. Challenging this system necessitated defining the relationship between blackness and disability for themselves in an effort to avoid the trap of the dominative narrative, where all too often, as Toni Morrison writes, "definitions belonged to the definers—not the defined."[65] What they did, as this book details, was simply ingenious. They crafted a means of survival and resistance out of the nation's offering of racial injustice by avowing disablement and disability—that which has been so often used to discriminate against them. In doing so, they offered a blueprint for the kind of coalition-building and cross-movement work that could possibly get us all free.

PART I

Age of Slavery

1

David Walker's Accessible *Appeal*

"Catalogue of Cruelties"

The message was ominous and emphatic. Near the conclusion of the third edition of *Walker's Appeal to the Coloured Citizens of the World*, the abolitionist David Walker inserted a warning to his Black antebellum readers and audiences about the dangers of literacy and worship in the nineteenth-century United States, where white supremacy ruled and anti-Black authority prevailed. He published this third (and final) edition in 1830, less than a year after publishing the first, in September 1829, and in that brief time, he had seen the pamphlet's circulation incite the ire of white authorities in southern states such as Georgia, Virginia, and North Carolina. Each state took extraordinary measures to prevent the *Appeal's* circulation. Upon discovering that sixty copies of Walker's *Appeal* had been delivered by a white mariner to a Black preacher for distribution in Savannah, the Georgia legislature enacted a new law quarantining Black sailors entering the state's ports and holding anyone found guilty of circulating seditious publications liable to the penalty of death. The Virginia House of Delegates narrowly passed a bill that made it illegal to write, print, or circulate incendiary publications, and North Carolina passed laws to imprison or whip any person who circulated materials that might stir up "a spirit of insurrection, conspiracy or rebellion" in a Black person (nominally free or enslaved) as well as to punish anyone who taught an enslaved person how to read or write.[1] Walker detested such measures, for he viewed knowledge as central to liberation, and he hoped his pamphlet would inspire the very spirit of insurrection that such laws attempted to squelch.

Walker's conflict of interest, however, did not stop him from alerting his readers and audiences about these stigmatizing and perilous obstacles, and he issued his warning in perhaps the most striking fashion ever: "☞ADDITION," Walker began: "They hinder us from going to hear the word of God—they keep us sunk in ignorance, and will not let us learn to read the word of God, nor write—If they find us with a book of any description in our hand, they will beat us nearly to death—they are so afraid we will learn to read." "They" refers to "the white Christians of America, who hold us in slavery" (also described as "pretenders to Christianity"), and their fear of Black literacy produced a plethora of restrictions for enslaved people, who were barred not only from reading and writing but also from worshiping God, hearing Bible verses, or even possessing a book.[2] Prohibiting literacy, through the law, entailed extensive regulation of the body and mind. For an enslaved person in the antebellum United States, illiteracy was a sociolegal disability—one that was remediable but for the stringent legal prohibitions against literacy. Literacy is often considered as a matter pertaining solely to the mind, but antebellum antiliteracy efforts exacted a toll on the body as well.

Walker's *Appeal* helps fill a gap in the archive of slavery by disclosing both the scope and severity of that toll. In particular, the *Appeal* details the disabilities of extralegal antiliteracy measures, measures left unmentioned in antiliteracy laws. Walker included what he called a "catalogue of cruelties" consisting of corporeal injuries inflicted onto Black people. Immediately after citing barriers to literacy and worship, Walker delineated the extent of white slaveholding Christians' brutality: "They brand us with hot iron—they cram bolts of fire down our throats—they cut us as they do horses, bulls, or hogs—they crop our ears and sometimes cut off bits of our tongues." Walker's parallel sentence structure spotlights white Christian enslavers' violent acts. Branding, cramming, cutting, and cropping: these are not the kind of punishments listed in antiliteracy laws; rather, these are the kind of punishments listed in slave laws for fugitives, where amputation was a cited practice. But, as the historian Janet D. Cornelius argues, "the most common widely known penalty for learning to read and write was amputation," even though "it was not true that amputation was a legal penalty."[3] Although the record of antiliteracy laws is extensive, it does not account for the penalty of amputation. The *Appeal* does, though, and Walker's pamphlet is not the only piece of evidence that described such punishments.

Testimonies of the formerly enslaved, particularly those interviewed for the Works Progress Administration (WPA), included similar details

of brutal assault, disablement, and amputation.[4] Doc Daniel Dowdy declared, "The first time you was caught trying to read or write, you was whipped with a cow-hide, the next time with a cat-o-nine tails and the third time they cut the first jint offen your forefinger."[5] And Samuel Hall stated that in North Carolina, "if the Negro ever learned to write and it was made known the law was that he or she must suffer the loss of a finger to keep him from writing."[6] Although such a law did not exist, it is easy to see why Hall understood this punishment as an attempt to prevent the purported crime. These punishments functioned as acts of terror designed to produce the sort of bodily deformities and disabilities that would perpetuate illiteracy.

The significance of Walker's acute attention to literacy suppression and disability is manifold. Walker recognized how the discourse of incapacity was often used as an impediment to freedom, and he understood legal and extralegal literacy suppression as highly hypocritical. Proslavery advocates, he observed, not only stigmatized Black people "as a tribe of TALKING APES, void of INTELLECT!!!!! *incapable* of LEARNING . . . incapable of acquiring knowledge!!! . . . incapable of self government!!" but also "instituted laws to hinder us from obtaining our freedom" and passed laws to "prohibi[t] all free or slave persons of colour, from learning to read or write."[7] They engaged in a two-pronged approach: first, they claimed that Black people lacked the intellectual capacity to learn; second, they enacted laws to prohibit literacy and hinder Black people from acquiring knowledge. It was the ultimate catch-22—no freedom without literacy, no literacy without freedom. The bodily amputations that ensued are significant because they suggest a link between de jure and de facto, between the strong arm of the law and the terror of the streets.

Walker considered the connections between antiliteracy laws and extralegal disablement as he composed and revised his *Appeal* between 1829 and 1830, and various narratives of disability have greatly shaped the third edition of Walker's *Appeal*, which aimed to reach as capacious an audience as possible: free and enslaved people; white and Black folks; literate, semiliterate, and illiterate people. I argue that the design of David Walker's *Appeal*—from its intended readership and audiences and its emphasis on recitation, performance, and emotion to its purposeful typography and the way the text mimics and revises the language and

structure of US founding documents as well as lambastes Thomas Jefferson's *Notes on the State of Virginia*—considers the interplay of blackness, disability, and accessibility at almost every turn. Walker's *Appeal* is accessible insofar as it provides a guide for engaging it in multiple modalities that work for a wide range of people. While the verso of the third edition's title page urges Black readers to turn the solitary, private act of reading into a communal, public performance, the punctuation and typography of Walker's *Appeal* instruct us in written form how to do it: the dashes signal where we can pause or take a slight breath; the exclamation points prompt us to elevate our voice in order to emote; the capitalizations compel us to modulate our vocal register for emphasis; the italics draw our attention to certain keywords; the bracketed and parenthetical phrases function as either asides or stage directions; the asterisks are notational; and the pointing index fingers or severed hands (what manuscript specialists call "manicules") denote not only which passages have been added to the most recent edition but also the performative cues readers could take when reciting Walker's *Appeal*—that is, the pointing index fingers function as an embodied *j'accuse*, telling readers which individuals (Jefferson foremost among them) we can point our finger at to accuse of wrongdoing in addition to which texts we can cite as evidence of the injurious color line or use as props for the staging of our performance. Likewise, Walker's invitation to recite to others (and the insistence that public recitation and performance are just as important to our reading practices as the solitary textual form) makes *Appeal* accessible to people who cannot read because of either illiteracy or another impairment.

Walker's typography, then, is an essential part of his *Appeal*, for it foregrounds a common lineage between writing and speech, print and orality, and words and communication that is as central to the Black oral tradition and the work of African American literary societies as it is to the elocution movement of the late eighteenth century, both of which deeply informed Walker's pamphlet. Yet, apart from occasional references that describe his typographic changes across editions as "minor" or refer to his stylistic form as "quirks," Walker's typography has not received the scholarly attention it deserves.[8] In fact, Walker's typography is often misprinted, and certain typographical elements are omitted entirely in reprints of his work.[9] The literary scholar Marcy J. Dinius

argues that "none of this scholarship has looked closely enough at the print itself to discover that the typographic radicalism of *Walker's Appeal* lies less in its exceptionality as a typographically unusual document than in the relation of its typographic form to its informational and argumentative content and to its performance."[10] I aim to uncover another typographic radicalism, one that explicitly links the *Appeal's* form to the disablement of slavery in order to demonstrate how Walker's accessible pamphlet exhibits interability compassion and cross-ability communication by imagining Black and disability futurity. I also show how the accessibility of Walker's *Appeal* is important to the fields of Black literary studies, disability studies, and performance studies, for the *Appeal* is a model for how to critically engage the lives of people who have been disabled by the regime of slavery.

The Design of Walker's *Appeal*

We do not have to wonder whether David Walker intended for the *Appeal* to be read aloud and heard. He told us that it was several times. At the beginning of the *Appeal*, on the verso of the title page in the pamphlet's third edition, Walker primed his readers with a set of instructions: "☞ It is expected that all coloured men, women and children,* of every nation, language and tongue under heaven, will try to procure a copy of this Appeal and read it, or get some one to read it to them, for it is designed more particularly for them." His address to "all coloured men, women and children" comes with a caveat. The notation next to the asterisk explains that this collective includes only those "who are not too deceitful, abject, and servile to resist the cruelties and murders inflicted upon us by the white slave holders, our enemies by nature." Nevertheless, readers can discern the gist of Walker's message: Black people are expected to acquire the *Appeal* and read it or arrange to have someone read the *Appeal* to members of the Black diaspora. Near the conclusion of the *Appeal*, Walker reiterated this point in a footnote in the fourth article, in which he took his anticolonization stance. He asked, "Why do the Slave-holders or Tyrants of America and their advocates fight so hard to keep my brethren from receiving and reading my Book of Appeal to them?" This rhetorical question was a commentary on how southern states were strengthening laws against slave literacy, and it also articulated one of Walker's most adamant appeals: to read his pamphlet aloud.[11]

Recitation and listening were integral to the composition and writing of the *Appeal*. Walker's work, after all, was meant to be heard. That is why Walker supposed his assailment of enslavers was "perhaps . . . too harsh for the American's delicate ears." That is why, in the midst of condemning Thomas Jefferson's *Notes*, he included bracketed stage directions—"[Here, my brethren, listen to him.]"—to his Black readers. That is why he twice implored white Americans, "Hear your language," when pointing out the hypocrisy of the Declaration of Independence. That is why Walker portrayed himself as both writer *and* speaker of his *Appeal*, declaring at one pivotal moment, "Here I pause to get breath, having labored to extract the above clause of this gentleman's speech, at that colonizing meeting."[12] In this moment, he practiced what he preached: he did not just instruct readers to recite his work to Black people; he also recorded his own act of recitation within his written text for everyone to read, recite, and hear.

Walker's declarations to recite and listen to his *Appeal* are clear, but his remarks regarding whom his *Appeal* is "more particularly" designed for are cryptic. In particular, his use of the pronoun "them" on the verso of the third edition's title page has vexed scholars—largely because the antecedent to the pronoun "them" in the final clause on the verso is confusing. As a result, many scholars have attempted to answer the question, Whom does "them" refer to?[13]

I wish I could say Walker made it easy to answer this question. But he made a number of competing statements about book design and intended audience that challenge even the most discerning critics. For instance, Walker's other references to his audience and book design in the second and fourth articles of the *Appeal* (both of which were included before the publication of the third edition) do not make the antecedent to "them" in the final clause on the title page verso any less ambiguous. In the third article, in which Walker addressed American preachers of Christianity, he stated, "Men of colour, who are also of sense, for you particularly is my APPEAL designed. Our more ignorant brethren are not able to penetrate its value. I call upon you therefore to cast your eyes upon the wretchedness of your brethren, and to do your utmost to enlighten them—*go to work and enlighten your brethren!*" And in a footnote near the end of *Appeal*, he wrote, "Some of my brethren, who are sensible, do not take an interest in enlightening the minds of our more ignorant brethren respecting this B O O K, and in reading it to them, just as though they will not have either to stand or fall by what is written in this book."[14]

These lines are easily misinterpreted, especially if one assumes (as a number of scholars have) that Walker's use of the term "ignorant" referred only to illiterate people and that his understanding of "sense" and "sensible" behavior applied solely to literate readers. In the *Appeal*, having "sense" is not synonymous with literacy, and being "ignorant" is not synonymous with illiteracy. These terms have multiple meanings in his pamphlet that make them difficult to pin down. In his second article, which focuses on the consequences of ignorance, Walker revealed the extent to which a person being "ignorant" or lacking "sense" was often determined by their "treachery and deceit" or "servile and abject submission," not their degree of literacy.[15]

Walker did not provide a definitive answer to the pressing question, Whom does "them" refer to? Yet his equivocation is understandable: any explicit instructions to teach illiterate enslaved people to read or to circulate his pamphlet (which lawmakers considered inflammatory) would have been considered a crime, one punishable by disablement or death. A careful review of the evidence, however, suggests that "them" on the title page verso most likely refers to "all," as in "all coloured men, women and children,* of every nation, language, and tongue." It is a democratic yet particularized "all," one that does not hierarchize literate and illiterate Black people. Again, the only Black people whom this "all" excludes are the ones who are "too deceitful, abject, and servile to resist." Everyone else is welcomed.

The inclusivity and accessibility of Walker's *Appeal* are a marvel. In the early nineteenth century, it was a rare and remarkable thing for a Black author to write explicitly to and for Black readers and auditors— let alone an enslaved, illiterate, and disabled Black audience. Consider, for example, the number of slave narratives that required authentication from white editors and amanuenses before publication and that focused on evoking the sympathy of white readers and eliciting their support for abolition. Toni Morrison reflects on this topic in the 2019 documentary *The Pieces I Am*. Morrison explains that many American books (even those written by ex-slave writers or twentieth-century Black writers) do not imagine Black people as their primary audience: "You could feel the address of the narrator talking to somebody white. I could tell because they're explaining things that they didn't have to explain if they were talking to me. The assumption is that the reader is a white person, and that troubled me. . . . Even Frederick Douglass—he's not talking to me. I can feel him holding back, and I understand that because the people supporting him were abolitionists, white people."[16] The implied white reader is an all-too-common feature of American literature, Morrison asserts, because of the invasive presence of the white gaze, an intractable force, which acts as though Black "lives have no meaning and no depth" without it.[17]

Walker's *Appeal* does not privilege the white reader. Black people are the primary audience in his pamphlet. From the outset, Walker announced his audience loud and clear in his title: *Walker's Appeal, in Four Articles; Together with a Preamble, to the Coloured Citizens of the World, but in Particular, and Very Expressly, to Those of the United States of America*—a gallant, audacious title to be sure—addresses the citizenry of the Black diaspora. Any nineteenth-century Black reader or auditor who saw or heard this title in full would have known that the author was addressing them as well as conferring citizenship on them. It was a bold move, claiming citizenship for all Black people in the world even as citizenship was being denied to Black folks in the United States. It was also an outright rejection of white supremacy writ large. As the literary critic David Kazanjian outlines, "By addressing the 'Coloured' as 'Citizens' both 'Of The World' and 'Of The United States Of America,' and by quoting and revising the Declaration of Independence in the final pages of the *Appeal*, Walker rewrites America's racially and nationally particularized claims to universal equality. Against the racialist articulation of whiteness with citizenship and the imperial articulation of the United States with the world, Walker offers a counterarticulation: 'coloured' particularity with the 'citizen's' global equality." This counterarticulation, Kazanjian adds, is "an appropriation and a rewriting, a critique of U.S. white supremacy from within the terms of its own discursive practices."[18] Walker railed, "ALL MEN ARE CREATED EQUAL!!" "Compare your own language above," he wrote, "extracted from your Declaration of Independence, with your cruelties and murders inflicted by your cruel and unmerciful fathers and yourselves on our fathers and on us."[19] Because the words *slave, slavery, Black,* and *colored* are not included in the Declaration of Independence, Walker revised that document in his *Appeal* to highlight the ways that free and enslaved Black people are left unaccounted for.

The persistent disregard of Black people in founding documents like the Declaration makes Walker's explicit regard for them a triumph in so many ways—especially so because he considered how the intersecting identities of blackness and disability made illiterate Black people particularly vulnerable to exclusion and designed a text to mitigate their marginalization and bring them into the fold. The radical thing about the *Appeal's* inclusive design is that it is accessible for illiterate and literate Black folks, and that accessibility counteracts the ways the nation imposed disabilities and exclusions on free and enslaved Black people. This inclusivity and accessibility are yet other reasons I consider it important to think of "them" on the title page verso as a reference to "all." As Walker pointed out in his revision of the Declaration, if "ALL" are "EQUAL!!" then why are Black people not included in that number? Walker's *Appeal* is more concerned with uniting Black folks (particularly disabled and nondisabled people with a will to resist) together for a common cause and survival than with creating a divide between them.

The sweeping measures deployed to maintain the illiteracy of enslaved people compelled Walker to craft a pamphlet that would be accessible to them. The dashes, exclamation points, italics, all caps and small caps, parentheses, brackets, and pointing index fingers that pebble his pamphlet are more than a measure of Walker's sermonic flourishes or dramatic flair. They aided in the recitation and performance of his words by others, and that performance and recitation had the potential to reach more members of his target audiences. The form of Walker's *Appeal* takes enslaved people's history of disablement into account. He wrote for a literate audience, and his writing was constructed in a way that could be relayed to an illiterate or otherwise impaired one.

Elizabeth McHenry discusses Walker's literary goals in her analysis of the two public spheres he accessed with his *Appeal*:

> It is important to note that for Walker the imperative that the literate read the *Appeal* to the illiterate was not a straightforward endorsement of the

already-scripted Western idea that those without literacy skills were also without logic. He did not assume that those without the ability to themselves read the *Appeal* were definitively without the presence of mind and sophistication of thought to eventually understand it. Rather than viewing literacy exclusively as a sign of an elevated state of reason, Walker recognized it as a powerful apparatus that might be deployed in various ways by black Americans to further their pursuit of civil rights.[20]

McHenry's reading of how Walker viewed literacy as a powerful apparatus to be variously deployed rather than as a sign of reason and logic is incredibly instructive. Her argument explains one way that Walker dislocated literacy from "sense" or, as she puts it, from "reason." It also shows the extent to which Walker valued Black folks who could not read.

The *Appeal* indicates that Walker not only appreciated illiterate Black voices but also thought that they had significant contributions to make to the nation. This message is encoded within another source: Thomas Sheridan's *A General Dictionary of the English Language* (1780). Sheridan was an influential Irish actor, rhetorician, and member of the elocution movement. In the *Appeal*, Walker encouraged his readers to turn to Sheridan's *Dictionary* to look up the meaning of the word *apathy*, a word used by Elias B. Caldwell, a lawyer who served as executive secretary of the American Colonization Society (ACS), in a speech in support of colonizing free Black people to Liberia. Walker wrote,

> ☞ See Mr. Caldwell's intended blessings for us, O! my Lord!! "No," said he, "if they must remain in their present situation, keep them in the *lowest state of degradation and ignorance*. The nearer you bring them to the condition of brutes, the better chance do you give them of possessing their *apathy*." Here I pause to get breath, having labored to extract the above clause of this gentleman's speech, at that colonizing meeting. I presume that everybody knows the meaning of the word "*apathy*,"—if any do not, let him get Sheridan's Dictionary, in which he will find it explained in full.[21]

Per Walker's instructions, I picked up Thomas Sheridan's *A General Dictionary of the English Language*—not because I did not know the meaning of the word but because I was hoping to find a lengthy definition of *apathy* that would trump the one in *Merriam-Webster*. I had no such luck. The definition of *apathy* in Sheridan's *Dictionary* simply reads, "Exemption from passion." That is an adequate definition, certainly, but not one I would describe as "explained in full." So I wondered if there might be another reason Walker directed us to *this* dictionary; there were certainly other existing dictionaries, including Noah Webster's more recent and comprehensive *An American Dictionary of the English Language* (1828), that he could have cited. As I mentioned earlier, this section of the *Appeal* caught my attention because of the way it showcases Walker as not only a writer but also a speaker. It is especially striking because he stated that he was so out of breath that he had to pause from speaking. This moment is significant, for at no other point in his *Appeal* does Walker reference his labored breathing or mention a need to "pause to get breath." It seemed like a sign, especially for a text that focuses so extensively on recitation and orality.

Flipping through a massive hardcover copy of Sheridan's *Dictionary* in search of another explanation, I discovered that his book is more than a dictionary in the modern sense of the word. It is also a guide on grammar, pronunciation, and oratory and includes excerpts from two of Sheridan's previous works, *Lectures on Elocution* (1762) and *Lectures on the Art of Reading* (1775). In the section on grammar, in particular section 7, "Of the Art of Delivery," Sheridan has a subsection titled "Pauses or Stops," which includes an extended discussion on pausing, punctuation, tones, and gestures and a remarkable passage about the passion—not apathy—of the "illiterate man":

> The source of these abuses may be farther traced, by attentively weighing the following observation—That no illiterate man ever uses false emphases, tones, or stops, in speaking; it is only the literate, those who have learned to read, that can fall into errors of that sort. For, as our ideas pass in train in our minds, and are there connected or divided, the illiterate man . . . exhibits them exactly as they pass in his mind. To the idea that makes the most forcible impression there, he gives the greatest force of expression in utterance; and therefore the strongest emphasis to the word which stands as its mark. And whatever emotions are excited in him by those ideas, he cannot help manifesting in suitable tones, looks, and gestures; as these necessarily proceed from an original law of his constitu-

tion, and without pains cannot be suppressed. Whereas the man who has learned to read, has been taught to connect or separate his words, by arbitrary rules of stopping, which are not taken from the natural train of our ideas. . . . It is here therefore the remedy is to be fought for, by supplying and correcting what is erroneous and defective in the art of reading. . . . Confirmed bad habits in a thing which we daily practice, can be removed only by a right method, and daily practice according to that method.[22]

The "abuses" to which Sheridan refers are the "erroneous" and "defective" delivery of literate men, who are inclined to speak in the way they read—in a "monotonous manner" that "is at once discordant to the ear, and disgusting to the understanding." Reading and speaking are two different skill sets, and the rules that apply to one do not apply to the other. Reading is accompanied with the "arbitrary rules of stopping," an unnatural and artificial expression of ideas. Speaking, on the other hand, is fueled by "emotions" and expressed through "suitable tones, looks, and gestures." With regard to speaking, the illiterate man never fails to deliver "the greatest force of expression in utterance." He has more natural ability, Sheridan observes, than the literate man: speaking comes "from an original law of his constitution."[23]

I imagine Walker would have been fascinated by Sheridan's observations about the passionate expressions of illiterate men. Sheridan's comments align with Walker's own sensibilities—with his decision to design an accessible pamphlet for literate and illiterate folks, with his disagreement with Caldwell about the apathy of the enslaved, and with the way he valued the voice of illiterate Black people. What Walker understood (and what Sheridan's remarks clarify) is that illiterate folks have an important contribution to make to American discourse. Walker's call for his literate brethren to recite his text aloud to illiterate auditors should not be misconstrued as a form of charity or pity. Those who were illiterate could bring their own unique skills—their distinctive tones, looks, and gestures—to bear on the material. In fact, a literate person's delivery or performance of the *Appeal* could be enhanced by the performance or delivery of an illiterate person, who, Sheridan argues, outshines the literati when it comes to public speaking and forms of expression. Performing the *Appeal* for illiterate folks could also contribute to the *Appeal*'s afterlife, its ability to be retold and reperformed even by people without access to the printed text or those who cannot read. The literati need their illiterate brethren as much as the latter need the former. Walker's pause because of loss of breath, in the middle of his own recitation no less, embodies just how much he needed his illiterate brethren too.

While I cannot verify that David Walker read "Pauses or Stops" in Thomas Sheridan's *Dictionary*, I am confident that he would have enjoyed reading a rhetorician like Sheridan discuss speaking and writing as two distinct art forms with two different sets of rules. I also think he would have taken a particular interest in Sheridan's alternative "method" for remedying the "chief defect" in writing in order to restore the art of speaking.[24] Sheridan's method for marking pauses in speech patterns broke with the conventional rules of punctuation. He created a system of diacritical accent marks that were to be used in place of more standard punctuation marks, such as commas, semicolons, colons, and periods. His system was well known in the late eighteenth century. For instance, Sheridan's diacritical marks are "identical" to the ones used by Thomas Jefferson in his extant rough draft of the Declaration of Independence, and they also appear in the proof copy of John Dunlap's official broadside printing of the Declaration.[25] Sheridan used a "small inclined line" (´) to signal a short pause, two lines (´´) for a pause "double the time of the former," three (´´´) for a "full stop," two horizontal lines (=) "to mark a pause longer than any belonging to the usual stops," and a "sloping line inclining to the right" (`), a grave accent, to "mark each emphatic word." "D`early belo`ved brethren = The scripture moveth us ´ in su`ndry places ´ to acknow`ledge and confe`ss our manifold sins and wickedness´´" is an example of how Sheridan would mark a sentence to signal pauses.[26] This line is an excerpt from the Evening Prayer from *The Book of Common Prayer*, and the addressee is the same one that Walker used for the preamble and first and fourth articles in his *Appeal*.

Walker's especial citation of Sheridan's *Dictionary* implies that his *Appeal* was informed by the work of the elocution movement. He did not adopt Sheridan's diacritical accents, but his use of punctuation marks was accretive, as Sheridan's lines were: each additional punctuation mark amplified or influenced the speaker's delivery. Walker's technique was in accordance with Sheridan's method, which suggests that they both thought the formal rules governing modern punctuation were unfit to capture the art of speaking and discourse. Walker's typography, similarly to Sheridan's marks, reflected his understanding of the imperfections of modern punctuation. Both men, consequently, flouted convention religiously.

Sheridan's *Dictionary*, however, was neither the only nor the main work to influence the design of Walker's pamphlet or to prime his interest in orality, elocution, and public speaking. Walker's *Appeal* was also informed by the organizing and activism of African American literary societies in the late eighteenth and early nineteenth centuries. According to the literary scholar Frances Smith Foster, these literary societies were the product of Afro-Protestant churches, which took initiative to create their own publishing spaces, newspapers, schools, and societies to help "foster literacy" within the Black community.[27] The practices of reading aloud, recitation, memorization, and public speaking were central components of these societies. They developed literary activities to cultivate critical thinking and spark intellectual debates. "They, therefore, encouraged the creation and expression of elocution and oratory, of reading and writing, of public articulation of ideas and ideals about personal and public concerns," argues Foster.[28] Because pamphlets were affordable and portable, they were effective at facilitating public expression as well as aiding in the practice of elocution and oratory, especially within enslaved communities that used covert means for engaging, enacting, or attempting literacy because they were barred from learning to read. As Gene Jarrett puts it, "Pamphlets were a flexible literary technology."[29] They were so flexible and portable, in fact, that Walker sewed copies of his *Appeal* into the lining of garments worn by sailors traveling to the South to assist the pamphlet's circulation beyond literary societies.[30]

The literacy work of African American literary societies was tied to a larger American project of nation building. In the eighteenth- and nineteenth-century United States, literacy marked something more than merely an education; literacy was emblematic of freedom and citizenship, power and independence. To withhold literacy was to withhold all the privileges that came with it—a fact that was known to members of African American literary societies. "In the years leading up to the American Revolution," McHenry observes, "reading, writing, and print were increasingly seen to be technologies of power. Colonists turned to written texts in the form of pamphlets and broadsides as a medium of public expression." Members of African American literary societies were cognizant "of the centrality of written texts of national construction to both the legitimacy of the new nation and to their status in it," and "they sought effective avenues of public access as well as ways to voice their demands for full citizenship and equal participation in the life of the republic," argues McHenry.[31] Walker understood all too well how reading, writing, and public expression functioned as "technologies of power." He conspicuously noted how the Declaration could include "ALL" yet exclude some, and he wanted Black folks to be included by any means necessary.

Thus, Walker was a rebel with a cause. His instruction for Black people to recite his pamphlet for enslaved people to hear is essentially a directive to engage in what was deemed unlawful behavior. Yet he instructed them to do so anyway both to make his pamphlet accessible to those who could not read and to make it possible for all Black people to gain access to citizenship. If literacy was a prerequisite for citizenship, then it was a valuable skill worth cultivating and acquiring to reach a desired goal. In *Accessible Citizenships*, the disability studies scholar Julie Avril Minich asks, "What does it mean to make citizenship accessible?" According to Minich, accessibility necessitates that citizenship "functions as a way of making the distribution of rights more equitable, not as a fixed relationship to a defined nation-state."[32] Equity, not equality, is key to accessible citizenships. The Declaration, after all, effectively emptied the word *equality* of all meaning, particularly for Black and Native people. Minich's definition, with its focus on rights distribution and equity, dovetails with Robert McRuer's description. In *Crip Theory*, McRuer argues, "An accessible society, according to the best, critically disabled perspectives, is not simply one with ramps and Braille signs on 'public' buildings, but one in which our ways of relating to, and depending on, each other have been reconfigured."[33] Accessibility, in other words, is not merely structural; it is relational. It requires that a society reconfigure its understanding of interdependent and interpersonal relationships. What good is US citizenship if a person born in the country can be enslaved? How useful is freedom if, according to *Dred Scott*, Black people have access to "no rights which the white man was bound to respect"?[34] What does *criminal* mean in a country that criminalizes the rights to literacy and free speech *only* for particular racialized and Indigenous groups?

The Performative and Political Character of Walker's Punctuation and Typography

With repeated calls for recitation and listening, Walker's *Appeal* aimed to reconfigure the interpersonal relationships between "*Christian* Americans!" and free and enslaved Black folks.[35] Given how cruelly white Christians had behaved toward Black people, Walker knew it would be a difficult task. To demonstrate how challenging it would be, Walker enumerated a litany of injuries that these Christians have inflicted on Black people:

> ☞ ADDITION.—I will give here a very imperfect list of cruelties inflicted on us by the enlightened Christians of America.—First, no trifling portion of them will beat us nearly to death, if they find us on our knees praying to God, ...—they chain and hand-cuff us, and while in that miserable and wretched condition, beat us with cow-hides and clubs—they keep us half naked and starve us sometimes nearly to death under their infernal whips or lashes (which some of them shall have enough of yet)—They put on us fifty-sixes and chains, and make us work in that cruel situation, and in sickness, under lashes to support them and their families. ... They take us, (being ignorant,) and put us as drivers one over the other, and make us afflict each other as bad as they themselves afflict us—and to crown the whole of this catalogue of cruelties, they tell us that we the (blacks) are an inferior race of beings! incapable of self-government!!—We would be injurious to society and ourselves, if tyrants should loose their unjust hold on us!!! That if we were free we would not work, but would live on plunder or theft!!!! that we are the meanest and laziest set of beings in the world!!!!! That they are obliged to keep us in bondage to do us good!!!!!!— That we are satisfied to rest in slavery to them and their children!!!!!!— That we ought not to be set free in America, but ought to be sent away to Africa!!!!!!!!—That if we were set free in America, we would involve the country in a civil war, which assertion is altogether at variance with our feeling or design, for we ask them for nothing but the rights of man, viz. for them to set us free, and treat us like men, and there will be no danger, for we will love and respect them, and protect our country—but cannot conscientiously do these things until they treat us like men. ☜[36]

It cannot be stressed enough that it took a tremendous amount of labor to produce this passage. First, it required extensive reading and research of a variety of sources on Walker's part to recount the disablement of Black people during the antebellum period. Second, it required extensive effort on the part of a compositor, who would have had to manually add the accretive exclamation points strategically placed throughout this passage. Dinius reminds us that "in the age of word processing, strings of exclamation points are not rare; to signify anger, absurdity, or excitement, we have only to hold down two keys to add as many exclamation points as desired. It is easy to forget that when *Walker's Appeal* was published, a compositor would have set each point manually, as an individual piece of type."[37]

Each exclamation point added essential meaning to Walker's message, and each aimed to elicit a reaction and performance from readers and auditors alike. As he recorded the arguments used to maintain and defend the institution of slavery, Walker added an exclamation point to punctuate his claims. Each additional exclamation point in the passage was meant to mark Walker's rising fury in his *Appeal*, a fury that reached seemingly cataclysmic levels as the number of exclamation points increased from one to eight. Yet Walker was not the only one who meant to be moved by his punctuation. Readers and auditors were expected to respond or emote to each of his exclamation points as well. As Tara Bynum argues, his "punctuation narrates" anger and "invites us to witness ourselves as part of his affective community."[38] Likewise, Walker's repeated references to "us" and "our," interspersed between his exclamation marks, made readers and auditors the direct object of the action, not just him.

Punctuation marks extract and shepherd performances. That is what they are intended to do, as a number of literary theorists have argued. In "Punctuation for the Reader," Paula Backscheider utilizes a sports analogy to convey this point. She compares punctuation to elements of football to reveal its performative aspects: "Punctuation marks are like signals given by football referees. Everyone in the stadium cannot hear the referee call 'offside,' but they can see the signal. We cannot hear the writer, but we can see that the comma means that he wants us to pause. Just as the referees cannot make up their own signals, so the writer must

—They will not suffer us to meet together to worship the God who made us—they brand us with hot iron—they cram bolts of fire down our throats—they cut us as they do horses, bulls, or hogs—they crop our ears and sometimes cut off bits of our tongues—they chain and hand-cuff us, and while in that miserable and wretched condition, beat us with cow-hides and clubs—they keep us half naked and starve us sometimes nearly to death under their infernal whips or lashes (which some of them shall have enough of yet)—They put on us fifty-sixes and chains, and make us work in that cruel situation, and in sickness, under lashes to support them and their families.—They keep us three or four hundred feet under ground working in their mines, night and day to dig up gold and silver to enrich them and their children.—They keep us in the most death-like ignorance by keeping us from all source of information, and call us, who are free men and next to the Angels of God, their property!!!!!! They make us fight and murder each other, many of us being ignorant, not knowing any better.—They take us, (being ignorant,) and put us as drivers one over the other, and make us afflict each other as bad as they themselves afflict us—and to crown the whole of this catalogue of cruelties, they tell us that we the (blacks) are an inferior race of beings! incapable of self government!!—We would be injurious to society and ourselves, if tyrants should loose their unjust hold on us!!! That if we were free we would not work, but would live on plunder or theft!!!! that we are the meanest and laziest set of beings in the world!!!!! That they are obliged to keep us in bondage to do us good!!!!!!!— That we are satisfied to rest in slavery to them and their children!!!!!!—That we ought not to be set free in America, but ought to be sent away to Africa!!!!!!!!!—That if we were set free in America, we would involve the country in a civil war, which assertion is altogether at variance with our feeling or design, for we ask them for nothing but the rights of man, viz. for them to set us free, and treat us like men, and there will be no danger, for we will love and respect them, and protect our country—but cannot conscientiously do these things until they treat us like men.

How cunning slave-holders think they are ! ! !— How much like the king of Egyptwho, after he saw plainly that God was determined to bring out his people, in spite of him and his, as powerful as they were. He was willing that Moses, Aaron and the Elders of Israel, but not all the people should go and serve the Lord. But God deceived him as he will Christian Americans, unless they are very cautious how they move. What would have become of the United States of America, was it not for those among the whites, who not in words barely, but in truth and in deed, love and fear the Lord ?— Our Lord and Master said :—† " Whoso shall of " fend one of these little ones which believe in me, " it were better for him that a millstone were hang " ed about his neck, and that he were drowned in " the depth of the sea." But the Americans with this very threatening of the Lord's, not only beat his little ones among the Africans, but many of them they put to death or murder. Now the avaricious Americans, think that the Lord Jesus Christ will let them off, because his words are no more than the words of a man ! ! ! In fact, many of them are so avaricious and ignorant, that they do not believe in our Lord and Saviour Jesus Christ. Tyrants may think they are so skillful in State affairs is the reason that the government is preserved. But I tell you, that this country would have been given up long ago, was it not for the lovers of the Lord. They are indeed, the salt of the earth. Remove the people of God among the whites, from this land of blood, and it will stand until they cleverly get out of the way.

---

* See St. Matthew's Gospel, chap. xviii. 6.

Figures 1.1. (facing page) and 1.2. Excerpts from *Walker's Appeal*, third ed. (Boston, 1830; courtesy of the Wilson Special Collections Library at the University of North Carolina at Chapel Hill).

use the 'standard' signals of punctuation if he is to be understood."[39] Walker did not abide by the standard rules of punctuation in *Appeal*, but his marks transmitted signals and evoked affective responses all the same.

Exclamation points are especially good at soliciting affective, dramatic responses from readers and audiences. In an imaginative dialogue about semicolons, colons, and exclamation points, the literary scholar Jennifer DeVere Brody writes of the latter that "when [they are] encountered, audiences almost invariably react—widening their eyes, raising an eyebrow, skipping a heartbeat, rushing in (to the text) to help. We see the exclamation point hopping its dance, its action and appearance are in effect one—performing in a singular gesture." "The exclamation point," Brody continues, "certainly solicits a reaction from an addressee. It can be an element of surprise, pain, fear, or anger (all affective states). . . . It is, however, resolutely emotional. The exclamation point is an amplifier; it pumps up the (visceral) volume."[40] The range of emotions is important to note. In the pantheon of punctuation marks, the potential for such varied reactions is what gives the exclamation point its distinctive character.

Even the shape of the exclamation point appears both dangerous and sportive. As Theodor Adorno puts it, "An exclamation point looks like an index finger raised in warning."[41] Or, as Joseph Lasky states, "Exclamation-mark or Exclamation-point. This mark consists of a short line at the top, that tapers like a billiard-cue, and a period directly under it."[42] The form of the exclamation point is such that a reader might be unsure if it is an instrument of play or of pain. The context matters. Such confusion is not all that surprising given that, according to Lasky, the exclamation mark comes with a competing set of nicknames: "It is called, for short, an *exclam*, a *bang*, and a *screamer*. This mark is said to have been formed from the Latin *Io*, joy."[43] These nicknames suggest both displeasure and delight. The stark contrast between these two feelings is enough to perplex any reader or speaker. My point is that the exclamation marks in the *Appeal* could provoke a variety of emotions. But, at the very least, they should spark you to do something.

Walker's exclamation points—along with his dashes, parentheses, periods, and pointing index fingers in the passage—all ply his prose with performative gestures. The dashes, for instance, that splice each sentence or phrase "capture both connection and detachment," Adorno observes.[44] The fragmentary form of dashes could seduce readers into a slight, subtle pause, but their connecting quality should quickly propel us to the next sentence. And it is hard for me to envision that anyone could read the line "they tell us that we the (blacks) are an inferior race of beings!" and choose not to recite the parenthetical "(blacks)" in a hushed (or similarly modulated) tone that later rises once it meets the exclamation point. It is also hard to envision that "(blacks)" is the word "they" would use to describe a people they believe "are an inferior race of beings!" (Perhaps that is why Walker chose to enclose that particular word within parentheses.)[45]

Of all the aforementioned marks and symbols, the pointing index fingers or severed hands (☞ ☜) have the most peculiar history. William H. Sherman's *Used Books* provides a useful gloss of the history and function of this symbol, explaining that the symbol "often served to mark noteworthy passages" or "to highlight passages that were added to a new edition of an old text."[46] Walker used both methods of the pointing index finger in the *Appeal*. Yet he highlighted passages that were added to a new edition by using ☞ at the beginning of the passage with "ADDITION" in small caps immediately following that pointing index finger and using ☜ at the conclusion of the new passage. (See my last block quotation for an example.) These severed hands, though rare in modern literature, "may have been the most common symbol produced both for and by readers in the margins of manuscripts and printed books" between the twelfth and eighteenth centuries, Sherman observes.[47] Since that time, though, these pointing index fingers have fallen into comparative disuse. It is a pity given the momentous gestural and performative function of pointing index fingers—the way they embody the movement and comportment of speakers and writers in the absence of archival visual or phonographic recordings. We do not know the sound or timbre of Walker's voice, and there is no footage of his mannerisms, gait, or oratorical style. But every pointing finger leaves a discernible trace of his authorial expression and speaking demeanor.[48]

The various names used to describe this pointing index finger also have a distinctive history. Even though most readers could infer its function, Sherman explains that "there is no single word that will conjure it up for everyone." In fact, many names have been given to the severed hand. Sherman reveals, "I have now found no fewer than fifteen English names for what I prefer to follow the manuscript specialists in calling the manicule: hand, hand director, pointing hand, pointing finger, pointer, digit, fist, mutton fist, bishop's fist, index, indicator, indicule, maniple, and pilcrow."[49] Despite this list of varied names, Sherman makes a pitch for why the word *manicule* should be the one that scholars adopt to describe this symbol.[50]

However, I have decided not to use the word *manicule*. I have chosen instead to refer to this symbol either as a *pointing index finger* or a *severed hand*. The image of a severed hand takes on a symbolic meaning once we consider the history of disablement within slavery, particularly as it relates to antebellum efforts to thwart literacy. As Walker described, the punishments for enslaved people who learned to read included whippings and dismemberment. And, as the testimonies of the formerly enslaved such as Doc Daniel Dowdy and Samuel Hall reveal, the punishment for literacy could be the amputation of the forefinger, also known as the index finger. Henry Nix, who was a slave in Upson County, Georgia, also recalled what happened after his uncle stole a book in an attempt to learn to read and write: "Marse Jasper had the white doctor take off my Uncle's fo' finger right down to de 'fust jint' . . . as a sign for de res uv 'em!"[51] Consequently, I prefer to describe the symbol in a way that refers to the body parts that it visually represents. Within this context of slavery and punishments for literacy, the visual representation of pointing index fingers or severed hands on the printed page signaled more than just a noteworthy passage or new addition. They also signified the risks that every enslaved person took if they were caught reading or caught in possession of the *Appeal* as well as the risks that every free Black person took if they recited this pamphlet aloud to enslaved people. The pointing index finger, then, indicated both a passage and a punishment. Neither free nor enslaved Black people were exempt from that punishment. The sight of these severed hands probably influenced the performances of Black antebellum readers and auditors.

For these reasons, Walker's *Appeal* is a "scriptive thing," what the performance studies scholar Robin Bernstein defines as "an item of material culture that prompts meaningful bodily behaviors." "The set of prompts that a thing issues," Bernstein explains, "is not the same as a performance because individuals commonly resist, revise, or ignore instructions. In other words, the set of prompts does not reveal a performance, but it does reveal a *script* for a performance. That script is itself a historical artifact. Examination of that artifact can produce new knowledge about the past."[52] Walker provided a script for Black performance and orality. He directed Black readers to procure, read, and recite his *Appeal*, and he provided them with cues in the text that prompted a particular recitation to their illiterate brethren who could, in turn, perform the work again in their own way. These performances provide new insights about Black resistance during the antebellum period. First, they transformed antebellum Black readers and auditors into outlaws. Since it was illegal to teach enslaved people how to read and write as well as illegal for enslaved people to learn how to read and write, recitation and listening were acts of rebellion. Walker's request to read and recite his pamphlet was a direct instruction to break the law and become political dissidents; his instructions elicited the very resistance that the *Appeal* demanded. Second, they made Walker's *Appeal* accessible to an inclusive audience: not just literate readers but also semiliterate, illiterate, and other disabled audiences. Third, they allowed Black people to enact one of Walker's most effective arguments against the racist ideas sketched in Jefferson's *Notes*: Black people express a range of emotions, feel pain, and deliver orations; their capacity to do so serves as evidence that Black folks of mixed abilities are capable of self-governance, that they are of sound constitution, and, thus, that they are fit for freedom.

David Walker cited sources aplenty in the *Appeal*—including the Bible, *Freedom's Journal* and other periodicals, letters, speeches, Thomas Sheridan's *General Dictionary*, Murray's *English Grammar*, the Declaration of Independence, and so on—but the source that received the most attention is Thomas Jefferson's *Notes on the State of Virginia*. According to Gene Jarrett, "the pamphlet cites Jefferson about twenty times explicitly (such as by name, in reference to *Notes*, and through quotations) and implicitly (such as in reference to Jefferson's colleagues)."[53] On several occasions, Walker pointed the index finger directly at Jefferson, so we do not have to guess whom he blamed or why he blamed him. We also do not have to wonder why Walker critiqued him, for he stated explicitly, "unless we try to refute Mr. Jefferson's arguments respecting us, we will only establish them." And by "we," Walker was referring specifically to Black people: "We, and the world wish to see the charges of Mr. Jefferson refuted by the blacks *themselves*, according to their chance; for we must remember that what the whites have written respecting this subject, is other men's labours, and did not emanate from the blacks."[54] Following Walker's instructions once again, I turn my attention to Jefferson's *Notes* to offer my own refutation of his arguments against Black people, particularly the way his arguments frame Black folks as inherently disabled.

"The Injuries They Have Sustained": Thomas Jefferson's *Notes on the State of Virginia*

Five years after Thomas Jefferson composed the original draft of the Declaration of Independence and several years before he would observe the creation and ratification of the new Constitution of the United States from his diplomatic post in Paris, Jefferson, in 1781, had written a draft of *Notes on the State of Virginia*. First published without his name in 1785 as a limited French edition (in an effort to maintain his anonymity) and then published in London in 1787 as the first English edition (once he realized that effort was futile), *Notes* was Jefferson's first book. It was written as a response to a set of "Queries" posed by Francois Barbé-Marbois, then secretary of the French delegation in the United States, who was requesting geographical, populational, cultural, military, legal, scientific, political, financial, and historical information about the states. The text is sometimes understood as a corollary to the Declaration of Independence or as a rich, focused sourcebook on the extent to which the largest and most influential state in the union could fulfill, according to the historian Peter S. Onuf, "the American Revolution's promise."[55]

Yet the Jefferson who wrote the Declaration of Independence was not the Jefferson who wrote *Notes*. For one, during the writing and publication of *Notes*, Jefferson underwent cataclysmic changes in his personal and professional life: his wife, Martha Wayles Jefferson, who suffered from illness and the effects of frequent childbirth, died in 1782. Second, after enduring a brutal two-year term as governor of Virginia—during which he was branded as a coward, nearly censured for his irresponsible wartime tactics, and seriously considered retiring from public service—Jefferson experienced a sudden course correction in his career when he assumed broader governmental responsibilities: he served as a Virginia delegate in the Confederation Congress (1783–84) and later as the new nation's minister to France (1785–89). Such professional and personal experiences altered Jefferson's orientation, making him more aware of the fragility of the human body, the vagaries of political life, and the vulnerability of the body politic. Unfortunately, Jefferson's life experiences did not translate into a newfound compassion for his fellow Black citizens, including those he enslaved.

Jefferson pursued a different goal in *Notes* than he did in the Declaration. As Jarrett observes, while the Declaration of Independence proclaimed the "unalienable Rights" of US citizens to "Life, Liberty, and the pursuit of Happiness," *Notes*, particularly in its focus on slavery and the incorporation of Black folks, scrutinized whether Black people in the United States were *capable* of exercising those rights.[56] Independence, Jefferson knew, had to be declared before he could attend to matters of constitution, but one's constitution mattered for the formation of the nation. And, in *Notes*, the term *constitution* had a dual meaning. It referred both to the system of beliefs and laws by which a state is governed and to the physical health and condition of its citizens.

In "Query XIV: The Administration of Justice and Description of the Laws?," in which Jefferson offered his most famous views on slavery, he made clear his belief that Black people suffered from defective constitutions in both mind and body. While he qualified his views of Black inferiority "as a suspicion only," the certainty with which he spoke about Black corporeality and cognition gave the impression that he advanced his argument on much more than a mere hunch. Regarding the mind, he argued that the "faculties" of Black folks were inherently inferior to those of whites in both "reason" and "imagination," claiming that Black people "could scarcely be found capable of tracing and comprehending the investigations of Euclid," nor could they utter "a thought above the level of plain narration." Citing Phillis Wheatley and Ignatius Sancho (an eighteenth-century Afro-British writer who documented his enslavement) as examples of Black writers who did not meet certain literary standards, Jefferson aimed to challenge the mental ability of Black people and to explain why they could not be included in the national body politic.[57]

Jefferson's shift from rights to capability unjustly portioned out freedom in the United States along sharp racial lines, bestowing white citizens with legal and moral authority while subjecting Black folks to a litmus test of competency and fitness. It was a crafty and calculated move, a feint that transformed the meaning of independence. It was the difference between understanding freedom as a privilege or as a burden, as an asset or a debt, as something that is owned rather than something that is owed, as immunity or a disability. Jefferson did not question the rights of white US citizens, but he wanted to make sure that Black people possessed the requisite skills to employ their rights, that they had the cognitive capability for logic, oration, and imagination, something he assumed was necessary in order for them to exercise their rights. His message: that which was assumed and guaranteed to white folks must be earned and achieved by Black folks.

A root word of *capable* is *able*, the same as for *disable*—an etymology that Jefferson understood and exploited in his critique of not only the mental capabilities of Black people but also their presumed physical disabilities. In an effort to prove that Black people were "inferior to the whites in the endowments of both body and mind," Jefferson wrote that "a difference of structure in the pulmonary apparatus, which a late ingenious experimentalist* has discovered to be the principal regulator of animal heat, may have disabled them from extricating, in the act of inspiration, so much of that fluid from the outer air, or obliged them in expiration, to part with more of it." Although Jefferson's syntax was reckless and unruly, his sentiment was clear. He wanted to situate disability as something innate in the bodies of Black folks, to prove that "it is not their condition, then, but nature, which has produced the distinction."[58]

The "pulmonary apparatus" was not the only part of the anatomy where Jefferson attempted to locate disability. Moving from a discussion of racial difference to racial ability, Jefferson appraised both external and internal features of the Black body and, with each component part, discerned either a deficiency or deformity: skin color "which covers all the emotions"; "less hair on the face and body"; a lack of "elegant symmetry of form"; kidneys that secrete too little with glands that secrete too much, a combination that produced a "very strong and disagreeable odour." He, in effect, played the role of scientist, donning his "Optical glasses," sharpening his "Anatomical knife," and examining Black people "as subjects of natural history."[59] Yet his version of science was natural and social, and it included a measure of racism substantial enough to crack that poetical creed of American human rights that he once composed in the Declaration.

On those rare moments in *Notes* when Jefferson conceded that Black people were equal or superior to whites in some capacity (a concession that the historian Fawn M. Brodie regards as evidence of his "quixotic"— even "radical"—politics, given his status as a white person in the eighteenth century), he would undercut his praise by spotting anew another supposed malady, one that usually called into question the mental, physical, or emotional competency of Black people.[60] Jefferson wrote that Black folks were "at least as brave, and more adventuresome" than white people but quickly added that their bravery and sense of adventure probably emerged from "a want of forethought." He claimed their "love is ardent," but it lacked "sentiment," "reflection," and "imagination." His remark that Black folks "in music . . . are more generally gifted than the whites with accurate ears for tune and time" came on the heels of his proclamation that they, in reason and imagination, ranked far below not only whites but also Native Americans, who could "astonish you with strokes of the most sublime oratory; such as prove their reason and sentiment strong, their imagination glowing and elevated." In "Query VI," in which Jefferson discussed his encounters with Black "Albinos" who were "born of parents who had no mixture of white blood," he described them as "well formed, strong, healthy, perfect in their senses" before quickly noting that "their eyes are in a perpetual tremulous vibration, very weak, and much affected by the sun: but they see better in the night than we do." The remarkable endurance and resilience of Black people were even characterized as inabilities to feel pain and suffering to the same degree as other racial and ethnic groups. "Their griefs are transient," he wrote. "Those numberless afflictions, which render it doubtful whether heaven has given life to us in mercy or in wrath, are less felt . . . with them."[61]

Even when Jefferson wrote of Black people that "in memory they are equal to the whites," his claim worked to affirm his conviction that there could be no racial and national reconciliation without the separation of Black and white people. The differences between Black and white folks were simply too great for Jefferson to imagine them living together in harmony. His compliment served as an answer to the central metaquestion posed in "Query XIV": "Why not retain and incorporate the blacks into the state, and thus save the expence of supplying, by importation of white settlers, the vacancies they will leave?" As Jefferson explained, neither retention nor incorporation would be promising solutions: "Deep rooted prejudices entertained by the whites; ten thousand recollections, by the blacks, of the injuries they have sustained; new provocations; the real distinctions which nature has made; and many other circumstances, will divide us into parties, and produce convulsions which will probably never end but in the extermination of the one or the other race."[62] The emancipation of Black people must be followed by their emigration from the United States; otherwise, Jefferson warned, the nation would run the risk of a cataclysmic race war, in which one race would probably be exterminated by the other.

Jefferson's focus on memory was another example of how a Jeffersonian compliment can turn out to be condemnatory. Elsewhere in "Query XIV," Jefferson described memory as the most fundamental cognitive function for learning Greek, Roman, European, and US history and languages: "The memory is then most susceptible and tenacious of impressions; and the learning of languages being chiefly a work of memory, it seems precisely fitted to the powers of this period, which is long enough too for acquiring the most useful languages antient and modern."[63] He clearly understood the relationship between memory and education, especially with children. Yet Jefferson not only questioned the mental capacity of Black folks but also used his remark about their ability to remember against them.

What Jefferson feared was not merely Black people's ability to remember but, more specifically, their ability to remember "the injuries they have sustained." The content of their memories, that is, was just as important as their acts of remembrance. In "Query XIV," Jefferson devoted a tremendous amount of time to tallying the inherent mental and physical disabilities of Black people. But in this one telling moment, he implied that their "injuries" were not innate, that they had been "sustained" from outside forces. Unfortunately, he did not elaborate on which injuries he was referring to. The list of injuries, in truth, could have been quite long. Did the injuries refer to the slave codes that mandated fugitives be hamstrung and branded for running away for freedom? Could the injuries have referred to sexual assault, maiming, or disfiguring, all crimes that Jefferson notably listed in *Notes* as part of Virginia's revised legal code? Whatever the reference, Jefferson's recognition of Black people's sustained injuries was one of those moments when he deviated from his script. It was on par with his point that "it will be right to make great allowances for the difference of condition, of education, of conversation, of the sphere in which [Black people] move."[64] Rather than absolve Jefferson, however, these claims provide insight into just how calculated his other observations were. They prove both that he knew about the theories of environmentalism and that the lion's share of his commentary was meant to dispute them. His emphases on internal and external features, inherent and innate defects, were an attempt to undermine one of the main arguments for Black equality. As Winthrop A. Jordan states, "Jefferson was thoroughly aware that the environmentalist argument could serve (and actually had) to make a case for Negro equality, and hence he went to great lengths to prove that Negroes' lack of talent did not stem from their condition."[65]

One of Jefferson's ultimate purposes was to frame Black people as a corporeal threat to the safety and security of the state, and he did so by priming his readers to link the legal distribution of justice in Virginia to the regulation of contagion and disorder. Included in his description of Virginia's laws was a key passage about the necessity of protecting that state's citizens from harm. He wrote, "The laws have also descended to the preservation and improvement of the races of useful animals, such as horses, cattle, deer; to the extirpation of those which are noxious, as wolves, squirrels, crows, blackbirds; and to the guarding our citizens against infectious disorders, by obliging suspected vessels coming into the state, to perform quarantine, and by regulating the conduct of persons having such disorders within the state."[66] Jefferson's transitions from "animals" to "vessels" to "persons" were incredibly quick, but all were listed as potential dangers that the law must expunge, isolate, or regulate. If you compare the language in this passage to Jefferson's observations about Black people, you will notice his striking reliance on the lexicon of disability. Words like *noxious, infectious, quarantine*, and *disorders* are related to words like *disabled, injuries, diseased*, and *condition* (terms he used to describe Black people and enslaved people). Such strong similarity in language suggests Jefferson's reliance on the power of suggestion and, thus, the power of metaphor. If "disorders" must be guarded against, quarantined, or controlled to protect the citizenry and Jefferson described Black bodies as "disabled" and abnormal, then, by association, the intense social regulation of Black people would be warranted because it was necessary to ensure the safety of the citizens of the nation-state. This logic had detrimental consequences for Black people. It shaped the meanings of blackness, slavery, citizenship, mobility, and freedom for Black folks in the United States, and it contributed to the fraught history of race and disability—even well after formal emancipation. Injuries were sustained indeed, and David Walker took great care to point them out.

"They Have Done Us So Much Injury": David Walker's Refutation of Jefferson's *Notes*

The unnamed and unattributed "injuries" mentioned in Thomas Jefferson's *Notes* were the primary source of David Walker's attack in the *Appeal*. Unlike Jefferson, however, Walker identified what those injuries were and who was responsible for them. Each section of the *Appeal*—the preamble and four articles—detailed the injurious treatment Black people had endured as a result of enslavement, illiteracy, poor education, slaveholding religion, and colonization as well as identified those guilty parties involved. Some individuals—such as Henry Clay, Elias B. Caldwell, and Thomas Jefferson (although Jefferson died before Walker published his *Appeal*)—were addressed by name and roundly condemned for their racist remarks about Black people. Some groups—such as white American Christians, enslavers, schoolmasters, and preachers—were mentioned by affiliation or occupation and denounced for their behavior toward enslaved people. As Walker stated in the *Appeal*'s first article, one of his goals was "to demonstrate to the satisfaction of the most incredulous, that we, (coloured people of these United States of America) are the *most wretched, degraded* and *abject* set of beings that *ever lived* since the world began, and that the white Americans having reduced us to the wretched state of *slavery*, treat us in that condition *more cruel* (they being an enlightened and Christian people,) than any heathen nation did any people whom it had reduced to our condition."[67] This sentiment is one that Walker expressed throughout the *Appeal* (especially at the outset, on the verso of the title page, and in the preamble)—but the italics alter the emphasis of the line and call attention to the reordering of key words conjuring up images of slavery's debilitating conditions in addition to the comparative form, marking chattel slavery and manumission in the United States as distinct from (and "*more cruel*" than) earlier forms of slavery and manumission elsewhere.

For Walker, the distinction between the condition of slavery and the nature of enslaved people was paramount to disproving Jefferson's claims about the presumed innate disabilities of Black bodies and minds. While Jefferson argued that Black people, by nature, were inherently inferior to white people, Walker argued that the conditions of slavery were debilitating and disabling. It was a distinction that made a monumental difference, yet one that Jefferson virtually ignored in his assessment of Black people's external and internal features, finding deficiencies or deformities in everything from their skin, hair, and physique to their kidneys, glands, respiratory system, cognition, and imagination.

One key example of this distinction between condition and nature that Walker critiqued in Jefferson's *Notes* concerns Jefferson's take on the differences between enslaved Romans and enslaved Black folks in the United States. Jefferson insisted, "We know that among the Romans, about the Augustan age especially, the condition of their slaves was much more deplorable than that of the blacks on the continent of America. . . . The American slaves cannot enumerate this [the selling of "sick and superannuated slaves"] among the injuries and insults they receive."[68] Walker outright rejected this claim in the *Appeal*, asserting, "The world knows, that slavery as it existed among the Romans, (which was the primary cause of their destruction) was, comparatively speaking, no more than a *cypher*, when compared with ours under the Americans."[69]

Despite this rebuttal, Walker felt that Jefferson's opinions regarding Roman slaves required more deliberation, that they revealed something about his views of the constitution of Black people:

But let us review Mr. Jefferson's remarks respecting us some further. Comparing our miserable fathers, with the learned philosophers of Greece, he says: "Yet notwithstanding these and other discouraging circumstances among the Romans, their slaves were often their rarest artists. They excelled too, in science, insomuch as to be usually employed as tutors to their master's children; Epictetus, Terence and Phaedrus, were slaves,—but they were of the race of whites. It is not their *condition* then, but *nature*, which has produced the distinction."* See this, my brethren!! Do you believe that this assertion is swallowed by millions of the whites? Do you know that Mr. Jefferson was one of as great characters as ever lived among the whites?[70]

Per usual, Walker's typography tells us how to read Jefferson, guiding us to the section of utmost importance and instructing us on how to respond. The most salient words in this passage, as Walker's italics stress, are "*condition*" and "*nature*," and the most appropriate response to Jefferson's comments, as Walker's punctuation suggests, is a combination of anger and astonishment. The distinction drawn between the words *condition* and *nature* aims to depict the capacity of Roman slaves to excel in the arts and science as natural, as an essence so inherent to their character and constitution that not even a "more deplorable" form of slavery could root it out. Yet Jefferson's depiction relied on a false equivalency; he juxtaposed the "natural" capacity of enslaved Romans against the "natural" incapacity of enslaved Black people for the purpose of excluding Black people from political representation and citizenship. This sleight of hand is what Walker implored his "brethren" to "see": the way that Jefferson framed this racial competition between "the race of whites" and "the blacks on the continent of America" not only in terms of excellence but also in terms of biology.[71]

Considering the matter of emancipation and incorporation, Jefferson returned to the Romans to make yet another comparison: "Among the Romans emancipation required but one effort. The slave, when made free, might mix with, without staining the blood of his master. But with us a second is necessary, unknown to history. When freed, he is to be removed beyond the reach of mixture."[72] Given what we know about Jefferson's sexual relationship with Sally Hemings, one must wonder if the pronoun "he" here included her too. It is certainly plausible, especially if we consider, as the feminist, queer, and critical race theorist Sharon Patricia Holland does, "that *racism has its own erotic life*," and Jefferson's racism is no exception.[73] Part of the reason emancipation necessitated racial segregation in Jefferson's opinion was because even as he diagnosed Black bodies as defective in *Notes*, he also recognized some Black folks as objects of sexual desire. His call for the separation of the races could be understood as a ruse, as a wily attempt to erase his own coerced relationship with Sally Hemings. Similarly to the Confederacy, he tried, as Holland argues, "to convince an entire nation to look toward the future for events that had already taken place in the past; to believe that emancipation would result in rampant miscegenation," although interracial sexual relations already existed during slavery.[74]

Another Jeffersonian ruse involves his rhetoric concerning the blood of Black people, which he described as both dynamic and dormant. Sometimes Jefferson figured the blood of enslaved Black people as potent and communicable, as a substance imbued with the power to soil or "stai[n] the blood of his master." In the language of genetics, Black blood would be considered dominant, and white blood would be considered recessive. To mix Black blood with white blood, then, is to prioritize Black over white, to produce a population that more closely resembles Black people than white people. This understanding was probably what led Jefferson to propose a second requirement as essential to his postemancipation plan. The requirement—that formerly enslaved people, when granted freedom as Americans, must "be removed beyond the reach of mixture," effectively expelled from their home country—was so outlandish and nonsensical that even he had to acknowledge that it was heretofore "unknown to history." Yet he floated the idea as "necessary," for his studied calculations confirmed that a predominance of white blood was required to dissolve blackness, while only a fraction of Black blood was sufficient to cancel out whiteness. Later, in 1815, Jefferson configured what the historian Lucia C. Stanton calls a "series of algebraic formulas" to ascertain the amount of white blood necessary for a slave to be considered white.[75] He drafted these formulas after reviewing a 1785 statute in Virginia law, which stated that "every person who shall have one-fourth part or more of negro blood, shall, in like manner, be deemed a mulatto."[76] Jefferson's formulas had inadvertently given the blood of Black people superior power.

At other times, however, Jefferson depicted Black blood as inactive and recessive, as a malleable fluid that can be modified when mixed. Take, for example, his unfortunate views about the "improvement" of mixed-race people: "The improvement of the blacks in body and mind, in the first instance of their mixture with the whites, has been observed by everyone, and proves that their inferiority is not the effect merely of their condition of life."[77] In typical Jeffersonian fashion, he did not specify precisely here what the improvement was or whether "mixture" was a euphemism for miscegenation; but given his appraisal of Black beauty, fitness, talent, and intelligence in *Notes*, we can surmise that he felt that mixed-race people (like, say, the enslaved Hemings family) possessed more beauty and sounder bodies and minds than did Black people who presumably did not have white blood. Still, his identification of mixed-race folks as "blacks" reiterated the idea of a Black person's blood being a dominant gene. As Michelle M. Wright argues, "Jefferson begins by observing that 'Blackness' can be altered when mixed with white blood. His rhetoric already assumes Black inertia and white activity, for this intermixture and the resultant change is accredited to the white blood; yet the fact that the issue is considered Black, not white or even half-white, points to the impossibility of trying to change or transform this inert Blackness."[78] According to Jefferson, the blood of Black people could be dominant or recessive, immutable or moribund; it was merely a matter of which racist argument one wanted to make.

Jefferson, unfortunately, made many; and his stature as a revered member of what would later become known as the "founding fathers" meant that his observations carried considerable weight and captured transnational attention.[79] "Sometimes one wishes," writes the legal historian Annette Gordon-Reed, that Jefferson had not "observed black people" or "fancied himself an expert on the subject." "Of all the white southern members of the founding generation," she observes, "he devoted the most time to thinking about blacks as a group—what they did, what they were like, and how they responded in certain situations."[80] His devotion was riddled with contradictory claims. Jefferson's notes on Black people and their blood were so shifty that any attempt to pin them down could quickly turn into a hellish enterprise. Still, David Walker wanted to take Thomas Jefferson's racist remarks to task. He saw Jefferson as an influencer with tentacular reach, a public figure whose work and writings extended beyond the United States to enthrall the world. "See his writings for the world, and public labours for the United States of America," Walker wrote. "Do you believe that the assertions of such a man, will pass away into oblivion unobserved by this people and the world?"[81] Walker most certainly did not, and he took pains to poke holes in each one of Jefferson's flawed arguments.

Regarding the matter of blood, Walker emphasized what Jefferson failed to observe: the blood of Black enslaved people has sustained, not stained, white Americans; their blood has been the nation's richest, most precious resource. On at least half a dozen occasions, Walker stated that Black people have been "enriching [white Americans], from one generation to another with our *blood* and our *tears*!!!!" He punctuated his assertion with italics and exclamation points for a reason: he did not want readers to overlook the connection between the generational wealth of white Americans and the blood and tears of Black people.[82]

Walker reprised his argument in the fourth article of *Appeal*, in which he rejected the colonization plan proposed by Henry Clay, Elias Caldwell, and John Randolph by relying once again on the discourse of blood. Clay, Caldwell, and Randolph planned to separate enslaved people from nominally free Black people by sending free Black folks to the "Coast of Africa," namely Liberia, in a bid to maintain the institution of slavery in the United States without disruption or retaliation "from those of the coloured people, who are said to be free." In 1816, at a meeting in Washington, DC, to inaugurate the American Colonization Society, Clay gave a speech explaining his position. Clay claimed, "That class of the mixt population of our country [coloured people] was peculiarly situated; they neither enjoyed the immunities of freemen, nor were they subjected to the incapacities of slaves, but partook, in some degree, of the qualities of both. From their condition, and the unconquerable prejudices resulting from their colour, they never could amalgamate with the free whites of this country." Clay had a special knack for equivocation and opacity, for there are lines in his speech—such as "the unconquerable prejudices resulting from their colour"—that would have benefited from further clarification. Even Walker admitted that there were parts of Clay's speech that he had "never been able to conceive."[83] But one thing Clay was clear about was his take on colonization. Given that "coloured people," by which he meant free people of color, were "peculiarly situated," Clay concluded that a return to Africa would constitute "a peculiar . . . moral fitness."[84] His references to the "immunities of freemen" (by which he meant the immunities of "the free whites of this country") and the "incapacities of slaves" (which to some extent, according to Clay, included free Black folks too) recalled Jefferson's language in *Notes*. He aligned "immunities" with freedom and whiteness, and "incapacities" with enslavement and blackness, just as Jefferson aligned capacity with freedom and disability with blackness. And, similarly to Jefferson, Clay contended that colonization was the most feasible plan, rationalizing that Black folks were fit for freedom in Africa but, somehow, unfit for freedom in the United States.

This colonization plot was centered on a fallacious, filial narrative presented by enslavers—that a return to Africa would "restor[e] [Black folks] to the land of their fathers," that a return would reconcile the past with the present and stop "a civil war" from erupting in the country, that a return would repair the interminable injuries wrought by slavery. Walker renounced the call to return to Africa, preferring instead to remain in the United States. He knew that no return could restore all that had been stolen and lost due to the violence and terror of the Middle Passage; no return could undo or repair the cruelties of enslavement. A return to Africa would be misconstrued as a forfeiture of Black people's birthright and entitlement in the United States. A return would have been misread as an exoneration of the wrongdoings of white Americans for all the injurious deeds they had done. A return would have been misunderstood as an endorsement of a plot that perpetuated slavery in the name of reconciliation. Any return without proper reparations would have been a regression, and if any Black person was "ignorant enough to let the whites *fool* them off to Africa," Walker scoffed, "the coloured people ought to be glad to have them go." "Oh! my coloured brethren," he proclaimed, "let no man of us budge one step, and let slave-holders come to beat us from our country. America is more our country, than it is the whites—we have enriched it with our *blood and tears*. The greatest riches in all America have arisen from our blood and tears:—and will they drive us from our property and homes, which we have earned with our *blood*? They must look sharp or this very thing will bring swift destruction upon them. The Americans have got so fat on our blood and groans, that they have almost forgotten the God of armies."[85]

Walker yoked the prosperity, vitality, and excess of the United States and of white Americans to the blood, tears, and groans of Black people. He did so by purposefully repeating certain words and phrases. Due to the italics, the phrases "our *blood and tears*," "our blood and tears," "our *blood*," and "our blood and groans" are not stated exactly the same, but there is symmetry in Walker's repetition of these words. They spotlight the possessive form and a syntactical parallelism: "our *blood*" equates to "our country," and "our blood and tears" equates to "our property and homes." Or, in algebraic form, "our *blood*" = "our country," and "our blood and tears" = "our property and homes." "The greatest riches in all America," he informed Black readers, are ours—having been "earned with our *blood*" and bought with our labor.

For all the ways Black folks' blood had been fractured, divided, spilled, and shed, Walker presented an alternative narrative of blood that differed from how it had been depicted and regulated by the color line in the nineteenth century. The color line restricted Black life by drawing a distinction between the blood of white and Black people. It besmirched the blood of Black folks in a myriad of ways.

But Walker restored our blood.

In all the ways the color line demarcated Black blood as dormant, contagious, deficient, and lacking, Walker marked the blood as dynamic, salutary, opulent, and live. His assertion that Black folks' blood had "enriched" the nation and been the source of the United States' and white Americans' "greatest riches" revised the sordid racial history of blood. Everything white Americans own is owed to Black folks, he implied. Anyone who suggests otherwise is simply mistaken.

Walker's account of blood was propelled not only by advocates of colonization but also by adversaries. It was a direct rejection of the colonization plan posed by Clay, Caldwell, Randolph, and others, a way of staking claim in the plot of land called the United States. It was also an explicit nod to Richard Allen, bishop of the African Methodist Episcopal Church in the United States, a man whom Walker affectionately referred to as "Reverend Divine" and touted as having "done more in a spiritual sense for his ignorant and wretched brethren than any other man of colour has, since the world began."[86] Allen was a man with many titles—bishop, minister, community leader, and preacher—but what caught Walker's attention was a letter he wrote in November 1827 to the editor of the *Freedom's Journal*, the first African American newspaper, repudiating the "Colonizing of Africans in Liberia." Bishop Allen opened his letter by stating, "We are an unlettered people, brought up in ignorance, not one in a hundred can read or write, not one in a thousand has a liberal education; is there any fitness for such to be sent into a far country, among heathens, to convert or civilize them, when they themselves are neither civilized or Christianized?" He closed his letter by stating, "I have no doubt that there are many good men who do not see as I do, and who are for sending us to Liberia; but they have not duly considered the subject—they are not men of colour.—This land which we watered with our *tears* and *our blood*, is now our *mother country*, and we are well satisfied to stay where wisdom abounds and the gospel is free."[87] Both the beginning and the ending of his letter responded to language mentioned in Clay's 1816 speech—in particular, the references to there being "a moral fitness" to relocating free Black folks to Liberia and about colonization "restoring them to the land of their fathers." Allen questioned the "fitness" of the colonization plan, and he pinpointed the United States, not Liberia, as "our *mother country*," land that Black folks had "*tilled . . .* with our *tears* and *our blood*."[88]

While there are minor differences between Bishop Allen's original letter and Walker's transcription, the italicized words and phrases in Walker's extract are in the published version of the letter. Walker's italics, then, are citational. They direct us to the original source Walker used for his argument against colonization. There is no need to ponder which of the two opposing positions—Henry Clay and his "slave-holding" party's or Bishop Allen and his "righteou[s]" party's—Walker agreed with.[89] His endorsement of Bishop Allen's anticolonization stance is evident in his language and font.

Walker expressed his stance to all who supported colonization—what he also called "the colonizing trick." While he explicitly named Clay, Caldwell, and Randolph in his treatise on colonization, he spoke implicitly to Jefferson too. His assertion that supporters of colonization believed that "if we [Black people] were set free in America, we would involve the country in a civil war" jibes with Jefferson's warning that "ten thousand recollections, by the blacks, of the injuries they have sustained; . . . will divide us into parties, and produce convulsions which will probably never end but in the extermination of the one or the other race." This consistent refrain was the threadbare lie of the colonization plot. It was the quintessence of the "trick" of colonization: it blamed survivors for the cruelties of their perpetrators. It held the people who had sustained injuries responsible for the behavior of those who had inflicted injuries. It made Black folks believe that a relocation that would cause them harm would do them good. It forced those who had been hurt by the nation to sacrifice themselves for its health and well-being. To all supporters who promoted this lie—in particular, the Society for the Colonization of Free People of Color of America—Walker delivered a surprising message: "America is more our country, than it is the whites."[90]

To claim possession of a nation that has done you harm is a wayward act of defiance. To tether your feelings of possession to your experiences of disablement, deformity, and atrocity is a citation of injury. From the Latin root *injuria*—"wrong, hurt, detriment"—the feminine noun of *injurius*, which means "unjust, wrongful," the term *injury* has a mixed meaning.[91] To claim an injury is to acknowledge you have been wronged and to ask for restitution; it is to recognize that you have rights, to enumerate a violation of your rights, and to demand redress. *Injury*, then, includes both a complaint and an appeal. It is no wonder Walker used that word so much.

Indeed, the word *injury* came to be crucial to Walker's critique—a way of undoing some of the harm caused by Jefferson's *Notes*. One passage, in particular, stands out:

How could Mr. Jefferson but say,* "I advance it therefore as a suspicion only, that the blacks, whether originally a distinct race, or made distinct by time and circumstances, are *inferior* to the whites in the endowments both of body and mind?"—"It," says he, "is not against experience to suppose, that different species of the same [genus], or varieties of the same species, may possess different qualifications." [Here, my brethren, listen to him.] ☞ "Will not a lover of natural history, then, one who views the gradations in all the races of *animals* with the eye of philosophy, excuse an effort to keep those in the department of MAN as *distinct* as nature has formed them?"—I hope you will try to find out the meaning of this verse—its widest sense and all its bearings: whether you do or not, remember the whites do. This very verse, brethren, having emanated from Mr. Jefferson, a much greater philosopher the world never afforded, has in truth injured us more, and has been as great a barrier to our emancipation as any thing that has ever been advanced against us. I hope you will not let it pass unnoticed.[92]

Let me begin at the end, where Walker implored his readers to review the various meanings of Jefferson's verse, the "very verse" that "has in truth injured us more" than anything. The injurious line is from Jefferson's "Query XIV" in *Notes*, and in the original publication, no words were italicized or capitalized. Walker's typography is instructive. The words *"animals," "*MAN*," and "distinct"* leap off the page, and they highlight a fundamental reordering of the human species in Jefferson's book, which posited "the races of *animals*" as "*distinct*" from "the department of MAN" and thereby positioned "MAN" above all other biological life forms, all the while maintaining that this new order was how "nature has formed them."

A lover of natural history with a penchant for philosophy would know that Jefferson's reordering of life is not ordained by nature. Examining European culture since the sixteenth century, the philosopher Michel Foucault, for instance, tells us that "man is a recent invention" and "is neither the oldest nor the most constant problem that has been posed for human knowledge."[93] The philosopher Sylvia Wynter argues the West reinvented itself in terms of the rational "Man" on more than one occasion, whereby "Man" functioned as an "overrepresentation" of the human itself and created an "Other" as a "physical referent." As Wynter states, "Man was to be invented in its first form as the rational political subject of the state," whereas "the 'Indians' were portrayed as the very acme of the savage, irrational Other, [and] the 'Negroes' were assimilated to the former's category, represented as its most extreme form and as the ostensible missing link between rational humans and irrational animals."[94] Jefferson attempted to turn the conception of man—which Foucault and Wynter argue was a recent invention of the imagination— into a supernatural human in order to transform Black folks collectively into an Other: an irrational and inferior Other. What Walker wanted to point out is how Jefferson's verses aimed to remove Black folks from "the HUMAN FAMILY."[95] Considering Jefferson's quoted lines as a whole, it is clear that Jefferson outlined something like an Aristotelian syllogism, such that "the blacks" are to "the whites" as "the races of *animals*" are to "the department of MAN."

It is difficult to definitively say whether David Walker supported or rejected Jefferson's concept of Man. In one moment, Walker asserted that white Americans "are waiting for us to prove to them ourselves, that we are MEN, before they will be willing to admit the fact."[96] This line suggests an affinity for Jeffersonian logic, a wish for white Americans to see Black folks as part of the "department of MAN" rather than a renunciation of the overrepresentation of "MAN" as the paramount human. In another moment, Walker undercut Jefferson's suspicion that Black folks are inferior to white folks as well as his endeavor to distinguish Man from animals by comparing both Black and white people to a nonhuman animal. Meditating on Jefferson's comments about racial inferiority, Walker wrote, "I do not know what to compare it to, unless, like putting one wild deer in an iron cage, where it will be secured, and hold another by the side of the same, then let it go, and expect the one in the cage to run as fast as the one at liberty."[97] This analogy suggests a resistance to Jeffersonian reasoning, an understanding of all human species as part of a larger animal family. Walker depicted white and Black people as the same "wild deer," while the "iron cage" symbolizes the chief difference between the two deer. That difference amounted to the unrestrained freedom of one and the confining immobility of the other.

Although Walker's understanding of the human species shifted, he was consistent in his framing of discursive and material violence as an injury throughout his *Appeal*. Though Jefferson was his main target, he was not his only one. Jefferson served as a sort of a specimen of racialism, a man who modeled for others the distinct ways to degrade and devalue Black life. Walker wrote, "I pledge you my sacred word of honour, that Mr. Jefferson's remarks respecting us, have sunk deep into the hearts of millions of the whites, and never will be removed this side of eternity."[98] Walker knew that Jefferson's words would live long after his lifetime. Even after Jefferson's death, Walker found himself contending with descendants of Jefferson's clan: proslavery American preachers and colonizers.

Walker chose the keyword *injury* to describe the violent acts of slaveholding Christians and colonizers alike, and he repeated that word within the same phrase with effective frequency. In the third article, Walker berated American preachers who professed that "slaves must be obedient to their masters—must do their duty to their masters or be whipped." To these Christians, Walker delivered a warning: "I tell you Americans! that unless you speedily alter your course, *you* and your *Country are gone!!!!!!* For God Almighty will tear up the very face of the earth!!! . . . I hope that the Americans may hear, but I am afraid that they have done us so much injury, and are so firm in the belief that our Creator made us to be an inheritance to them for ever, that their hearts will be hardened, so that their destruction may be sure."[99] Walker's emphatic proclamation of American destruction but for cosmic change was a damning premonition, and his determined use of italics, capitalization, and exclamation points matched the dramatic flair of his prophecy. Meanwhile, the phrase he reiterated in his subsequent excoriation of slaveholders—"they have done us so much injury"—is left unadorned: no exclamation points, no italics, no capital letters, no pointing index fingers or severed hands.

The phrase accrues import, though, through repetition. In the fourth article, Walker wrote, "Some of you have done us so much injury, that you will never be able to repent.—Your cup must be filled.—You want us for your slaves, and shall have enough of us—God is just, *who will give you your fill of us.*"[100] Here, in these lines directed toward Clay and his slaveholding party, the phrase gains more traction as an omen of the enslavers' demise, for their inability to repent is directly correlated to the scope of the injury they have inflicted. Walker cemented this idea in his final articulation of the phrase: "They (the whites) know well, if we are *men*—and there is a secret monitor in their hearts which tells them we are—they know, I say, if we *are* men, and see them treating us in the manner they do, that there can be nothing in our hearts but death alone, for them. . . . The whites knowing this, they do not know what to do; they know that they have done us so much injury, they are afraid that we, being men, and not brutes, will retaliate, and woe will be to them."[101]

This recurrent injury to which Walker referred is a racial one, engendered by anti-Black sentiments and actions; it can be located in the words and deeds of the slaveholding world. It lies in the verses of a revered American statesman, whose words limned Black folks' blood and bodies as diseased and deformed. It rests in antebellum newspapers, periodicals, or founding documents that failed to mention American chattel slavery, a practice that Walker reckoned "is ten times more injurious to this country that all the other evils put together." It arises when a preacher of Christianity professed a gospel "of blood and whips," not of peace and love.[102]

Walker's recurring line "they have done us so much injury" acts as a corrective to Jefferson's "the injuries they have sustained." The divergence in their verses is notable. Walker's phrase utilizes the active voice, while Jefferson's phrase uses the passive one. Walker's line pinpoints injurious actors, while Jefferson's line obscures agency and absolves blame. Walker chose the singular form of the word *injury*; Jefferson chose the plural. Even their use of the pronoun "they" has a different racial meaning. Walker's "they" refers to white Americans, whereas Jefferson's "they" refers to Black people. Essentially, Walker's verse does everything that Jefferson's does not. It honors the lives and memory of the enslaved by telling the truth about the brutal actions of their enslavers.

Walker's repetition of the word *injury* also mimics the language of the Declaration of Independence, which Jefferson penned. "The history of the present King of Great Britain is the history of repeated injuries and usurpations. . . . Our repeated Petitions [for Redress] have been answered only by repeated injury," Jefferson wrote. The man who decried injury in the Declaration of Independence to free the colonies from British rule was the same one who inflicted injury on Black people in the United States in order to maintain slavery in the country. The man who lamented that his British brethren "have been deaf to the voice of justice and consanguinity" and every appeal from "the good People of these Colonies" had been met with silence was the very man who failed to listen to the admonitions of Black people, the one who summarily dismissed Wheatley's warning in "On Being Brought from Africa to America": "Some view our sable race with scornful eye, / 'Their colour is a diabolic die.' / Remember, *Christians, Negros*, black as *Cain* / May be refin'd and join th' angelic train."[103] Such willful disregard was enough to make Walker call into question white Americans' sensorial capacity for compassion and understanding. He urged them to perceive otherwise: "See your Declaration Americans!!! Do you understand your own language? Hear your language, proclaimed to the world, July 4th, 1776."[104]

There is something apt and satiric about using the very word deployed by enslavers—*injury*—to combat the harmful treatment caused by that language. Walker and Jefferson shared the same vocabulary but not the same intent or impact. Walker's *Appeal* countered and resisted the most salient attacks in Jefferson's writings through a process of revision and redirection, and Walker's radical typography enhanced the significance of his message. As Dinius argues, "with each stab of an ex-clamation point, each pointing manicule (or punch of a printer's 'fist'), every letter that rises up to become a capital or that rushes forward as an italic, the text graphically acts out its resistance. In the visually and rhe-torically radical text that results, the master's house is dismantled with one of his most historically significant tools—moveable type."[105] The key to dismantling the master's house lies both in moveable type and in the rebellious performances that such stunning typography produced— reading, recitation, listening, and performing—actions that increased the accessibility of his pamphlet. Walker's expectation that the literate would read and recite his pamphlet aloud for illiterate people to hear invited illiterate Black folks into the literacy process and, thus, into the realm of citizenship. His polemical *Appeal* was thoughtfully designed to make citizenship accessible to all. In Walker's *Appeal*, racial injury was a disability, and Walker's response to such racial injury was not a repudia-tion of disability but rather a call to imagine and create a world capable of accommodating all abilities. Walker said as much to his readers and auditors on the verso of the third edition's title page: "Let them remem-ber, that though our cruel oppressors and murderers, may (if possible) treat us more cruel, as Pharoah did the children of Israel, . . . the day of our redemption from abject wretchedness draweth near, when we shall be enabled, in the most extended sense of the word, to stretch forth our hands to the LORD our GOD."[106] Be enabled, Walker commanded the coloured citizens of the world, encouraging them to empower them-selves and mobilize against their oppressors. To those same citizens, I say, in the spirit of Walker, recite these words aloud to yourself and your fellow Black folks as a reminder or as an affirmation of another world worth fighting for.

2

Fugitives' Disabilities

The Extraordinary Escapes of Henry Box Brown and
William and Ellen Craft

He sacrificed his body in the pursuit of freedom. The day before Henry
Box Brown mailed himself in a small, cramped wooden crate from
Richmond, Virginia, to Philadelphia, Pennsylvania, in March 1849, he
intentionally burned his finger to the bone with sulfuric acid. The burn
was a crucial element of Brown's escape from slavery. To avoid arous-
ing suspicion of his plans, Brown knew he would need to be excused
from his work in the fields and determined that only a severe, visible
injury would provide sufficient justification for a leave of absence. His
plan worked. After inspecting Brown's injury, Mr. Allen, his overseer,
granted him permission to stay home and advised him to apply "a
poultice of flax-meal to it, and keep it well poulticed until it got better." With his leave of absence secured, Brown had sufficient time to
execute his escape.[1]

William and Ellen Craft relied on poultices in their escape from slavery too. Several months earlier, in December 1848, the Crafts absconded
from Georgia to Philadelphia, utilizing disability to enact their escapes.
Ellen disguised herself as Mr. "William Johnson," a disabled, white male
planter: she made a poultice to bind her right hand in a sling and made
another one to tie around her face and hide her beardless chin.[2] Her
husband, William, played the role of her slave, assisting Ellen along their
journey and highlighting the frailty and fragility of the white slaveholder
in the process.

Given the extraordinary details of these escapes, it is hardly surprising that the narratives of Henry Box Brown and the Crafts have received
scholarly attention. But one key detail of their stories is often underexplored: they all relied on disability as a crucial part of their escapes.
This chapter examines the intersections of blackness and disability in

the slave narratives of Brown and the Crafts, focusing specifically on how these narratives frame disability as a crime, as punishment, and, significantly, as a means of liberation. Positing the escapes of Brown and the Crafts and the accompanying bodily transformations as challenges to the presumed connections between Black freedom and disease, illness, and incapacity, I analyze how the narratives' authors engage with and demonstrate their knowledge of the legal and social forms of disability inflicted on the bodies of Black people in the United States, in defiance of such stereotypical tropes. In their slave narratives, Brown and the Crafts cited several slave laws, including those that prescribed disability as a punishment for runaways. So with the full knowledge that escape carried risks of disablement, Brown and the Crafts embodied and inhabited disability with the intention of escaping enslavement.

Yet each author employed disability in two notable ways, each of which reflected their preoccupation with citizenship and personhood. The Crafts exploited disability through performance—incorporating it into their disguises and artfully deploying it in combination with other social identities and performances. Henry Box Brown enacted his escape by inflicting physical disability and disabling pain on himself. His narrative reveals that the treatment of a disabled Black slave was markedly different from that of a disabled white gentleman. What their stories share, though, is an ironic manipulation of disability and corporeality to disprove two interrelated proslavery arguments: that enslaved people lacked all sense of self-possession and that freedom would lead to their disablement.[3] Rejecting those arguments and inverting them instead, both Brown and the Crafts found beauty in disability: a plot for their escapes.

The Burned Finger of Henry Box Brown: Claiming Legal Personhood through Criminality and Disability

None of the proposed escape plans felt quite right. Henry Box Brown consulted at length with the white local storekeeper Samuel Smith as well as his friend and co-choir member James C. A. Smith about possible escapes, but he struggled to decide on a viable plan. Samuel Smith discussed several successful escape plans with Brown, but "none of them," wrote Brown in the 1851 edition of his slave narrative, "exactly suited my taste." His trusted confidant J. C. A. Smith "did not approve" of them either, leaving Brown with the ultimate task of inventing a plan that did not rely on their input.[4]

Brown did not provide any details about the other plans that were under consideration. In fact, the 1849 edition explicitly makes a point of showing discretion: "Perhaps it may not be best to mention what these plans were, as some unfortunate slaves may thereby be prevented from availing themselves of these methods of escape."[5] Although Brown does not discuss these other plans, he certainly would have had options to pick from.

Which plans could have been his source material? Would the feigned disabilities of James Pennington (who pretended to have smallpox) or Lewis Clarke (who wore green spectacles and tied handkerchiefs around his forehead and chin) have been as familiar to Brown as Ellen Craft's performances of disability? Did he consider disguising himself as a sailor and securing a Seaman's Protection Certificate like Frederick Douglass? Would he have known that Harriet Jacobs spent seven years confined in the small crawlspace of her grandmother's attic before escaping in 1842? While it is unclear which specific plans Henry Box Brown discussed with Samuel Smith and J. C. A Smith, it is clear that his plot borrowed from some of the most famous recorded escapes: all of them relied on disability, disguise, performance, or confinement.

Henry Box Brown's *Narrative* artfully appropriates all of these fundamental elements, but the particular way he foregrounds self-inflicted disability and disabling pain as a combination of tactics for fugitives from slavery distinguishes his narrative from the rest. In *Bodies in Dissent*, Daphne Brooks argues that Brown "manipulate[d] the corporeal to produce a renegade form of 'escape artistry.'"[6] While Brooks focuses primarily on the staging of his moving panorama, *Mirror of Slavery*, an exhibition that opened in Boston in April 1850 and was presented throughout New England, Brown's deft manipulation of the corporeal was also evident in his intentional use of disability, a core feature of his escape that has received virtually no scholarly attention. For all the accounts of Brown as a magician, scientist, showman, performance artist, and mesmerist, perhaps his most impressive magical trick (or experiment) was to make people forget how central disability was to his freedom.[7]

This lack of attention to disability in Brown's *Narrative* has resulted in glossing over the distinct role of disability in the lives of enslaved people. Brown's *Narrative* offers several key insights into the treatment of disabled slaves as well as the relationship between an enslaved person's bodily value, labor, and disability. First, Brown presents disability as a tool of emancipation. Focusing on the relative inattention that incapacitated slaves received from their enslavers, Brown observed that disability offered prospective runaways from slavery the incredibly precious resource of time. Second, Brown's self-inflicted disability and descriptions of disabling pain not only aimed to oppose the slander of insentience (a prominent proslavery argument that claimed Black people could not feel pain and lacked consciousness) but also revealed his resilient sense of personhood in the midst of being regarded as property by the law. To execute his plan, Brown gathered intelligence about the connections among disability, value, labor, and time for the enslaved, and he used that information to secure everything he needed for his extraordinary escape—not only his box, which was so legendary that it eventually became a central part of his name, but also his leave of absence, which was obtained through a deliberate act of disablement.

The first action Brown undertook after procuring his box was an attempt to secure a temporary discharge from work. "It was deemed necessary," Brown wrote, "that I should get permission to be absent from work for a few days, in order to keep down suspicion until I had once fairly started on the road to liberty."[8] While enslaved people were occasionally granted time off from work, they generally had to receive permission, which was granted at the slaveholder's sole discretion and usually out of self-interest. For instance, in the *Narrative of the Life of Frederick Douglass, an American Slave* (1845), Douglass recounted that on some plantations, enslaved folks were not forced to work during the Christmas holidays. From Christmas to New Year's Day, slaves could spend their time as they wished. But Douglass did not mistake this time off as an act of benevolence on behalf of the slaveholders. "The holidays," he wrote, "are part and parcel of the gross fraud, wrong, and inhumanity of slavery. . . . [Slaveholders] do not give the slaves this time because they would not like to have their work during its continuance, but because they know it would be unsafe to deprive them of it." Holiday breaks, Douglass believed, were "the most effective means in the hands of the slaveholder in keeping down the spirit of insurrection."[9]

The holidays were not the only occasions when an enslaved person received time off from work; a slaveholder might also grant a furlough if a slave was suffering from an illness or a disabling injury. Having observed an enslaved person suffering from an unspecified disease receive days off from work, Brown was aware that an illness or disability would serve as a permissible excuse for a leave of absence. In fact, the circumstances surrounding an unnamed slave's illness and the subsequent treatment he received from his overseer provided Brown with key intelligence: Brown learned that a sick or incapacitated slave could expect, at most, a few days off from work before his overseer came looking for him or her. He also observed that one consequence of taking too much time off because of an illness or injury could be a severe lashing, especially from his overseer, Mr. Allen, who was as cruel as they came.

This crucial information about the way slaveholders and overseers handled sick enslaved folks served Brown well as he plotted different parts of his escape. "This man was taken sick," Brown explained, "and although he had not made his appearance at the factory for two or three days, no notice was taken of him; no medicine was provided nor was there any physician employed to heal him. At the end of that time Allen ordered three men to go to the house of the invalid and fetch him to the factory; and of course, in a little while the sick man appeared; so feeble was he however from disease, that he was scarcely able to stand."[10] While Brown's attention to the amount of unmonitored time and lack of medical care that this enslaved man received might seem inconsequential within the context of his larger story, these details were essential for his eventual escape from slavery. Brown discovered that a sick or injured slave received less attention and care, not more. Acquiring an illness or becoming injured would provide a potential runaway with an invaluable asset: time. Brown was not the only ex-slave narrator who recognized a correlation between acquiring an illness or disability and the lack of supervision. In *Twelve Years a Slave* (1853), Solomon Northup observed the same. After becoming seriously ill, declining in health, and sustaining injuries as punishment for his sluggish labor, Northup could no longer work in the fields. "Finally, in September," Northup wrote, "when the busy season of cotton picking was at hand, I was unable to leave my cabin. Up to this time I had received no medicine, nor any attention from my master or mistress."[11]

Brown realized, however, that unmonitored time was limited. Taking more than a few days off could be dire. After Mr. Allen had sent three men to fetch his "invalid" slave and bring him to the factory, he, "for no other crime than sickness, inflicted two-hundred lashes upon his bare back; and even this might probably have been but a small part of his punishment, had not the poor man fainted away: and it was only then the blood-thirsty fiend ceased to apply the lash!"[12] To avoid the lash and to travel from Richmond to Philadelphia, Brown would not need two full days; his narrative recounts that he traveled "twenty-seven hours in the box."[13] Brown planned to make every hour count, for he had no time to waste.

Similarly to Douglass, Brown observed that time off for an illness or disability was not an indication of the benevolence of slaveholders. "The advocates of slavery will sometimes tell us," he wrote, "that the slave is in better circumstances than he would be in a state of freedom, because he has a master to provide for him when he is sick." "But what is the real fact?" he asked rhetorically. "In many instances the severe toils and exposures the slave has to endure at the will of his master, brings on his disease, and even then he is liable to the *lash for medicine*, and to live, or die by starvation as he may, without any support from his owner; for there is no law by which the master may be punished for his cruelty—by which he may be compelled to support his suffering slave."[14] Slavery, according to Brown, engendered disease. The illness of the enslaved was not innate but rather caused by the "severe toils and exposures" of slavery. Moreover, the treatment of disabled slaves ran counter to the treatment of disabled white gentlemen. As Ellen Craft witnessed when she embodied "Mr. Johnson," a white disabled man yielded special protections from his fellow citizens, who offered him assistance and acted on his behalf. Disabled slaves—perhaps because of their diminished market value, labor, or both—were often sold away or severely whipped with the cat-o'-nine-tails *"for medicine."*

Accordingly, Brown had to be strategic about the kind of disability he inflicted on himself, and his decision to burn his finger was calculated. Brown twice tried to use his disabled finger to secure a leave of absence. The first time he approached his overseer about getting time off from work, Mr. Allen refused his request. After glancing at Brown's "gathered finger," which Brown had previously injured, Mr. Allen told him "it was not so bad as to prevent [him] from working." Brown refused to be denied a second time. He enlisted the help of his friend Dr. Smith and procured sulfuric acid "with a view of making [his finger] bad enough." While his decision to burn his finger was intentional, he admitted that he did not plan to burn it so severely. He had planned to pour only a few drops of acid, but, in his haste, he poured much more, making his injury "worse than there was any occasion for." The acid seared his flesh to the bone, and it took Brown "some weeks" to recover "from the effects of the oil of vitriol with which [he] dressed it" before he left Richmond.[15]

Brown's self-inflicted disability and subsequent escape came with incredible risks—risks that potentially could have led to indebtedness and further liability. Any person who disabled or maimed a slave was legally required to pay the enslaver for medical expenses and interrupted labor, while runaways were often punished with disability or disfigurement, including a severed ear, a cut hamstring, or a brand on the skin. With the 1851 publication of his *Narrative*, Brown signaled his appreciation of these risks. This edition of his *Narrative* included an appendix, which cited a "few specimens of the laws of a slave-holding people" that detailed both how the law protected enslaved people from disablement and how it punished runaways with disablement. A state law in South Carolina, for example, stated that "if any person cut out the tongue, put out the eye, cruelly burn, or deprive any slave of a limb, he shall be liable to a penalty not exceeding five hundred dollars." Additionally, "if a slave be attacked by any person not having sufficient cause for so doing, and be maimed or disabled so that THE OWNER SUFFERS A LOSS FROM HIS INABILITY TO LABOUR, the person so doing, shall pay the master of such disabled slave, for the time such slave shall be off work, and for the medical attendance on the slave."[16] This law outlined that enslaved people had legal protections from persons who were not their slaveholders, while simultaneously indicating the degree to which they were not protected from the violence of their slaveholders. In short, it was a finable offense to maim or disable someone else's slave, but the law did not outline restrictions regarding what an enslaver could do to their own slave.

What I find striking about this South Carolina state law is how frequently it linked personhood to criminality—particularly the criminal act of disabling an enslaved person. The law stipulated that "any person" who "cruelly burn[ed]" a slave was liable to a penalty and "any person" who maimed or disabled a slave was required to pay the slave's "master" for both loss of labor and medical care. Considering this context, Brown's self-inflicted disability—the burning and maiming of his finger—raises a number of pertinent questions: What happened if the person who injured the enslaved was the slave himself? In what way did these laws inform Brown's precarious sense of his personhood and value even as he recognized that the law regarded him as chattel personal? That is, to what degree did Brown recognize that, within the law, a criminal act of disablement could render the enslaved a person? Such questions are especially significant if we also factor in how the legal personality of slaves was contingent on two kinds of action: civil and criminal. With respect to civil action, according to the legal historian Colin Dayan, slaves were determined to be "utterly deprived of civil capacity," for "no act of *self-possession* [was] legally possible." With respect to criminal action, however, a slave was deemed "capable of crime, hence recognized as a willful being with a consciousness that extended through time."[17] Given how slave laws granted self-possession to the enslaved depending on their civil and criminal actions, Brown's fugitivity via self-mutilation could be understood as a means of achieving legal personhood *through* criminality and disability. With this disabling act, Brown became, as the ethnomusicologist and Black studies scholar Shana L. Redmond argues, part of that "dark, mutinous class of U.S. society, those who would rather be permanently disfigured by their own hand than be made in someone else's image."[18]

Indeed, Brown's self-inflicted disability suggests that he recognized himself as more than his enslaver's property; his self-mutilation was related to his own resilient sense of personhood despite enslavement. The fact that he committed this act of bodily harm with the full knowledge that fugitivity carried with it risks of further disablement is critical too. Brown's appendix also included a law that prescribed graduated punishments for recalcitrant runaways: "If a slave let loose a boat from where it has been made fast, he shall for the first offence be liable to a penalty of thirty-nine lashes, and for the second, to have one ear cut from his head—for being on horseback, without a written permission from his master—twenty-five lashes; for riding or going abroad at night, without a written permission, a slave may be cropped or branded in the cheek, with the letter E, or otherwise punished, not extending to life, or so as to render him unfit for labour."[19] According to this slave law, enslaved folks who sought freedom could find themselves with body parts that were branded and slashed as a sadistic form of retribution. The law thus framed disability not only as a crime but also as a punishment. Runaways from slavery were subjected to severe lashings, dismemberment, and disfigurement. These punishments marked the enslaved with a permanent sign of criminalization, and they were meant to deter repeat offenders and to instill fear in other slaves who might be considering escape.

Undaunted by these laws, Brown used disability to enact his escape. It provided him with an opportunity to exert possession of his own body, to express himself differently than the law permitted. These actions do not mean that Brown did not wrestle with the tensions between personhood and property for the enslaved. If anything, he took the interplay between personhood and property during slavery seriously when he disguised himself as precious cargo enclosed in a wooden crate. The law regarded him as property, and he fashioned himself as property in disguise. But his artful appropriation of property was not robbed of any sense of personhood. As Brown reflected in the 1849 *Narrative*, his box contained "a *male*," "not the *mail*."[20]

The exact dimensions of Brown's box varied across different accounts. The title of the 1849 edition of *Narrative* listed the dimensions as "Three Feet Long, Two Wide, and Two and Half High." The pictorial representation of the box at the end of the 1849 version listed the dimensions as "3 feet 1 inch long, 2 feet wide, 2 feet 6 inches high."[21] In the 1851 *Narrative*, Brown wrote that the box "was three feet one inch wide, two feet six inches high, and two feet wide."[22] James Miller McKim wrote that it was "3 feet by 28 in high & 23½ wide," and Charles W. Morgan heard it described as "one foot eleven inches deep, two feet six inches wide, and three feet two inches long."[23] By all accounts, the box was small—certainly too small to comfortably accommodate a man of Brown's size.

Although the precise dimensions of the box varied, the descriptions of Brown's disabling pain while he was enclosed in it remained consistent. While en route to Philadelphia, Brown was often tossed around, and the box was frequently placed in precarious positions. On two different occasions, he was upside down in the box for nearly ninety minutes, and the pain was difficult to bear. "I was resolved to conquer or die," Brown wrote. "I felt my eyes swelling as if they would burst from their sockets; and the veins on my temples were dreadfully distended with pressure of blood upon my head. In this position I attempted to lift my hand to my face but I had no power to move it; I felt a cold sweat coming over me which seemed to be a warning that death was about to terminate my earthly miseries."[24]

Brown's emphasis on deformity, pain, and disability—his swollen eyes, distended veins, and temporarily paralyzed hand—during his boxed journey delegitimized one of the main proslavery claims: that enslaved people were impervious to pain, that they were insensate. The belief of Black insentience was widespread. In 1853, William Goodell recorded how the narrative of insentience was included in US slave codes. He wrote, "The slave has no rights. Of course, he, or she cannot have the rights of a husband, a wife. The slave is a chattel, and chattels do not marry. 'The slave is not ranked among sentient beings, but among things,' and things are not married."[25] Here, Goodell showed how slave codes excluded enslaved people from the category of "sentient beings" and characterized them as inanimate objects and property, who, by rule, could not marry. Such designations allowed slaveholders to rationalize slavery and deny enslaved people essential rights. In particular, the claim that the enslaved were unable to feel pain and lacked consciousness served to explain and excuse the oppressive violence of slavery.

Brown's escape wrought a spectacular performance of Black pain through self-inflicted disability in a manner that exhibited the consciousness and sensibilities of Black folks. As Robin Bernstein and others have pointed out, expressions of visible pain became a way for Black abolitionists to signal Black people's eligibility for humanity and citizenship. Bernstein argues, for instance, that "one of abolitionism's most organized, long-standing, and successful arguments [was] that slaves feel pain, and that this ability to feel pain demonstrates African Americans' fitness for freedom." Abolitionists "showcased emotional, physical, and spiritual suffering of enslaved people" to "combat the libel of black insensateness."[26] Brown's self-inflicted disability and boxed escape show that he was keenly aware of how expressions of pain demonstrated Black feelings and their fitness for citizenship.[27] Being attentive to how Brown's slave narrative conveys the centrality of disability to the experiences of the enslaved helps to clarify the relationship between disability and ideas of health, pain, and personhood. Such attention also challenges the idea that "disability . . . would not be represented in a traditional slave narrative as central to their personhood or experience" and, if ex-slave writers did represent disability, "such representations had to be limited since emphasizing the disablement of black people at large could, once again, limit collective group claims to the rationality, morality, and citizenship denied black subjects during this period," as Sami Schalk asserts.[28] While I acknowledge that slave narratives have competing aims—one of which includes the aim of proving rationality and morality—it is important to highlight the moments when ex-slave writers represented disability and disablement in their work. This acknowledgment underscores how enslaved people understood the intersections of race and disability as well as demonstrates how slave narratives aimed to accomplish multifaceted radical goals simultaneously. In the case of Brown, more particularly, disability was a key element of his escape from slavery, allowing him to claim liberation and birthright citizenship elsewhere.[29] His plot was carefully researched, planned, and executed—that is, disability was central both to his pursuit of emancipation and to his expression of personhood. And Brown was not the only enslaved person who relied on disability for his escape. For William and Ellen Craft, disability played a crucial role in their escape as well—with, however, one significant difference: their disability was not self-inflicted.

An "Invalid Gentleman" and His "Attentive" Slave: Scripted Disabilities in *Running a Thousand Miles for Freedom*

Theirs was a spectacular escape north—the denouement of eight days' worth of deliberation and execution. On Sunday, December 25, 1848, William and Ellen Craft, two runaways, arrived on free soil in Philadelphia, donning disguises that relied not only on performances of race, gender, and class but also on performances of disability: Ellen posed as a white "invalid gentleman" named Mr. William Johnson who feigned deafness and inflammatory rheumatism, while William, her husband, acted as her—the gentleman's—valet, attending to and aiding his wife-cum-slaveholder throughout their perilous journey. The roughly one-thousand-mile trip from Macon, Georgia, had taken them four grueling days, grueling in part because of a constant fear that they may not make it to the North—twice it seemed as if their elaborate plan might be thwarted by officers—and in part because their trip required taking a combination of trains and steamers across several different cities and states, traveling from Macon through Savannah, Georgia; Charleston, South Carolina; Wilmington, North Carolina; Richmond, Virginia; Fredericksburg, Virginia; Washington, DC; Baltimore, Maryland; and, finally, across the Mason-Dixon line into Pennsylvania.[30]

The length of the Crafts' escape, coupled with travel across slave states into a free state, required meticulous planning. Several plans were discussed, a number of different scenarios were imagined, and the risks of each underwent careful consideration. First, the Crafts set out to obtain passes from their enslavers that would grant them permission for time off during the holidays. "We knew it would not do to start off without first getting our master's consent to be away for a few days," wrote William and Ellen Craft. "Had we left without this, they would soon have had us back into slavery, and probably we should never have got another fair opportunity of even attempting to escape." Second, they needed to devise an escape plan that would be suitable for both of them. "We thought of plan after plan," narrated William Craft, "but they all seemed crowded with insurmountable difficulties." Despite these difficulties, "a plan suggested itself," one that involved sartorial disguises and strategic props, as well as intersectional performances of race, gender, class, and disability. He narrated, "Knowing that slaveholders have the privilege of taking their slaves to any part of the country they think proper, it occurred to me that, as my wife was nearly white, I might get her to disguise herself as an invalid gentleman, and assume to be my master, while I could attend as his slave, and that in this manner we might effect our escape." Ellen agreed. She told William, "if you will purchase the disguise, I will try to carry out the plan." So William procured her disguise "piece by piece," including a "waistcoat," "a fashionable cloth cloak," "a pair of green spectacles," and "boots." He also cut her hair "square at the back of the head" in the style of an aristocratic southern gentleman. The only piece of clothing he did not purchase was a pair of "trowsers," which Ellen decided to make herself. And although William credited himself as the architect of their escape plan, he acknowledged that Ellen suggested the use of two poultices, important additions to the disguise that would ultimately help them implement their plot. After Ellen realized that "it was customary for travellers to register their names in the visitors' book at hotels, as well as in the clearance or Custom-house book at Charleston," and knowing that signing their names would have been difficult since neither she nor William were literate at the time, she offered a critical solution: "I think I have it!" she said. "I think I can make a poultice and bind up my right hand in a sling, and with propriety ask the officers to register my name for me." The other poultice, which would "be worn under the chin, up the cheeks, and . . . [tied] over the head," was intended to hide her smooth skin, facial expressions, and "beardless chin."[31]

With all clothing and props assembled, the Crafts felt more prepared to act out their escape. Ellen would assume the alias "William Johnson," and she would play the role of slaveholder to her husband and namesake, William, who would play the role of her slave. Outfitted in attire and styled in a manner befitting what her husband described in *Running* as the "most respectable looking gentleman," Mrs. Craft would embody "Mr. Johnson": a disabled upper-class white male planter, traveling from Georgia to Philadelphia with his male slave as his primary caretaker.[32]

While each aspect of the Crafts' disguises played a significant role in their escape from slavery, the critical ways that they deployed disability within their narrative and disguise as well as the larger implications of their engagement with disability have been underexamined. The reasons for this lack of scholarly attention are manifold. Some critics have refrained from fully examining the relationship between blackness and disability out of both a concern that addressing the intersections of race and disability might engage too closely with the language and logic of scientific racism and a recognition that disability was often used as a justification for inequality against people of African descent. The disability studies scholar Nirmala Erevelles argues that "the concept of disability justified oppressive social, political, cultural, and economic policies based on the argument that racial difference and class inequalities represented pathological defects otherwise known as 'disability.'"[33] The desire to challenge the particular ways that disability has been used in proslavery arguments as well as other forms of racial inequality has led some Black writers to attempt to rehabilitate the Black body by avoiding an examination of the relationship between race and disability and instead engaging in an ideology of racial uplift.[34] As the literary and disability studies scholar Ellen Samuels argues, "Both abolitionists and freedmen of the Crafts' time and African Americanist scholars and critics today appear deeply invested in the recuperation of the black body from a pathologizing and dehumanizing racism that often justified enslavement with arguments that people of African descent were inherently unable to take care of themselves—in other words, disabled."[35] This avoidance of disability has resulted in less engagement with the diverse ways that Black writers and abolitionists have purposefully deployed disability.

Notwithstanding this complex historical relationship between blackness and disability, the centrality of disability in the Crafts' narrative makes it difficult to overlook it entirely. Some scholars have offered nuanced approaches to the subject by focusing specifically on the significance of performance to disability in *Running*. Samuels, for instance, highlights how the "disability con," which she defines as "the masquerade of a nondisabled person who deceptively and deliberately performs disability, often for material gain," functions as the "central enabling device" in the Crafts' narrative, allowing for their escape and presenting disability "as a social identity that can be manipulated or interpreted, as can race and gender."[36] The literary and performance studies scholar Uri McMillan examines Ellen Craft's escape as both a "form of fugitive performance art" and a "*prosthetic performance*," which "repurposed objects (such as the green spectacles and two poultices Ellen wore) *and* embodied behaviors (feigned deafness, slowed gait, and frustrated chirography)" to transform disability from a "mere bodily impairment into an elastic and *mobile* aesthetic device and a set of tactical performances."[37] And although the literary and cultural theorist Lindon Barrett neither uses the term *disability* nor cites scholars of disability studies in his analysis of the Crafts' narrative, his reiteration of the significance of Ellen Craft's "bandaged hand" captures what he describes as the "pantomime of literacy," a bodily performance that "derives . . . from the legally enforced conflation of race and literacy" during slavery.[38] Samuels's analysis of the "disability con," McMillan's focus on "prosthetic performance," and Barrett's examination of the "pantomime of literacy" all highlight the ploys of performance to illuminate more fully the import of disability in the Crafts' narrative.

Yet each of these scholars' examinations either hedge on or disclaim a key factor that prompted the Crafts' disguise: that William and Ellen Craft's illiteracy exemplified one way that they were disabled by the color line. Barrett, for instance, is evasive in his discussions of Ellen's disability. Barrett's references to Ellen's bandaged hand, as Samuels points out, "repeatedly evokes but endlessly defers the presence of disability as fundamental to Ellen's disguise—and thus to her racial meaning."[39] And both McMillan and Samuels figure Ellen as nondisabled. McMillan states so outright, while Samuels's disavowal is less direct. As a means of emphasizing Ellen's prosthetic performances, McMillan claims that "Ellen Craft herself was not disabled."[40] While Samuels posits illiteracy as a "possible intellectual disability," her description of Ellen Craft's disability con—which Samuels defines as a *nondisabled* person feigning disability—characterizes Craft as not disabled as well.[41] This misrepresentation is tied to the fraught and strained history of blackness and disability, since acknowledging the illiteracy of enslaved people was all too often erroneously interpreted as evidence of their innate defects.[42] It is also likely tied to a belief that the provisional aspect of illiteracy is not tantamount to a disability because, for many people today, illiteracy can be remedied. Yet, for the enslaved Black person in the antebellum United States, illiteracy was a sociolegal disability that, if disobeyed, came with material consequences. As I argue in chapter 1, illiteracy was a corrigible condition, yet if an enslaved person attempted to remedy their illiteracy, they were often punished with disabling violence designed to perpetuate that condition.

Ellen Craft's disability, along with her race, class, and gender, animated her disguise, and the intersectionality of these identity categories was pertinent to the Crafts' escape. I examine how the Crafts regarded disability not only as a social identity that is just as constructed, malleable, and performative as gender, race, and class but one that creates distinctive synergies with other social identities. I argue that the Crafts embraced disability as a means of emancipation rather than dismissing it wholly as a hindrance and that their incorporation of disability into the persona of a white male upper-class body both called attention to and defied the disabilities imposed on Black bodies. In what way did Ellen's performances of disability intersect with her cross-racial, cross-class, and cross-dressing performances? How did performances of disability and able-bodiedness function together in their escapes to Philadelphia and, later, Boston and England? How did the legal and discursive ascriptions of the enslaved Black body—which rendered enslaved Black people as property, as noncitizens, as illiterate, and as nonwomen and nonmen—arouse the Crafts' radical imagination to such an extent that they felt empowered to disguise themselves in direct opposition to such designations? These questions are central to my analysis of *Running a Thousand Miles for Freedom* (1860), the slave narrative of William and Ellen Craft, as well as of the Crafts' abolitionism in Europe.

Running a Thousand Miles for Freedom captures how enslaved Black people existed in what Elizabeth Alexander calls "a counter-citizen relationship to the law," one that "contradicts the histories our bodies know."[43] The Crafts' narrative shows how information about their bodies and lives has been erased from US narratives of citizenship, civilization, and personhood.[44] One way "that African Americans have been scripted out of narratives of American national belonging," argues the literary critic Candice M. Jenkins, is through the stigmatization of the Black family and sexual behavior. Jenkins states, "African American sexual and familial character has traditionally been stigmatized as *un*civilized in the United States, from the days of slavery onward," and it has excluded them from concepts like "the republican family ideal," the "cult of True Womanhood," and "true manhood," concepts that bear a relation to who Black people are as "civic subjects."[45] These concepts are flush with raced and gendered conceptions of fitness, and they stigmatize Black people by compromising their health and mobility.

This stigmatization is rooted in various forms of limitations placed on the enslaved—some of which motivated Ellen Craft's disguise as Mr. Johnson. William narrated,

> My wife had no ambition whatever to assume this disguise, and would not have done so had it been possible to have obtained our liberty by more simple means; but we knew it was not customary in the South for ladies to travel with male servants; and therefore, notwithstanding my wife's fair complexion, it would have been a very difficult task for her to have come off as a free white lady, with me as her slave; in fact, her not being able to write would have made this quite impossible. We knew that

no public conveyance would take us, or any other slave, as a passenger, without our master's consent. This consent could never be obtained to pass into a free State.[46]

Here, William Craft described in more detail how the idea for their escape was conceived and why they chose to assume their particular disguises in order to seek their freedom. Because it was not customary for white women and Black male slaves to travel as companions, because Ellen Craft was unable to write, because the enslaved could not travel on public transportation without their enslavers' consent, and because consent alone was insufficient to grant a slave traveling sans their slave-holder entry into a free state, the Crafts decided to disguise Ellen as a disabled white gentleman in order to travel from a slave state to a free one with William in tow as a Black male servant. Their plot had to reconcile all the restrictions waged against their Black bodies, individually and collectively.

The legal and social restrictions imposed on the Crafts as well as other enslaved Black people exemplify the disabilities of the color line. In *Running*, these disabilities entailed the enforced illiteracy of the enslaved, restrictions on their movement and mobility, the threat or punishment of dismemberment and severe wounding, and the implicit stigmatization of Black womanhood and manhood as an emblem of disease, illness, and contamination. In the nineteenth century, the disabilities of the color line attempted to excise Black people from the national body politic, and each attempt utilized the concept of disability as its modus operandi. As I have argued in my introduction, the metaphor of the body politic is so effective at producing racial stigmatization in part because it frames the nation as a body vulnerable to contamination and harm, and anyone who poses or is perceived as a threat to the nation's health could be punished or contained. Black bodies have been stigmatized as disabled and diseased in order to remove them from US national belonging.

The genius of the Crafts' insurrectional performances is its diversion: embodying the white male body with physical disabilities as a means of seeking their freedom connected and undermined the disabilities that have been inflicted on Black bodies. Each aspect of Ellen's disguise highlighted what she was not at the time of her escape: literate, male, socially mobile, legally white, and physically disabled. Additionally, each aspect of her disguise spotlighted the disabilities of the color line, including the Crafts' legally enforced illiteracy, restricted mobility, the stigmatization of Black manhood and womanhood, and prescribed punishments—all of which deserve our extended attention.

Running addressed the enforced illiteracy of enslaved folks before the Crafts assumed their disguises and embarked on their escape. After relating how both William and Ellen secured passes from their enslavers for a furlough during Christmas, William informed the reader that they were once illiterate: "On reaching my wife's cottage she handed me her pass, and I showed mine, but at that time neither of us were able to read them. It is not only unlawful for slaves to be taught to read, but in some of the States there are heavy penalties attached, such as fines and imprisonment, which will be vigorously enforced upon any one who is humane enough to violate the so-called law."[47] Although William did not mention it, the heavy penalties to which he referred also included bodily dismemberment and injury, since Black enslaved people's attempts at literacy could result in a broken index finger or whippings. While it was not true that all slaves were illiterate, literacy in the antebellum period had become associated with freedom and civil rights, both of which had been legally denied to enslaved people.

The denial of literacy functioned as a means of denying citizenship to Black people in the United States, of claiming that they did not have the capacity or authority to exercise their inalienable rights.[48] This line of reasoning was certainly used in Thomas Jefferson's *Notes*, in which he claimed that Black people lacked the cognitive capacity for reason, logic, and imagination that he deemed necessary for inclusion into the national body politic. Enforcing illiteracy on Black people also had an effect on the significance of Black physicality. As Barrett argues, "If literacy is the most manifest formalization of the life of the mind, if it provides testimony of the mind's ability to extend itself beyond the constricted limits and conditions of the body, then to restrict African Americans to lives without literacy is to immure them in bodily existences having little or nothing to do with the life of the mind. It is an attempt to create a social reality in which the physicality of African American bodies is taken as the entire measure of their significance."[49] Illiteracy and physical able-bodiedness were closely connected for enslaved Black folks. Without the ability to access the life of the mind, the Black body became overdetermined, known only for its physicality and little else. To avoid that fate and escape from slavery, the Crafts had to develop a strategy that would give them the pretense of inhabiting literacy (or the life of the mind), of extending themselves "beyond the constricted limits and conditions of the body." Their plan accomplished this goal by assigning physical disability onto the white male body.

Ellen Craft's feigned physical disability was ingenious because it deflected attention from another disability: her illiteracy. The sole reason she bound her right hand in a poultice was to avoid having to register her and William's names during their interstate travel. To perfect her performance as Mr. William Johnson, the white upper-class male planter, Ellen had to pantomime literacy; she had to give the impression that she could sign their names even though, at the time, she could not. Paying close attention to all aspects of Ellen's varied performances of disability is crucial. Using the sling as a theatrical prop and acting frustrated with her temporary impediment, Ellen performed literacy that she did not yet possess, and her props and performances enticed some witnesses to sympathize with her fabricated Mr. Johnson and, on occasion, invited them to act on his behalf.

One such occasion occurred at the customhouse office in Charleston, South Carolina, where Mr. Johnson purchased tickets to Philadelphia for him and his slave. After the officer distributed tickets to and collected money from Mr. Johnson, he requested Mr. Johnson's signature: "I wish you to register your name here, sir, and also the name of your nigger, and pay a dollar duty on him." Mr. Johnson paid the dollar, but, "pointing to the hand that was in the poultice," he did not sign his name; instead, he "requested the officer to register his name for him." The officer, however, refused to grant Mr. Johnson's request: "He jumped up, shaking his head; and, cramming his hands almost through the bottom of his trousers pockets, with a slave-bullying air, said, 'I shan't do it.'" The officer's brouhaha attracted the attention of the passengers and crew, and, fortunately, two men intervened on behalf of Mr. Johnson and his slave. The first was one of Mr. Johnson's new acquaintances, a "young military officer" who had conversed with him while traveling from Savannah. Having witnessed the way Mr. Johnson was being treated, the military officer vouched for his credibility: "I know his kin . . . like a book." Despite the fact that the young officer was drunk, his endorsement of Mr. Johnson was sufficient evidence for the captain of the steamer, the second person to intervene. The captain told the detaining officer, "I will register the gentleman's name, and take the responsibility upon myself." He signed the names of Mr. Johnson and his slave, and both of them were allowed to board the steamer.[50]

In this exchange, we can see how Ellen Craft's performance of literacy was a performance of disability as well as how the efficacy of her performance depended on others' participation. Although the sling did not work precisely as Ellen imagined, it did solicit the help of others (a function the sling was always intended to do). Ellen initially thought the sling would prompt the officers to register her name for her. She was wrong. Yet it did prompt a passenger and the steamer's captain—both acting as witnesses and participants—to rescue Mr. Johnson. Accordingly, the sling functioned as what Bernstein calls a "scriptive thing," a thing that instructs or invites individuals to do something. "Items of material culture *script*," Bernstein explains, "in much the same sense that literary texts *mean*: neither a thing nor a poem (for example) is conscious or agential, but a thing can invite behaviors that its maker did and did not envision, and a poem may produce meanings that include and exceed the poet's intention."[51] In *Running*, the sling exceeded Ellen's intention. She thought it would invite the sympathy and actions of particular state actors. But, instead, the sling aroused the sympathy of fellow citizens, such that the young military officer claimed an intimate relationship with Mr. Johnson (even though William considered the young officer to be a "stranger"), and the captain of the steamer, by endorsing the names of Mr. Johnson and William, assumed responsibility for them both (even though they had never met before).[52] Mr. Johnson's race and disability solidified his national belonging, his membership within a community that protected and cared for his well-being.

This incident was neither the first nor last time when Mr. Johnson's accoutrements of disability enlisted the actions of others. The first time occurred when Mr. Johnson and William arrived at one of the hotels in Charleston, and the landlord provided unsolicited assistance to Mr. Johnson: "On arriving at the house the landlord ran out and opened the door: but judging, from the poultices and green glasses, that my master was an invalid, he took him very tenderly by one arm and ordered his man to take the other."[53] Neither Mr. Johnson nor his slave asked for help; but Mr. Johnson's scriptive things invited the landlord to move, and the landlord commanded the assistance of his servant. Herein lies another example of how the poultices surpassed Ellen's expectations. The poultice wrapped around her face was intended primarily to disguise her gender. Yet in combination with the sling and eyeglasses, the poultice worked to enhance Mr. Johnson's disability. The landlord took his cue from Mr. Johnson's green glasses, poultices, and the impression of Johnson's body, and he, like most people who came in contact with Mr. Johnson, acted accordingly.

William, of course, played a significant role in shaping others' perception of Mr. Johnson as well. As Mr. Johnson's slave, William acted on behalf of his disabled slaveholder throughout their journey: carving his food, supporting him while walking, assisting him when entering train carriages and buildings, preparing his poultices, and heating his opodeldoc to soothe his rheumatism. William was even tasked with fielding questions about his enslaver's health and speaking for him. "It is clear," Samuels argues, "that William's presence as the servant of 'Mr. Johnson' is as fundamental to Ellen's successful performance of invalidism as are the sling, poultice, and green spectacles she wears."[54] Their performances mutually reinforced each other, emphasizing Mr. Johnson's disability at every turn.

The final occasion when Mr. Johnson's disability prompted the actions of others occurred the day before the two arrived in Philadelphia. In Baltimore, on December 24, 1848, an officer detained Mr. Johnson for failure to show proof that William was, in fact, his slave: "It is against our rules, sir, to allow any person to take a slave out of Baltimore into Philadelphia, unless he can satisfy us that he has a right to take him along." In this encounter, Mr. Johnson benefited from a number of different participants, some of whom sympathized with him because of his disability. First, several passengers expressed discontent with the way the officer treated Mr. Johnson: "because they thought my master was a slaveholder and invalid gentleman," they thought that "it was wrong to detain him." Second, the train conductor confirmed that Mr. Johnson and his slave had just come by train with him from Washington, information that apparently weakened the resolve of the detaining officer. Finally, after the bell rang for the train to depart and with everyone staring, the officer caved: "I really don't know what to do; I calculate it is all right," he said.

"As he is not well, it is a pity to stop him here." Thankfully for the Crafts, the officer miscalculated. What ultimately compelled the officer to break the rules was Mr. Johnson's disability and race. Mr. Johnson's "not well" appearance was misconstrued as a presumption of innocence and elicited the officer's pity. The combination of Mr. Johnson's race, class, gender, and disability bolstered this presumption of innocence. A sick or disabled enslaved Black person did not receive the same treatment, as Henry Box Brown's narrative explained. Mr. Johnson and William, perhaps both recognizing how disability functioned as a motivating factor in the officer's decision, sharpened their performances. "My master thanked him," William narrated, "and stepped out and hobbled across the platform as quickly as possible. I tumbled him unceremoniously into one of the best carriages, and leaped into mine just as the train was gliding off towards our happy destination."[55]

Mr. Johnson's social mobility and the manner in which his disability encouraged the movement of others spotlight the distinct ways that the law immobilized the Black body. The Crafts, having assembled Mr. Johnson from their imaginations, surely must have marveled at the extraordinary mobility of their creation. He could travel any place he pleased: from South to North, from a slave state to a free one, inside the best railway carriages and hotels across the United States. His physical disability did not impede his social and legal mobility. Indeed, it invited others to move for him. The same could not be said for William and Ellen Craft, Henry Box Brown, or any other slave. As enslaved people, their legal and social immobility was an impediment. Additionally, as an elderly white female traveler informed Mr. Johnson, a disabled or "ill" slave was more likely to be discarded and sold down south rather than protected and cared for like that of a disabled white gentleman.[56] The law inscribed severe limits on what enslaved bodies could do: when, where, and with whom they could travel; how they could behave; whether they could read or write; whom they could marry. The law also inscribed limits on who they could be, demarcating who was a person and who was a thing, who was a man and who was a woman.

In fact, slavery's denial of Black womanhood was a pivotal reason Ellen decided to escape with her husband. William claimed that initially Ellen "shrank from the idea" of running away, thinking it would be "almost impossible for her to assume that disguise." But, upon further contemplation, Ellen "saw that the laws under which we lived did not recognize her to be a woman, but a mere chattel, to be bought and sold, or otherwise dealt with as her owner might see fit. Therefore the more she contemplated her helpless condition, the more anxious she was to escape from it."[57] Ellen's reflection on how slave laws had refashioned womanhood for enslaved Black women is of significant import. Her realization that, within the law, her status as chattel had superseded her status as a woman encouraged her to assume the disguise of Mr. Johnson.

One way that slavery rendered Ellen as a nonwoman was by positioning her outside "the cult of True Womanhood," which the historian Barbara Welter argues consisted of four attributes: "piety, purity, submissiveness and domesticity."[58] The conditions of Black women's enslavement and the frequent representations of Black female sexuality in nineteenth-century visual iconographies as "the source of corruption and disease," as Sander Gilman observes, made it difficult for Black enslaved women to meet such criteria.[59] This difficulty, it seems, was the point of constructing true womanhood in the first place. "The cult of true womanhood," argues Candice Jenkins, "relied upon this backdrop of black female 'nonwomen' in order to more clearly define true womanhood as white, frail, and virtuous—everything that black women supposedly were not."[60] Black manhood, of course, was not exempt from this brand of stigmatization either. Enslaved Black men, figured as "sexually rapacious savages," were excluded from notions of "normative manhood," which was defined as "rational, industrious, civilized, and virtuous—in a word, manly."[61]

The stigmatization of Black womanhood and manhood was difficult to resist, particularly since disobeying the law often resulted in disabling bodily consequences. At the conclusion of *Running*, William Craft observed, "I have often seen slaves tortured in every conceivable manner. I have seen them hunted down and torn by bloodhounds. I have seen them shamefully beaten, and branded with hot irons. I have seen them hunted, and even burned alive at the stake, frequently for offences that would be applauded if committed by white persons for similar purposes."[62] Torture, dismemberment, lashings, brandings, and burning at the stake—punishments that resulted in pain, disability, injury, disfigurement, or death—were often used to discipline runaways who had been captured as well as to deter others from running away.

The Crafts were well aware that their fraudulent performances came with considerable risks. If caught, they too could experience extreme torture. Under the Georgia state constitution, as the Crafts outlined in *Running*, runaways from slavery risked not only captivity and death but also disability and dismemberment: "Any person who shall maliciously dismember or deprive a slave of life, shall suffer such punishment as would be inflicted in case the like offence had been committed on a free white person, and on the like proof, except in case of insurrection of such slave, and unless SUCH DEATH SHOULD HAPPEN BY AC- CIDENT IN GIVING SUCH SLAVE MODERATE CORRECTION."[63] Enlarged typography notwithstanding, the operative words here are "except" and "unless." Malicious dismemberment of an enslaved person was punishable *except* if administered to forestall insurrection. Killing was a punishable offense *unless* it occurred while offering the enslaved moderate correction. The Crafts' inclusion of these details in their slave narrative signaled their astute awareness of the dangerous consequences of running for freedom.

These exception clauses are similar to the exception clause that would later be included in the Thirteenth Amendment, which states, "Neither slavery nor involuntary servitude, except as a punishment for crime whereof the party shall have been duly convicted, shall exist within the United States, or any place subject to their jurisdiction." One way of ensuring that a set of practices continued was to insert a loophole that could be exploited by contemporary or former white slaveholders who flouted the rule of law. According to the Thirteenth Amendment, slavery and involuntary servitude could continue if they were called by another name: criminal punishment. According to Georgia's state law, dismemberment and death of enslaved people could continue as long as they were done with the expressed intent to foil insurrections. This fundamental law of slavery was one of several that the Crafts cited "in order to give some idea of the legal as well as the social tyranny" from which they fled.[64]

The ways the laws of slavery attempted to reshape the bodies of Black people, to talk them "out of what their bodies know" (as Alexander puts it) about their manhood, womanhood, subjecthood and their physical and mental abilities, enlivened the Crafts' imagination.[65] Because their legal representations clashed with their experiential understandings of themselves as a Black woman, a Black man, a married Black couple, and whole human beings with the capacity for literacy but for the law's disablement, the Crafts reimagined themselves entirely. If the law could so easily attempt to transform their bodies through scripted narratives of disability, then why could they not transform their bodies, too, by revising these narratives? What made the Crafts' disguises so intellectually brilliant was not merely that they acquired their emancipation by redirecting disability onto the white male body but also that they achieved it through such counterintuitive and ironic means. For Ellen Craft to claim her Black womanhood in the North, for example, she embodied white southern manhood. To disguise her illiteracy (a legal disability), she feigned physical disabilities (deafness, rheumatism, poulticed hand, and hobbled gait). And for the Crafts to contest notions of their *unfitness* for freedom and their *incapacity* to exercise their rights, they relied heavily on performances of disability, invalidism, and illness. Although their escape was undeniably dangerous and risky, there is something bitterly funny about the ruse the Crafts played on slaveholders by having Ellen pass as a disabled white gentleman. Through wit and irony, they enacted a daring, rebellious escape. If we peel back the layers of their disguise and their performances of disability, we can detect not only a courageous enslaved couple willing to make sacrifices for their freedom but also a furtive-yet-firm "fuck you" from the Crafts to their enslavers and the institution of slavery.[66] Parallel to David Walker, who pointed an index finger at Jefferson, the Crafts pointed the middle finger at their slaveholders via their disguises and performances. The Crafts' performances, then, register as a radical form of political action, and it situates them within a group of performance artists who, as the disability and performance studies scholar Petra Kuppers argues, "use performance as a means to break out of allocated spaces" and "utilize public spaces outside the theater in order to challenge ever more effectively the concept of allocation and categorization."[67]

The Crafts' 1848 escape from Georgia to Philadelphia was only their first recorded one, not their last. Shortly after traveling to Philadelphia, they moved to Boston, where they stayed for nearly two years. William was employed as a "cabinet-maker and furniture broker," and Ellen was employed as a seamstress.[68] Alongside the fugitive William Wells Brown, they participated in antislavery lectures throughout New England, gaining a reputation for themselves and winning over audiences with tales of their bold escape. Their work in Boston ended after the passage of the Fugitive Slave Act of 1850, which made it illegal for residents of free states to aid fugitives from slavery and required that the fugitives be returned to their slaveholders. Since slave hunters were searching for the Crafts, they left Boston and fled to Liverpool, England, via Halifax, Nova Scotia.

The Crafts' 1850 escape to England, however, required no performance of disability: no sling, no poultices, no green glasses, no feigned deafness or rheumatism, no hobbled gait, no attending servant. Instead, they made it their mission to display their extraordinary abilities to the world. Under the auspices of the American Anti-Slavery Society (AAAS), the Crafts traveled throughout Europe, according to the literary and cultural studies scholar Britt Rusert, "to help strengthen networks of transatlantic abolitionism between the AAAS and the mainstream wing of British abolition."[69] On one momentous occasion, they staged a demonstration against US slavery by exhibiting their abled bodies at the 1851 Great Exhibition of the Works of Industry of All Nations in Hyde Park, London.

In a letter dated June 26, 1851, the white abolitionist William Farmer wrote to William Lloyd Garrison, offering a detailed personal account of his collaboration with three formerly enslaved people—William Wells Brown and William and Ellen Craft—at the 1851 world's fair. According to Farmer, the occasion was a highly orchestrated affair. On Saturday, October 4, 1851, the day they selected because "the largest number of the aristocracy and wealthy classes attend the Crystal Palace," Brown and the Crafts walked arm-in-arm with white British abolitionists, intending to rouse the slaveholders in the US section of the exhibition. William Craft walked with Miss Amelia Thompson and William Farmer. Miss Thompson requested to walk with William Wells Brown, and Mr. McDonnell escorted Ellen Craft and Mrs. Thompson. "This arrangement was purposely made," wrote Farmer, "in order that there might be no appearance of patronizing the fugitives, but that it might be shown that we regarded them as our equals, and honored them for their heroic escape from Slavery."[70]

In addition to presenting "the fugitives" as social and intellectual equals and as heroes, this intimate, interracial promenade served two additional purposes. First, the demonstration was intended to condemn white US slaveholders for their continued participation in slavery, a system that even their British rivals no longer condoned. As Barbara McCaskill argues, their public exhibition highlighted the "irony of encountering more racial tolerance in England—a country that had banned slavery from its Caribbean colonies by 1838—than in the so-called democratic United States."[71] Second, the demonstration offered the Crafts another opportunity to use their bodies to prove one of the most enduring arguments of abolitionism: that Black folks are fit for freedom. Farmer noted that "friends" of both Brown and the Crafts "resolved that they should be exhibited under the world's huge glass case, in order that the world might form its opinion of the alleged mental inferiority of the African race, and their fitness or unfitness for freedom."[72] The exhibition, then, was approached as a chance to counter the myths of Black mental and physical ineptitude. The Crafts, using their minds and bodies, refuted these myths on both fronts: they not only planned and organized what has been described as "one of the most memorable and influential spectacles of the nineteenth century" but also *walked* for six to seven hours in the largest international exhibition in the world.[73] Presenting themselves as thinking, perambulatory people, the Crafts' bodies served as yet another prodigious feat against slavery.

McCaskill claims that abolitionists initially had grander plans for the 1851 world's fair. They hoped "they could seize the event as a forum for a conspicuous confrontation with American slaveholders" and wanted to display "whips and chains and collars . . . to embarrass the American contingents."[74] In addition to William Wells Brown and William and Ellen Craft, Henry Box Brown was among the other abolitionists expected to attend. Brown was expected to display his crate, while the Crafts were supposed to show up in their disguises. This plan, however, never materialized. William Wells Brown, Henry Brown, and the Crafts "would cross paths on the anti-slavery podium only once in their lifetimes": on May 30, 1849, "before an assembly of New England abolitionists" organized by William Wells Brown.[75] The Crafts may not have met Henry Box Brown at the Great Exhibition, but their plots shared key features with each other, making the pairing of Brown's story with the Crafts' productive and worthwhile, particularly with regard to the visual representations of themselves in their frontispieces, the illustrations that proceeded the title of their slave narratives.

The Precarity of Fugitivity and the Missing Poultices of Henry Box Brown's and Ellen Craft's Frontispieces

The 1851 edition of Brown's *Narrative* included a frontispiece that captured what many commentators have described as the most compelling aspect of Brown's extraordinary escape: the signature moment when he emerged from his famous box (figure 2.1). In the lithograph, by Peter Kramer and titled *The Resurrection of Henry Box Brown at Philadelphia*, an interracial coterie of Philadelphia abolitionists surrounds Brown, who is partially enclosed in a crate. According to the literary historian John Ernest, to the far left stands Lewis Thompson (holding a handsaw), with James Miller McKim (who appears to be holding a hammer) next to him. Thompson and McKim were both white abolitionists, and McKim played an influential role in enabling Brown's escape and was present when Brown emerged from the box. To the right are William Still and Charles D. Cleveland. Cleveland, a white abolitionist who helped with the Underground Railroad after the passage of the Fugitive Slave Act of 1850, holds a cane to support himself and points at Brown in the box. William Still, the Black author of the influential text *The Underground Rail Road*, who is often dubbed the "Father of the Underground Railroad," holds the top of the crate, which includes the name and address that originally appeared on the box, along with a set of instructions: "This side up with care." In Kramer's depictions of Brown and the crate, he replicates the fundamental design of the 1850 print, which, though the print is not signed, most "scholars generally agree . . . is the work of Samuel Worchester Rowse" (figure 2.2).[76] Brown is centered in the lithograph, depicted from the chest up and appearing to rise out of the crate with his fingers gripping its edge. He is dressed in fine garments, and of all the people represented in the image, he is the only one who stares at the viewer, commanding our full attention.

This visual image played a significant role in Brown's ensuing fame as an author, lecturer, abolitionist, and antebellum performance artist. Audiences were mesmerized by the sensational details of his daring escape, and many were eager not only to see Brown but also to see his box (or representations of them). Brown's subsequent transatlantic staging of his moving panorama, *Mirror of Slavery*, confirms that he recognized the power of the visual. As John Ernest states, "Brown understood the value

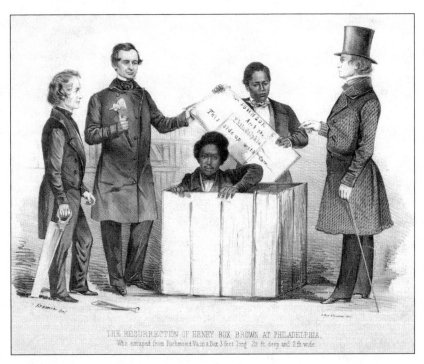

Figure 2.1. *The Resurrection of Henry Box Brown at Philadelphia, Who escaped from Richmond Va. in a Box 3 feet long 2½ ft. deep and 2 ft. wide*, lithograph by Peter Kramer, Philadelphia, ca. 1851. Courtesy of the Library Company of Philadelphia.

Figure 2.2. *The Resurrection of Henry Box Brown at Philadelphia. Who escaped from Richmond Va. in a Box 3 feet long 2½ ft. deep and 2 ft. wide*, lithograph, deposited for copyright in Boston on January 10, 1850.

of visual representations. His was a story that inspired and provoked the imagination, leading the mind's eye to re-create unimaginable pain and striking determination in the form of a box, and spiritual jubilation and political resistance in an office scene, with a box newly opened and a man just emerging into his new life of freedom."[77]

Given the political significance of the visual to Brown's career, it is noteworthy that this crucial visual representation of Brown's escape obscures signs of his disability and pain. The image was intended to represent Brown upon his arrival in Philadelphia, immediately following the removal of the box's lid. Yet, even though the *Narrative* described that Brown was in excruciating pain during his journey and that he felt the effects of his disabled finger (which was wrapped in a poultice) for weeks before recovering from his burn, there are no signs of bandages or paralysis, and his fingers (at least the ones that are visible) all appear to be intact in this visual representation. Here, Brown appears healed, healthy, and pain-free. The only person with a visible disability is Charles Cleveland, who holds a cane in his left hand, thus positing a link between whiteness and disability rather than blackness and disability. While it is unclear to what extent Brown was involved in the creation of Kramer's lithograph (or, for that matter, Rowse's print) or whether Kramer depicted it without soliciting advice or feedback from Brown, it does depict a transformation of Brown's body that is markedly different from the one we read about in his *Narrative*—since, in the lithograph, Brown is seemingly unmarked by injury.

Yet the lithograph also crucially represents something more: it shows how the specter of violence and disablement continued to haunt fugitives from slavery even after they had made it to the North. The depiction of Brown's body in such close proximity to white men holding a hammer and a saw—tools that could easily be turned into weapons—hints at Brown's ongoing precarity as a fugitive. Given the passage of the Fugitive Slave Act of 1850, Brown's sense of freedom would have been elusive. This reading is not meant to suggest that the white men depicted in this image (Thomson, McKim, and Cleveland) intended to do Brown harm; they were all abolitionists and supporters of Brown. But the image calls attention to how the law conferred on them the power to assist in Brown's capture and return him to his enslaver; in fact, the law compelled them to do so or suffer the consequences. Brown's positioning in the image demonstrates his intermediary state as well. He is more inside the box than outside it—a positioning that implies that he is not completely out of danger. Indeed, for viewers who have no context of the lithograph or the men represented in it, it might be unclear if Brown is being enclosed within the box or released from it. This point is clearer once we observe one of the key differences between Rowse's 1850 print and Kramer's 1851 print: in Rowse's print, McKim and Still are represented as holding the weapons (or tools) in their hands; in Kramer's, Thompson and McKim hold the hammer and saw. The political power granted to white men in the antebellum period, combined with the circumscribed status of free Black men during this period, enhances the significance of this swap, particularly for those viewers without context of the occasion.

A similar kind of alteration also occurs in the visual representation of Ellen Craft, presumably posing as "Mr. Johnson" (figure 2.3). The same year that she planned and participated in the Great Exhibition in London, Ellen posed for an engraving that was printed in the *London Illustrated News* on April 19, 1851; it would be used nine years later as a frontispiece to the Crafts' *Running a Thousand Miles for Freedom*. As William claimed in *Running*, the engraving was intended as a representation of his "wife in the disguise in which she escaped."[78]

But the engraving is an adaptation, not a replica, of Ellen's disguise, and traces of disability are removed, altered, or obscured. In the engraving, Ellen–cum–Mr. Johnson is wearing what appear to be clear eyeglasses, not green spectacles. The poultice worn around the face, which spectators perceived alongside the green spectacles and sling as a sign of Mr. Johnson's compromised health, is completely removed. According to William, "the poultice is left off in the engraving, because the likeness could not have been taken well with it on."[79] Finally, the sling that was supposed to bind the right hand is hanging loosely around the neck, like a tartan sash.

The manner in which Ellen's disguise was modified in this engraving—which, as a frontispiece, framed the reader's interpretation of the Crafts' escape narrative as well as authenticated the veracity of their tale—has preoccupied critics. Interrogating William's

Figure 2.3. *Ellen Craft, The fugitive slave*, engraving, *London Illustrated News*, April 19, 1851. The engraving was later used as the frontispiece for *Running a Thousand Miles for Freedom*.

explanation for why one of the poultices has been removed, Sterling Bland Jr. poses a provocative set of questions that several critics have attempted to answer: "What is unclear is whose likeness would be obscured by the poultice. Is the engraving intended to represent Ellen, William's wife? Or is the engraving intended to show Ellen in the disguise she used to pass as a white gentleman traveling with his black slave? The engraving fully succeeds at neither, thus forcing the reader to ponder the reason for the apparent deviation."[80] Samuels and McMillan both ponder these questions regarding the engraving's striking deviation from the Crafts' original disguise.[81] Samuels argues that the engraving represents "the 'most respectable-looking gentleman' so beloved of critics": it captures "the aspects of Ellen's disguise that subvert nineteenth-century assumptions regarding the immutability of race and gender, while removing those aspects that even by implication show the African American body as unhealthy, dependent, and disabled."[82] McMillan asserts that the unfinished quality of the engraving "suggests the performativity of both her *and* her white male avatar." The "engraving's in-between state," McMillan continues, "its incomplete rendering of Mr. William Johnson—with a top hat and spectacles, but not the full poultice—enables viewers to discern the seams of this performance, the *constructedness* of Ellen Craft's white gentleman."[83] Both Samuels and McMillan highlight aspects of the Derridean deconstructive "incommensurability or tension between presence and absence" at play in the engraving.[84] Ellen's pose as Mr. Johnson exposes the engraving as acutely constructed, as a visual artifact that manipulated several social identities at once. Far from being fixed or stable, disability, in particular, is revealed in the engraving as just as malleable and performative as race, gender, and class. But what if "the likeness" that William and Ellen Craft were attempting to capture was neither Ellen Craft (a once-enslaved Black woman who escaped to freedom by traveling to England) nor Mr. Johnson (Ellen's respectable-looking white male avatar) but rather the precarious life of "Ellen Craft, The fugitive slave" as the engraving's title suggests? That is, the engraving's in-betweenness parallels Ellen's liminal status between enslavement and freedom within the United States. As a fugitive from slavery living outside the United States, Ellen, at the time of the engraving, would not have needed to be in full costume or disguise, but her elusive sense of freedom would have probably compelled her to keep certain parts of her costume and props at the ready in the event that yet another escape was necessary in the future. Indeed, the missing poultices in the frontispieces of Brown and Ellen Craft reveal as much about their own precarious status as fugitives from slavery as they do their varied deployments of disability within their extraordinary escapes.

PART II

Age of Jim Crow

3

The Curious Case of Jim Crow

The historian C. Vann Woodward's *The Strange Career of Jim Crow* rightly called attention to the oddities and peculiarities of Jim Crow, a paradoxical period when the historic achievement and progress of civil rights was met by "violent racial explosions all over the country."[1] Another underexamined curiosity of that period concerns the origin of the term *Jim Crow*, for the term for the system of racial segregation that effectively immobilized Black Americans turned out to have disability embedded within its etymology. Although Woodward claimed that "the origin of the term 'Jim Crow' applied to Negroes is lost in obscurity," there are sources that, thankfully, clarify the root of the term's meaning.[2] One significant source is the account of Edmon S. Conner, an American actor who, in a June 1881 *New York Times* profile about his career, described what he remembered about the emergence of minstrelsy and Jim Crow. Conner traced the term *Jim Crow* back to a theater in Louisville, Kentucky, where Thomas Dartmouth "Daddy" Rice, a white American performer and playwright who wore blackface, siphoned material for his routine. Conner stated,

> Back of the theatre was a livery-stable kept by a man named Crow. The actors could look into the stable yard from the theatre, and were particularly amused by an old decrepit negro, who used to do odd jobs for Crow. As was then usual with slaves, they called themselves after their owner, so that old Daddy had assumed the name of Jim Crow. He was very much deformed, the right shoulder being drawn high up, the left leg stiff and crooked at the knee, giving him a painful, but at the same time, laughable limp. He used to croon a queer old tune with words of his own, and at the end of each verse would give a little jump, and when he came down he set his "heel a-rockin." He called it "jumping Jim Crow."[3]

Conner's description of the elderly enslaved man's deformity and impairment—his drawn right shoulder, his stiff left leg, his crooked left knee, and his decrepitude—reflects the cavalier way that Black people's pain was often misconstrued as a fount of entertainment. Conner's observations that the actors were "amused" by Crow and his acknowledgment of Crow's "painful" limp, which he nevertheless described as "laughable," exemplify one way that white spectators took pleasure in Black pain and disability and how Black suffering became the wellspring of popular performances.

Given the phenomenal success of T. D. Rice's well-known Jim Crow persona, Conner certainly had a model for such "innocent amusements."[4] According to historical accounts, Rice closely watched this enslaved man's performances and adapted them for the stage. The term *Jim Crow*, thus, became part of the American lexicon as a result of the minstrel performances of Rice, who based his popular "Jump Jim Crow" act on the routine of Crow, a disabled, elderly stableman. Although the historian Leon F. Litwack concedes that it is not clear "how a dance created by a black stableman and imitated by a white man for the amusement of white audiences became synonymous with a system designed by whites to segregate the races," it is clear that the Jim Crow system distorted the representation of Black people through subordination, exclusion, and violence and that the rhetoric and practices of disability played a crucial role in this distortion.[5]

Plessy v. Ferguson, the 1896 landmark US Supreme Court case that upheld the constitutionality of racial segregation, was a foundational part of that process. In *Plessy*, the imprimatur of segregation came from Justice Henry Billings Brown's majority opinion, which legitimized racial separation in public facilities, including railways, bathrooms, restaurants, and schools. Similarly to Rice, *Plessy* relied on the category of disability to make a case for the separation of the races. My examination of the majority and dissenting opinions in *Plessy* demonstrates how disability shaped the Court's understanding of racial inequality during the regime of Jim Crow. And my consideration of the plot that led Homer Plessy to violate Louisiana's Separate Car Act of 1890 shows how Plessy and his team attempted to unsettle the racial logic of that period.

The "Onerous Disabilities and Burdens" of *Plessy*

The *Plessy* ruling cited disability as one of the most formidable tools of racial injury and subjection, and then the Court masked the deployment of disability by behaving as if it could offer no protection against disability and by framing the unnatural hierarchy of the races as natural. Justice Brown explained this process when he refuted the claim that the 1890 Louisiana statute that required separate railway carriages for white and Black folks was unconstitutional because it violated the Thirteenth and Fourteenth Amendments. He wrote that the Thirteenth Amendment was intended primarily to abolish slavery and involuntary servitude and not "to protect the colored race from certain laws which had been enacted in the Southern states, imposing upon the colored race onerous disabilities and burdens, and curtailing their rights in the pursuit of life, liberty and property to such an extent that their freedom was of little value."[6] While Justice Brown argued that the Thirteenth Amendment intended to emancipate enslaved people, he claimed that the amendment cannot be held responsible for either protecting the citizenship rights of the newly freed or ensuring that the freedom it grants them was of any value. Brown ironically also stated that, although the Fourteenth Amendment forbade states "from making or enforcing any law which shall abridge the privileges or immunities of citizens of the United States," the enforced separation of the two races in Louisiana railroad cars did not infringe on the privileges and immunities of citizenship because the statute applied equally to both races.[7]

The words that effectively fueled the Jim Crow racial imagination were "disabilities" and "immunities." Justice Brown's acknowledgment that "onerous disabilities and burdens" were imposed "upon the colored race" alongside his claim that the "privileges or immunities" of Black folks were not abridged belied his later assertion that the law has no power to create social equality between Black and white people. He wrote, "If the two races are to meet upon terms of social equality, it must be the result of natural affinities, a mutual appreciation of each other's merits and a voluntary consent of individuals." "Legislation," he wrote, "is powerless to eradicate racial instincts or to abolish distinctions based upon physical differences, and the attempt to do so can only result in accentuating the difficulties of the present situation. If the civil and political rights of both races be equal one cannot be inferior to the other civilly or politically. If one race be inferior to the other socially, the Constitution of the United States cannot put them upon the same plane."[8]

In Justice Brown's opinion, "social equality" was distinct from "civil" and "political" equality, and the aura of his "social" sphere was flush with an intoxicating sentimentality. Brown attached social equality to racial feelings for at least two reasons. First, it allowed him to frame the nineteenth-century social realm as a private and intimate world, one ruled by pleasure, desire, admiration, and impulse, an exclusive and close-knit coterie that could be penetrated only if granted permission. Second, it aimed to portray racial hierarchy as natural, as an anticipated consequence of some unbeknown legitimate and divine order. (Clearly, Brown had not carefully read the literature of David Walker or Frederick Douglass, both of whom could have helped Brown revise his views of the social sphere and the law.) As a result, Brown surmised that the law could not invade a private entity like the social realm, for it produced consensual, affective attachments—or, as he put it, "natural affinities," "racial instincts," "mutual appreciation," and "voluntary consent"—that were too intimate for intrusion and too natural for enforcement. In this manner, the Supreme Court imagined the social world as a lawless, free-standing zone, located somewhere on the outskirts of its immediate domain and well beyond the orbit of lawful interference.

The main problem with the Court's assertion regarding the law's limited reach is that none of it was true. The distinction Justice Brown drew between civil, political, and social equality was erroneous, for civil and political rights are social matters. In the eighteenth and nineteenth centuries, the law customarily outstretched its arms toward social matters, extending its hands and dipping its fingers into the most intimate and mundane details of Americans' personal lives. The ability to travel, to work, to learn, to touch, to mate with any person—all rights that if denied under the law would become legal disabilities—were under intense legislative surveillance and control. At the same time that the Court upheld Louisiana's constitutional right to create separate "colored" and "white" train compartments, it claimed that the law was unable "to abolish distinctions based upon physical differences." Segregation laws sorted individuals by race; yet the Court believed legislation was powerless to rescind laws that make distinctions based on racial differences. It, in effect, argued that the law could not undo what the law has already done.

Disability was ensnarled within the confines of this strange social milieu, functioning as a yardstick for measuring racial health as well as an instrument for inciting fear of racial contamination. Segregation laws, like the Louisiana statute under consideration in *Plessy*, were designed to sort and regulate citizens along racial lines. They aimed to restrict the contact and proximity of the races and embraced a separate-but-equal doctrine that was neither wholly separate nor equal. The "white" train cars were often in better condition than the "colored" train cars, and the law primarily intended to impair the mobility of Black people, not the mobility of white folks. According to Justice Marshall Harlan, the lone dissenter in *Plessy*, "Every one knows that the statute in question had its origin in the purpose, not so much to exclude white persons from railroad cars occupied by blacks, as to exclude colored people from coaches occupied by or assigned to white persons." "The fundamental objection," he added, "to the statute is that it interferes with the personal freedom of citizens."[9]

This conspicuous interference with the personal freedom of Black citizens was deeply immobilizing and stigmatizing. What everyone knew, as Harlan put it, was the original intent of Louisiana's segregation statute, the limits it placed on Black people. By denying African Americans the right to move freely into white-designated spaces, *Plessy* effectively diagnosed casual contact and intimacy with Black folks as a contagious affair, and it transformed commonplace activities of everyday life into public health matters of the highest order: eating a meal nearby Black customers or families, sitting too close to a Black person on the train, drinking water from the same fountain as Black people, sleeping in a hotel bed or swimming in a pool previously occupied by African Americans, receiving medical treatment at the same hospital as Black patients, or learning in the presence of Black folks apparently tainted the experiences of white people—diminishing their reputation, jeopardizing their privilege, and compromising their immunity. The health and vitality of white citizens were so essential that separate facilities were created throughout the late nineteenth and early to mid-twentieth centuries to ensure their safety. Accordingly, the law was doubly injurious. It stigmatized Black folks as contagious and diseased, stirring fears of racial contamination, and then capitalized on that fear to justify the immobilization and quarantine of Black citizens as compulsory measures for the protection of the greater body politic. In this regard, *Plessy* virtually mirrored the spirit of Thomas Jefferson's colonization plan outlined in *Notes* almost to the letter.

Saidiya Hartman explains how health and safety matters became attached to both the physical body and the body politic at the close of her book *Scenes of Subjection*. She writes, "If the fundamental task conducted under the cover of the state's police power was the protection of the health of the populace, then, as this duty took shape in the emergent era of Jim Crow, ensuring the public health required the state to attend to bodily matters, particularly the policing of blackness and the tracking down of all its ascertainable traces, as well as regulating legitimate forms of intimacy, association, and reproduction and, if and when necessary, imposing onerous but warrantable hardships."[10] The health of the republic hinged on the regulation of the Black body, and such regulation bore a close resemblance to the intimate and natural social world of Justice Brown's imagination.

The body was a central part of the social system in *Plessy*. The Court's understanding of the social sphere was teeming with "affinities," "appreciation," "instincts," and "consent," feelings that electrified the body with a potent and polarizing magnetism capable of either attracting or repelling any person within its force field. The wellspring of these feelings and the key substance of this magnetism was the color of one's skin, the largest and likely the most legislated organ of the human body. The Court neglected to mention this detail, perhaps fearful that it might blur its vision of racial hierarchy as part of the natural order. Nevertheless, skin color is a significant element informing the reasoning in *Plessy*.

Although Justice Brown aimed to emphasize racial hierarchy as a natural bodily phenomenon, even he, in his remarks about the "onerous disabilities and burdens" of African Americans, could not disregard how the law created barriers for Black people. Brown's pairing of the noun "disabilities" with the verb "imposing," a word that suggests that disabilities were inflicted and not innate, illuminated how racial and physical distinctions were highly constructed. And it undermined his claim that the way individuals think about race is purely instinctual.

Brown's language struck a similar chord to that of Chief Justice Roger B. Taney in the infamous 1857 Supreme Court case *Dred Scott v. Sandford*. In the majority opinion, Taney described Black people as a racial group "separated from the white by indelible marks, and laws long before established" and later as one on whom the framers of the Constitution had "impressed such deep and enduring marks of inferiority and degradation" that it can be assumed that "they had deemed it just and necessary thus to stigmatize."[11] These remarks were offered in support for Taney's larger claim that Black folks "had for more than a century before been regarded as beings of an inferior order, and altogether unfit to associate with the white race, either in social or political relations."[12] Indeed, in *Dred Scott*, Taney marshaled the Declaration of Independence, the Constitution, and an armada of state laws as his most compelling evidence to "show that a perpetual and impassable barrier was intended to be erected between the white race and the one which they had reduced to slavery."[13] Taney's rhetoric was highly metaphorical, as his language, like that of Justice Brown, tried to make the social relationship between the races into something corporeal and biological. It appears that Brown wanted his impressionistic words about the barriers established by law to leave an imprint on the public's imagination, to change the way the public conceptualized blackness. "Taney's argument," the literary scholar Eric J. Sundquist clarifies, "was not, strictly speaking, biological, but it blurred the biological into the constitutional in an even more unsettling and philosophically rigid way. The legal justification of racial inferiority, that is to say, was constructed and discursive; the law of slavery was branded into African American beings by 'indelible' marks that, having been already 'impressed' on blacks at the time the Declaration of Independence and the Constitution were drafted, could not, according to Taney's logic, be erased except by constitutional amendment."[14]

The influences of *Dred* and *Plessy* were visible in the nineteenth century, when sentiments about race, disability, and fitness flourished. Taney, Brown, and others of their ilk produced a distinct history of blackness and disability. If you align Taney's language of "impressed" and "indelible marks" of stigma in *Dred* with Brown's deployment of "disabilities" in *Plessy*, then you can hear the repetition of an eerily familiar refrain. What they did was frame the Black body as dangerous to the health of the nation-state. Their shared vocabulary and modus operandi show that they understood the metaphorical power of race and disability in a racist and ableist world.

One key difference between Brown and Taney was their approaches to the social sphere. Brown argued that the social was an arena that the law could not touch; Taney claimed that the law not only meddled in social relations but also created them. One key similarity between them was the way they focused on the biological in their examinations of racial relationships. The turn to the biological animated the history of blackness and disability. It tangled together notions of blackness, disability, unfitness, and inferiority that were difficult to unravel, and it largely connected these notions to the body rather than to racially discriminatory laws or other acts of discrimination and subjugation.

How could the *Plessy* Court not see this? It is almost as if the justices suffered from willful disregard. Or perhaps they refused to see the law's involvement in social relations and racial matters so that they could, as Hartman argues, hide behind the ruse of innocence and noninterference in the name of parity and equality. The professed "innocence of the law (it did not create prejudice and thus could not change it) and the state (it merely protected the public safety, health, and morals and promoted the general prosperity) was maintained," she says, "by denying the public character of racism and attributing it to individual prerogatives."[15] This denial of the public life of racism even extended to Justice Harlan's dissent.

Although Harlan disagreed with the main arguments in *Plessy*, he neither sufficiently distanced himself from the majority nor adequately remedied the Court's oversight. In fact, Harlan's dissent invoked a disability of a different kind when he prescribed color blindness as a solution to racial segregation. On the one hand, he wrote, "The white race deems itself to be the dominant race in this country. And so it is, in prestige, in achievements, in education, in wealth and in power." On the other, Harlan proclaimed, "Our Constitution is color-blind, and neither knows nor tolerates classes among citizens. In respect of civil rights, all citizens are equal before the law. The humblest is the peer of the most powerful."[16] One of the chief problems with Harlan's dissent is the manner in which he tried to separate the operation of race in the nation from its operation in the law. He essentially claimed that dominant races did exist in the country but that they do not exist within the law—creating a distinction that was hard to uphold. This distinction also made it difficult to determine what Harlan meant when he invoked the word "colorblind." Did Harlan mean that the law should pretend as if it does not see race, that it should perform an act of disability? Or did he mean that the law should treat people equally regardless of skin color, race, or ethnicity, and, if so, how would the law accomplish that goal in the face of a stratified US racial caste system and overwhelming racial subordination (both of which Harlan knew existed)? I explore these questions in part 3 of this book. For now, I want to point out how, in many ways, Harlan's call for a legal color blindness worked in lockstep with the Court's refusal to interfere in racial relations. Harlan probably would not have expected that color-blind constitutionalism would become a significant doctrine of the twentieth and twenty-first centuries, further exacerbating the racial injuries inflicted on Black people in the United States. But, whether he anticipated it or not, it did.

The Citizens' Plot

Plessy's opinion and dissent were devastating, but the plot that forced the Supreme Court to wrestle with issues of race was genius. It required meticulous planning to execute and was engineered by the activism of the Citizens' Committee (Comité des Citoyens)—a group of eighteen local writers, politicians, and ex-Union soldiers—who actively recruited Homer Adolph Plessy to challenge Louisiana's recently enacted Separate Car Act. Plessy, on June 7, 1892, boarded an overnight train on the East Louisiana Railway traveling from New Orleans to Covington, Louisiana, and took a vacant seat in a coach designated for white passengers. Plessy entered the train car fully aware of the railroad segregation laws. In 1890, the Louisiana legislature passed a "separate railroad cars" law, stipulating, "No person or persons, shall be permitted to occupy seats in coaches, other than, the ones, assigned, to them on account of the race they belong to."[17] The law mandated that railroads provide "equal but separate" facilities to different races, but, as Peter Irons points out, "it did not define 'race' and left to conductors the job of assigning passengers to the proper cars."[18] Upset by the new legislation, the Citizens' Committee crafted a well-organized experiment to challenge the Louisiana statute.

In order to execute the plan, the committee, led by Albion W. Tourgée and Louis Martinet, needed someone who could exploit the Louisiana legislature's failure to define race, someone who could not only confound the murky constructions of race but also challenge ideas of racial categories circulating in the late nineteenth century.[19]

Homer Plessy certainly looked the part. With his light skin and European features, Plessy had all the conventional appearances of a white man, and at thirty, he was sufficiently old enough to "project an image of 'manly resistance'" that the committee was looking for in a candidate.[20] His parents were classified as free people of color or Creoles of color, with African and French forebears, which made him light enough to pass—so much so that the conductor on the train could not immediately tell if Plessy was Black. When the conductor, J. J Dowling, asked Plessy if he was a Black man, Plessy responded (as rehearsed) that he was seven-eighths white. The conductor then told Plessy to move into the "colored" car.

The choice of a mixed-race figure was an important legal strategy. As the theater historian Joseph Roach argues, the committee had at least two goals that it wanted to accomplish: the most immediate concern "was to challenge the constitutionality of the discriminatory public accommodations act of 1890"; the second and perhaps more provocative "goal was to challenge the legality of the concept of race itself."[21] To this end, Albion Tourgée asked in his brief a number of questions about the standard for racial classifications, some of which the Court actually attempted to answer: "Is the officer of a railroad competent to decide the question of race?" "Is it a question that *can* be determined in the absence of statutory definition and without evidence?" "Is not a statutory assortment of the people of a state on the line of race, such a perpetuation of the essential features of slavery as to come within the inhibition of the XIIIth Amendment?" "Is it not the establishment of a statutory difference between the white and colored races in the enjoyment of chartered privileges, a badge of servitude which is prohibited by that amendment?" "Is not *state* citizenship made an essential incident of *national* citizenship, by the XIV Amendment, and if so are not the rights, privileges and immunities of the same within the scope of the national jurisdiction?"[22] Tourgée's list of questions was designed to give the Court several things to consider in the case, but the bulk of his argument rested on two claims: Jim Crow laws not only violated the rights and privileges of national citizenship guaranteed by the Fourteenth Amendment but also disregarded the prohibition of involuntary servitude stated in the Thirteenth Amendment.

In addition to attempting to make the Court think harder about the law, Tourgée also sought to make the justices reconsider the racial implications of this case. To do so, he asked them to imagine themselves as Black in appearance. Here was his scenario:

> Suppose a member of this court, nay, suppose every member of it, by some mysterious dispensation of providence should wake to-morrow with a black skin and curly hair—the two obvious and controlling indications of race—and in traveling through that portion of the country where the "Jim Crow Car" abounds, should be ordered into it by the conductor. It is easy to imagine what would be the result, the indignation, the protests, the assertion of pure Caucasian ancestry. But the conductor, the autocrat of Caste, armed with the power of the State conferred by this statute, will listen neither to denial or protest. "In you go or out you go," is his ultimatum.[23]

Understanding Tourgée's appeal to racial empathy and impersonation is critical to understanding his distinctive view of race in the law. With his speculation of racial mutability, he wanted the justices to "feel and know" what it was like to appear Black in the United States in the hope that they would understand that the law was nothing but a blatant attempt to "humiliate and degrade" Black people.[24] In this regard, Tourgée requested that the Court shed their skin and don a racial mask. He attempted to put them in a disguise. It was a risky proposition, one that the Court did not participate in. Rather than entertain Tourgée's fanciful imagination, the justices would stick to their discriminating version of the law.

The majority and dissenting opinions in *Plessy* and the Citizens' Committee's plan greatly informed the work of Charles Waddell Chesnutt and James Weldon Johnson, the two authors I examine in chapters 4 and 5. Both chapters focus on how each author challenges constructions and perceptions of race, and both frame the Jim Crow train car as a site of disablement and disability. Chesnutt's essays took a satiric approach to the matter of race, as he revised Tourgée's imaginative scenario to profound effect. Rather than ask white Americans to imagine themselves as Black (as Tourgée did), Chesnutt asked them to define and defend the category of whiteness. And his fiction—both *The Conjure Stories* and *The Marrow of Tradition*—took up the subject of disability by spotlighting the injuriousness of slavery and Jim Crow and the fragile and interdependent racial health of his white and Black characters. James Weldon Johnson described the disabilities of Jim Crow in his fiction and nonfiction as well—focusing not only on how disability was racialized within the US race-based caste system but also on how disability was defined, constructed, and produced, particularly in segregated spaces within the United States.

4

Losing Limbs in the Republic

Charles Waddell Chesnutt

Remixing American Blood

So determined to dismiss the false narrative of white racial purity sweeping across the nation and to overturn the crude belief that Black folks would disappear postemancipation because of an innate biological defect, Charles Waddell Chesnutt inquired about the construction of "the disability of color" within US culture.[1] Aiming to dispute the notion of Black blood as diseased, he seized on a satirical and circuitous line of reasoning. During the late nineteenth century, while several white southerners were deeply concerned about the ubiquitous "Negro question," he decided to look in a wholly different direction when he asked another question that others were eager to overlook: "What is a white man?"[2]

On May 30, 1889, when Chesnutt published his seminal essay with this query as its title, the general tenor of US racial relations was almost as fraught as it had been before the Civil War. Despite regional and national attempts among white and Black people to secure equal political rights for African Americans during the postbellum period, most southerners maintained a defensive posture in spite of defeat, holding steadfast to their belief in white supremacy.[3] This southern creed of white authoritarianism inflamed the ire of Chesnutt, whose essay interrogates who precisely can lay claim to whiteness. "The fiat having gone forth from the wise men of the South that the 'all-pervading, all-conquering Anglo-Saxon race' must continue forever to exercise exclusive control and direction of the government of this so-called Republic," he wrote, "it becomes important to every citizen who values his birthright to know who are included in this grandiloquent term."[4]

The "grandiloquent term" under consideration was *Anglo-Saxon*, and its loftiness had as much to do with its overdetermination as it did with its sense of superiority. As Chesnutt outlined, the term was certainly meant to include "Celts," "Slavs," "Teutons," "Gauls," and Jewish people.[5] In fact, its application had been so loose and unruly that Chesnutt later described this racial designation as a "social fiction," a fanciful invention with the sensational ability to selectively pluck members out of thin air.[6] Recognizing the fluidity of the term *Anglo-Saxon* and understanding that the color line separating Anglo-Saxons from non-Anglo-Saxons was "the line which separated freedom and opportunity from slavery or hopeless degradation," Chesnutt had good reason to engage in such a scholarly pursuit.[7] In his view, *Anglo-Saxon* was a not-so-secret code word for anyone who *appeared* white.

With "What Is a White Man?" and his subsequent serialized three-part essay "The Future American" (1900), Chesnutt hatched a plan for racial intermixture that he thought would subvert racial hierarchy and create racial harmony. He wrote, "There can manifestly be no such thing as a peaceful and progressive civilization in a nation divided by two warring races, and homogeneity of type, at least in externals, is a necessary condition of harmonious social progress."[8] His plan of racial amalgamation was certainly controversial—and, given the nation's fierce determination to keep Black and white races separated, grossly absurd—but his derisive tone made it difficult to discern which parts of his plan were meant to be implemented and which not. Teetering between the personal and the political, his essays contain all the essential ingredients of a racial satire: there are expressions of piercing irony sprinkled throughout with a dash of sarcasm tossed in for good measure. Yet his essays are also grounded in an astute knowledge of law, science, and history, and they capitalize on the anxieties of some white Americans about the nation's racial and ethnic futurity. As the literary, gender, and sexuality studies scholar Marlon B. Ross points out, "Pursuing and exploiting the logic used by white progressive writers who have attempted to turn anxiety over southern and eastern European immigration into a benefit by promising the immigrants' assimilation into a perfect American union, Chesnutt want[ed] to extend this idea to the two most maligned and marginal groups, American Indians and Negroes."[9] Chesnutt's goal was twofold: he wanted to expose how racial amalgamation had been under way for centuries and to show the futility of using phenotype and blood quantum as markers for racial and ethnic identity (especially for light-skinned Black folks and Indigenous people).

Chesnutt's plan, however, was not foolproof, for it did not fully consider the role of dark-skinned Black people within it. That is, his distinctions between dark-skinned and light-skinned African Americans worked at cross-purposes, and his emphasis on racial mixing was too rash in its promotion of racial erasure, which sounded dangerously close to the anti-Black rhetoric of white supremacists who were advocating for Black emigration to Africa and endorsing notions of Black extinction. Indeed, his essays carry a strain of racial logic that has given some literary critics extended pause. For instance, SallyAnn H. Ferguson argues that Chesnutt's cursory dismissal of dark-skinned African Americans from his consideration of racial amalgamation in "The Future American" essays made it appear as if he was willing to forsake a large number of southern Black folks in the name of achieving racial equality for light-skinned Black people who could engender his type of assimilation.[10] And Arlene A. Elder remarks that Chesnutt's impulse to eliminate "the marker of color, the semiotic of skin" through assimilation was "an understandable, if unfortunate, position for a mulatto writer living during the racially-turbulent turn-of-the-century."[11] Ferguson and Elder rightly point out the flaws of Chesnutt's plan, particularly at the beginning of the twentieth century, when violent extralegal lynchings were executed to maintain white supremacy.

Yet Chesnutt's skewed vision should not completely obscure his premise. His emphasis on racial hybridity and his strategy for producing a "future American" body politic were part and parcel of a more egalitarian mission: to eradicate the "social stigma," "social disability," and "social injury" imposed on Black folks and "to disprove the theory that people of mixed blood, other things being equal, are less virile, prolific, or able."[12] By putting "forth a biological solution to the cultural dilemma of race," Ross asserts, Chesnutt issued a novel idea: "Sex between the races produces not the monstrous half-breeds of legend and fantasy but instead productive individuals, like himself, who possess the best characteristics of the combined races and ensure the amplified diversity of the American species."[13] Chesnutt figured cross-racial sex and reproduction as a possible solution, "even if tongue-in-cheek," for eradicating the idea of blackness as innately defective or diseased, and he did so by emphasizing that racial hybridity—a phenomenon the law staunchly regulated and restricted by meting out severe punishments to Black folks—was already in existence.[14] By questioning the social system that made "mixed blood a *prima-facie* proof of illegitimacy," he attempted to upend the legal regime, practically forcing it to answer for the discourse and practices of disability that were of its own making.[15]

Tracing Chesnutt's various avowals of disability throughout his body of work is the primary objective of this chapter. While his essays largely address disability via a scrupulous accounting of blood, his fiction tackles disability by scrutinizing the matter of blood as well as the varied contingencies of the Black body and mind. In particular, Chesnutt's work exhibits an acute and extensive theorization of loss within the Black community—insofar as bodily dispossession, literal and figurative dismemberment, legal immobilization, and the fracturing of the family tree reside at the core of his *Conjure Stories* and his second novel, *The Marrow of Tradition* (1901). In both his tales and his novel, he reveals disablement as part of Black sociality but avoids recapitulating racist depictions of the Black body and mind as inherently defective. And similarly to his essays, Chesnutt's fiction crucially sutures the health and progress of Black people with that of white folks in a manner that both demonstrates the manufactured and material aspects of disability as well as frames racism and white supremacy as a national health crisis. None of his characters are immune to the toxic force of racism, for toxicity in Chesnutt's work is configured, to borrow from the theorist Mel Y. Chen, "as already 'here,' already a truth of nearly every body, and also as a biopolitically interested distribution" that assumes "both individual and collective vulnerability" and "suggests an ulterior ethical stance."[16]

What follows is an engagement with Chesnutt's work through the lens of disability in an effort to offer a nuanced analytical framework, one that does not depend solely on his fiction at the expense of his nonfiction, or outright dismiss him as an assimilationist who advocates for Black racial extinction, or disregard the political savviness and subversiveness of his literary work. Whether he focuses on the racist narratives of Black blood as contaminated (as he does in his essays), the dismemberment and deformities inflicted onto enslaved people who are deemed disobedient (as he does in *Conjure Stories*), or the literal and figurative disablement of Jim Crow via segregation and lynching (as he does in *Marrow*), Chesnutt remains especially attuned to how disability is imposed by the perils of slavery, segregation, and white supremacy.

Dissolving Limbs in Chesnutt's *Conjure Stories*

In December 1916, while delivering a lecture to the National Buy-a-Book Campaign in Philadelphia, Charles Chesnutt offered a retrospective account of the particular kind of Black characters he incorporates into his literary work as well as a glimpse of how disability and blackness intersect in US culture. His talk, "The Negro in Books," demanded fairer and more balanced portrayals of Black people. Rather than depicting the "servile, groveling menial or the absurd buffoon," two stock character types that flooded the literary market of his era, Chesnutt urged writers to create more diverse images of Black folks and to produce bold and daring characters who resist authority in the face of "many hardships, many handicaps."[17] George Washington Cable's Bras-Coupé in *The Grandissimes* ranked high on Chesnutt's list. "The story of 'Bras Coupé,'" said Chesnutt, "is a masterpiece; the character of the Negro who defied the lash, defied his master, and who preferred death to slavery, is a refreshing departure from the popular literary convention of the cringing, fawning menial who would lick the hand that struck him."[18]

Chesnutt's interest in Cable's Bras-Coupé was manifold. As a Black writer who wrote about the intense violence of slavery in his stories, essays, and novels and whose fiction includes a number of characters that resist systemic oppression, Chesnutt was enthralled by Bras-Coupé's willingness to defy his enslaver and his display of courage despite the possibility of death. Yet Cable's engagement with the law in his novel also caught Chesnutt's attention. Given Chesnutt's professional interest in the law, he paid close attention to Bras-Coupé's body, which undergoes a gruesome transformation for violating an old French slave code.[19] As punishment for running away and for striking his slaveholder, Bras-Coupé is "mutilated" and "maimed."[20] In accordance with the *Code Noir*—slave codes that were enforced in the nineteenth-century US South and mandated dismemberment and disfigurement as punishments for fugitives—Bras-Coupé's enslaver severs his ears and hamstrings. Here, the weaponization of disability within these codes serves as evidence of what Jasbir Puar calls "'the right to maim': a right expressive of sovereign power that is linked to, but not the same as, 'the right to kill'" as well as "a practice of rendering populations available for statistically likely injury."[21]

These codes reveal the centrality of disablement within US law, and the transformation of the Black body due to the slaveholder's cruelty and the imposition of the law holds a special resonance for Chesnutt's *The Conjure Stories*.[22] In his stories, Chesnutt depicted characters like Uncle Julius McAdoo, a freedman whose body is susceptible to disablement, alongside characters like Henry in "The Goophered Grapevine," Sandy and Tenie in "Po' Sandy," Primus in "The Conjurer's Revenge," Dave in "Dave's Neckliss," and Viney in "The Dumb Witness," Black women and men whose vulnerability to deformation and madness is tied directly to the precariousness of slavery.

Upon publication, Chesnutt's conjure stories immediately captured the attention of the literary world. Some of the individual stories were published in major periodicals including the *Atlantic Monthly* and *Overland Monthly*, and in 1899, Houghton Mifflin published seven of the stories as a collection titled *The Conjure Woman*. The stories were so popular that they captured the eye of William Dean Howells—an American realist author who, in his 1900 *Atlantic Monthly* review, wrote that the stories were "the creation of sincere and original imagination, which is imparted with a tender humorousness and a very artistic reticence."[23] Howells was not alone in his praise. Chesnutt's stories have continued to fascinate contemporary scholars of African American literature, who have commented on his use of Black dialect, African American folklore, and the transformative power of conjure in his tales.[24] Paying close attention to the racialized embodiment of Chesnutt's characters, I focus on his representation of disability, an often ignored but essential feature of his stories.

In alignment with the disability studies scholar Anna Mollow, I examine the "intersections of forms of oppression" in Chesnutt's stories to show how they elucidate the multiple ways that disability influenced Black lives in the antebellum and postbellum periods and to "guard against the dangers of a 'disability essentialism,' in which the experiences, needs, desires, and aims of all disabled people are assumed to be the same and those with 'different' experiences are accommodated only if they do not make claims that undermine the movement's foundational arguments."[25] First, by depicting Sandy's limbless body, Tenie's madness, Viney's mutilation and illiteracy, and Primus's clubfoot, Chesnutt portrays both visible and invisible disabilities in *The Conjure Stories*. Second, because Chesnutt was aware of the racist narratives surrounding Black bodies, he took care to present disability as imposed through enslavement and racial segregation. I argue that Chesnutt's attentiveness to the various forms of disability stemmed from his recognition that a portrayal of blackness and disability posed a particular set of challenges for African American authors, especially given the racist assumptions circulating about racial degeneracy. By examining the intersections of blackness and disability in *The Conjure Stories*, I show how Chesnutt depicts visible and invisible disabilities via slavery and Jim Crow while maintaining distance from the racist claims that Black folks are innately inferior. Rather than disassociate disability from race, he acknowledges disability to gain a better understanding of how and why particular Black bodies are disabled. If we fail to interrogate the intersections of blackness and disability, then we run the risk of putting Black studies at odds with disability studies and of misinterpreting the work of Black authors like Chesnutt as a repudiation of disability rather than as a critique of how the institutions of slavery and Jim Crow relied on disability as an essential part of their brutal regimes. While several of the conjure stories spotlight disability, I focus primarily on three stories—"Po' Sandy," "The Dumb Witness," and "The Conjurer's Revenge"—by exploring Chesnutt's engagements with physical and cognitive disabilities imposed on the bodies and minds of both his white and Black characters.

Dismemberment and Madness in "Po' Sandy"

In the 1931 essay "Post-Bellum—Pre-Harlem," Chesnutt stated that one of his principal aims was to capture "the alleged incidents of chattel slavery" in his tales.[26] *The Conjure Stories* fulfills this aim by offering a nuanced account of how these "incidents" impede the freedom and mobility of Black folks. Each story typically includes two narrators (John, the white Yankee businessman; and Uncle Julius McAdoo, the ex-slave and storyteller), two narratives (an outer frame story, which Chesnutt refers to as the introduction and "wind-up" and which is set after the

Civil War; and an inner conjure tale, which is set before the war), and white northern audience members (John; his wife, Annie; and sometimes her sister, Mabel).[27] Shifting from one point of view to another, Chesnutt's stories yield a blend of cultural and regional perspectives, mixing the Standard English of a transplanted northern entrepreneur and the sentimentality of his genteel wife with the local southern dialect of a formerly enslaved man who has a superb gift for storytelling. Portraying how the antebellum period endures in the postwar South, Chesnutt's *Conjure Stories* tap into an occult and wondrous world where Black folks (and sometimes white folks) undergo a metamorphosis so uncanny and bizarre as to border on the grotesque. The power of conjure enables such dramatic metamorphoses. "Conjure," the historian Dylan C. Penningroth notes, "straddled this world and the next; it was all about social relationships that knit together the living and the dead."[28] Several of Chesnutt's stories capture this liminal state through a range of bodily transformations. Humans become birds, mules, insects, trees, houses, or other objects either as a form of escape or occasionally as punishment for some transgression.

The Conjure Stories emphasizes not only the transformations of the characters' physical bodies but also the environment in which these characters live. For instance, Chesnutt takes full measure of how the conditions and surroundings of a particular place at a specific time affect the varying experiences of its inhabitants. Despite such lush and rich conditions in Patesville (the setting of the conjure stories)—its temperate weather, the fertile soil, and ripe and succulent grapes—the former McAdoo plantation (which the narrator, John, eventually buys) bears serious signs of deterioration. As a "victim to the fortunes of [the Civil] war," the old plantation is insufferably marked by "exhausted" soil, "ruined chimneys," "decayed and broken-down trellises," "neglected grapevines," and "gnarled and knotted fruit-trees."[29] Parts of it are in disuse, while other parts are simply misused to the point of depletion and desolation. The ecological deformities of the former plantation parallel the inflicted bodily injuries in the tales. Black bodies become abused to the point of destruction just as much as the soil, trellises, and trees of the McAdoo plantation.

In "Po' Sandy," Chesnutt clarifies the extent of the deformation that both slavery and the war have wrought on the old plantation and its residents. This tale focuses primarily on white access to and destruction of plantation resources, and it details the manner in which the enslaver exploits with impunity enslaved labor, human bodies, personal property, and natural resources alike. As a parable for this exploitation, Julius recounts the story of Sandy, the eponymous character whose physique undergoes a drastic change in appearance. Disgruntled with being moved from one slaveholder to another, Sandy requests that his second wife, Tenie, a conjure woman, turn him into a pine tree, which, at the behest of his enslaver, later gets cut down and used as lumber, first for the slaveowner's kitchen and then for his schoolhouse.

Sandy's transformations from a man to a tree, from a tree to a kitchen, and from a kitchen to a schoolhouse reveal the relentless cycle of abuse rooted in the setting. In the opening description of the neighboring schoolhouse, which exhibits a frame that is worse for wear, John observes the considerable disrepair: "Its weather-beaten sides revealed a virgin innocence of paint"; "the crumbling mortar had left large cracks between the bricks . . . leaving the chimney sprinkled with unsightly blotches"; and the "wooden shutter, which had once protected the unglazed window, had fallen from its hinges, and lay rotting in the rank grass and jimson-weeds beneath."[30] Here Chesnutt presents a property twice defaced since this anthropomorphic abode doubles as reconstituted Sandy. Its "weather-beaten sides," its "unsightly blotches," its "crumbling mortar," and its "rotting" shutter all refer to the various skinned and dismembered parts of Sandy's body. "Po' Sandy" gives full import to the term *chattel slavery*, where persons and property, humans and things, blur into each other and bear the brunt of the slaveholder's intractable violence. By focusing on the fantastical transformations of Sandy's body, Chesnutt, not unlike the Black women writers of a later generation that Rosemarie Garland-Thomson examines in her work, establishes "the extraordinary body as a site of historical inscription rather than as physical deviance" and repudiates "such cultural master narratives as normalcy [and] wholeness."[31]

Just as the gaunt schoolhouse evokes Sandy's dismembered body, Sandy's dismembered body evokes the racial injuries of slavery. Before Tenie transforms Sandy into a pine tree, before the pine tree is felled, and before field hands saw the pine logs into boards and scantlings, Sandy's slaveholder, Marrabo McSwayne, figuratively pulls him apart.

To honor his children's wishes, McSwayne bestows Sandy upon them as a wedding present. Sandy consequently shuttles from one household to another on a monthly basis.

This constant shuffling back and forth frustrates Sandy to such an extent that he makes the following confession to his new wife, Tenie:

> I'm gittin' monst'us ti'ed er dish yer gwine roun' so much. Here I is lent ter Mars Jeems dis mont', en I got ter do so-en-so; en ter Mars Archie de nex' mont', en I got ter do so-en-so; den I got ter go ter Miss Jinnie's: en hit's Sandy dis en Sandy dat, en Sandy yer en Sandy dere, tel it 'pears ter me I ain' got no home, ner no marster, ner no mistiss, ner no nuffin. I can't eben keep a wife: my yuther ole 'oman wuz sol' away widout my gittin' a chance fer ter tell her good-by; en now I got ter go off en leab you, Tenie, en I dunno whe'r I'm eber gwine ter see you ag'in er no.[32]

Here Sandy discovers the unfavorable consequences of being a good and dutiful slave: diminishing returns. Having more work or expending more energy offers less reward, or in the words of Sandy, having more equals having "nuffin": "no home, ner no marster, ner no mistiss," and certainly no familial ties protected by the law. This labor accentuates Sandy's paralyzing sense of bodily dispossession. Under McSwayne's rule, to be "lent" is to be stolen anew—since Sandy's borrowed hands and borrowed feet are not rightfully returned to him but rather given to multiple slaveholders. Compelled to do "dis," "dat," and the other and forced to be "yer," "dere," and everywhere, Sandy is almost unable to do anything or be anywhere on his own volition. It is this sense of alienation that prompts Sandy's personal confession to Tenie, but it is the fear of possibly losing another wife that propels him into an act of resistance.

The tragic irony of this tale lies in the fact that Sandy's effort to gain control of his body exacerbates his disability. When Tenie offers to fulfill Sandy's wish to be turned into "sump'n w'at could stay on de plantation fer a w'ile" so that he can spend more time with her, it is with the hope that they can possibly save their family from ruin and destruction.[33] But when McSwayne's wife loans Tenie to one of their sons while Sandy is in tree form and before Tenie turns them both into foxes so that they "could be free en lib lack w'ite folks," it becomes clear that Tenie's particular brand of conjure ultimately falls short against the potency of southern slavery.[34] After Tenie returns to the plantation, she discovers Sandy's "stump standin' dere, wid de sap runnin' out'n it, en de limbs layin' scattered roun', [and] she nigh 'bout went out'n her min.'"[35] This cruel twist of misfortune confirms Sandy and Tenie's fatal miscalculation: their misguided assumption that any living, natural being could thrive long in such close proximity to the perilous environs of a slave plantation.

Granted, Tenie's conjure demonstrates that the slaveholder's sovereignty is not absolute. In fact, conjure was often the principal way that enslaved people were able to exert their own autonomy and retaliate against each other as well as their slaveholders; it, thus, showed that there were limits to the power of white folks. As Penningroth observes, the enslaved probably used special objects such as "patent medicine bottles, coins, buttons, mirrors, musical instruments, chalk, bird skulls, ocean shells, scales, and small cloth bags filled with plants" to "channel supernatural power into 'fixing' people's problems with one another. Some kinds of conjure targeted other black people, as when the teenaged Henry Bibb bought something to make girls fall in love with him. Other kinds of conjure were aimed at whites."[36] For instance, in order for Frederick Douglass to win his epic battle against his overseer, Mr. Covey, he carried with him "a certain *root*" that he believed "would render it impossible for Mr. Covey, or any other white man, to whip [him]."[37] He received this root from an enslaved man named Sandy Jenkins—perhaps a possible source for the name of the titular protagonist in "Po' Sandy." Acknowledging that the use of conjure offered enslaved people a certain kind of power does not render the slaveholder's authority ineffective, however. Although Tenie's power turns Sandy into a pine tree, it is the enslaver's power that hews his body into gnarled "limbs" and chops him down to a bloody "stump."

Sandy, it deserves mentioning, is not the only victim in "Po' Sandy." If the response of the narrator's wife, Annie, in the outer frame story functions as a barometer for measuring the narrative's larger meaning for one of the tale's listeners, then Uncle Julius's inner conjure tale provides us with at least two casualties: Sandy and Tenie. "What a system it was," Annie says at the conclusion of Julius's story, "under which such things were possible!" When the incredulous John asks his wife, "Are you seriously considering the possibility of a man's being turned into a tree?" Annie whispers, "Oh, no . . . not that . . . Poor Tenie!" Her response to Julius's "gruesome narrative" reminds us that after Sandy's dismemberment, Tenie spirals downward into a state of madness until she eventually dies in the schoolhouse.[38] Sandy's body parts are severed, while Tenie loses her mind. Although the use of sympathy toward disabled characters is often criticized in disability studies, since it tends to reinforce an unfortunate hierarchy between the disabled and the nondisabled, Annie's sympathy for Tenie demonstrates how sympathy can, as the disability studies scholar Howard Sklar observes, turn into compassion, involving a "'heightened awareness' of . . . discrimination, as well as the simultaneous recognition that that situation of discrimination ought to be 'alleviated.'"[39] While Chesnutt's title marks Sandy as the key sympathetic figure, Annie's response emphasizes Sandy and Tenie's mutual suffering. The brutal assault of slavery breaks both Sandy's body and Tenie's mind, and such systematic violence irrevocably fractures the limbs of their genealogical tree, fulfilling the enslaver's careless attempt "ter break up de fambly."[40]

Tenie's madness functions as a corollary to Chesnutt's ulterior motive, allowing him to elaborate further on the wide-ranging effects of slavery and racism. Her madness registers not only as a psychological equivalent to Sandy's physical dismemberment but also as a muted reminder of Annie's fragile mental and physical state. At the outset in "The Goophered Grapevine," John tells us that he and Annie move to North Carolina primarily because of her "poor health," which John closely monitors throughout The Conjure Stories.[41] She suffers from a fatigue and melancholy that is engendered by her surroundings, which the literary critics Robert Stepto and Jennifer Rae Greeson have described as neurasthenia, a condition characterized by physical and mental exhaustion and typically associated with depression or emotional distress.[42]

The close proximity between Tenie's madness and Annie's malady suggests that even white residents fall victim to Patesville's sordid past. Similarly to "Mars Jeems's Nightmare," the story in which a cruel white slaveholder is conjured and thus comes to appreciate the violent plight of his slaves, "Po' Sandy" depicts a white woman whose particular ailment makes her especially sympathetic to Tenie's grief. Chesnutt's inclusion of details regarding Annie's health spotlights a significant point that proves crucial to understanding one of the story's key morals: Annie is no more immune to the malevolence of slavery and racism than is Tenie, and Annie's health and quality of life are bound to Sandy and Tenie's as well as to the condition of Black people writ large.

By using Sandy and Tenie as examples of slavery's barbarity, Chesnutt demonstrates how the institution relies on disablement as an integral part of its oppressive system. In fact, Chesnutt's parallel between slavery and disability recalls the severe practices of the *Code Noir*. Like George Washington Cable's Bras-Coupé, Chesnutt's Sandy discovers the high bodily price that the enslaved must pay for attempting to elude his slaveholder's sway. Article 32 of the *Code Noir* outlined, "The runaway slave who shall have been absent one month from the day reported to the Court by his master shall have his ears cut off, and shall be branded on one shoulder with the fleur-de-lis. If he repeats the offense during another month from the day of reporting, he shall be hamstrung and branded with the fleur-de-lis on the other shoulder; and the third time, he shall be punished by death."[43] According to the logic of the *Code Noir*, an enslaved person who attempts to reclaim their own body can, to their dismay, find their body branded and dismembered. Focusing on the enslaved person's experiences of deformation in "Po' Sandy," Chesnutt conceivably harks back to the *Code Noir*.

Chesnutt's desire to create Black characters willing to risk life and limb for freedom, equality, and respect is an essential feature of his literary project. Sandy and Tenie sacrifice their lives and bodies, enduring both physical and psychological disabilities in the process. Sandy's attempt to escape figures him as a fugitive and leads to his dismemberment; his dismemberment results in Tenie's madness until she eventually "grieve' herse'f ter def."[44] Their inflicted disabilities are figured as part of the slavery regime, and the different ways disability is deployed in Chesnutt's story show the comprehensiveness of slavery's violence and trauma.

Mutilation and Illiteracy in "The Dumb Witness"

In "Po' Sandy," Charles Chesnutt captured the bodily dispossession of the enslaved and the injurious practices of slavery by focusing on an enslaved couple; in "The Dumb Witness," he delineated how the law affects a single, Black woman by focusing on her relationship with her former slaveowner as well as her mutilation and illiteracy. John narrates this tale without Julius, and he summarizes "The Dumb Witness" as a "story of old man Murchison's undoing" and as a "story of jealousy, revenge and disappointment."[45] Although not inaccurate, John's description notably deemphasizes the role of one of the story's main characters: Viney, a formerly enslaved woman who is freed after the war. From her view, "The Dumb Witness" can also be described as a story about her enslaver's wayward violence and unyielding power or as a tale about the enslaved's vulnerability to disability. Such descriptions are more apropos, for the heart of the tale centers not only on Viney's "mutilation" but also on the subsequent ways she is "handicapped . . . by her loss of speech."[46]

The reader is introduced to Viney during a heated postwar dispute between her and her former slaveholder, Malcolm Murchison. While Murchison demands that Viney disclose the whereabouts of his uncle's will (which, among other things, names him as the sole heir of the plantation), Viney remains mute, offering no verbal reply to Murchison's demand. When Murchison calls her a "hussy" and threatens to have her "whipped," Viney becomes enraged and speaks up. Her speech, unfortunately, is indecipherable. According to John, Viney speaks in what he originally thought was "some foreign tongue." "But after a moment I knew," says John, "that no language or dialect . . . could consist of such a discordant jargon, such a meaningless cacophony as that which fell from the woman's lips." The "discordant jargon" and "meaningless cacophony" of sounds that Viney exhibits after the war result from the violence that Malcolm Murchison inflicts on her before the war. As punishment for discreetly talking to one of his female acquaintances and convincing her to dismiss Murchison's advances, Viney receives a beating from Murchison that is apparently so horrible she suffers from defective speech.[47]

Explicit details about Viney's assault and disability are unknown to the reader. Part of the reason there are no specifics about Viney's mutilation might be the fact that "The Dumb Witness" was posthumously published and the story is composed from two partial transcripts. As Stepto and Greeson point out, there is a marking near the description of Viney's assault that "indicates that Chesnutt intended that another passage be inserted at the end of this sentence," but the "passage does not survive with the extant typescript."[48] However, it is also possible that

Chesnutt withholds details about the incident to increase the story's dramatic tension, offering the reader enough information to suture together a narrative about what might have happened. For instance, we know that Murchison, in an effort to teach Viney a lesson about telling "tales about your master," threatens her with violence. He states, "I will put it out of your power to dip your tongue in where you are not concerned." We can surmise that Murchison makes good on this threat, since when he later pleads to Viney for information about his uncle's will, Viney points "to her mouth" as an explanation for her inability to speak. And we discover that Murchison laments his own violent behavior, for "he had begun to feel, in some measure, that there was not sufficient excuse for what he had done" and he admits to Viney, "it was wrong, and I've always regretted it."[49] In spite of all the things we know, there is no definitive description of "what he had done" or what "it" is, and neither Murchison nor Viney enlightens us about the matter. The act is so ghastly that "it" is presumably unspeakable within the narrative of the story.

The story's lacuna inevitably compels the reader's imagination to run wild with speculation: Was Viney bludgeoned so badly that her mouth was disfigured or deformed? Or did Murchison attempt to excise Viney's tongue? "The Dumb Witness" does not answer any of these questions, but the story's notable silence regarding precisely how Murchison disciplined Viney reminds the reader that Murchison could have done anything to Viney without fear of being reprimanded by the law. "There was no one to say him nay," Chesnutt wrote. "The law made her his . . . and no angel of mercy stayed his hand."[50] Slave law imbues Murchison with the authority to possess and control the enslaved—his property—as he wishes. The law's transmutation of "her" into "his" grants the slaveholder an "irresponsible power" that he can exercise with impunity, and Murchison certainly makes use of this power against Viney (though, as the story informs us, his assertion of power comes at a cost).[51]

One likely source for Chesnutt's story is William Lloyd Garrison's 1863 essay "The Dumb Witness," which not only bears the same title as Chesnutt's tale but also describes how the violence of slavery deforms and mutilates the enslaved body. Garrison's essay focuses on the photograph of Gordon, an enslaved man who escaped from a Louisiana plantation in 1863 and whose scourged back was depicted as visual evidence of slavery's brutality. Garrison claims that Gordon's back represents a "testimony" against the terrors of slavery: "Scarred, gouged, gathered in great ridges, knotted, furrowed, the poor tortured flesh stands out [as] a hideous record of the slave-driver's lash." In addition to focusing on Gordon, Garrison's "The Dumb Witness" is also a story about the denial of a "Copperhead" to see evidence of slavery's barbarism as well as his attempt to erase the visual archive of the suffering slave. After purchasing a photograph that features Gordon's scourged back, the Copperhead "tore the card into fragments, and scattered them on the floor," presumably to destroy evidence of slavery's torture. But as Garrison points out, the man's actions were futile: "the damning fact of slavery's cruelty still remained when the harmless card was gone." The abolitionist photographer who sold Gordon's photograph to the Copperhead reiterated this point when he informed the buyer that there are many other photographs available for purchase. Garrison interprets the actions of the Copperhead as an attempt to alleviate his "troubled conscience," but he assures his readers that "as long as the flesh lasts will this fearful impress remain."[52]

Chesnutt's "The Dumb Witness" similarly spotlights the inescapability of slavery's brutality and how its violent regime has the potential to haunt slaveholders. In Chesnutt's tale, Viney does not let Murchison forget his violent act, and the violence he exacts leads to his own undoing. His beating robs Viney of her speech, and when Murchison is informed that Viney is the only person who knows the "hiding place" of the will, Murchison believes her speech is necessary to determine the will's location. Of course, Viney's speech is not essential in order to find the will; that is, she does not need to speak to show Murchison where the will is located. Nevertheless, this dilemma tortures Murchison until his death, for he never finds his uncle's papers. Hoping that Viney will be able to speak once she has healed from her injury, he takes pains to aid her recovery. He moves her out of the cabin and returns her to his house. He arranges for her to receive the utmost attention, feeding her and making sure that the best "care as was possible was given to her wound." When these efforts fail, he even decides to hire someone to teach Viney to read and write.[53]

This final attempt to circumvent Viney's disability reveals her illiteracy, which Chesnutt figures as a legal disability. According to the narrator, "It occurred to [Murchison] more than once how simple it would be for her to write down the few words necessary to his happiness. But, alas! she might as well have been without hands, for any use she could make of them in that respect. Slaves were not taught to write, for too much learning would have made them mad."[54] The line regarding how education and literacy lead to madness recalls the justifications of slavery, particularly those made by medical doctors in the nineteenth century. Dr. John Van Evrie wrote in the late 1860s that there are severe penalties and "consequences of negro education." He claimed that while some Black people "seem as well educated as white men, . . . it must be at the expense of the body, shortening the existence, just as we sometimes witness in the case of children when the pride, vanity, or ignorance of parents have stimulated their minds, and dwarfed or destroyed their bodies."[55] And earlier, in 1851, Dr. Samuel A. Cartwright claimed that runaways suffered from a mental illness known as "drapetomania," which he described as a "disease of the mind causing [enslaved people] to abscond."[56] Of course, this line of reasoning was racist. The link between mental illness and notions of disease and disability suggests the particular ways that both are ensnarled in justifications for slavery, which underscore that an examination of visible and invisible disabilities is crucial for understanding the myriad ways disability has been deployed during and after slavery. As the literary and disability studies scholar Therí Alyce Pickens argues, "the charges of cognitive disability and mental illness (i.e., *drapetomania* as a mental illness causing Black slaves to run away) or congenital, race-based neuroatypicality (i.e., all Blacks are mentally deficient) bear repercussions for imagining, analyzing, and theorizing Blackness and madness."[57] Murchison's link between literacy, madness, and disability also highlights the connection between medical and legal discourses, for Chesnutt does not construct illiteracy as a congenital defect but as something enforced by law and imposed by the enslaver. He does not concede that Viney is incapable of becoming literate. Rather he imagines that, were it not for the law's prohibition, she would be literate.

Throughout the tale, Chesnutt shows that Viney is no dumb witness. Her strategic silence shows how the enforced illiteracy of slaves could drive their masters into poor health and madness, for Murchison not only "worrie[s] himself into a fever" and serious "illness" but also succumbs to dementia.[58] Murchison's condition undermines the idea that literacy would lead to the slave's madness. Chesnutt's use of silence, then,

Eric Sundquist observes, "turns the diagnosis of madness back on the masters" for Murchison eventually goes mad and later dies as a result of Viney's refusal to tell him the will's location.[59] Although "The Dumb Witness" demonstrates Chesnutt's awareness of how disability was meted out to recalcitrant enslaved people, it also depicts the ways that enslaved men and women attempted to resist their masters and exert their own authority. Viney disobeys her master by intervening to prevent Murchison's relationship with another woman. In fact, she becomes enraged when Murchison tells her to prepare the house for a new mistress. Therefore, Viney's silence can be interpreted both as retaliation for her mutilation and as revenge for Murchison's disloyalty.

Similarly to "Po' Sandy," "The Dumb Witness" demonstrates Chesnutt's extensive engagement with how both disability and race are connected in *The Conjure Stories*. The tale focuses on bodily dispossession in Viney's relationship with Murchison as well as on the physical and cognitive disabilities that are embedded in the institution of slavery. It also parallels the health of the slave's body with that of the master's. Murchison's illness and madness are tied to Viney's mutilation in "The Dumb Witness" just as Annie's health is tied to Sandy and Tenie's in "Po' Sandy." This link between the health of enslaved people and their enslavers allows Chesnutt to show that both white and Black people were vulnerable to disability. Their vulnerability was not the same, and comprehending the different ways that disability has affected Black enslaved people involves a close examination of the intersections of disability and race, one that accounts for, as the historian of medicine Dea H. Boster claims, the "interactions between bodies and their physical, social, cultural, and aesthetic environments." "This relational view of disability," Boster argues, "rejects the notion that those who are disabled have always been defined in contrast to a central, unproblematic, able-bodied norm and seeks ways to examine how both disability and able-bodiedness were culturally constructed, performed, racialized, commodified, and negotiated."[60] In "The Conjurer's Revenge," Chesnutt employs a similar approach, depicting how both disability and animality are constructed and racialized.

Mule and Man in "The Conjurer's Revenge"

While "Po' Sandy" strikes a sentimental chord in Annie, "The Conjurer's Revenge" does not elicit quite the same emotional response. Unlike Sandy's and Tenie's stories, which produce in Annie a heartfelt sense of empathy, Uncle Julius's yarn about Primus (an enslaved male whom an unnamed conjure man turns into a mule for allegedly stealing his charmed shoat) apparently lacks the desired amount of pathos and significance required for her taste. After Julius concludes the first part of his tale, Annie states bluntly, "That story does not appeal to me, Uncle Julius, and is not up to your usual mark. It isn't pathetic, it has no moral that I can discover, and I can't see why you should tell it. In fact, it seems to me like nonsense."[61] Her criticism of Julius's tale as "nonsense" should not be interpreted as an adequate justification for her outright rejection of it. For even though Annie claims earlier that Julius's anecdote in "Po' Sandy" is indisputably "absurd," she nonetheless takes his advice not to build her new kitchen from the schoolhouse lumber and allows him and other "seceders" of the Sandy Run Colored Baptist congregation to use the old schoolhouse as their new church, with the understanding that "religious worship" will do "Sandy's spirit" some good.[62] Her other concerns do, however, deserve our attention: What is the primary moral of Julius's tale, and why is it that Annie, who, in comparison to John, represents Julius's most sympathetic listener, either cannot detect it or does not think it warrants recounting?

The possible morals of "The Conjurer's Revenge" run the gamut, but at its core the story is concerned with bodily deformation and human-animal relations. It can be characterized as a narrative about the precariousness of slavery, a system that treats human and nonhuman animals as, according to the poet and literary studies scholar Joshua Bennett, "saleable, living beings . . . that are certainly used for labor, entertainment, and breeding but also possess an interiority that is, by the rule, denied."[63] It can be summarized as a story about deception, punishment, and atonement—since the unnamed Guinean conjurer from Africa turns Primus into a mule for supposedly stealing his enchanted pig; but, after the conjurer becomes sick with rheumatism, he later attempts to transform Primus back into his original form and nearly succeeds except for Primus's retention of a clubfoot. Alternatively, "The Conjurer's Revenge" may be described as a story about the risks of entrepreneurship—since John buys a defective horse, based on the appearance of the horse's flesh, that is blind in one eye and unable to plow the land. All of these versions share a common thread. Whether we focus on the parallels of human and nonhuman animal life on the plantation, the significance of a man as a mule, Primus's clubfoot, or a horse that turns out to be both blind and diseased, the story underscores bodily dispossession, deformity, and disability as central to its narrative about the deception of appearances and the various representations of race in the pre– and post–Civil War South.[64]

The pretext for Primus's transformation into a mule rests in a dispute between Julius and John as to whether a horse or a mule should be purchased for the plantation. John believes that a "mule can do more work, and doesn't require as much attention," but Julius advises him to buy a horse, offering this explanation: "I doan lack ter dribe a mule. I's alluz afeared I mought be imposin' on some human creetur; eve'y time I cuts a mule wid a hick'ry, 'pears ter me mos' lackly I's cuttin' some er my own relations, er somebody e'se w'at can't he'p deyse'ves."[65] Julius's link between "some human creetur" and "a mule" spotlights the shared subjection of mules and enslaved Black people within the confines of the plantation. Since Black people were perceived as property and valued for their labor within slave law, Julius imagines both human and nonhuman animal as sharing a sense of fellow feeling, a common understanding of the injuriousness of enslavement. In this instance, then, Julius observes what the literary and visual culture scholar Zakiyyah Iman Jackson refers to as "trans-species precarity." That is, his imaginative vision of being human "disrupt[s] the human-animal distinction and its persistent raciality" and resists "animality as abjection" by forming a kinship between the enslaved person and the nonhuman animal—one forged through a recognition of how the violent disablement (or wounding) of a fellow species can appear (or feel) like a disablement against the self or, as Julius puts it, "my own relations."[66]

Julius's association between "a mule" and his family "relations" is full of possibilities. What if, for instance, Julius's connection suggests a reimagining of human-animal relations to envision another cosmos, one that does not impose a binary between human and nonhuman animal and does not adopt the dominant ideology as a means of being in the world? Jackson's work helps to clarify the importance of such an imaginative practice. She argues "that the recognition of humanity and its suspension act as alibis for each other's terror, such that the pursuit of human recognition or a compact with 'the human' would only plunge one headlong into further terror and domination." Rather than ask, "Is the black a human being?" Jackson poses a "better question" for consideration: "If being recognized as human offers no reprieve from ontologizing dominance and violence, then what might we gain from the rupture of 'the human'?"[67] Julius's subversive analogy between human and nonhuman animal life seeks to incite that rupture.

Julius's strategy of subversion relies on both Annie's and John's disbelief in his story. Hence, when John asks Julius, "What put such an absurd idea in your head?" he, like Annie, who comments that the tale seems like "nonsense," plays into Julius's hand—granting him the opportunity to expand on his story of mules as kinfolk. "I doan ha'dly 'spec' fer you ter b'lieve it," Julius responds, but "did you eber see a club-footed nigger befo' er sence?"[68] His rhetorical question helps him segue into his narrative, for it piques John's interest just enough that he begs for an explanation. Julius, the consummate storyteller, is more than willing to oblige.

To ease John's and Annie's doubts about the tale's veracity, Julius turns for corroboration to Primus's physical body, a body that is significantly reshaped postconjure. Before Primus's transformation into a mule, he is described as "de livelies' han' on de place, alluz a-dancin', en drinkin', en runnin' roun', en singin', en pickin' de banjo."[69] But when he returns to the plantation after his absence, Primus does not retain the same appearance or function: a clubfoot mars his former unparalleled body, and it hampers his earlier frenetic mobility.

The reason for Primus's clubfoot arises from the conjure man's untimely death. Before he can complete the task of turning Primus back to his old self, the conjurer dies from an accidental poisoning. According to the literary scholar Henry B. Wonham, the conjure man's premature death leaves Primus on "unsure footing, literally straddling two worlds with his two feet, one animal and the other human. As a parable about black life in the American South, then, the story describes Primus's incomplete recovery of manhood in the postwar aftermath of his dehumanizing experience as a beast of burden under the rule of slavery."[70] By reconsidering the relationship between the human and the category of the animal and by focusing on the myriad representations of disability and deformity, Chesnutt's story comments on the lingering repercussions of slavery, given that neither the conjurer's wicked deeds nor Primus's malformed body can be entirely undone. Primus's misshapen foot stands as evidence of collateral damage; as visual proof of a sustained racial injury; as an imprint of something that cannot be fully repaired, restored, or reconstructed postwar no matter the amount of repentance, religion, or reconciliation. This instance of conjure effectively reproduces a kind of violence that is emblematic of slavery, which places all living beings—human and nonhuman animal—in precarious situations. Yet what if we consider Chesnutt's decision to retain Primus's clubfoot as a radical practice of worldmaking, of imagining an otherwise world where the relation between the human and nonhuman animal, between disabled and nondisabled people, is avowed rather that repudiated? Primus's clubfoot certainly functions as confirmation of something lost and transformed, but such loss and transformation could also signal the demise of the dominant social hierarchy and the rise of a new ideology in which beings are not hierarchized by their abilities or their relation to the human.

Perhaps Annie's inability to detect this moral stems from the fact that it lies outside her immediate interest, or perhaps Julius's vision of this other world is simply too unsettling for her. As a listener, she seems more fascinated with tales that prioritize romance and domesticity rather than ones that foreground the transformations of slavery and its afterlife, and a protracted discussion between Julius and John about purchasing a horse or a mule does not appeal to her. However, by highlighting Annie's skepticism and indifference, Chesnutt implores the reader to uncover the alternative meanings of Julius's tale. He demands that we find a moral where she cannot. At times, this demand offers a gratifying challenge to the reader's sensibility, allowing the reader to consider all the narrative possibilities at Julius's disposal. At other times, as Wonham argues, Chesnutt's call is simply too much for some readers to bear, particularly since his double-edged rhetoric could be interpreted as teetering on the brink of recapitulating the very racist images that it seeks to undermine: "In narrating the story of a black man's fluid transformation into a mule," Wonham asks, "doesn't Julius purchase symbolic resistance . . . at a terrific price, in that his tale perpetuates a racial stereotype?"[71] To effectively answer Wonham's question, the reader must consider to what extent Julius (and, to some extent, Chesnutt) endorses the ideology of the dominant social order or to what extent he rejects it. Indeed, to comprehend any of Julius's stories, the reader would have to determine the degree to which he challenges the dominant ideology at any given moment.

Even if Chesnutt's stories *appear* to depict a fictional Black body and mind in a manner that resembles a "racial stereotype," their subversiveness resists such a reading. To mistake the author's representations of Henry's rheumatism, Sandy's limbless body, Tenie's madness, Viney's mutilation, and Primus's clubfoot as replicas of the dominant racial iconography is to conflate correlation with causation. Unlike the predominant racist portrayal of Chesnutt's own time, which largely characterized blackness as inhuman or innately disabled, Chesnutt's stories disrupt, not perpetuate, those racial stereotypes by pushing us to ask a different set of questions about human-animal relations and to think about disability differently within the oppressive systems of slavery and Jim Crow.[72]

Reducing Chesnutt's depictions to a stereotype similarly overlooks his intricate and multifaceted use of Julius's narrative voice. Julius has economic, political, and personal reasons for uncovering the dangers of perception and for highlighting the exploitative potential of language in a world obsessed with categorizing and hierarchizing bodies and minds. On the one hand, Julius's stories function as a counter to John's—as tales that challenge the flawed and myopic viewpoint of his employer and reveal the invidious truths about slavery's ramifications before and after the war. On the other, as Sundquist argues, his stories "function as 'lies' in the classic African American folkloric sense—as tales that destroy the barrier between redaction and invention in order to place all discourse in the realm of manipulation and power."[73] Given this range of narrative objectives, Julius's stories necessarily place his listeners (and readers) on unstable ground, forcing them to be attentive to the diverse meanings of each narrative, since Julius usually juggles numerous agendas at once. As a result, he often tells one tale to upset another. To enable John and Annie to grasp the "deceitfulness of appearances," he tries to make them understand the repercussions of judging someone or something on the basis of looks and the drawbacks of believing everything one sees and hears.[74]

Julius delivers versions of these messages throughout the conjure stories. The effectiveness of these lessons resides in their undertones: the less explicit their messages, the more likely that Julius's stories will compel his listeners to decipher the sensible from the absurd, the moral from the trick, and the truths from the untruths. John and Annie do not always register his particular meaning, but their incomprehension is not a sign of Julius's failure to express such multiplicity. Chesnutt explores a wide range of disabilities in his stories without shunting disability or capitulating to stereotypes regarding the innate degeneracy of Black bodies and minds. By highlighting Sandy's limbless body, Tenie's madness, Viney's mutilation and illiteracy, and Primus's clubfoot, Chesnutt acknowledges the disablement of enslavement not only to illuminate the consequences of racial inequality but also to uncover the ways the law itself enacts disability. In this regard, his stories function as a repository for a complex history regarding the association of blackness and disability.

Procrustean Measures in *The Marrow of Tradition*

If Chesnutt had misgivings about the political effectiveness of his conjure stories, if he had serious qualms about what the literary scholar Ben Slote refers to as the possible "irresponsible consumption" of his highly allusive tales, then he put most of those concerns to rest with the publication of his 1901 novel *The Marrow of Tradition*.[75] In *Marrow*, Chesnutt offers an unapologetic account of the 1898 Wilmington riot, and some writers at the time could not manage much enthusiasm for it.

Take, for example, the case of William Dean Howells. The publication of Chesnutt's conjure tales and stories about the color line initially caught the attention of Howells—who, in his 1900 *Atlantic Monthly* review, described Chesnutt's stories as "remarkable" works of art.[76] However, after reading *Marrow*, Howells took a dim view of Chesnutt's novel. Writing for the *North American Review* in December 1901, Howells critiqued Chesnutt's decision to render Black and white relations during the North Carolina riot, and he characterized the novel as an intensely "bitter, bitter" book that was more concerned with revenge and retribution than with mercy and forgiveness.[77]

For the most part, Howells was right: *Marrow* is a bitter book. But given what transpired during the Wilmington riot, Chesnutt had a good reason to express such bitterness. Commenting on the mayhem in an 1898 letter to Walter Hines Page, Chesnutt wrote, "It is an outbreak of pure, malignant and altogether indefensible race prejudice, which makes me feel personally humiliated, and ashamed for the country and the State."[78]

As a fictional account of this historical event, *Marrow* corresponds in tone and content to the wretched conditions of the riot, and it bridges the gap between history and fiction with imaginative flair. Perceptively weaving the story of familial tension between the white Carterets and the Black Millers with the story of the racial massacre in Wellington, North Carolina (which is the fictional name for Wilmington), Chesnutt carefully links the political plot with the familial plot of the novel. With regard to the political plot—in particular, the series of events leading up to the race riot that erupts near the conclusion of *Marrow*—Chesnutt delineates how white southerners used the allegation of "negro domination" to arouse an unruly white mob that felt that it was losing economic and political power.[79] The fear that Black folks had taken over the city stirs a chaotic outbreak in Wellington, and Chesnutt's novel recounts the varied tactics of intimidation and discipline implemented in order to secure white control.

The riot, though, constitutes only a small section of the novel. Chesnutt's *Marrow* is just as concerned with capturing the sinister social fabric of Wellington and the mundane, routinized discrimination that African Americans experience as it is with describing the racial violence that culminates with the riot at the novel's end. The text thus closely scrutinizes the fraught interracial encounters in Wellington, paying attention to when, where, and how Black people inhabit a variety of spaces, from the homes of white aristocrats and segregated southern hotels to segregated trains and the streets of Wellington. At almost every turn in the novel, Chesnutt limns Black people as under constant danger from white supremacists, who deem African Americans as unfit for citizenship and suffrage and who take several measures to bring about their "unfitness." The "unfitness of negro," they claim, is "due to his limited education, his lack of experience, his criminal tendencies, and more especially to his hopeless mental and physical inferiority to the white race"—all of which are promulgated by the very actions of the white bigots in the text.[80] From endorsing racial segregation on trains to promoting anti-

Black violence on the streets, white supremacists spare nothing in order to achieve their goal of racial dominance.

In an effort to describe in the novel the unreasonable and unjust standard that white supremacists impose on African Americans, Chesnutt inserts a seemingly trivial reference to Greek mythology. But because the reference turns out to be so central to the novel's dramatization of Black representation, his Greek allusion is important to examine. Focusing on the disabilities of the color line that Dr. William Miller, one of the main Black protagonists in the novel, experiences on a segregated train, Chesnutt writes,

> Surely, if a classification of passengers on trains was at all desirable, it might be made upon some more logical and considerate basis than a mere arbitrary, tactless, and, by the very nature of things, brutal drawing of a color line. It was a veritable bed of Procrustes, this standard which the whites had set for the negroes. Those who grew above it must have their heads cut off, figuratively speaking,—must be forced back to the level assigned to their race; those who fell beneath the standard set had their necks stretched, literally enough, as the ghastly record in the daily papers gave conclusive evidence.[81]

Moving from the figurative to the literal, this passage exposes the manner in which Chesnutt's novel is absorbed by the linked concerns of race, politics, mythology, and bodily disintegration, which are sutured together here under the guise of a gruesome image of decapitation and the grim allusion to lynching. In deploying the Procrustean metaphor within his political novel, Chesnutt discloses how the enactment of racist violence results in dramatic transformations of the Black body.

But who is Procrustes? There are two important biographical details of the Procrustean story that inform Chesnutt's *Marrow*. The first detail concerns his profession. Procrustes is a robber and rogue blacksmith dwelling somewhere in Attica and, in some versions, the city of Eleusis. The second detail involves his method of punishment. In Greek mythology, he is known for compelling strangers to lie on his iron bed and making them fit it either by stretching their limbs with a hammer if they are too short or by amputating their limbs with an ax if they are too tall.[82] Though his actions are extreme beyond measure, they match in intensity his principal objective: to exact conformity and to afflict violence at all cost. In this regard, Procrustes's method corresponds to the tactics of *Marrow*'s white supremacists, who, on separate occasions, claim that their chief mission is to teach "negroes" how "to keep their place" and who profess a desire to "kill or maim a Negro" by any means necessary.[83] Accordingly, these white supremacists simultaneously articulate "the right to maim" and "the right to kill" as their modus operandi.

Couched within a scene in which Dr. Miller is separated from his white colleague (Dr. Alvin Burns) and occupies the same train car with Black farm laborers, Chesnutt's Procrustean metaphor spotlights the relationship between "the right to maim" and "the right to kill" in an effort to obtain conformity. First, it shows the stark difference in treatment between Black folks who have achieved a certain level of success and wealth and those who have not. Second, it illustrates how lynching was used as punishment for any Black person who did not conform to the color line standard. Chesnutt's metaphor, then, captures the social and legal minefield of Jim Crow that severely restricted the movement and functionality of Black folks through bodily violation.

The literary scholars Susan Gillman and Gerald Ianovici offer two notable views on the diverse meanings of Chesnutt's Procrustean metaphor. Gillman states that the "forced conformity of interracial relations, which subjects all blacks to versions of the same ghastly treatment, also intensifies the divisions inherent in the differences between figurative and literal punishments."[84] For Gillman, the punishment is the same in degree but different in kind—at least to the extent that "all blacks" sustain a "ghastly" injury but some injuries are "figurative" and others are not. Ianovici provides another stance. "The white supremacist denial of black success effects a symbolic decapitation, or, more properly, psychological mutilation," he states. As a result, the "figurative quality of the dismemberment represents turn-of-the-century black success as a state marked by a horrific negation of being, an ontology experienced in gothic terms as a living death . . . [because] success for a black person yields the psychological equivalent of lynching."[85] In contrast to Gillman, Ianovici observes both sameness in degree and kind insofar as Chesnutt's reference to figurative decapitation doubles as a psychological counterpart to a literal lynching.

Though *Marrow* draws several lines of distinction among Black people—distinctions in age, skin color, and class—they often buckle at the point of interracial conflict or unrest. At this juncture, every Black American, no matter what their socioeconomic background or level of success, is subject to a loss of life and limb. Under the "arbitrary," "tactless," and "brutal drawing of a color line," Chesnutt's Black characters are a reminder that, in the moment of crisis, your class and stature will not save you. And Chesnutt is not just commenting on the servant class and the professional class; he also considers the persecution of the Black working class. As Bryan Wagner points out, "Between Sandy and Mammy Jane [representatives of the servant class], on one hand, and William and Janet Miller [representatives of the professional class], on the other, are characters like Josh Green, representatives of the African American working class who are no more welcome in the house of white supremacy than is Dr. Miller."[86]

None of the African American characters in *Marrow* has complete immunity from abuse, violence, or death. This vulnerability is why the safety of William and Janet Miller is in as much jeopardy as that of Watson, Barber, and Sandy Campbell. This is also why Mammy Jane and Jerry Letlow die alongside Josh Green and the Millers' anonymous son. From this cast of characters, I primarily focus my attention on Dr. William Miller and Josh Green, two key Black male figures who are often thought of as antithetical to each other because of their radical political differences. Substituting the Procrustean bed for the segregated train car and swapping Procrustes's hammer and ax for fists, knives, pistols, and muskets during scenes of racial violence, *Marrow* offers a modern version of a bygone tale and uncovers a standard that wields its power with authority by legal and extralegal means. In so doing, Chesnutt provides the reader with access into the interconnected, relational network of the novel, one that remains faithfully attuned to not only how the disabilities of the color line affect both Black and white people but also how the collective health of the Wellington community is dependent on the individual health of its citizens.

Staring Signs of Disability

As a young, handsome, well-educated man, Dr. William Miller is portrayed as an African American who, to borrow Chesnutt's language, is figured as above the Procrustean standard. In part because of his enslaved grandfather's frugality and in part because of his father's impressive business acumen, Miller is a Black man of means. He lives with his wife in a mansion formerly owned by the white Carteret family, and with his inheritance, he establishes a hospital with the hope of adding a nursing school, medical college, and a school of pharmacy. Yet even he is not exempt from the legal disabilities of Jim Crow. In the chapter "A Journey Southward," which offers an explicit engagement with *Plessy v. Ferguson*, Chesnutt describes how the law disables the Black professional.

Returning home to Wellington from a business trip in New York, William Miller meets his white former professor Dr. Alvin Burns on the train. Eager to get reacquainted, Miller and Burns become engrossed in good conversation, discussing everything from the marvels of the medical profession to their shared sense of social responsibility for the African American community. Once the train travels farther south, however, their congenial exchange comes to a screeching halt. In Virginia, the conductor requests that all passengers relocate from the sleeping car to the day coach because the hot box in the sleeping car has to be turned off.

This relocation turns out to be a crucial turning point in the scene. Since segregation does not apply to the sleeping car, Miller can rest easy knowing that his communication with and proximity to Burns is not a violation of the law. But when he has to transfer to the day coach, where the segregation law does apply, Miller's sense of repose is swiftly effaced as he notices a marked change in their treatment. Under the protection of the sleeping car, Miller and Burns bear a pronounced resemblance: they are members of the same profession; they have the same education; they are well mannered and well traveled; and they are described as physically fit. But in the segregated space of the day coach, Miller beholds the one indisputable feature that distinguishes them both, a difference the law regards as a profound disability: his color. Unfortunately for him, the train conductor notices too. Recently empowered by the state to regulate and enforce racial segregation, the conductor takes a piercing glance at Miller, makes a beeline for his seat, and responds accordingly. "I'm sorry to part *friends*," he says, "but the law of Virginia does not permit colored passengers to ride in the white cars. You'll have to go forward to the next coach. . . . This is a day coach, and is distinctly marked 'White,' as you must have seen before you set down here. The sign is put there for that purpose."[87]

The "White" sign, like the sign marked "Colored," exposes the blurry line between the signifier and the signified since it serves as both the caution and the tale. On the one hand, it is a stern reminder of the racial demarcation of space on the railroad; on the other, it presents a damning narrative about the compulsory subordination of Black folks (particularly the Black professional) in relation to whiteness, a narrative so formidable that no one in this scene—not the conductor, Burns, or Miller—can subvert it without suffering consequences. In response to Burns's query regarding why Miller cannot remain in the white train car, the conductor explains, "The law gives me the right to remove him by force. I can call on the train crew to assist me, or on the other passengers. If I should choose to put him off the train entirely, in the middle of a swamp, he would have no redress—the law so provides." Though this news is upsetting to Miller and Burns, Chesnutt shows that they have little recourse against the letter of the law. When Miller explains to Burns that the separate train cars are "the law, and we are powerless to resist it," he, like the train conductor, accepts the law's restrictions. When Burns insists on moving to the colored car to stay with Miller, he learns that even certain white men can forfeit their rights if they dare to stand in the way of Black legal subordination. The conductor, ever more "conscious of his power," informs Dr. Burns that "white passengers are not permitted to ride in the colored car." He states, "The beauty of the system lies in its strict impartiality—it applies to both races alike."[88]

Almost as if to disprove the conductor's obligatory yet misguided claim regarding the law's "beauty," Miller observes that while the law may be strict in its enforcement, it is anything but impartial in its distribution. During his train ride, he notices two instances of legal favoritism with respect to racial segregation along with the relentless degradation that the law metes out to African Americans.

First, immediately after being informed that Virginia law utterly forbids white and Black passengers from riding in the same train car, Miller must contend with the smoking, cursing, spitting, littering, and altogether disruptive behavior of the one-eyed Captain George McBane. McBane, along with Major Philip Carteret and General Belmont, is a member of the "Big Three"—a group of white bigots who are responsible for engineering the campaign for white supremacy in Wellington.[89] After playing an instrumental role in expelling Miller from the white day coach, McBane enters the colored coach and turns it into a smoking car. To test the law's impartiality, Miller asks the conductor to remove McBane from the colored train car just as McBane removed Miller from the white one. Significantly, Miller objects to McBane's smoking, not to his disability. He states, "This car is plainly marked 'Colored.' I have paid first-class fare, and I object to riding in a smoking car." Despite his appropriation of the conductor's language, Miller's protest is dismissed by McBane. McBane lends no credence to the conductor's warning that "it's against the law for [him] to ride in the nigger car." He instead retorts, "Who are you talkin' to? . . . I'll ride where I damn please. . . . [And] I'll leave this car when I get good and ready, and that won't be till I've finished this cigar."[90] McBane's actions convey his impregnable sense of standing above the law, and they remind Miller just how much he is under the law's heavy foot.

Second, when the train picks up more passengers from a different station, Miller realizes that McBane is not the only passenger permitted to cross the color line. Noticing that a Chinese man and a Black nurse accompanied by her mistress are allowed to enter the white train car without objection, Miller recognizes the discretionary nature of the law. The approval of the Chinese man and the Black nurse aiding her mistress supplies Miller with a revelatory moment, for he states to himself that "white people . . . do not object to the negro as a servant. As the traditional negro,—the servant,—he is welcomed; as an equal, he is repudiated."[91] Miller discovers by the novel's end that the distinction he draws along the lines of race and class virtually dissolves during the racial massacre; however, in this moment on the train, he makes an astute observation about the way the law begets Black subservience. As Julia H. Lee argues, "The reason whites do not want to mingle with blacks is not because of a natural aversion between the races; rather whites only want to be around those blacks who occupy subservient positions and can thus reassure whites of their own superior niche within racial hierarchies."[92]

Miller's articulation of this racial hierarchy—his understanding of what his nonsubservient position to whites means in a society that does not honor such status—offers no solace to him. Rather, it unnerves him and produces a "queer sensation" that, like the "peculiar sensation" of Du Bois's double consciousness, compels Miller to see himself through the eyes of others. For instance, upon seeing the African American porter walking in his direction with a white passenger's German shepherd, he briefly questions his own humanity. He wonders "whether the dog would be allowed to ride with his master, and if not, what disposition would be made of him." He admits that he "would not have objected to the company of a dog, as a dog," yet he is "consciously relieved when the canine passenger [is] taken on past him into the baggage-car ahead."[93] Miller's relief probably indicates that he fears that the German shepherd's presence on the Jim Crow train car would alter the dog's and, by extension, his own subjectivity. His experience on the train is so overwhelming that nearly all of his relationships are placed under scrutiny. He is as disturbed by his positioning in relation to white folks, to the Black nurse, to her mistress, to the Chinese man, and to a dog as he is by his proximity on the Jim Crow train car to the other passengers. His mixed emotions give a glimpse into the psychological stress that segregation law foists on him and show the extent to which the law cuts across class, gender, race, disability, and behavior. What begins mainly as an interracial problem transitions into an intraracial and class issue, threatening to unsettle even further William Miller's outlook on his surroundings.

Dr. Miller learns the measure of his own worth from these experiences, and he sees clearly just what the system of segregation is intended to impart. Reflecting more on the law's influence, he reaches the following conclusion about the coded meaning hidden behind segregation: "should a colored person endeavor, for a moment, to lose sight of his disability, these staring signs would remind him continually that between him and the rest of mankind not of his own color, there was by law a great gulf fixed."[94] In response to the creed of separate but equal, this passage bears an ominous message to African Americans who suffer from Jim Crow's continual assault: segregation is more than a social system that separates white folks from Black folks, servants from professionals, North from South, and friends from each other; it also separates along lines of disability (legal or otherwise).

Chesnutt's personification of the segregation signs emphasizes this message, since they police bodies through their disquieting and oppressive stare. Staring, Garland-Thomson argues, can be "aggressive," "hostile," and "corrupt": it is a "form of nonverbal behavior that can be used to enforce social hierarchies and regulate access to resources."[95] Functioning as a form of social and corporeal regulation, the "staring signs" on the train work to render Miller's fit and unblemished body into an unfit and sullied one. At the beginning of the chapter, he is described as having an "erect form, broad shoulders, clear eyes, fine teeth, and pleasingly moulded features [that] showed nowhere any sign of that degeneration which the pessimist so sadly maintains is the inevitable heritage of mixed races." However, under the probe of the "American eye" and the "signs" of "disability," he is depicted as being "branded and tagged and set apart from the rest of mankind upon the public highways, like an unclean thing" near the chapter's end.[96] Like the Jim Crow train car, which is disfigured and defaced by "torn" and "faded upholstery," thick layers of "dust" on the "window sills," and Captain McBane's spit and phlegm on the floor, Miller sustains a figurative transmutation.[97] Here (and elsewhere) his form reflects the train's shoddy conditions, for his body suffers from a monstrous brand of social stigma.

Segregation law, then, closely resembles US "ugly laws," which generally stipulated that "any person who is diseased, maimed, mutilated, or in any way deformed, so as to be an unsightly or disgusting object, or an improper person to be allowed in or on the streets, highways, thoroughfares or public places in this city, shall not therein or thereon expose himself or herself to public view, under the penalty of one dollar for each offense."[98] According to the disability studies scholar Susan M. Schweik, "The ugly laws are part of the story of segregation and of profiling in the United States, part of the body of laws that specified who could be where, who would be isolated and excluded, who had to be watched, whose comfort mattered."[99] Such laws have a long history of regulating alleged improper and unseemly bodies. One reason why ugly laws have been used as a powerful device for subjugating Black and disabled people is that their language is so ambiguous and indeterminate. The laws cast a net so wide that nearly anybody can be snarled in their intricate web of exclusion and containment. The discursive excess of the ugly laws marks them as discretionary and inane: their attempt to target such a large group of people empties them of any specificity, and yet they can be applied narrowly when such an application fulfills their purpose. In this regard, ugly laws mirror the Procrustean standard of the color line. Shifting from "diseased," "maimed," and "mutilated" to "deformed," "unsightly," and "disgusting" before settling finally on "improper," the ugly laws yield a minefield of arbitrary recalibrations that is not unlike Procrustes's twofold method of cutting and stretching limbs to fit his ever-adjustable iron bed. Both measures are primarily about categorizing bodies, and within the context of *Marrow*, they intimately tether narratives of blackness to narratives of disability. As Schweik observes, "Ugly laws in practice functioned to sort people on the streets and into institutions by race as well as disability; the two kinds of segregation were not so much comparable as inseparable."[100]

Chesnutt's reference to the disablement of segregation laws in "A Journey Southward" indicates that he recognized one way in which the concept of disability is inseparable from race. His train scene captures the slipperiness and deceptiveness of racial segregation law by offering a description of the differences between the "White" and "Colored" train cars. Even though the conductor tells Miller that the separate-but-equal system is a "beauty," Miller's experience depicts the law's bias as remarkably "ugly." Admittedly, Miller is not fined a monetary penalty for "expos[ing] himself to public view," but the price he pays is prohibitive: hidden from the view of certain white people, separated from his friend and colleague, forced into the filthy and dilapidated train car, and "set apart" in "public highways" and "public spaces," Miller is ostracized and stigmatized all the same.

The Memory of Racial Injury

Dr. William Miller, however, is not the only one who is disabled by the toxicity of racism in *Marrow*. Josh Green, who comes closest to serving as Dr. Miller's opposite in the text, is disabled too. If Miller represents an African American who needs to be figuratively cut down to size and who must learn "to keep [his] place," then Josh Green, returning to Chesnutt's Procrustean standard, represents an African American in danger of being stretched to his bodily limits, as someone who falls under a constant threat of lynching.

Notwithstanding these distinctions, Jim Crow did not discriminate when it came to imposing disability onto Black people who challenged the standard set by the system. Though Green, unlike Miller, has "stolen a ride to Wellington on the trucks of a passenger car," Green's marks of stigmatization are no less visible than Miller's. In what constitutes the reader's introduction to Josh Green in "A Journey Southward," we notice the degree to which the vigilant stare of segregation law stigmatizes him. He is described as "covered thickly with dust," and he is smeared with a "grimy coating" that somewhat masks his facial features.[101] To be sure, it is a crude and somewhat primitive depiction of Green, but this description makes plain that any person tangentially connected to the soiled and stained "colored" train car is begrimed by association.

Throughout *Marrow*, Green is figured as vulnerable to disability and death. As a dockworker and laborer, he falls on the lower rung of the socioeconomic hierarchy depicted in the novel, far removed from Miller's wealth, status, and privilege. But it is not his different socioeconomic background that makes him intimately familiar with the ways that disability and race intertwine in US regimes of oppression; two other biographical details reveal his unique awareness of the vulnerability of Black bodies and minds in the United States. First, Green is a Black radical, who is more inclined to use violence as a form of redress and thus more likely to be on the receiving end of violence as well. Second, Green possesses a comprehensive and graphic memory of US racist practices, which allows him to connect the dots between the violent tactics of the Ku Klux Klan (KKK) in the immediate aftermath of the Civil War and the viciousness of the "Big Three" at the turn of the twentieth century. As Green confides to Miller, "I was a chile, too, but I wuz right in it, an' so I 'members mo' erbout it 'n you does. . . . One night a crowd er w'ite men come ter ou' house an' tuck my daddy out an' shot 'im ter death, an' skeered my mammy so she ain' be'n herse'f f'm dat day ter dis." Here "it" refers to the violence of the Ku Klux Klan, which Green witnesses firsthand. He watches members of the KKK shoot and kill his father, and he observes the traumatic effect that his father's death has on his mother, whom some Wellington residents call "Silly Milly" because she has effectively lost her mind, "wandering aimlessly about the street, muttering to herself incoherently." Green's memory of his father's death and his mother's madness not only festers like an "old wound still bleeding" but serves as the primary rationale for his radical political bent.[102]

In sharp contrast to Miller, who has developed a reputation for being the "very good sort of a negro, [who] does n't meddle with politics, nor tread on any one else's toes," Green is depicted as the one of the "bad negroes."[103] Or, as Sundquist observes, Green "has something in common with the 'bad nigger,' a hero figure that appears throughout much black folklore and the blues in characters such as Railroad Bill or Stagolee, as well as in literary adaptations from Henry Blake in Martin Delany's *Blake; or, The Huts of America* (1859) to Bras-Coupé in George Washington Cable's *The Grandissimes* (1880)."[104] Like Bras-Coupé, who was maimed as punishment for his attempted escape, Green later discovers that the white mob in Wellington has a similar goal.

In the chapter "Another Southern Product," which presents the first interaction between Miller and Green within the context of novel, we get a good sense of Green's violent tactics and also his specific political motivation. Purposefully, Chesnutt constructs their encounter as a meeting between a doctor and his patient: "One morning shortly after the opening of the hospital, while Dr. Miller was making his early rounds, a new patient walked in with a smile on his face and a broken arm hanging limply by his side. . . . He perceived, from the indifference with which Josh bore the manipulation of the fractured limb, that such an accident need not have interfered seriously with the use of the remaining arm, and he knew that Josh had a reputation for absolute fearlessness."[105] Green's injured body—his "broken arm" and "fractured limb"—functions as a site where Chesnutt can test the limits of two competing strains of racial ideology represented through Miller and Green. In fact, as the literary scholar Richard Yarborough argues, "the ideological tension between the two men forms the center of Chesnutt's novel."[106] Green's willingness to sacrifice his body for a cause is different from Miller's acquiescence on the train. Green shows us what can happen to a Black man who does not obey the law or stay in his place. Upon hearing that Green received his injuries in a scuffle with a white South American labor worker, Miller warns, "These are bad times for bad negroes. You'll get into a quarrel with a white man, and at the end of it there'll be a lynching, or a funeral. You'd better be peaceable and endure a little injustice, rather than run the risk of a sudden and violent death. . . . What has any man in this town done to you, that you should thirst for his blood?"[107] Miller's attempt to distance himself rhetorically from "bad negroes" seems somewhat misguided, especially since the earlier train scene exposes what Miller should, at this point, already know: to incur the wrath of white supremacists in the social world of Wellington, you do not have to be bad, only Black. Nevertheless, Miller's question compels Green to respond.

Green's response to this question offers us a better insight into his personal and political reasons for participating in the riot. After he identifies Captain McBane as the object of his vengeance, we realize that Green is not just a bloodthirsty martyr motivated by an intense desire to kill the white people of Wellington, but rather he is personally motivated by a determination to avenge his father's death and his mother's subsequent psychological impairment at the hands of the Ku Klux Klan. As Chesnutt writes, Green is "a negro who could remember an injury, who could shape his life to a definite purpose, if not a high or holy one." He feels an indelible marking that recalls Miller's sense of being "branded" after his slight on the train. Remembering how his father was killed, Green states, "I hid in de bushes an' seen de whole thing, an' it wuz branded on my mem'ry, suh, like a red-hot iron bran's de skin."[108] Green's memory of racial violence serves as an explanation for why he so readily participates in the riot at the novel's end. Unable to get Miller to serve as a leader during this time of crisis, Green is the one who spearheads an effort to lead the Black community.

Having witnessed the violence of the Ku Klux Klan and his mother's subsequent madness, Green is more than a little intolerant when it comes to meeting the expectations of white folks. He states,

A w'ite man kin do w'at he wants ter a nigger, but de minute de nigger gits back at 'im, up goes de nigger, an' don' come down tell somebody cuts 'im down. If a nigger gits a' office, er de race 'pears to be prosperin' too much, de w'ite folks up and kills a few, so dat de res' kin keep on fergivin' an' bein' thankful dat dey 're lef' alive. Don' talk ter me 'bout dese w'ite folks,—I knows 'em, I does! Ef a nigger wants ter git down on his marrow-

bones, an' eat dirt, an' call 'em "marster," *he's* a good nigger, dere's room fer
him. But I ain' no w'ite folks' nigger, I ain'. I don' call no man "marster." I
don' wan' nothin' but w'at I wo'k fer, but I wants all er dat. I never moles's
no w'ite man, 'less 'n he moles's me fus'. But w'en de ole 'oman dies, doc-
tuh, an' I gits a good chance at dat w'ite man,—dere ain' no use talkin',
suh!—dere's gwine ter be a mix-up, an' a fune'al, er two fune'als—er may
be mo', ef anybody is keerliss enough to git in de way.[109]

If the reader was unsure about the differences between Miller and Green
up to this point, then Green's bold statement regarding political violence
and retaliation makes the distinction between the two men crystal clear.
Here, Green further explains how the Procrustean standard operates
within Wellington's segregated world. According to Green, this standard disciplines successful and defiant Black people differently than it
does Black folks who are subservient to white supremacists. If a Black
person acquiesces to the demands of "w'ite folks," then "*he's* a good nigger, dere's room fer *him.*" But if a Black person gains political power,
achieves too much economic success, or resists the dictates of white
people, then that person is lynched or killed. Green's observations align
with the argument of the literary scholar Koritha Mitchell, who clarifies
the "cause-and-effect relationship" between Black success and white-
supremacist violence in the United States: "Black people pursue and
achieve success, white aggression counters their progress, and then violence becomes part of any accurate representation of African American
communities." Mitchell insists that "white supremacy is reactionary" to
Black success and achievement, not the other way around.[110] Josh Green
understands the reactionary nature of white supremacy quite well, and
he plans to respond with violence in equal measure.

Preferring to "be a dead nigger any day dan a live dog!" Green refuses
to behave as the "w'ite folks' nigger." His reference to a "live dog" recalls
the train scene in "A Journey Southward," in which Miller becomes anxious about his proximity to the German shepherd and in which Green
is described as a "wet dog." Green's preference for death over dehuman-
ization indicates his frustration with being forced to live like an animal.
Rather than waxing philosophically about his unfair treatment, Green
outlines a plan of attack and anticipates a "mix-up," a violent conflict
that could lead to multiple funerals. Green's rage is not without provoca-

tion, but that does not mean his desire for retribution is any less dangerous. Perhaps his extreme approach is meant to counter notions of Black
subservience and to oppose the image of Black people postslavery kow-
towing and referring to white people as "marster." His response, then,
serves as a way to separate himself from other Black characters who are
not willing to die for a cause. In the end, Green does die from a bullet
wound, but not before he exacts his revenge against his main enemy,
Captain McBane. "Armed with a huge bowie-knife, a relic of the civil
war," Chesnutt writes, Josh Green makes his way through the riotous
mob, "raise[s] his powerful right arm, [and] burie[s] his knife to the hilt
in the heart of his enemy."[111]

Ultimately, the riot results in the death of Josh Green and several
members of his crew and leaves "many more disabled." Described variously as a *"coup d'état,"* "demonstration," and "revolution," the riot is
emblematic of the extreme measures taken to ensure the reign of white
supremacy.[112] It uncovers the crucial link between white control and
Black bodily disintegration, and it spotlights how disablement functions
as one of the main objectives of white supremacists. William Miller and
Josh Green are more than familiar with such objectives, for both have
endured their injurious effects.

No Immunity for White Folks

The determination of white supremacists to inflict disability onto Black
bodies in *Marrow* sheds light on the white community's disabilities,
deformities, and diseases. Just as Chesnutt ties the precarious health of
Annie (the white sympathetic listener of Uncle Julius's stories) with the
health of Black folks in his conjure tales, he, in *Marrow*, shows that Black
people are not the only ones who are disabled. The white characters are
disabled as well. For instance, Old Man Delamere is crippled by three
paralytic strokes—the last of which takes his life. Polly Ochiltree suffers
from "bodily infirmities" that affect both her mind and body. Captain
McBane, a member of the "Big Three," has only "one eye." Olivia Carteret, who is the half sister of Janet Miller, is in "delicate health" and is
reproductively challenged, and when she does conceive, she gives birth
to her son, Theodore "Dodie" Felix, who is perpetually ill and later
requires a tracheotomy for his "membranous croup."[113]

This litany of disabled white bodies is wide-ranging and purposeful. Here, disability affects the old and the young, men and women, enemies and allies; and it is acquired and congenital, psychological and physical, permanent and temporary, and visible and invisible. And, perhaps most importantly, the disability of Chesnutt's white characters functions as his critique of the myth of innate Black degeneracy, which he addresses in his earlier essays "What Is a White Man?" and "The Future American" series. His inclusion of white disabled bodies proves that the white community is no more immune from disability than the Black one is, and it disrupts the narrative of whiteness as an exemplar of legitimacy, physicality, and able-bodiedness. The vulnerabilities of the body and mind are shared among the entire Wellington community because of the toxic force of racism.

In addition to exposing the disabilities of white bodies, Chesnutt also addresses the deterioration of white behavior. Though the political leaders in Wellington are obsessed with the notion of Black inferiority, Chesnutt, according to Ianovici, makes "plain that white racism, not inner corruption or innate degeneracy, is what condemns blacks to the southern abyss."[114] Chesnutt shows how the white mob comes to embody the very same monstrous and barbaric traits that they frequently attempt to imprint on Black bodies: "The qualities which in a white man would win the applause of the world would in a negro be taken as the marks of savagery. So thoroughly diseased was public opinion in matters of race that the negro who died for the common rights of humanity might look for no meed of admiration or glory. . . . They would applaud his courage while they stretched his neck, or carried off the fragments of his mangled body as souvenirs, in much the same way that savages preserve the scalps or eat the hearts of their enemies."[115] Making yet another allusion to lynching, this final image of human fragments, of the "mangled body as souvenirs," sums up a genuine concern that Chesnutt examines throughout the novel. By analyzing the legal discourse, the constant threat of lynching, and the racial violence that erupts during the Wellington riot, Chesnutt reveals the tangible links between the insatiable desire for power and authority and the violent acts of dismemberment, consumption, and bodily excavation. According to the logic of the white mob in *Marrow*, one cannot be achieved without the other since white authority relies heavily on Black dematerialization.

No one in the novel quite understands this logic like William Miller, who stands as one of the few principal Black characters left alive at its conclusion. Surveying the cauterized terrain of Wellington immediately after the riot, Miller comes face-to-face with instances of death and disability, which all serve as a "gruesome spectacle" of the expendable nature of Black bodies and minds.[116]

Despite the gloom and terror of these images, Chesnutt manages to offer a glimmer of cautious optimism in the novel's last scene through the actions of William Miller. Though Miller's child has been killed by a stray bullet from the riot, he is called on, as the only available doctor in the city, to save the son of Major Carteret, one of the men responsible for igniting the riot. After much contemplation and at the urging of his wife, Janet, Dr. Miller eventually decides to attempt to save the child's life. As a result, he is pictured as a savior to the Carteret family and to the future of Wellington. While it is unclear whether Miller saves Dodie's life—though, the fact that his nickname is inscribed with a mandatory death sentence (do die) makes it seem unlikely—that detail would little change the final image of the novel. Although the novel concludes with Miller holding a knife in his hand as he prepares to perform a tracheotomy on Dodie, he wields his knife in order to spare a life, not to take one. Chesnutt thus leaves us with a visual of Dr. Miller fulfilling his professional duty to the very end and exhibiting a standard of benevolence and magnanimity toward white people that is less exacting and injurious than the Procrustean standard inflicted on him and his people.

5

The Disabilities of Caste

James Weldon Johnson

Recasting Race and Disability

While participating in the annual Quiz Club in English Composition and Oratory contest held during commencement week at Atlanta University, James Weldon Johnson delivered a winning oration in May 1892 that illustrated the myriad ways that blackness was tethered to disability in the Jim Crow United States. His speech, "The Best Methods of Removing the Disabilities of Caste from the Negro," offered a measured response to the racist rhetoric of white supremacists, who held that African Americans were inherently disabled, who claimed that their innate depravity made them unsuitable for full citizenship, and who argued that they would simply disappear from existence postemancipation.[1] These beliefs of racial degeneracy and extinction provoked Johnson's political rage, and he wanted nothing more than to put such nonsense to rest. With this objective in mind, he told his audience that the roots of disability lay not in the false theories of racial contamination but rather in the racist violence and injuriousness of the US caste system of slavery, a "slavery which tended not only to crush out of [the Negro] every semblance of manhood, intelligence and virtue but also to inscribe in his very nature every form of vice, superstition and immorality."[2]

Transitioning from India's caste system and its emphasis on religion and profession to the European caste system and its emphasis on rank and pedigree, Johnson outlined an alternative form of caste in the United States by highlighting its crude racial hierarchy. He wrote, "Caste in America is the distinction between two great races, the white and the black. The whites make this distinction. It is not mutual."[3] Here caste is intertwined with race in the United States to such an extent that it burdens race with a wide range of other signifiers. What is noteworthy about Johnson's theory is not his claim regarding the differences of caste in the United States; several critics have articulated this understanding of caste in more detail.[4] What is noteworthy is the manner in which he understood blackness and disability as dynamic categories that inform each other. His speech highlights how disability was racialized and how racial subjects were susceptible to disablement during Jim Crow.

In Johnson's articulation of the "disabilities of caste," where caste is informed by race and where race is marked by skin color, phenotype, and blood, he cited several examples of legal subordination as his evidence. In particular, he examined Jim Crow through the lens of disability. As he put it, "The disabilities of caste under which the Negro labors are many, especially in the South. He is not allowed in hotels, restaurants, or any other such public place, however wealthy he may be. He is compelled to ride in a dirty, smoky railroad car, however refined and cultured. He does not get justice in the courts; and for every slight offense the fullest extent of the law is meted out to him. . . . In fact he is subjected to every form of humiliation and oppression which humanity and a republican form of government will allow."[5] This litany of sociolegal "disabilities"—the denial of access to public social spaces, the foul and shoddy conditions of the segregated train car, the disproportionate administration of punishment, the lack of opportunities for upward social mobility, and the subjection to humiliation, suffering, and racial injury—all serve the ultimate purpose of stigmatizing African Americans and restricting their movement, of thrusting them into a system that conspires to tarnish both their reputation and their bodies. The law's proclivity to disable functions as another way to discipline and control bodies that it considers unruly—Black bodies. Shifting from segregation and punishment to humiliation and oppression, Johnson offered an expansive understanding of disability—one that aligns with historical definitions of the term *disability* as a restrictive system.[6]

Johnson's use of disability also aligns with how other Black writers during the late nineteenth and early twentieth centuries were using such language. For instance, in the 1892 volume *A Voice from the South*, Anna

Julia Cooper invoked the language of disability in her critique of the US government's "color-phobia."[7] Fully aware of the grim and uncompromising measures foisted on Black folks, Cooper argued that the nation owed "an enormous pecuniary debt" to Black people: "our present poverty is due to the fact that the toil of the last quarter century enriched [the country's] coffers, but left us the heirs of crippled, deformed, frost-bitten, horny-handed, and empty handed mothers and fathers."[8] Similarly to Johnson, Cooper emphasized how disability was imposed on Black people. Their focus on the imposition of disabilities could be understood as an attempt to, as Nirmala Erevelles describes, "situate disability not as the condition of 'being' but of 'becoming.'"[9] This reframing challenges the sociomedical and sociolegal racialism that attempted to frame blackness as inherently disabled. It entails, as Erevelles argues, a shift from considering the process of "becoming disabled" as more than merely a discursive hap to considering it as a "historical event," one with significant material consequences and, I would add, one that demonstrates how disability was central to Jim Crow.[10]

Johnson engaged in a critical exploration of the intersections of race and disability to enhance our knowledge of citizenship and the racialized embodiment of African Americans. "In emphasizing not only the accelerated mobility but also the handicapping circumstances," Marlon Ross argues, "new-century activists [like Du Bois, Chesnutt, and Johnson] hoped to reconceptualize radically the worth, status, and iconography of the race" by fostering attention to "the race's rapid progress despite the severe handicap posed by segregation, anti-black violence, disenfranchisement, unequal economic opportunity, and other barriers erected by the Jim Crow regime."[11] Johnson's focus on the race's progress and mobility despite the "severe handicap" often meant demonstrating his exceptionalism and agency both to maneuver out of Jim Crow restraints and to expose the intricate relationship between notions of race, property, immunity, and disability.

Within the Jim Crow regime lay a racialized narrative of property and value that was underpinned by a discourse of disability and that set up a correlation between white supremacy and antiblackness in the United States.[12] Reflect again on *Plessy v. Ferguson*, the 1896 Supreme Court case that upheld the constitutionality of racial segregation by claiming that the 1890 Louisiana statute that required separate railway carriages for white and Black people did not violate the Thirteenth and Fourteenth Amendments. The majority opinion in *Plessy* shows that, in late nineteenth-century jurisprudence, notions of property and value became part of an intricate web of legal correlatives in which, as the African American literature scholar Stephen M. Best observes, "one person's 'immunity' or freedom from the legal control of another correlated with the latter's powerlessness or 'disability.'"[13] The coupling of "immunity" with "disability" suggests how these terms informed each other at the turn of the nineteenth century, making it difficult to examine one without the other. The system of Jim Crow not only constructed this coupling but also exploited it to maintain white supremacy, inflicting disabilities on Black folks while attempting to offer immunity to non-Black people.

Johnson offered in his oeuvre multiple examples of the disabilities that Jim Crow imposed on Black Americans while aiming to protect the privileges and immunities of people who were not African American. Speaking at the age of twenty, Johnson emphasized in his Quiz Club speech the social and legal disabilities that African Americans experienced. But the elder Johnson, the Johnson of *The Autobiography of an Ex-Colored Man* (1912) and *Along This Way* (1933), would account not only for legal disabilities but also for physical and psychological impairments. He would do so by identifying the line between one person's presumed "immunity" and another person's presumed "disability," as well as by revealing the interlaced relationship between value, property, and race. In order to understand fully how the discourse and experience of disability fits into the lives of African Americans, Johnson would have to examine race and ethnicity in terms of fluidity and variability, not fixity and rigidity. In *The Autobiography of an Ex-Colored Man*, Johnson accomplished these goals via his protagonist, the ex-colored man, who by virtue of his Black-to-white racial passing functions as a cipher of discordant qualities: both insider and outsider, both familiar and foreign, and thus simultaneously both exempt from and vulnerable to disability. In *Along This Way*, Johnson spotlighted this line between immunity and disability by offering instances of his own Black exceptionalism (moments when he circumvents legal and social disabilities) alongside an encounter with violence that nearly leads to his lynching.

Focusing on scenes of racial exclusion, coercion, and violence in *The Autobiography of an Ex-Colored Man* and *Along This Way*, this chapter shows how Johnson exposed disability as an integral, not incidental, element of the Jim Crow regime. Demonstrating that Jim Crow was more than a social system that separated white people from Black people, Johnson detailed the disabilities of Jim Crow—how the system stigmatized African Americans writ large, restricted their geographical mobility and movement in public spaces, inflicted physical and psychological wounds, disciplined their bodies as a form of control and regulation, and sanctioned the practice of lynching. We must understand how disability functioned as a conduit for racial oppression during Jim Crow for several reasons: it calls attention to how social and legal restrictions inflicted physical and psychological injuries; it shows how Jim Crow produced disability via the enforced immobility of segregation and the bodily deformation and psychological trauma of lynching; it uncovers how Jim Crow constructed notions of disability to manufacture racial hierarchies, particularly during moments of racial indeterminacy; and it challenges our understanding of US citizenship and blackness, marking citizenship as a positional good while highlighting the ingenuity of Black resistance that enabled African Americans to survive despite the onslaught of disabilities posed by Jim Crow.[14]

The ex-colored man's story is not James Weldon Johnson's, but as the scholar of African American literature and culture Valerie Smith argues, "any consideration of Johnson's novel must address . . . the connections between the simulated autobiography and Johnson's actual autobiography, *Along This Way*" to avoid conflating the life of Johnson with that of his character.[15] This chapter takes Smith's instructions seriously. I illustrate how disablement was one of the Jim Crow caste system's most effective tools of racial injury by closely examining Johnson's fiction and nonfiction. First, I consider Johnson's personal encounters with the system of Jim Crow in *Along This Way*—focusing on an incident in which he narrowly escapes the legal disability of the color line, one in which he posits the Jim Crow rail car as the locus of disability, and another in which the National Guard nearly beats him to death and leaves him with physical and psychological injuries. Second, I analyze how disability and stigma function in Johnson's only novel, paying close attention to the ex-colored man's witnessing of a lynching and its connection to other instances of disability, racial violence, and exclusion. Given how influential Johnson's own experiences were to his understanding of the relationship between blackness, caste, and disability, I begin with his story.

Racial Stigma, Immobility, and Injury in *Along This Way*

It was the quintessential version of a spectacular departure. In the fall of 1887, the year James Weldon Johnson began at Atlanta University, he and his childhood friend Ricardo Rodriguez were preparing to board an overnight train traveling from Jacksonville, Florida, to Atlanta, Georgia. At the train station, Johnson arrived with his parents, his girlfriend, and several of his friends—all of them eager to bid him farewell on what promised to be a momentous and celebratory occasion.

The roughly three-hundred-mile trip would take several hours, and his parents wanted to ensure that the send-off for their son was nothing short of perfect. His mother securely packed his bags and prepared him a meal that would satisfy the most demanding palate. His father made sure to purchase him a first-class ticket for his trip to Georgia, presumably to protect him from the smoking, drinking, gambling, and unclean conditions of the Jim Crow car or perhaps to provide him with a comfortable train ride before his official introduction to college life. Whatever the reason, his son could not have asked for a more auspicious start. Sitting in the first-class car of an interstate train, a modern symbol of US progress, Johnson, the Renaissance man who nearly three decades later would become a spokesman for international diplomacy and who would eventually succumb to the sweet seductions of cosmopolitanism, probably imagined that these were the kind of accommodations he could get used to.[16]

Unfortunately, his trip turned sour. No sooner had the train pulled out of the station than Johnson was forced to confront the abrasiveness of southern racial politics. Johnson and his Afro-Cuban friend Ricardo were approached by the conductor, who, suspecting that they were occupying the wrong seats, asked to see their tickets. (In 1887, Florida began requiring railroads to provide separate cars for Black and white passengers, and it could charge conductors and railroad companies a $500 fine if they did not comply with the law.) The subsequent exchange went as might be expected between a Black southern teenager and a white adult male in the Jim Crow United States. Recently empowered by the state to enforce racial segregation, the conductor inspected James and Ricardo's first-class tickets, took a quick glance at them, and responded accordingly. "You had better get out of this car and into the one ahead," he said brusquely. "You'll be likely to have trouble if you try to stay in this car."[17]

The conductor's warning was more than a little confusing to both James and Ricardo, who were not aware of Florida's railroad segregation laws.[18] Johnson's response was tinged with a good measure of naïveté: "We have first-class tickets; and this is the first-class car, isn't it?" This was the kind of comment that in most cases could have been easily misinterpreted as insolence and could have possibly provoked physical violence. But, on this occasion, it was ignored—largely because of the question that followed. Not fully understanding the situation because of the language barrier, Ricardo, in his native language, asked James to clarify: "*¿Que dice?* (What is he saying?)." James explained in Spanish that they were being asked to relocate. When the conductor overheard their conversation, his demeanor suddenly switched. As Johnson remembered it, "As soon as the conductor heard us speaking a foreign language, his attitude changed; he punched our tickets and gave them back, and treated us just as he did the other passengers in the car." Notwithstanding the shift in tone, Johnson never forgot the conductor's antagonism and quickly recognized the exchange as a product of racism. Indeed, he conclusively marked the incident as his "first impact against race prejudice as a concrete fact."[19]

That Johnson recognized his experience as an act of resistance and remembered it as a challenge against racial prejudice emphasizes how he understood this incident as a form of legal disability. His experience paralleled the ones he described in his 1892 speech regarding the "disabilities of caste," which illuminated the particular ways de jure segregation injured African Americans and ranked them as second-class citizens. It also foreshadowed what the Supreme Court would eventually acknowledge in *Plessy*: that the "Southern states [were] imposing upon the colored race onerous disabilities and burdens."[20] Albion Tourgée, one of the litigants in *Plessy*, would reiterate this link between "onerous disabilities" and racial value when he argued that Homer Plessy was being denied the property of his white-colored skin. Johnson's early encounter with racism on the segregated train in the South not only revealed the close relationship between race, property, freedom, and value but also exposed how racial and national identification were imbricated within the practice of disability insofar as Johnson's Americanness mattered just as much as his blackness did.

What is remarkable about this scene of racial misidentification is how much the conductor participated in it.[21] Neither Johnson nor Rodriguez set out to sway the conductor's attitude, and yet the conductor made conclusive assumptions regarding their race, assumptions that enabled them to remain in their first-class seats and that allowed them admission to an otherwise inaccessible domain. This moment illustrates how the US construction of race extended beyond mere skin color to encompass other racial and ethnic markers and how these markers functioned as important signifiers for the assortment of bodies, the permissible extent of the state's social intrusion, the threat of racial contagion, and the degrees of deviance associated with blackness. The difference between Johnson's access to a first-class car and his expulsion from it hinged on his linguistic proficiency: had Johnson not spoken in Spanish to Ricardo, he would have been evicted from the train car or hauled off to jail and fined or, if deemed insubordinate, lynched.

Johnson's experience was certainly atypical, but it nonetheless demonstrates precisely whom Jim Crow policies were intended to target and whom not. It also clarifies the relationships among disability, immunity, and exceptionalism. Granted, there were not many African Americans who had Johnson's language skills and who could skirt the enforcement of the law in this fashion. Johnson's story thus figured him as an exemplary race man, demonstrating his extraordinary ability to evade Jim Crow constraints. Yet his racial exceptionalism also allowed him to observe the difference between freedom from legal control and subjection to it. "Johnson's fluency in a foreign language," Monica Miller argues, "simultaneously exposed and allowed him to bypass the turgidity, arbitrariness, and cruelty of America's racial system and color line, the full experience of which his larger cosmopolite self-concept and its psychosocial sign, dandyism, was designed to avoid."[22] If he had not been able to circumvent the law, he would not have been able to understand how the other side of the color line felt or to experience the privileges afforded to non-Black Americans. Here, Johnson's racial exceptionalism offered him temporary immunity from the disabilities of the color line.

Accordingly, Johnson's encounter taught him a valuable lesson about the intricate nature of US race relations in the nineteenth century: "The experience with this conductor drove home to me the conclusion that in such situations any kind of a Negro will do; provided he is not one who is an American citizen."[23] Johnson's comment illustrates the subtle yet significant way African *American* identity was being imagined as a severe impediment during Jim Crow. Indeed, if you were identified as a Black American in the late nineteenth and early twentieth centuries, then you were often denied a sense of mobility that was granted to others. As an African American man, Johnson recognized how his ability to move, to think, to act, or to speak without hindrance or restraint was curtailed on a segregated train. His observation that "any kind of a Negro will do" indicates that neither he nor the conductor was oblivious to how a number of identity factors (such as phenotype and language) informed assumptions about race, ethnicity, and nationality. Although Johnson was not light enough to pass as white, his conversational Spanish elided his Black American identity. As *Plessy* has shown, this misidentification worked in Johnson's favor largely because in the nineteenth-century United States non-US citizens (in particular, Chinese people) were allowed to ride in the same cars as white people, whereas African Americans were not. The misidentification that Johnson experienced in this instance was only temporary, however.

Nine years later, traveling from New York to Jacksonville, Florida, in 1896, Johnson endured what he described as one of his most "ridiculous" encounters with Jim Crow's legal disability, an "injustice" so profound that only the realization of its "absurdity" could quell Johnson's bitterness.[24] Part of what made his experience so absurd was the sheer volatility of late nineteenth-century segregation laws—the drastic manner in which Jim Crow laws varied from state to state and how they compromised the movement of Black Americans (often stigmatizing them as contagious and isolating them in public spaces), while extending whites' freedom of mobility and safeguarding their immunity. Traveling while Black during Jim Crow was, thus, a deeply disorienting experience. Depending on the segregation laws in each location of Black people's interstate travel, they were often shuttled from one train car to another at a moment's notice.

Johnson's path to Florida entailed traveling by steamer from New York to Charleston, South Carolina, and then by rail from Charleston to Jacksonville, which meant passing through the state of Georgia along the way. Johnson's journey from North to South, by boat and then train, from New York to Charleston through Georgia to Jacksonville, demanded both a familiarity and compliance with various state segregation laws. His life, liberty, and health depended on it. As Johnson wrote, "South Carolina had not yet enacted its separate car law," so he could ride comfortably in the first-class car for which he paid. But "it was against the law in Georgia for white and colored people to ride in the same railroad car," and after the train crossed the Georgia state line, the white conductor asked Johnson to move into the Jim Crow car. Because outright recalcitrance, Johnson knew, would lead to imprisonment (or worse), he reluctantly agreed to switch train cars—but not before taking "a look at the car designated for [him]."[25]

What Johnson discovered after inspecting the other car reveals the significant role of stigma and disability in the history of Jim Crow, a history in which familiar details of unequal accommodations and unjust treatment unfold anew. Johnson's coerced relocation exposes two noteworthy aspects of the Jim Crow system. First, his relocation shows that the separate-but-equal doctrine of racial segregation was neither wholly equal nor separate: the cars designated for Black folks were in worse shape than the cars designated for white people; and, as Justice Marshall Harlan argued in his dissent in *Plessy v. Ferguson*, segregation laws were intended primarily to impede the mobility of Black citizens, not the mobility of white citizens. This tragic irony of Johnson's relocation would not have been lost on him; he recognized how technologies of progress (such as the train) converge with technologies of oppression (such as the separate and dilapidated "colored" train car). Second, Johnson's forced relocation crucially reveals that race was not the sole determining factor considered when white and Black people were separated into separate train cars. Disability was considered, too.

Upon inspection of the "colored" car, Johnson immediately noticed its poor conditions and paltry accommodations—familiar features of the Jim Crow car that aimed to stigmatize Black people. Johnson wrote,

"It was the usual 'Jim Crow' arrangement: one-half of a baggage coach, unkempt, unclean, and ill smelling, with one toilet for both sexes. Two of the seats were taken up by the pile of books and magazines and the baskets of fruit and chewing gum of the 'news-butcher.'"[26] With less space, more dirt, foul smells, and one toilet, the "Jim Crow" car paled in comparison to the "white" first-class car. Comfort was hard to come by in this space. The conditions might have elicited more of a reaction from Johnson if they were not such a common sight and if he had not understood them as an integral element of Jim Crow: the need to subject Black passengers (even those who paid for first-class accommodations) to vile conditions and demand that they either bear it or suffer the consequences. Indeed, Johnson's description of the "colored" car is noticeably similar to the way Charles Chesnutt describes it in his novel *The Marrow of Tradition*, in which his protagonist, Dr. William Miller, becomes besmirched by the dirt, dust, grime, and spit covering the train car (see chapter 4). This condition of the Jim Crow car is what leads Miller, in part, to consider his relocation to the segregated train car as a stigmatizing enterprise. Johnson's Jim Crow experience in Georgia was no exception to this rule.

Johnson's relocation also exposes how under Jim Crow laws, the "colored" car functioned as the locus of disability. During his inspection of the Jim Crow car, Johnson observed the presence of two white men. The sight of white men in a Jim Crow car was not especially unusual. Johnson wrote, "It was—and in many parts still is—the custom for white men to go into that car whenever they felt like doing things that would not be allowed in the 'white' car. They went there to smoke, to drink, and often to gamble. At times the object was to pick an acquaintance with some likely-looking Negro girl."[27] The way Johnson tells it, the Jim Crow car was a breeding ground for white male debauchery—a loathsome, sometimes lascivious, space where white men displayed wanton and unscrupulous behavior and subjected Black passengers, particularly Black women, to potential harm and racial injury. "If white men frequented the car for the purpose of soliciting black women for sex," the historian Blair L. M. Kelley argues, "the racial and sexual mores of the day meant that black women risked their safety when resisting or rejecting such advances."[28] Segregation law required that the races remain separated in public spaces, but it generally only enforced that separation rule for

Black people, placing limits on their mobility by quarantining them in
the Jim Crow car. White people, on the other hand, could move between
the train cars; and white men, as Johnson observed, did so with reckless
abandon, engaging in activities not permitted elsewhere on the train and
occasionally making sexual advances toward Black women, opening up
the possibility of miscegenational relations that historically racial segregation was designed to prevent.

Although it was a customary practice for white men to occupy the
colored car, Johnson did not miss this opportunity to use their presence
to challenge the reasoning of racial segregation. Before switching train
cars as the conductor requested, Johnson demanded legal parity, calling on the conductor to enforce the doctrine of separate but equal for
all railroad passengers—white as well as Black people. He informed the
conductor that he could not ride in the "colored" car because there were
white passengers located in that car. Riding with white passengers in the
"colored" car, Johnson suggested, would put him in violation of the law
just as much as riding with white passengers in the "white" car would.
As a result, Johnson insisted that the law be applied equally.

The conductor's response to Johnson's complaint as well as his explanation for why the two white male passengers were placed in the "colored" car spotlight the complicated relationship between race, disability,
and class during Jim Crow. The conductor explained to Johnson that
the "two men were a deputy sheriff and a dangerously insane man, who
was being taken to the asylum." Consequently, the conductor exclaimed,
"I can't bring that crazy man into the 'white' car." From this exchange,
Johnson learned the principal reason that these two white men were
located in the "colored" train car was because one of them had a psychiatric disability. Another reason was because the disabled man was considered dangerous and had to be shepherded by the sheriff to an asylum.
In the surveilled and policed environment of the Jim Crow car, the white
man's psychiatric disability motivated the conductor to place him in the
"colored" car, not the "white" car.[29]

The conductor's explanation indicates that Jim Crow was more than
a system that separated white and Black people; it also defined the line
between disabled and nondisabled and first-class and second-class citizens. Johnson's exchange with the conductor reveals that the "white"
and "colored" signs were not the only differences between the train

cars. More specifically, the presence of the disabled white man in the Jim Crow train car encoded disability with race (especially blackness) in such a manner that both blackness and disability figured as threats to the health of the white citizenry and had to be excluded from the "white" car. Thus, Jim Crow cars exemplified what Snyder and Mitchell call the *"cultural locations of disability"* or what Michael Davidson refers to as the "sites" of disability—the spaces in which disability is constructed, defined, and produced.[30] That Johnson was forced to leave the "white" first-class car and relocate to the "colored" train car, only to find it occupied by a disabled white man, reveals how Jim Crow authorized, authored, and enforced segregation by race and disability—grouping and isolating African Americans and people with disabilities together in the "colored" car to constitute whiteness as a normative category.

This observation becomes clearer once we recognize how the conductor refused to identify the race of the man that the sheriff held in custody, emphasizing instead how that man's psychiatric disability was what led to his placement into the Jim Crow car. Put differently, Johnson's complaint was based solely on the *whiteness* of the two men, not the disability of one of them. The conductor, however, identified the sheriff's prisoner only by his disability and sex (as an "insane man" and a "crazy man"). The disabled white man's race was virtually erased in the conductor's response to Johnson, a move that disassociated disability from the white race and, therefore, attempted to reinforce the privilege, immunity, and able-bodiedness of whiteness. A similar move occurred when the conductor initially decided not to seat the disabled white man in the "white" train car.

Unmoved by the conductor's response, Johnson, fortunately, remained firm, insisting that the conductor fulfill his legal obligations and offering him an ultimatum. Within the flawed logic of Jim Crow, Johnson's final appeal to the conductor could be considered as advocating for his limited rights as much as the rights of the two white men. "Maybe you can't [move the two white men]," Johnson stated, "but if I've got to break this law I prefer breaking it in the first-class car." It is difficult to pinpoint precisely what led the conductor to move the disabled white man and his warden. Did Johnson persuade the conductor by conveying his point in language that the conductor could understand—the language of legal parity? Could the conductor sense implicit pressure from the white passengers—who smiled and nodded in approval after he removed Johnson from the first-class car but did not initially utter explicit threats toward Johnson or wage any public protest against his presence? Either way, both Johnson and the conductor came to an agreement. Johnson stated, "The conductor was, after all, a reasonable fellow; and he decided to stand squarely by the law, and bring the two white men into the 'white' car." The white passengers immediately regretted this switch. According to Johnson, as soon as the man entered the first-class car, he "thrust his manacled hands through the glass of the window, cutting himself horribly," and then he proceeded to yell and curse. Although the passengers protested the change and were upset that they were subjected to the man's "ravings," both Johnson and the conductor "stood squarely by the law."[31] On this occasion, Johnson collaborated with the conductor, who was essentially acting on behalf of the state, in holding the law to its own subpar standard.

In an encounter with the National Guard several years later while walking in a public park, Johnson would not be nearly as fortunate. While his experiences on the train exhibited his racial exceptionalism— his astute knowledge of segregation laws as well as his ability to challenge and subvert them—his violent encounter with the National Guard confirmed that, despite his linguistic skills and legal knowledge, it was difficult for a Black person to elude disability during Jim Crow. In the case of Johnson, disability meant not only legal restraint but also physical and psychological trauma. First, the circumstances surrounding his encounter with the National Guard must be contextualized. In May 1901, a massive fire swept across Jacksonville, beginning in the part of the city where the majority of African Americans lived. Starting from the western end of town one morning and spreading east, north, and south during the day, the fire was a "breath-taking pyrotechnical show" that by nightfall had reduced over 150 blocks to ash and rubble. The fire was so catastrophic that martial law had been declared, which meant that military men from central and western counties poured into the city— military men who were unaccustomed to interacting with urban Black people and who had "many unnecessary clashes with the colored people of Jacksonville."[32]

Johnson soon experienced firsthand a violent clash of his own. His conflict with the militia occurred at Riverside Park in Jacksonville, Flor-

ida, where he agreed to meet a young, fair-complexioned female journalist, who solicited Johnson's advice on an article she was writing about
the fire and its effects on the Black community. The choice of this public
location turned out to be a critical misstep, for a cadre of onlookers assumed that Johnson was escorting a white woman into the park and
reported the activity to the authorities, leading to the dispatch of national troops. Charged with the task of protecting a white woman from a
Black man, the militiamen, armed with combat weapons, tracked down
Johnson and attacked him near a barbed-wire fence. Johnson recalled,
"Just across the fence in the little clearing were eight or ten militiamen
in khaki with rifles and bayonets. The abrupt appearance of me and
my companion seemed to have transfixed them. They stood as under a
spell. . . . The spell is instantly broken. They surge round me. They seize
me. They tear my clothes and bruise my body; all the while calling to
their comrades, 'Come on, we've got 'im! Come on, we've got 'im!' And
from all directions these comrades rush, shouting, 'Kill the damned nigger! Kill the black son of a bitch!'"[33] This assault had all the essential
elements of a potential lynching: The troops shouted death threats. They
bore rifles and bayonets in close proximity to a barbed-wire fence with
trees looming just behind the clearing. They mercilessly beat Johnson.
They yelled terroristic sounds, "hallooing back and forth."[34] And at the
center of this maelstrom was Johnson, a Black man who was presumed
guilty of being in the park with a white woman and who feared that
this attack would cause his imminent death. Indeed, the brutality was so
severe that Johnson, who was writing about this incident in his memoir
decades after it occurred, could not resist shifting from past to present
tense when describing the violence he endured. The only way Johnson
could convey accurately the impact of his assault was by transforming
the past into the present, reliving blow by blow how the military "surge,"
"seize," "tear," "bruise," and "rush" his body. His active verbs animate the
scene and signify how the trauma of his near-lynching experience per-
sisted in his mind several decades later. The African American studies
scholar Jacqueline Goldsby argues that "until this moment—and only
with this moment—*Along This Way* had been narrated in the past tense."
This abrupt tense shift signals that Johnson could not "find the language
to partition off the incident as a mere past event while preserving its
transformative effect."[35]

Although Johnson survived his assault, he did not survive it un-scathed; alongside his physical injuries, Johnson suffered intense psy-chological trauma. After he revealed that his female companion was not white and the National Guard released him from custody, he remained haunted by his racial nightmare: "For weeks and months the episode with all of its implications preyed on my mind and disturbed me in my sleep. I would wake often in the night-time, after living through again those few frightful seconds, exhausted by the nightmare of a struggle with a band of murderous, bloodthirsty men in khaki. . . . It was not until twenty years after through the work I was then engaged in, that I was able to liberate myself completely from this horror complex."[36] That Johnson paralleled his physical attack with that of his psychological one demonstrates how racial violence affected both his mind and his body. Not unlike his shifting from the past to present tense to describe his physical assault, here Johnson collapsed time when describing his men-tal state. While he initially stated that the assault "preyed" on his mind for "weeks and months," it is clear that the psychological trauma lasted much longer, for he ultimately admitted that it would take two decades and his antilynching work with the NAACP before he could really feel free. Johnson's various shifts in time expose the disorienting and de-bilitating power of anti-Black violence: it made an assault by "a band of murderous, bloodthirsty men" feel like a "few frightful seconds"; it made "weeks" of terrifying nightmares indistinguishable from "months"; and it took "twenty years" to recover fully from what Johnson described as a "horror complex."

Despite the significance of this near-death experience to Johnson's life and writing, he did not publicly disclose details about the encoun-ter. In the immediate aftermath of the assault, the only person he told was his brother, Rosamond; he refused to tell his parents or anyone else in his family.[37] According to Goldsby, the first person to divulge Johnson's secret to the public was W. E. B. Du Bois. Speaking in 1931 at Johnson's resignation dinner from the NAACP, Du Bois surprised the audience with shocking news about Johnson's incident: "Mr. John-son . . . was once nearly lynched in Florida, and quite naturally lynching to him, despite all obvious excuses and explanations and mitigating cir-cumstances, can never be less than a terrible real."[38] Du Bois probably shared this story to show that Johnson's fifteen-year commitment to the NAACP antilynching campaign was personal as well as political. Yet Johnson's intentional silence about the assault—even as he was fighting to protect others from experiencing this kind of violence—calls attention to his own need to suppress this painful experience. Goldsby argues that "the assault steeled Johnson to accept lynching as his 'terrible real,' a force which clarified the ways in which literal, violent enactments of racial power demarcated the boundaries between experience ('Life') and its aesthetic expressions (the things 'enjoyed' from Life)."[39] The distinction Goldsby makes between life and the things enjoyed from life mirrors the strained relationship between blackness and whiteness that was a central part of Jim Crow—like the difference between survival and freedom, between duty and rights, and between disablement and immunity. In this regard, the "terrible real" of lynching—its ability to harm, disfigure, and kill—demarcates clearly the violence of Jim Crow's varied forms of oppression. This brand of violence is something that Johnson was willing to interrogate in his work (particularly in his antilynching activism and his novel) as long as his personal life was not at the center of it.

The "Terrible Real" and "Terrible Handicap" in *The Autobiography of an Ex-Colored Man*

While Johnson was too traumatized to share his near-lynching experience with the world immediately, the assault did not prevent him from depicting the physical and mental consequences of lynching in his only novel, *The Autobiography of an Ex-Colored Man*. First published anonymously in 1912, the novel was republished in 1927 with Johnson's name attached to it, marking *The Autobiography of an Ex-Colored Man* as a paradigmatic passing text. More than a novel about racial passing, *Autobiography*, as several scholars have noted, addresses other permutations on passing as well: it is a novel that passes as an autobiography and borrows key tropes from slave narratives; it is a text that, despite its title, pertains as much to the malleability of gender, sexuality, and class as to race; it is a migration narrative that traverses extensive geographical terrain from the United States to Europe; and, with its focus on the arts, it jumps between a number of different literary and musical forms, engaging fiction and nonfiction as well as Negro spirituals, classical music, and ragtime.[40] Focusing on the lynching scene in addition to other scenes of racial injury, I offer an account of Johnson's discursive, physical, and psychological representations of disability.

The lynching scene at its core represents a culmination of the anti-Black violence deployed throughout the novel, and it confirms what Johnson's protagonist-narrator, the ex-colored man, observes as he travels across the United States and abroad: that the intractable system of Jim Crow made the Black body especially vulnerable to bodily deformation and psychological disability. Although the Black lynch victim in Johnson's novel dies, his lynching is not only a representation of death. The manner in which he is captured, tied, displayed, and burned alive before a captive audience suggests an attempt to deform the Black body, to transform the way the body is visualized in the US cultural imagination. As a witness of the lynching, the ex-colored man is traumatized by the experience. Additionally, the lynching emphasizes other forms of anti-Black violence in the novel—particularly the ways blackness is stigmatized. Alluding to scientific and political discourses that figure Black folks as inherently disabled, the novel details the manner in which disability and stigma are inflicted on Black folks, via the watchful eye of the ex-colored man, whose visibly white skin allows him to experience life on various sides of the color line. As a Black man passing for white, he recognizes the "premium" placed on whiteness (or "lack of color") in the United States. As a Black man who does not pass as white, he experiences firsthand the disabilities of the color line, what he describes as "the dwarfing, warping, distorting influence which operates upon each colored man in the United States."[41]

This "dwarfing, warping, distorting influence" is certainly one of the reasons why the ex-colored man's white millionaire patron discourages him from returning to the United States as an African American composer, warning that his relocation and Black racial identification could potentially have disabling effects. The white patron states, "My boy, you are by blood, by appearance, by education and by tastes, a white man. Now why do you want to throw your life away amidst the poverty and ignorance, in the hopeless struggle of the black people of the United States? Then look at the terrible handicap you are placing on yourself by going home and working as a Negro composer; you can never be able to get the hearing for your work which it might deserve."[42] Although the white patron only gets it partly right when he observes that the ex-colored man is "by blood . . . a white man," since the infamous one-drop rule of racial identity places the narrator into the legal category of blackness, the patron nonetheless realizes that the ex-colored man's perceived whiteness provides a mobility, freedom, and financial advancement unavailable to the Black composer who ventures back to the United States, especially in the South. That the white patron describes such a return as "the terrible handicap" emphasizes the particular role that disability will play in the ex-colored man's racial identification and relocation. The patron's warning both foreshadows the southern lynching (what Du Bois described as the "terrible real" for Johnson) that will occur in the novel and recalls the ex-colored man's earlier experiences of racial violence and trauma. While in Paris, the ex-colored man has to field a question about the "ugly rumor" of lynching that he is not altogether prepared to handle. A man from Luxembourg asks him, "Did they really burn a man alive in the United States?"[43] The question embarrasses the ex-colored man so much that he cannot accurately remember his response. Lynching becomes the thing he cannot talk about in part because it is so terribly real and painful.

The lynching scene in Johnson's *Autobiography* sutures the "terrible real" and "the terrible handicap" in the penultimate chapter, in which the ex-colored man witnesses the lynching of an unidentified Black male in the South and watches both the graphic transformations of the victim's body and that of the white mob's behavior. It is not only the image of the Black man's burning body and the throng of animated spectators that terrifies and traumatizes the ex-colored man but also the ghastly sounds emitting from them. In the moment of crisis near the novel's conclusion, as the white men busily prepare for the lynching, the narrator recalls the rapid-fire sequence of events:

> The men who at midnight had been stern and silent were now emitting that terror instilling sound known as the "rebel yell." A space was quickly cleared in the crowd, and a rope placed about his neck; when from somewhere came the suggestion, "Burn him!" It ran like an electric current. Have you ever witnessed the transformation of human beings into savage beasts? Nothing can be more terrible. A railroad tie was sunk into the ground, the rope was removed and a chain brought and securely coiled

around the victim and the stake. . . . Fuel was brought from everywhere, oil, the torch; the flames crouched for an instant as though to gather strength, then leaped up as high as their victim's head. He squirmed, he writhed, strained at his chains, then gave out cries and groans that I shall always hear. The cries and groans were choked off by the fire and smoke; but his eyes bulging from their sockets, rolled from side to side, appealing in vain for help. Some of the crowd yelled and cheered, others seemed appalled at what they had done, and there were those who turned away sickened at the sight. I was fixed to the spot where I stood, powerless to take my eyes from what I did not want to see.[44]

Nearly every detail here contrasts with another to form a macabre and grotesque affair, and together they force the reader to interrogate the practice and meaning of lynching. Enacted partly as spectacle and partly as celebration, this instance of brutal public torture changes everyone in the scene: the white mob, the ex-colored man, and certainly the Black lynch victim. With respect to the white mob, its transformation from "human beings into savage beasts" is both volatile and routinized. The sudden and marked shift in the white men's deportment—from utter silence and relative inaction to screams and quick, lockstep movement—heightens the scene's explosiveness while showing how their behavior is methodical and strategic. The mere mention of violence—"Burn him!"—electrified the mob, and the "rebel yell," the "terror instilling sound" of Confederate soldiers, turns this violence into an act of war against the Black body. The juxtaposition of the cheering, yelling crowd alongside the crying, imploring victim frames this event as a spectacle of torture, as an infliction of pain intended to disable and kill the anonymous Black male victim as well as offer sadistic pleasure to some of the spectators. Yet not everyone is thrilled by the incitement of racial violence; some seem "appalled," while others are "sickened at the sight." Figured as an interloper, the ex-colored man does not consider himself as an active member of this crowd. His careful distinction between the third-person plural and the first-person singular makes clear that the Black man chained to the railroad tie and set aflame is "their" victim and that the orchestration of the lynching is something "they" had planned. The ex-colored man's unknown racial identity allows him to be a spectator—but he is only a witness, not a participant. The sight of the lynching leaves him transfixed, unable to avert his eyes from the "terrible" event he "did not want to see."

Although the ex-colored man witnesses this violent act, his physical presence is not quite enough to ensure its realness. To confirm the veracity and importance of this traumatic moment, the ex-colored man relies on lynching's remains—its tools, its aftereffects, and especially the mutilated corpse of its victim: "Before I could make myself believe that what I saw was really happening, I was looking at a scorched post, a smoldering fire, blackened bones, charred fragments sifting down through coils of chain, and the smell of burnt flesh—human flesh—was in my nostrils."[45] The "scorched post," the "smoldering fire," and the "coils of chain" constitute part of the story, relaying important details about what has transpired. But it is the decomposing body that immediately authenticates—that helps the ex-colored man "believe" in—lynching's ability to disable and kill. Torched, burned, writhing, and screaming for his life: here is visual proof of the disfigured Black male body. The sensorial experience of the lynching overwhelms the ex-colored man, traumatizing him. The sounds of the Black lynch victim, the sight of his decomposed body, and finally the smell of his burned flesh all collide in this scene to convey lynching's deadly power. While the victim's "bulging" eyes, "blackened bones," "charred fragments," and dissolving flesh offer the ex-colored man evidence of the transformation of the Black lynch victim, the victim's sounds and smell leave an indelible impression, too. The ex-colored man "shall always hear" the Black man's "cries and groans" just as certainly as he will always associate the smell of human flesh with that of the lynch victim. Before the lynching, the victim stands as a man "in form and stature"; after the lynching, the man's form and stature are radically altered, deformed in full view of a frenzied southern audience.[46]

The lynching scene in Johnson's novel demonstrates that lynching taxed more than just one's visual senses. As the historian Amy Wood points out, "lynching included not only the sight of black desecration but also other senses. Spectators heard the speeches of the mob, the shouts of the crowd," and the "dying shrieks and cries" of the victim. "In cases where the victim was burned," Wood adds, "to witness a lynching was also to smell it. And, in all instances, the feel and push of the crowd created the sense of belonging and commonality that sustained the violence. In this respect, spectators did not watch or consume a lynching as much as they *witnessed* it."[47]

The novel's lynching scene has as much to do with disability as it does with death and brutality. The line between brutality and disability was quite porous in the nineteenth and early twentieth centuries; and the term *lynching* had several different meanings, and its implementation took a variety of forms. During that time, lynching "did not apply, as it does now, exclusively to the infliction of the death penalty," Johnson states in his 1924 essay "Lynching—America's National Disgrace."[48] In the nineteenth and early twentieth centuries, Black people were lynched in myriad ways, including shooting, hanging, beating, burning, mutilation, dismemberment, and tar-and-feathering.[49] Moreover, the NAACP's photographic archive from the 1940s and 1950s includes a visual record of lynching's conspicuous depictions of disability. "In addition to images of brutalized black corpses," Goldsby observes, "the visual records in the [NAACP's] anti-lynching files are full of scopically sympathetic pictures (photographed at a remove, with the victim-subjects facing the camera's eye) that depict lynching's reappearance in blindings, amputations, and other corporeal mutilations that southern 'progress' was supposed to have made obsolete."[50] Johnson's evocation of disability in an event that is usually associated with brutality and death clarifies his expansive understanding of the various ways disability was deployed during the Jim Crow regime. Indeed, in the novel's lynching scene (as with other scenes of lynching), the lynching victim does not serve as the only instance of disability. The ex-colored man has to live with what he has just witnessed, and "living with lynching," Koritha Mitchell argues, entails being "traumatized by the sights and sounds of racial violence."[51]

Paralleling the metamorphoses of the white mob and the Black male lynch victim, the ex-colored man undergoes a physical and mental transformation as well. The lynching has a disabling effect on his body and psyche, for he is rendered temporarily immobile and debilitated. During the lynching, the ex-colored man is "fixed to the spot where [he] stood"; later he "was as weak as a man who had lost blood."[52] The effect on the ex-colored man's body is such that the lynch victim serves as his double. Both men are nameless, and both lose blood. While the victim literally loses blood, the ex-colored man figuratively loses Black blood, since it is the lynching that makes him decide to pass as a white man.

The ex-colored man's decision to pass as a result of the lynching raises the specter of another form of disability: castration. Although the novel's lynching victim is not castrated, the manner in which lynching alters our understanding of Black masculinity in the novel forces us to wonder, according to the race, gender, and sexuality studies scholar Hazel V. Carby, "if the ritual of dismemberment and the sadistic torture of black bodies is, in fact, a search to expose, and perhaps even an attempt to claim, an essence of manhood that is both feared and desired."[53] Carby interprets the practice of lynching as an invalidation of Black manliness. The literary scholar and cultural critic Phillip Brian Harper makes a similar point in his examination of the relationship between racial authenticity and gender. As Harper argues, insofar as Black racial authenticity is gendered as masculine and the lynching propels the ex-colored man to engage in Black-to-white racial passing (which, through the figure of the tragic mulatto, has been coded in "decidedly *feminine* terms"), the sensational violence of lynching—with its focus on disability, dismemberment, and torture—could be interpreted as an attempt to rob both the lynching victim and the ex-colored man of their masculinity, representing a form of figurative castration.[54] This line of reasoning is more compelling if we consider, as the disability studies scholar Michelle Jarman does, the overlap between the racial violence of lynching and the eugenic narratives of "cognitively disabled men as social menaces and sexual predators" in an effort "to promote public acceptance of institutionalization, surgical castration, and sterilization." Jarman writes, "I suggest that even as racist mob violence and surgical sterilization followed distinct historical trajectories, the ubiquitous presence of lynching in the public imagination during the period from 1890 to 1940 may have informed and helped naturalize the rationale used to support medical castration and asexualization."[55] The ritual of lynching is tied to a history of emasculation and asexualization, and this history intersects with the regulation of disability and blackness in the United States.

The parallel that Johnson creates between the ex-colored man and the anonymous victim spotlights an observation that he would later make in his "Lynching" essay, in which he writes, "no one can take part in a lynching or witness it and remain thereafter a psychically normal human being."[56] In his novel, no one in the scene—not the lynching victim, the perpetrators of the lynching, or the witnesses of it—survives intact. The victim is hanged, burned, and killed; the mob turns into savage beasts; and the ex-colored man suffers paralysis and endures a racial transmutation that impoverishes his racial authenticity and masculinity.

Blackness, Disability, and Stigma

What makes the lynching scene so pivotal to the rest of *Autobiography* is the manner in which it calls attention to the varied ways that the Black body is made vulnerable to disability and stigma during Jim Crow. The imprint of disability is nearly everywhere in the ex-colored man's life—in his home, at his school, in his personal relationships—but it is often overlooked or ignored in scholarly assessments of the novel, even though each example of disability sets up the lynching scene at the novel's end. The lynching, then, is not the ex-colored man's first encounter with disability. In both his adolescent and adult life, he encounters disability. For example, the ex-colored man confronts his mother's disability as well as that of a singer of spirituals. First, his mother suffers from a mysterious illness that greatly compromises her health, leaving her bedridden and eventually resulting in her death. Second, at the "big meeting," a weeklong gathering where various congregations unite at a centrally located church for a series of social and religious functions, the ex-colored man sees Singing Johnson, the powerful singer who leads the congregation in a number of Negro spirituals and who, the narrator notes, has only one eye.[57]

The illness of the ex-colored man's mother and her subsequent death have a profound psychological influence on him. Describing his mother's debilitating illness and death as "one of the two sacred sorrows of [his] life"—the second sacred sorrow being the death of his wife at the end of the novel—the ex-colored man experiences severe grief and loneliness.[58] After his mother's death, the ex-colored man effectively becomes an orphan—abandoned by his father, estranged from his other family members, and utterly alone for the first time in his life. Her death represents a distinct loss of familial roots and community for him. This feeling of rootlessness also offers him the possibility of reinvention and self-fashioning, which he takes up at the novel's conclusion after witnessing the lynching.

While the death of the ex-colored man's mother represents an irrevocable loss for him, his encounter with one-eyed Singing Johnson symbolizes the potential recuperation of a racial, ancestral, and cultural past that he deeply desires at certain points throughout the novel yet ultimately forsakes as a result of the violent lynching. At the big meeting, Singing Johnson's musical sensibility enthralls the ex-colored man. Reflecting on the wondrous quality of Negro spirituals and the importance of an accomplished lead singer to bring these songs to life, the ex-colored man exclaims, "Any musical person who has never heard a Negro congregation under the spell of religious fervor sing these old songs, has missed one of the most thrilling emotions which the human heart may experience."[59] Indeed, Singing Johnson's improvisation and ingenuity, his impressive memory of the Negro spirituals, and his remarkable complementarity with the preacher John Brown all mark him as an embodiment of those "unknown black bards" whom James Weldon Johnson honors in his poem "O Black and Unknown Bards" and discusses in his preface to The Book of American Negro Spirituals. Johnson's preface reveals a biographical connection to Singing Johnson, a man whom James Weldon Johnson would periodically see in church and whom he describes as "a small but stocky, dark-brown man . . . with one eye, and possessing a clear, strong, high-pitched voice."[60] This description of Singing Johnson in Johnson's preface is repeated almost verbatim in the novel. The literary critic Lucinda H. Mackethan argues that, in this scene in the novel, in which the narrator visits the "big meeting," James Weldon Johnson "wrests the voice from his narrator and, in his own 'singing' voice, goes into great detail concerning the way the song leader directed the spirituals at the meeting."[61] In his novel, Johnson transfers his own exuberance about the power of Black music and performers onto his narrator. The ex-colored man is so inspired by Singing Johnson's performance of these songs—what he calls "the most treasured heritage of the American Negro"—that one might expect the ex-colored man to defy the odds, challenge the directive of his white millionaire patron, and prosper as a Black composer in the South.[62] This future, unfortunately, never materializes, for the lynching follows shortly thereafter, and it changes the trajectory of the ex-colored man's life.

James Weldon Johnson's decision to pair the lynching scene with Singing Johnson's performance at the big meeting in the same chapter emphasizes how anti-Black violence via lynching destroys the ex-colored man's musical aspirations and spotlights how Black bodies are made susceptible to disablement. The ex-colored man's experiences at the big meeting enhance the dramatic effect of the lynching, generating a synergy between the two scenes. James Weldon Johnson's detailed description of bodily deformation in the lynching scene offsets the lack of particulars he provides about how Singing Johnson lost his eye. After reading Johnson's description of the lynch victim's "eyes bulging from their sockets," the reader has a good sense of the circumstances that could have led to Singing Johnson's missing eye and does not require further graphic details. What the lynching scene in *Autobiography* makes clear is that a Black person under the rule of Jim Crow could be subjected to all manner of violence and that the manifestations of that violence could take several forms: disability, lynching, and death.

Such disabling violence bears extraordinary transformative power, reshaping the fit, healthy, and mobile Black body into an unfit, feeble, and immobile one. This distortion of the Black body is of central importance to Johnson, as it is to several other African American writers who explore how blackness is deployed in opposition to whiteness. "In the America of Jim Crow," Sundquist asserts, "to be black was always to wear the distorted mask of blackness before the white world and to be, in legal and political terms, 'nobody.' To be black, in relation to the dominant white culture, was to be 'anonymous,' as Johnson has it, to be 'nothing,' as several of Charles Chesnutt's penetrating stories had argued, or to be an 'invisible man,' as Ralph Ellison would later contend in his own borrowing from Johnson's plot."[63] Such designations—nobody, nothing, anonymous, and invisible—emphasize the varied and complicated ways that blackness becomes reduced in relation to white supremacy.

In the case of Johnson's protagonist, to be "nobody," "nothing," or "invisible" differs from being "anonymous" in that racial anonymity is more a matter of agency. When the ex-colored man renounces his African American heritage, packs his bags, and heads to New York at the novel's conclusion, it is an option that his visibly white skin affords him. Unlike his dark double, who is burned and mutilated at the stake, or even Ellison's invisible man, whose invisibility stems from other people's refusal to see him accurately, the narrator inhabits his anonymous status by resolving to "neither disclaim the black race nor claim the white race . . . and let the world take [him] for what it would."[64] Although the ex-colored man posits his decision as neutral, he also takes measures to ensure that the world would take him for a white man. His reasons for ultimately deciding that he "was not going to be a Negro" are consistent: he wants to circumvent racial stigma, which he describes variously as "the 'brand,'" the "label of inferiority pasted across [his] forehead," and, in reference to the lynching victim, "every sign of degeneracy stamped upon his countenance."[65]

The brand, label, and sign represent marks that are imposed on the Black body, and they work to stigmatize Black people as inferior and degenerate. The ex-colored man could contest this social marking were it not for his own cowardice. As he puts it, "more than once I felt like declaiming, 'I am a colored man. Do I not disprove the theory that one drop of Negro blood renders a man unfit?'"[66] What the ex-colored man wants to disprove is the theory of unfitness, the presumption that Black blood is inherently diseased and that blackness is innately defective.

The theory that the ex-colored man probably refers to is the theory of biomedical racialism, or what George M. Fredrickson describes as "racial Darwinism," which applied biological concepts of natural selection to race and politics.[67] In the late nineteenth century, as Albion Tourgée reported in his 1884 manifesto *An Appeal to Caesar*, there was an "almost ineradicable belief of the white people of the South that the Negro is an inferior species of the human family and not fit or capable to exercise joint-sovereignty with the white race."[68] For instance, Thomas H. Huxley, a British disciple and advocate of Charles Darwin, maintained that "it is simply incredible that, when all his disabilities are removed, and our prognathous relative has a fair field and no favor, as well as no oppressor, he will be able to compete successfully with his bigger-brained and smaller-jawed rival, in a contest which is to be carried on by thoughts and not by bites."[69] Similarly, Frederick L. Hoffman, a German-born insurance statistician known for calculating Black mortality rates, argued that "the time will come, if it has not already come, when the negro, like the Indian, will be a vanishing race."[70] Huxley's and Hoffman's claims of innate Black degeneracy and racial extinction are representative of the theories that the ex-colored man refers to in his question about whether his existence disproves the myth that Black people are "unfit" citizens. As an exceptional Black man—one accustomed to hearing compliments about his beauty, one recognized as the "fastest 'stripper'" in the cigar factory, one whose quick language acquisition gets him selected as the "reader" for the Cuban workmen at the factory and whose musical skills earn him the title of "professor" of ragtime—the ex-colored man is capable of and fit for many tasks.[71] His ability to excel in and adapt to different environments explains why Johnson's brother, Rosamond, initially suggested "The Chameleon" as the novel's title. Despite the ex-colored man's exceptional abilities, though, he recognizes that as a Black man he is not immune to stigmatization. He becomes more aware of the connection between stigma and disability after the lynching, but it is something he observes even as a child and as a young adult.

The ex-colored man's recollection of early childhood experiences at school shows his familiarity with racial stigmatization as well as his understanding of the disabling and violent consequences that stigma has on the body and mind. One pivotal moment occurs when the ex-colored man is racially identified at school, which immediately results in his temporary blindness and deafness. In the novel's opening chapter, we discover that the ex-colored man has been living under the guise of whiteness until his elementary school teacher makes him painfully aware of his racial difference. When the narrator stands after the principal requests for all of the white scholars to rise, his teacher quickly puts him in his place. She says, "You sit down for the present, and rise with the others." This incident disorients the ex-colored man, who experiences not only shock but also a sudden loss of sight and hearing: "I sat down dazed. I saw and heard nothing. When the others were asked to rise I did not know it."[72] Stunned, the ex-colored man becomes stuck between the two sides of the color line in this classroom scene. Even though his teacher identifies him as not white, he does not rise with the other Black students, effectively placing him in a liminal racial category. The ex-colored man is unable to see his nonwhite color, and he is incapable of recognizing how his body marks him as Black. Moreover, the narrator remembers this moment of racial identification as not only a psychological assault but also a physical one, describing that unforgettable day in school as a "sword-thrust" that would take him years to heal from.[73] This instance of racial marking, both surprising and bewildering, turns race—which before now was an unproblematic point of identification—into the narrator's most immediate preoccupation.

In the ex-colored man's subsequent assessment of his and his mother's features, he relies on a racist scientific discourse that is underpinned by disability—searching for presumed abnormalities and defects in their features and relying on a rhetoric that marks Black blood as a source of contamination and social danger. As soon as he returns home from school, he closely examines himself in the mirror: "I noticed the ivory whiteness of my skin, the beauty of my mouth, the size and liquid darkness of my eyes, and how the long black lashes that fringed and shaded them produced an effect that was strangely fascinating even to me. I noticed the softness and glossiness of my dark hair that fell in waves over my temples, making my forehead appear whiter than it really was."[74] Crucially, the first thing the narrator notices as he is looking at his reflection in the mirror is the "ivory whiteness" of his skin, which suggests he is having a difficult time reconciling his new racial identification with his skin color. The narrator suddenly becomes obsessed with the color, texture, shape, and size of his features. He, without warning, allows this instance of racial marking to produce a "strangely fascinating" effect on himself; it is the strangeness of his racial difference that finally compels the ex-colored man to ask, "Mother, mother, tell me, am I a nigger?" Worse yet, before his mother finally discloses that she is not white, he scrutinizes her features through a much harsher lens. Although the narrator at one time considered his mother to be the "most beautiful woman in the world," he readily admits that he was "searching for defects" that he assumed her "nigger" blood would produce. Even after concluding that, despite her differences in color and hair texture, his mother is "very beautiful," the ex-colored man continues to examine her body. His mother's only recourse is to emphasize the fact that while she may not be white, her son's racial identity is somehow protected because he is the offspring of a white man: "No, I am not white, but you—your father is one of the greatest men in the country—the best blood of the South is in you."[75] To be sure, his mother's claim that the ex-colored man's father has the "best blood of the South" and her description of his father as "one of the greatest men in the country" are overwrought—especially when we consider that his father abandons them both, presumably because of his inability to overcome the racial barrier. His mother's reference to blood, much like his reference to defects, recalls a scientific racial discourse, which characterizes Black blood as a contamination to white blood and, as Huxley's and Hoffman's comments indicate, mark blackness as inherently defective and on the verge of extinction. Yet despite the ex-colored man's recognition of difference and reliance on this scientific discourse, it is significant to point out that he does not succumb fully to this white-supremacist rhetoric. As the literary scholar Steven J. Belluscio observes, the ex-colored man in this moment "cannot view these differences as 'defects'; his mother is still beautiful to him, much as he is still beautiful to himself." "Here," Belluscio adds, "Johnson debunks the verity of self-evident, racially determined beauty standards: for the protagonist, any notion that black is *not* 'beautiful' would have to be learned."[76] Put differently, the ex-colored man, even after his racist conflict at school, both embraces and finds beauty in blackness—that which the dominant social order deems defective.

If the ex-colored man's racial identification at school and his exchange with his mother do not fully educate him about racially determined beauty standards as well as the stigmatization of blackness, then his later exchange as an adult with his white girlfriend in the final chapter of *Autobiography* accomplishes that goal. In this scene of racial disclosure, when the narrator reveals his racial identity to his white girlfriend, her response is quite telling: "I felt her hand grow cold, and when I looked up she was gazing at me with a wild, fixed stare as though I was some object she had never seen. Under the strange light in her eyes I felt that I was growing black and thick-featured and crimp-haired. . . . Her lips trembled . . . but the words stuck in her throat."[77] Seeing himself through his girlfriend's eyes is different from seeing his own reflection in the mirror. The ex-colored man experiences a spectacular racial transformation that darkens his skin, distorts his features, and changes the texture of his hair. Under her "wild, fixed stare," his "ivory" skin turns "black," his proportional features become "thick," and his soft and glossy hair grows kinky.

The act of staring, Rosemarie Garland-Thomson argues, can "assign stigma to certain perceived traits," and it is capable of "hurdl[ing] a body from the safe shadows of ordinariness into the bull's-eye of judgment."[78] The ex-colored man's body is certainly under a bull's-eye in this scene. His perceived change in features, however, does not alone produce the stigma. His girlfriend's response stigmatizes his perceived racial traits. Her cold hand, her penetrating stare, her trembling lips, and her tight throat all convey disapproval of the ex-colored man's racial disclosure. In her eyes, he becomes monstrous and brutish. Reduced to a mere "object," the ex-colored man feels just as dehumanized and degraded as the Black lynch victim.

This exchange between the ex-colored man and his white girlfriend serves as another prime literary example of Du Bois's double consciousness. Describing his appearance through the eyes of his white girlfriend, the ex-colored man shows how racial stigmatization disfigures his mind and body, which elucidates key aspects of Du Bois's theory. Effectively capturing such racial exclusion and separation, Johnson's novel is certainly indebted to Du Bois's *Souls* in a number of ways. *Souls* is one of the few books that Johnson's narrator praises in *Autobiography*, and, as Henry Louis Gates Jr. has noted, the narrator's commentary on looking "out through other eyes" and on the "dual personality" of every Black man clearly echoes Du Bois's double consciousness.[79] Yet it is Johnson's depiction of the ex-colored man's interaction with his girlfriend that offers a fascinating perspective of double consciousness. Not only do we see the ex-colored man's image through the eyes of another, but we also see the injurious effect that image has on him. His girlfriend's initial rejection is traumatic for him largely because of his smugness and vanity, and her reaction ultimately influences his decision to pass as white and reconfirms a racial hierarchy. The ex-colored man shifts from one identity to another often for the sake of convenience and praise, and it sets him up as a self-serving character who will later betray Black folks.

Focusing primarily on what he would gain by passing as white, the ex-colored man fails to consider fully what he would lose in the process or how his decision to pass might harm African Americans writ large. A comprehensive understanding of the practice of racial passing, the historian Allyson Hobbs argues, must not only consider the "benefits accrued to these new white identities" but also reckon "with the loss, alienation, and isolation that accompanied, and often outweighed, its rewards."[80] The ex-colored man does not quite understand the significance of this loss, alienation, and isolation until it is too late—claiming at the novel's end that in disavowing his blackness for whiteness, he chose "the lesser part" and "sold [his] birthright for a mess of pottage."[81] His decision to pass as white—to, in effect, sever all Black racial ties by cutting himself off from his family, friends, and community—registers, thus, as a form of violence. The "ex-" that precedes the colored man's name is akin to a racial dismemberment, a negation of his name and his people.

* * *

The novel's success and the public's confusion as to whether *Autobiography* was the story of Johnson's life played no small role in Johnson's decision to write his memoir. He wanted to distinguish his own biography from that of his fictional narrator's. As he writes in *Along This Way*, "I continue to receive letters from persons who have read the book [*Autobiography*] inquiring about this and that phase of my life as told in it. That is, probably, one of the reasons why I am writing the present book."[82] Johnson's desire to separate himself from the ex-colored man was understandable; his protagonist exhibits a kind of cowardice that could have damaged the reputation of a race man like Johnson. Accordingly, his memoir and life serve as an example of an alternative and more promising route that a Black Renaissance man who experiences disablement could take rather than resorting to Black-to-white racial passing.

Yet putting Johnson's autobiography in conversation with his novel also demonstrates how the racial caste system of Jim Crow deploys disability. Shifting his focus from legal disability to the psychological and physical trauma of racial violence, Johnson examines the intricate and complex ways that blackness and disability intersect in US culture. Johnson's "The Best Methods of Removing the Disabilities of Caste from the Negro," *Along This Way*, and *The Autobiography of an Ex-Colored Man* illustrate that to be Black during Jim Crow was to be denied entrance into the US body politic, to witness firsthand how Black bodies were made vulnerable to physical and mental injury, and to experience the perilousness of US racism that functioned to discipline and quarantine African Americans.

The Jim Crow regime—its unidirectional and selective segregation of racial groups, its particular grouping and isolation of African Americans and disabled people apart from the train car designated for whites, its stigmatization of Black bodies as contagious subjects, its strict regulation of interracial contact, its deforming and disabling practices of lynching, and its relentless distortion of blackness—provides scholars with ample opportunity to examine more precisely how blackness and disability function as related social constructs. Black studies and disability studies are especially equipped to facilitate examinations of the shared subjection of blackness and disability during Jim Crow and to articulate how bodies designated as deviant have been disqualified historically from national belonging and social participation. The field of Black studies is flush with examples of how racial ideologies depend on discourses of disability from the antebellum period to the present, while the field of disability studies has recognized how other identity categories have informed cultural notions of disability. Together, Black studies and disability studies can, if employed productively, offer us a vital history about how disability has shaped the racialized embodiment of African Americans. This history is present in parts of James Weldon Johnson's corpus, which provides a narrative of the ways disability intersects with blackness to understand more fully the complexities of racial injury and subjection. This history is also present in the ongoing age of color blindness (the subject of chapter 6), an age that is just as relevant to Johnson's era as it is to the present day.

PART III

Age of Color Blindness

6

The Ableism of Color-Blind Racism

The problem of the twenty-first century is the problem of the
color-*blind*: those who wish to disavow the continued material manifestations of race in our society.
—Brandi Wilkins Catanese, *The Problem of the Color[blind]*

The Performance and Fashion of Color Blindness

In Patricia Williams's 1997 BBC Reith Lectures, titled "The Genealogy
of Race," the critical race theorist shared a captivating anecdote about
the sinister quality of color blindness, narrating a story about a racial
conflict between white and Black students at her son's nursery school
that illustrates how color blindness is fashioned and performed. At the
outset of her lecture, Williams detailed how her son's teachers misdiagnosed him as color-blind—as possessing a partial or total inability to
distinguish between certain colors—only to discover later that he did
not have a visual disability. Rather, he was dutifully following his teachers' instructions about how to talk about race, effectively demonstrating
how racial color blindness is a learned behavior.

To settle a dispute between the children concerning whether Black
people could play "good guys," the teachers at her son's predominantly
white nursery school directed their students to disregard color. "It
doesn't matter," the teachers said, "whether you're black or white or red
or green or blue."[1] Race, they implied, was of no consequence because
color has no significance. The phrase "It doesn't matter" is an evocative
refrain, especially among people who subscribe to the ideology of color
blindness, and it serves as one of the many common phrases that constitute a color-blind performance. As several scholars have pointed out,
some well-known phrases in the color-blind playbook include the following: "I don't see color." "I don't think about color." "I don't care if he's

black." "Color makes no difference."[2] These claims are based on the idea that racial harmony rests on the absence of racial recognition and regard, and they often aim to situate race and racism elsewhere, somewhere beyond the speaker's immediate purview. Yet, as Williams explained in her story, such claims are a powerfully apocryphal phenomenon. "The very reason that the teachers had felt it necessary to impart this lesson [that color doesn't matter] in the first place," said Williams, "was that it did matter, and in predictably cruel ways."[3] The children had been engaging in a heated debate about race, fighting about the meaning of blackness and its alleged goodness or badness; and the teachers evaded that debate about race by imparting a lesson about an assortment of colors.

Responding to this lesson, Williams's son resisted identifying the color of objects even though he knew what the color was. When asked the color of grass, he responded, "I don't know." And, on another occasion, he said, "It makes no difference." The latter response was especially peculiar to Williams, and it signaled to her that her son was placing a value on *not* noticing color. Instead of stating that the grass was green, her son relied on a color-blind script of circumvention, a memorized text marked by selective absence, denial, and silence. Only after Williams had taken her son to an ophthalmologist to determine if he had a color-blind condition and had conducted her own personal investigation at his school did she discover that his teachers were the source of this profound color-blind performance, not her son's ocular capacity.[4]

Williams's anecdote captures how key aspects of color blindness are both seductive and dangerous and how the ideology of color blindness can circulate with such vitality even though its consequences can be dire. The fact that Williams's son learned about color blindness in the space of the classroom and then applied that knowledge at home and his other surroundings exemplifies both how individuals are taught color blindness and how they are persuaded by its ideological power. The teachers at his school were certainly not immune to its lure. Rather than engaging in a substantive conversation about why some children felt that Black people could not play "good guys" or educating their students to resist imbuing racial groups with notions of goodness or badness, the teachers—because they believed in color blindness or because they sought a facile solution to the children's dispute or both—made the pedagogical choice of claiming that color does not matter.

In addition to showing how color blindness is learned, the teachers' lesson reveals the practice of color blindness as a highly performative act: it comprises a distinctive manner of expression and behavior, a familiar use of language and rhetoric, and a particular way of looking, listening, and talking about race and racism. In *Racism without Racists*, the sociologist Eduardo Bonilla-Silva describes this performance as "the basic style of color blindness." "Subscribing to an ideology," he states, "is like wearing a piece of clothing. When you wear it, you also wear a certain style, a certain fashion, a certain way of presenting yourself to the world. The style of an ideology refers to its peculiar *linguistic manners and rhetorical strategies* (or *race talk*), to the technical tools that allow users to articulate its frames and story lines."[5] When the teachers translated the children's racial dispute into a *non*racial matter about black, white, red, green, and blue colors on a spectrum, they were engaging in a performance of color blindness, donning a particular ideological style and reciting a well-worn script.

This performance of color blindness is not limited to speech or race talk, however. The response of Williams's son suggests that the performance concerns perception and consciousness just as much as sound and speech; it matters not only what is said about race and what is heard about it but also how a person views or understands it. In the case of Williams's son, his performance of not recognizing color was tied to his lesson about the insignificance of race and misdiagnosed as an inability to visually distinguish the difference between colors by teachers who probably were not listening closely to what he was saying about color or to how his comments mirrored the language they gave him during the racial dispute with his classmates.

His white schoolmates, however, were lulled into what Williams described as "the false luxury of [a] prematurely imagined community."[6] Because of their privilege, white people are afforded this false luxury, whereas Black people are not. This difference is why, in the span of one year, three teachers "pathologized" Williams's son as having an "individual, physical limitation."[7] For faithfully adhering to his teachers' instruction, he, ironically, was marked as deficient rather than proficient. His teachers, beguiled by their own racial fantasies, had so easily forgotten the color lesson they imparted on their students that they misdiagnosed him as having a visual disability even though he was obeying their rule to the letter. I am struck by the larger implications of this story: by how a conflict about race can be easily taken out of context, by how seductive the language of color blindness can be for teachers and their pupils, and especially by how a seemingly innocent exchange can unwittingly affirm disparaging stereotypes about Black people through a failure to dispute those stereotypes outright.

Williams's story reveals how performances of color blindness rely heavily on visual, auditory, and communicative disavowals of racial difference: they entail a refusal to perceive, listen to, or speak about race and racism. The practice of color blindness, then, is procedural and behavioral in form. It is a performative mode of being or a way of living in the world, in which the failure to recognize race and racism serves as a person's modus operandi. As the political scientist Naomi Murakawa states, "If the problem of the twentieth century was, in W. E. B. Du Bois's famous words, 'the problem of the color line,' then the problem of the twenty-first century is the problem of colorblindness, the refusal to acknowledge the causes and consequences of enduring racial stratification."[8] Or, as the comparative race studies scholar Lynn Mie Itagaki argues, color blindness "is something one merely *pretends* to have as if it were a fraud."[9] Murakawa's emphasis on refusal and Itagaki's emphasis on fraudulence spotlight a specious element of a color-blind ideology: those who engage in it typically do not have a visual impairment; they are merely imposters for the cause, playing a significant role in the production of a deleterious US lie.

This chapter investigates the varied discriminatory performances of color blindness by calling attention to their profound irony—that is, how performances of color blindness ostensibly embrace disability and often claim racial equality yet ultimately perpetuate ableism and racism. I argue that what sustains the disabilities of the color line—anti-Black acts of violence, trauma, and stigmatization—are the doctrine and practice of color blindness: ableist performances of disability that have been deeply injurious to Black lives in the past and in the present. The reasons for assuming a color-blind ideology could be well-meaning or sinister. Regardless of intent, color blindness has wreaked havoc on communities of color in general and on the Black community in particular. The ableism of color-blind racism manifests itself in manifold ways: it occurs when a person performs color blindness by acting as if they do not recognize the material consequences of race or racism; it occurs when the ideology of color blindness masks the racial injuries of Black, disabled people; and it occurs when that ideology pathologizes Black, disabled people or traumatizes people of color writ large. Racial color blindness is especially injurious because it places those who resist it into the burdensome position of having to prove the manifestations of race and racism in a world that attempts to deny the material realities of both. More specifically, this ideology obscures the way one perceives and processes blackness and racism, and in certain instances, color blindness nourishes and shrouds antiblackness, allowing it to thrive and providing it perfect cover by cloaking racial injury in a manner that requires tremendous effort to expose.[10]

Organized into three sections, this chapter shows how the realms of the legal and social and the doctrinal and cultural are deeply entangled in US life. The first section examines Justice Marshall Harlan's dissent in *Plessy v. Ferguson* (1896), while the second and third sections examine the death and afterlives of Emmett Till and Eric Garner, respectively. To understand the full import of color blindness, I examine not only the use of color-blind constitutionalism within the law by focusing on what Harlan might have meant by using the term *color-blind* in his dissent but also the performance of color blindness within US culture by focusing on the disabling and deadly consequences of color blindness in the cases of Emmett Till and Eric Garner, both of whom were disabled. I conclude this chapter by considering the inclusivity of the work of contemporary Black activists, whose use of various technologies and whose attention to intersectionality demand the world to perceive Black people otherwise. Before considering how activists resist color blindness in the twentieth and twenty-first centuries, though, we must return to the nineteenth century, a time when the term *color-blind* came into formation.[11]

The Fictions of a Color-Blind Constitution

"Our Constitution is color-blind," wrote Justice Marshall Harlan in his dissent of *Plessy v. Ferguson*, "and neither knows nor tolerates classes among citizens."[12] Harlan was the lone voice of opposition in *Plessy*, a case that the US legal scholar Akhil Reed Amar has included as part of the "anti-canon" of Supreme Court decisions, a set of opinions that are generally "reviled" and "occupy the lowest circle of constitutional hell."[13] Yet Harlan's dissent and his signature term "color-blind" have amassed significance well beyond the nineteenth century. A range of commentators have embraced the doctrine of color blindness, inspiring various interpretations of the idea that work at cross-purposes. Some conservatives interpret color blindness in terms of neutrality, arguing that race should not function as an explicit determining factor in employment and education decisions.[14] Some liberals interpret the idea in terms of either equality or equity, advocating for programs that combat racial discrimination, inequality, and disparity throughout the nation.[15] Some civil rights leaders imagine it as an aspirational vision of the US future, a dream of living in a world where, as Dr. Martin Luther King Jr. once proclaimed, his children "will not be judged by the color of their skin but by the content of their character."[16]

These versions offer competing views that all serve to romanticize color blindness in promoting the particular aims of each group, and all interpretations overlook one remarkable fact: despite Harlan's lofty proclamation, our Constitution is not color-blind and has always known and tolerated classes among citizens; any understanding of color blindness that does not acknowledge this reality is based on a lie.[17] When the Constitution was ratified in 1788, it calculated representation "by adding to the whole Number of free Persons, including those bound to Service for a Term of Years, and excluding Indians not taxed, three-fifths of all other Persons." Although the Constitution neither expressly used the words *white* or *Black* nor mentioned *slave* or *slavery*, the clause that prescribed provisions for "free Persons" and "three-fifths of all other Persons" who are unfree was understood to distinguish between white people and enslaved Black people. The Constitution also distinguished between taxed people and untaxed Native Americans, including within the supreme law of the United States a set of practices that relied heavily on a hierarchical and racialized structure. The Three-Fifths Clause of the Constitution, which was a compromise between southern and northern state delegates regarding how the enslaved should be counted within a state's total population for the purposes of representation and taxation, has certainly complicated the citizenship of Black people. As Elizabeth Alexander notes, enslaved Black folks historically have had to confront a Constitution that legally defined them as partial persons while simultaneously understanding themselves as whole persons.[18] And by the time Harlan wrote his dissenting opinion in *Plessy*, the Reconstruction Amendments were part of the US Constitution, and the Fifteenth Amendment prohibited discrimination explicitly "on account of race, color, or previous condition of servitude"—yet another example of how the Constitution is not color-blind.

These facts, along with the ambiguity of Harlan's discursive and citational practices, have made it difficult to determine exactly what Harlan meant by "color-blind." Harlan's color-blind sentiment was inspired by the brief of Albion Tourgée—an American writer, politician, and, significantly, the attorney for the plaintiff Homer A. Plessy in *Plessy v. Ferguson*. In his brief, Tourgée wrote, "Justice is pictured blind and her daughter, the Law, ought at least to be color-blind."[19] The historian Mark Elliott argues, "This arresting turn of phrase caught the attention of Justice John Marshall Harlan who borrowed it for his powerful lone dissent."[20] Tourgée's line is an artful turn of phrase, but it is imprecise on at least one point: Justice is pictured blindfolded; all she would have to do is put down her scales and lift up her cloth to wield her sword with impunity. It is unclear whether that detail regarding Justice's blindfold would have affected Harlan's dissent, for his stated language and reasoning in his dissent were both ambiguous and contradictory. He did not explicitly define the term "color-blind," explain how color blindness could be achieved, or intend for the idea of color blindness to apply to all races. In fact, as Elliott notes, "Justice Harlan never elaborated on his color-blind doctrine outside of his *Plessy* dissent," and "he never used this phrase either before or after it."[21] Harlan did, however, situate his claim about the color-blind Constitution between two other remarks in *Plessy* that complicate his understanding of race, vision, sensoria, and jurisprudence within the United States.

First, before commenting that the law is color-blind, Harlan attempted to disaggregate racial matters in the nation from racial matters in the law. He wrote, "The white race deems itself to be the dominant race in this country. And so it is, in prestige, in achievements, in education, in wealth and in power. So, I doubt not, it will continue to be for all time. . . . But in view of the Constitution, in the eye of the law, there is in this country no superior, dominant, ruling class of citizens. There is no caste here. Our Constitution is color-blind."[22] Here, Harlan essentially claimed that dominant races and classes of people did (and could) exist in the country, but this racial "caste" system did not (and could not) exist within the eye of the law. The law's visual acuity, according to Harlan, had to be detached from reality, narrowed in focus, and skewed in perspective. He thus created a distinction between the role of race within the law and within the country that was not only absurd but also nearly impossible to maintain.

Second, after claiming that "all citizens are equal before the law" and the "law regards man as man, and takes no account of his surroundings or of his color when his civil rights are guaranteed by the supreme law of the land," Harlan remarked that one ethnic group warranted special scrutiny. "There is a race so different from our own," he wrote, "that we do not permit those belonging to it to become citizens of the United States. Persons belonging to it are, with few exceptions, absolutely excluded from our country. I allude to the Chinese race. But by the statute in question, a Chinaman can ride in the same passenger coach with white citizens of the United States, while citizens of the black race in Louisiana, many of whom, perhaps, risked their lives for the preservation of the Union" cannot.[23] Harlan's commentary about Chinese people in *Plessy* in addition to his Chinese jurisprudence throughout his career demonstrate that his concept of color blindness was not all-encompassing; there was at least one group that he believed less deserving of the privileges and immunities of citizenship and personal liberty.[24] This anti-Chinese sentiment signals a problem in Harlan's vision, a deficiency in his interpretation of what constitutes US citizenship and racial equality.

Similarly to the Constitution, Harlan's racial vision was not color-blind—despite its pretense of being so. Harlan made a resounding call for racial inclusivity within the eye of the law even as he recognized and condoned white supremacy. He preached about the righteousness of racial equality as he supported inequality for certain ethnic groups. He proclaimed that the Constitution was color-blind even though he knew that the country was not. The roots of his concept of color blindness were clearly mired in a messy racial and ethnic politics. The legal scholar Gabriel J. Chin describes Harlan's color blindness as "backed by bad reasoning, bad policy, and bad principles" and states that after producing bad practices for over a century, his dissent "should be overruled."[25]

My focus on Harlan's *Plessy* dissent and, by extension, the Constitution is meant to highlight color blindness as a performance of disability and a catalyst for racial injury and trauma. Each text affected a racial blindness that contradicted its racist sentiments and policies. The Constitution that was ratified in 1788 made no explicit mention of Black people, Latinx folks, or Asian Americans and was markedly silent on the subject of slavery, yet it set in motion a legal system that would have injurious racial consequences for Black, Indigenous, and other people of color for centuries. Harlan professed in his dissent a wish for color blindness within the law and for an end to legalized racial segregation, but he deployed the law in a way that both distinguished between particular racial and ethnic groups and discriminated against them.

This brand of color blindness, in its selective omission and deceptive vision of race as well as its lack of concern about racial injustice, violence, and discrimination, has had just as detrimental of an effect on Black lives as did decades of racial segregation. One of Harlan's gravest missteps was failing to consider fully the consequences of a color-blind Constitution in an anti-Black United States. In *Plessy*, his principal argument was against racial segregation on trains, but he also understood that segregation laws would have reverberating effects in other key spaces, such as roads, neighborhoods, courtrooms, streetcars, vehicles, legislative halls, or any other space (public or private) where people of different races come in contact.[26] His decision to cast the law as blind, however, made it difficult for the law to remedy racial injustice, and it left people of color (including Black people, whose civil rights he was presumably fighting for in *Plessy*) subject to harm and injury throughout the twentieth and twenty-first centuries.

One would not think that a word with such a flawed and contradictory etymology would have become the standard by which we legislate the lives of US citizens. Yet color-blind constitutionalism has been utilized in antithetical ways for more than a century. Sometimes the doctrine has been used for the purpose of ending state-sponsored discrimination against people of color, and sometimes it has been leveraged for the purpose of asserting "that racially progressive policies [like affirmative action] were discriminating against white Americans," as Theodore R. Johnson, a senior fellow at the Brennan Center for Justice, observes.[27] On the one hand, arguing for the plaintiff in *Brown v. Board of Educa-*

tion, the case that ruled against racial segregation, Thurgood Marshall and his fellow appellants declared, "That the Constitution is color blind is our dedicated belief."[28] On the other hand, in the majority opinion in the US Supreme Court case *Parents Involved in Community Schools v. Seattle School District No. 1* (2007), Chief Justice John Roberts invoked color-blind constitutionalism to essentially rule against desegregation by relying on a tautology: "The way to stop discrimination on the basis of race is to stop discriminating on the basis of race."[29] The ability to use the same doctrine to achieve opposite goals stems, as Chin argues, from Harlan's bad reasoning and bad policy. Yet the lure of color blindness is not limited to the law. The doctrine has informed US culture and behavior, too. It has influenced how many Americans speak and think about race and race relations. Indeed, color blindness and antiblackness work as coconspirators.

This conspiratorial relationship has prompted several Black activists and scholars to call for a restoration of the senses, to insist on the recognition of race and racism as one means of challenging racial oppression and violence. According to the legal scholar and civil rights advocate Michelle Alexander, "Colorblindness, though widely touted as the solution, is actually the problem." What we need, she says, is "a commitment to color consciousness," one that "places faith in our capacity as humans to show care and concern for others, even as we are fully cognizant of race and possible racial differences."[30] The sociologist Alondra Nelson likewise believes that color consciousness could be the key ingredient for racial reconciliation and justice: "combating color-blind racism requires the restoration of color-*vision*—that is, the return to visibility of historic and continued racial inequalities."[31] There can be no reconciliation, Nelson argues, without a commitment to acknowledging the truth of historical injuries in need of repair.[32]

The activism of the family and supporters of Till and Garner—in particular, their use of technology—is meant to counter the practices of color blindness and antiblackness to make the truth known. Mamie Till-Mobley's decision to distribute photographs of her son's corpse and the Till family's decision to exhume Emmett Till's body to perform DNA testing almost fifty years after he had been buried were a response to conspiracy theories that he might still be alive. The Garner family's activism and wrongful death lawsuit, Ramsey Orta's recording of Garner's killing, and the wave of protests across the nation were responses to the New York Police Department's refusal to admit any wrongdoing and callous disregard for the lives of Black people. What precisely led Officer Daniel Pantaleo to imagine Eric Garner's body as such an imminent threat that he put him in a choke hold, and why did he and the other officers at the scene fail to regard Garner's gasps for air? Despite overwhelming evidence against the suspects in the cases of Till and Garner, why has no one been convicted of charges related to their deaths? What did the jurors fail to recognize, and what is the general public refusing to acknowledge? These are the questions I address in the next two sections, focusing first on Emmett Till and then on Eric Garner.

I focus on the tragic killings of Till and Garner for three primary reasons. First, they occurred when the ideology of color blindness was at a peak in US society: Till's lynching came on the heels of *Brown v. Board of Education*, the landmark 1954 US Supreme Court decision that weakened the separate-but-equal doctrine of *Plessy* and has been generally recognized as a watershed moment in color-blind constitutionalism. Garner's killing occurred during Barack Obama's presidency, a time that many political commentators misguidedly marked as the emergence of a postracial United States.[33] Second, the lack of care that Till and Garner receive is related to their intersectional identities as disabled, Black males, for it is not only their race that is disregarded but also their disabilities. In the cases of Till and Garner, their disabilities garnered no compassion or medical or therapeutic interventions from the people who killed them. Third, Till's and Garner's deaths galvanized two notable movements for social justice: the civil rights movement and the Movement for Black Lives (M4BL). In response to the varied performances of color blindness by local officials and state representatives—including those of Tallahatchie County Sheriff H. C. Strider (in the case of Till) and Republican congressman Peter Thomas King (in the case of Garner)—activists of both movements relied on technology to encourage those who engage in color blindness to recognize its dangers. These public performances are why Black scholars and activists have been calling for more awareness of the intersectional identities of Black people by demanding color consciousness, not color blindness.

"Let the World See What I've Seen": Looking Again at the Corpse of Emmett Till

His is a familiar story for many Americans. At the age of fourteen, in August 1955, Emmett Louis Till, while on summer vacation in Money, Mississippi, from his home in Chicago, Illinois, was killed after being falsely accused of flirting with a white woman. It is a narrative that many of us have heard or read or seen several times over. Some of us have had conversations with family and friends about his death. Some of us have read about him in newspapers, magazines, novels, poems, memoirs, and museums. Some of us have seen the horrific images of his mutilation. Some of us, who attended his open-casket funeral, have even bore witness to his maimed body—saw his corpse up close, smelled the stench of his dead flesh, and heard (or contributed to) the chorus of mourning emanating from within the Roberts Temple Church of God in Christ. And a few of us have been all of the above—a listener, teller, reader, spectator, and witness—and, therefore, intimately understand the compounding seriality of Till's death. The story of Till's lynching has been repeated so often that repetition is one of its aesthetic features—that is, it is difficult to talk about Till's injured body without describing the violence he endured or referring to what has already been said about his brutal death. To write a narrative about Till, according to Saidiya Hartman, is "to tell an impossible story" made more so by "the impossibility of its telling," for narrating Till's lynching entails wrestling with difficult questions, such as "What are the kinds of stories to be told by those and about those who live in such an intimate relationship with death?" and "How does one revisit the scene of subjection without replicating the grammar of violence?"[34] For those of us committed to telling these stories, our primary means of reconciling this tension involve selective narration and a reckoning with the limitations of loss: we can choose which stories to tell and which not, and when we tell those stories, we must do so with respect to "the limits of what cannot be known" and "fully cognizant that what has been destroyed cannot be restored."[35]

Attuned to these challenges, I return to Till's lynching in part to explain why we keep returning to Till's lynching and in part to consider how the ritual of looking at his corpse and of examining his death is rooted in and underpinned by the violence of color blindness, the persistent *disavowal* of and the utter *refusal* to acknowledge racism and racial terror. This violence is evident in the defense attorney's refusal to recognize or identify Till's body because of its decomposition. This violence is evident in Sheriff H. C. Strider's refusal to identify Till's body as Black, suggesting that the corpse could have been that of a white person. This violence is evident in the failure to believe the testimony of Till's mother and other family members, who gave crucial details about his abduction and identified the corpse as Till's. Because no credence was given to the family's testimony, they, like so many other Black people who have been disbelieved, turned to other resources to verify their testimony and authenticate their voices. The photographs of Till's corpse and the reliance on DNA testing attempt to compel the US public to recognize and speak about the racial violence enacted against Till's body that was apparently unrecognizable otherwise. This process of making visible that which is disavowed again and again is what makes color blindness so incredibly injurious; it incites mourners to use Till's body in a way that induces a compounding sense of loss in order seek a closure that is repeatedly denied. As the literary and material culture scholar Myisha Priest argues, "We endeavor to find meaning in the body to provide justice for the crime committed against Till, but what justice might be is contested, fraught, and, finally, at odds with the enactment of justice on behalf of black subjects constituted in pain."[36] Such "fugitive justice," a justice that is "elusive and perceptually dubious" and "call[s] attention to the incommensurability between pain and compensation," as Stephen Best and Saidiya Hartman put it, might be about as much as we can achieve in the face of such irreparable loss.[37] If so, what possibilities does fugitive justice provide that injustice inevitably forecloses? This is the work I undertake as I tell a story about the afterlife of Emmett Till, in which I consider what the family's turn to science and technology offers them in a country where color blindness operates as both doctrine and custom.

* * *

On June 1, 2005, nearly fifty years after Emmett Till's corpse was buried at Burr Oak Cemetery in Alsip, Illinois, the Federal Bureau of Investigation (FBI) exhumed it and performed an autopsy, dissecting his corpse for the purpose of uncovering additional details about his death. An autopsy, for some obscure reason, was not performed in 1955, the year of Till's death, which meant that neither the cause of Till's death nor the identification of his body had been corroborated by scientific evidence. Of course, Emmett Till's family and supporters had very little doubt about how he died or which main parties were responsible for killing him, and they had no doubt whether the battered body pulled from the Tallahatchie River was his. Moses Wright, Emmett Till's granduncle, identified J. W. Milam and Roy Bryant in court as the two men who abducted Till at gunpoint from his home. The National Association for the Advancement of Colored People (NAACP) and members of the Black press conducted a secret investigation in 1955 and secured testimony from several eyewitnesses including Willie Reed, who stated that he saw Milam in a truck with Till entering the farm on the Clint Shurden Plantation near Drew, Mississippi, and that he heard sounds of someone being whipped while inside a barn on the plantation the morning that Till was taken from Moses Wright's home. And in the absence of a coroner's report, Mamie Till-Mobley played the role, as she described in her memoir, of a "forensic doctor," examining her son's corpse from head to toe in order to provide a positive identification and to see with her own eyes what his killers had done to his body.[38]

Given that Till-Mobley identified Till's body and personal effects, that there were eyewitness accounts linking Bryant and Milam to the kidnapping of Till, and that both men confessed in 1956 (just months after being acquitted for his murder) to killing Till in *Look* magazine, the belated timing of the FBI's autopsy and investigation left commentators and family members befuddled, wondering, Why now? What precisely was the FBI hoping to resolve in a fifty-year-old case? What new information did it possess that caused it to reopen the case and exhume Till's body? What could it discern from his DNA or glean from his autopsy that was not already apparent in the testimonies of his family?[39]

"The first and foremost thing we're trying to do," said Frank Bochte, an FBI spokesman, "is to put to rest any theories that the body inside there is not Emmett Till. We would like to settle that issue once and for all." That theory was put forth by Tallahatchie County Sheriff H. C. Strider. Before the grand jury indicted Milam and Bryant for Till's murder, Sheriff Strider told the press that the body recovered from the river might not be Till's, that the body appeared to be that of a grown man rather than a boy, that the corpse was so badly deteriorated he could not discern whether the victim was Black or white, and that Emmett Till might still be alive. When he testified for the defense, which was a highly unusual move, he made similar claims in an effort to cast doubt on the identification of Till's body.[40]

But there was enough existing evidence at the time to disprove all of Strider's theories. First and foremost, Mamie Till-Mobley's identification of her son as well as the discovery of his ring, which had "LT" (the initials of Emmett Till's biological father, Louis Till) engraved on it, confirmed the identity of his body. Second, before testifying for the defense during the trial, Strider made key decisions that gainsaid his remarks about the uncertainty of Till's race and identity. For example, he released Till's corpse to a Black mortician, which, as Till-Mobley argues, "he never would have done if he thought the victim might not be black."[41] Then, he allowed the county to certify the death certificate, and he signed it on September 1, 1955, a couple of days before he spoke with the press and cast suspicions about the identity of Till's body. According to Till-Mobley, "The death certificate showed Emmett's full name, his race, his age, the names of his parents, the date of death, the cause of death," all the "information that contradicted everything he said" to the press.[42]

Taken together, Strider's actions are an example of color-blind racism in the twentieth-century United States. Strider merely pretended as if he did not know the race of Till's body, and his performance was enough to undermine the existing evidence against Bryant and Milam. When he signed Till's death certificate and released his corpse to a Black undertaker, Strider clearly identified Till's race, age, and lifelessness. Only after making these crucial decisions did Strider have difficulty distinguishing white from Black, man from boy, and the living from the dead. As implausible as Strider's theories seem, they were so effective that the FBI felt it necessary to address them fifty years later. Even in the twenty-first century, Strider's performance of color blindness was so persuasive that presumably only science could disprove his theory.

In addition to proving the identity of Till's body, the FBI also claimed that it wanted to determine the cause of death—even though it was widely believed that he had been shot, due to the gaping hole in his head—and that it hoped to find additional evidence that might link Till to his killers. Yet the age of Till's remains made it unlikely the FBI would recover much, if any, new evidence. In the end, the 464-page FBI autopsy report (which is part of an 8,000-page file accumulated during its investigation) confirmed two main findings: the casket contained Emmett Till's body, and the cause of death was a gunshot wound to the head. There were other details in the report about Till's skull, leg, and wrist fractures, and it included accounts of his killers' confessions and a few lesser-known allegations; but, in general, the report was so heavily redacted that it did not provide insightful information to those who were closely following the case. Names and identifying information about living people were removed, and the autopsy photographs of Till's injuries were not included in order to, according to FBI spokeswoman Denise Ballew, "protect the privacy interests of the surviving family members."[43] The investigation also did not lead to the arrest of additional suspects, and in February 2007, the grand jury in Leflore, Mississippi, declined to issue any new indictments.

This result was not the outcome hoped for by Till's family and supporters. Some considered the investigation as nothing more than a symbolic gesture or grandstand event, a delinquent act of atonement with almost no salutary benefits. Others expected more substantial evidence to be revealed and believed that DNA testing could be their holy grail. Simeon Wright—who is the first cousin of Emmett Till's mother and who shared a room with Till on August 28, 1955, the day he was kidnapped from Moses Wright's home in the wee hours of the morning— supported the exhumation of the teenager's body, hoping that others would be prosecuted if they were found to be involved. "If you can't prove that this is Emmett, the State of Mississippi is not going to reopen this case," said Wright. "I want to see someone prosecuted because if you wink at this, you might as well wink at every murderer."[44] Supporters like Keith Beauchamp felt similarly. "I truly believe," he said, "there's forensic evidence that could possibly link others who were involved." Beauchamp is one of the filmmakers whose documentary *The Untold Story of Emmett Louis Till* revived interest in the Till case, and he met with the Justice Department to encourage it to reopen the case: "I'm hoping it will bring justice for the family and bring them closure."[45] The particular kind of closure that Wright and Beauchamp expected from the FBI's investigation, however, never came. After the autopsy report was released, Wright conceded, "There are some things that will never be resolved about the Till case until someone comes forward." "Maybe," he added, "they'll just take it to the grave."[46]

Wright almost got his wish: for one of the participants involved in Till's death to come forward and clarify what happened decades earlier. A year after Wright's interview, Carolyn Bryant Donham (formerly Carolyn Bryant) reportedly confessed to the historian Timothy Tyson, in September 2008, that the most sensational parts of her testimony at trial—that Till "grabbed her hand forcefully across the candy counter," "chased her down the counter," "clutched her narrow waist tightly with both hands," and "uttered obscenities" toward her—were all fabricated. "That part's not true," she told Tyson, referring to her testimony recorded in the trial transcript, which was finally released in 2007 after it went missing immediately following the trial in 1955. "If that part was not true," Tyson asked, "what did happen that evening decades earlier?" "I want to tell you," Donham responded. "Honestly, I just don't remember. It was fifty years ago. You tell these stories for so long that they seem true." "But that part," she repeated, "is not true." These key details of Donham's confession were not revealed until 2017, nearly ten years after her interview with Tyson, when they were published in Tyson's book *The Blood of Emmett Till*.[47]

Carolyn Bryant Donham's belated confession, unfortunately, is shrouded in mystery. Donham, now in her late eighties, never publicly retracted her trial testimony or stated that she lied about what happened, and her current whereabouts are unknown, "kept secret by her family."[48] Donham's daughter-in-law, Marsha Bryant, who was present for the two tape-recorded interviews between Tyson and Donham, said that her mother-in-law "never recanted." And, apparently, the crucial part of Donham's interview, where she says, "That part's not true," was not recorded. Tyson admitted, "It is true that that part is not on tape because I was setting up the tape recorder"[49] Finally, according to a note in Tyson's book, Donham's unpublished memoir is being held in the Southern Historical Collection at the University of North Carolina at Chapel Hill library archives, which, at Donham's request, will be closed to the public until 2038.[50] It appears that Donham will take what happened to the grave after all, just as Simeon Wright suspected.

However, none of this information would have been known in 2007, when Till's family was still hoping that DNA testing would reveal crucial details about his death. Considering how DNA is regarded in our cultural imagination as well as how the authorities have invalidated the family's testimony, the expectation that the FBI's autopsy and use of DNA testing might produce the case's smoking gun was more than merely wishful thinking. As Alondra Nelson observes, DNA is granted a "special status" in the world, imbued with such an incredible social power that many people think of it "as the final arbiter of truth of identity." One need only look at the language we use to describe it: "code of codes," "the blueprint," the human "instruction book," and "the secret of life."[51] Although the "social life of DNA" has a diffuse and double-edged history, Nelson points out that it has often been the source of reconciliation.[52] DNA analysis has been definitively employed in biomedicine, genetic testing, and criminal justice settings. In the case of the latter, it has played a key, dual role in exoneration and conviction, sometimes producing outcomes that lead to social justice and racial reconciliation— restoring "lineages, families, and knowledge of the past" and making "political claims in the present"—and sometimes not.[53] Despite some initial familial tension regarding whether Till's body should be dug up from the grave, the possibility of justice and reconciliation (through either prosecution of other suspects or a desire for closure) was what led family members to authorize the exhumation—though they understood that it meant dredging up the past once again.[54]

DNA analysis, then, offered the Till family another way of looking at Till's body. Part of "the DNA mystique," as the sociologist Dorothy Nelkin and the historian M. Susan Lindee describe, is its "powerful, magical, and even sacred" ability to unveil the truth about a person's body.[55] Ellen Samuels agrees with Nelkin and Lindee. "The power of DNA in the cultural imaginary," Samuels states, "has already formed the basis for twentieth- and twenty-first-century fantasies of identification," in the attempt to "definitively identify bodies, to place them in categories delineated by race, gender, or ability status, and then to validate that placement through a verifiable, biological mark of identity."[56] An all-seeing, omnipotent, truth-telling technique like this one would have been useful for the Till family. DNA testing could have been used as indisputable proof of what they have been asserting all along. Testing Till's DNA would force the federal government to believe what it apparently could not accept from the testimony of Mamie Till-Mobley: the corpse pulled from the Tallahatchie River and buried in the grave was that of her son, Emmett Till. If any family has understood the power and significance of using technology, it is the family of Emmett Till. Their use of technology has been essential to their activism (even if it meant looking at the mutilated face of a child who was their own kin).

Indeed, the autopsy in 2005 was not the first time Emmett Till's corpse endured close scrutiny. In 1955, Mamie Till-Mobley made two crucial decisions that transformed the trajectory of the civil rights movement of the 1950s and '60s and inspired protests across the nation, particularly in the South. First, she decided to hold an open-casket funeral, where it has been estimated that somewhere between one hundred thousand and six hundred thousand people viewed Till's dead body over the course of four days.[57] According to the literary and sexuality studies scholar Dagmawi Woubshet, "Open caskets forced the public to see the dead it disavowed, while honoring those disprized dead with public rites and recognition."[58] These dual aspirations probably motivated Mamie Till-Mobley's actions. Her second important decision involved collaborating with the NAACP and the Black press (*Jet*, *Ebony*, and the *Chicago Defender*) and allowing the press to publish photographs of her son's corpse. These photographs provided a detailed portrayal of Till's brutal killing, and the depiction of racial violence in them left an indelible impression on the US public.

Mamie Till-Mobley instinctively knew that the public should no longer turn away from anti-Black violence. When A. A. Raynor, one of the most respected Black funeral directors in Chicago, asked Till-Mobley if she wanted to have a closed-casket funeral or whether she wanted him to retouch Till and make her son's body appear more presentable, she was firm in her reply. "No," she said. "Let the world see what I've seen." "I didn't really know," she added, "what was motivating me, what was making me do what I was doing during this period. It was something I can't explain, something working through me, something that would cause me to say things that would only become clear to me the instant I'd speak them." While it was difficult for her to imagine people looking in horror at the sight of her son's deformed corpse, her intuition told her that keeping his casket closed would diminish the public's view and understanding of the scope of racial violence. "We had averted our eyes far too long," she wrote, "turning away from the ugly reality facing us as a nation. I know, because I was guilty of the same thing. But to let that continue, to think that even one more mother, one more mother's son, would have to suffer, well, that was too much for me to bear. People had to face my son and realize just how twisted, how distorted, how terrifying, race hatred could be."[59]

Viewing Emmett Till's corpse and examining his death required understanding his killing as a lynching, as part of a long, heinous, and systemic history of US racial terrorism that was unexceptional in its violence, systematic in its approach, and methodical in its execution. In the case of Till, lynching referred to more than the beating, whipping, and mutilation of his body. The way Milam and Bryant snatched him from his great-uncle's home shows that lynching often entailed an invasion of the Black domestic space, a destruction of the home as either a safe or sacred place. The tools and techniques utilized in Till's killing—the .45 caliber pistol, M12 and M15 ammunition, and barbed wire lashed to the cotton-gin fan—demonstrate that the practice of lynching was a modern enterprise, not some relic from the past or throwback from some bygone era.[60] The fact that Milam and Bryant were acquitted of both the murder and kidnapping charges shows that the life of lynching thrived on exposure and secrecy, publicity and cover-ups. Lynching was a social practice that everyone knew of and some even witnessed but that very few publicly spoke about and others (even those who relished participating in it) outright denied. It was, as Jacqueline Goldsby persuasively argues in her book on lynching, "a spectacular secret."[61]

The NAACP and the Black press understood this double-sided dynamic of lynching and thus the importance of using the language of lynching to describe Till's killing. Roy Wilkins, the former executive secretary of the NAACP, did not mince words when he characterized what happened to Till: "It would appear from this lynching that the State of Mississippi had decided to maintain white supremacy by murdering children. The killers of the boy felt free to lynch him because there is in the entire state no restraining influence of decency."[62] In the issue that included photographs of Till's corpse, *Jet* magazine, a Black news and lifestyle publication, also described Till's death as a "lynching" and his killers as members of a "lynch party."[63] Mamie Till-Mobley did not initially consider it significant to characterize her son's torture as a lynching. In fact, she thought it was odd to debate whether his "vicious torture/killing" constituted a "lynching" or a "murder"; understandably, it was challenging for her to look beyond the bare fact that her son was brutally and senselessly killed. Eventually, though, she came to realize that this language matters, "that it could make a big difference" to see her "son's killing as part of a pattern" of US racism, as part of a network that linked her son's death to those who died before him and those who would die after.[64] Looking at the condition of Till's corpse involved not only viewing it (for those who saw the photographs) or witnessing it (for those who attended the funeral) but also describing it in ways that linked his death to the litany of other Black lives violently lost as a result of racism. Referring to his death as a lynching meant understanding it as symptomatic of US racial violence en masse rather than as a singular, isolated event. Because the criminal justice system failed to convict Bryant and Milam, the term *murder* in a strict legal sense does not apply to Till's killing—yet another cruel example of how an unjust color-blind legal system conceals crime. In the absence of *murder*, however, the term *lynching* records and archives a history of racial violence and holds the law accountable for the violence it often refuses to recognize. This "idea of 'looking'—together with the attendant practice of 'seeing' that [Till-Mobley] appealed to," argues Goldsby, "foregrounds how lynching importantly organized American ways of seeing." Goldsby asks, "What would 'the whole world' know that it couldn't comprehend otherwise without the aid of a photograph? . . . What discursive shifts had occurred . . . for [Till-Mobley] to insist on technologies of seeing and sight as the most effective way to express moral outrage and to mount political action to redress her loss?"[65]

One significant shift was the discourse and ideology of color blindness, which, I contend, compelled Mamie Till-Mobley to keep her son's casket open and distribute photographs of his corpse in the Black press as a form of redress. Her use of technologies that reproduce the sight of and demand recognizing antiblackness was incited by an ideology rooted in a refusal to see race and racism. The photograph offered a visual representation of the dangers of racial desegregation in a racist world. At a time when it appeared that the nation was making racial progress, Till's killing signaled a profound stasis in US racial relations. The timing of Till's death was significant because it followed the *Brown v. Board of Education* decision, which, largely due to the doll experiments of Mamie and Kenneth Clark, forced the Supreme Court to interrogate the suffering and pain of Black children.

In 1954, the year before Till was killed, *Brown v. Board of Education* declared racial segregation in public schools to be unconstitutional. The *Brown* decision is often perceived as fulfilling the promise of Justice Harlan's dissent in *Plessy*, which called for a color-blind society that "neither knows nor tolerates classes among citizens." But, similarly to Harlan, the Supreme Court justices in *Brown* had an obscured racial vision. In *Brown*, Chief Justice Earl Warren declared, "Separate educational facilities are inherently unequal," but he made no mention of the racism or racists that supported segregation.[66] *Brown* made it appear as if desegregation alone would undo the damage of *Plessy* by papering over the ongoing material consequences of racism. The Court interpreted racial oppression as a procedural matter, concluding that desegregation would eliminate the discrimination of and feelings of inferiority in Black children that stemmed from segregation, without acknowledging that segregation itself was a by-product of systemic racism. In large part due to the doll experiments of two African American psychologists, the Supreme Court in *Brown* declared racial desegregation as the key to ending the suffering of Black children.

The staged melodrama of the Clarks' doll tests provided a perfect backdrop for the Supreme Court's decision.[67] The Court argued in its opinion in *Brown* that racial segregation, which caused the suffering of Black boys and girls, must be terminated and that desegregation, which the justices believed could alleviate the children's suffering, must be implemented as quickly as possible. They effectively crafted a narrative that posited racial desegregation as a palliative for Black childhood suffering and trauma.

The photographs of Emmett Till's corpse, however, relayed an alarming story. Racial desegregation alone could not alleviate the pain and suffering of Black children. In fact, Till's death showed that the certain contact and interaction between Black and white people resulted in racial injury and death, particularly in the South. In *The Evidence of Things Not Seen*, James Baldwin situated Till's death within a historical context that partially explains why Till's story was so arresting and why it captured the nation's attention in such a dramatic way. "The *only* reason, after all, that we heard of Emmett Till," Baldwin wrote, "is that he happened to come whistling down the road—an obscure country road—at the very moment the road found itself most threatened: at the very beginning of the segregation-desegregation—not yet integration—crisis, under the knell of the Supreme Court's *all deliberate speed*, when various 'moderate' Southern governors were asking Black people to segregate themselves, *for the good of both races*, and when the President of the United States was, on this subject, so eloquently silent that one *knew* that, in his heart, he did not approve of a mongrelization of the races."[68] In this particular time and setting, the false accusation that Till flirted with a white woman prompted his kidnapping and killing, and it incited whites' anxieties about sexual violence and stoked their fears of free and gallant Black boys. Racial desegregation absent a commitment to racial justice was a bandage, not a cure. To end the violence against and the pain and suffering of Black children (and adults), the law would have to implement a plan that directly addressed racial animus. Till's lynching was an act of racism—something that racial desegregation could not completely resolve—and his mother's decision to display his corpse brought critical attention to this matter. The anti-Black violence during the crisis of desegregation, as Baldwin's book title describes, amounted to the evidence of things not seen by those who practice color blindness.

This anti-Black violence did not escape the notice of the Black community. In fact, the brutal lynching and racial violence depicted in Till's photographs haunted their memories and imaginations. A number of Black writers have written about the indelible quality of the photographs of Emmett Till's corpse that circulated in *Jet* magazine and the Black press. Muhammad Ali, John Edgar Wideman, Karla F. C. Holloway, Houston A. Baker Jr., and Charlayne Hunter-Gault have vividly recalled how the photographs and details of Till's story traumatized them as children and as adults, seeping into their dreams, nightmares, and consciousness. Wideman, for instance, describes a chilling nightmare that has troubled him since he was a boy, in which a monster with a face of terror stalks him until he awakes screaming: "I've come to believe the face in the dream I can't bear to look upon is Emmett Till's. Emmett Till's face, crushed, chewed, mutilated, his gray face swollen, water dripping from holes punched in his skull."[69] In *Turning South Again*, Baker describes the "grim details of an Illinois black teenager mutilated and killed in Money, Mississippi" as part of the "feverish ghoulish narrative collective unconscious of" what Baker calls the "Blue Man," a grotesque figure that he imagined as stalking and preying on the minds of Black southern boys like himself.[70] And in Hunter-Gault's memoir *In My Place*, she recounts Till's killing as an invasion of her childhood. "From time to time," she writes, "things happened that intruded on our protected reality. The murder of Emmett Till was one such instance. . . . Pictures of his limp, watersoaked body in the newspapers and in *Jet*, Black America's weekly news bible, were worse than any image we had ever seen outside of a horror movie."[71]

These writers' memories of Till's lynching reflect how his death lives on in the consciousness of Black folks and how it traumatizes them. This trauma is a long-standing and intergenerational one. According to Bessel van der Kolk, a professor of psychiatry at Boston University and founder of the Trauma Center in Massachusetts, "Trauma is not just an event that took place sometime in the past; it is also the imprint left by that experience on mind, brain, and body. This imprint has ongoing consequences for how the human organism manages to survive in the present." Understanding how "the body keeps the score" and how "the memory of trauma is encoded in the viscera, in heartbreaking and gut-wrenching emotions," as van der Kolk asserts, is significant because it stresses how Till's lynching should not be understood as a fleeting, individualized moment for Black folks.[72] Put differently, the spectacular violence of Till's killing has extensive transference. Clearly, his lynching left an imprint on the memories of Wideman, Baker, and Hunter-Gault that they would always remember. How could they forget?

For a Black person in the United States, looking at Emmett Till's photographs required confronting your own looming mortality, recognizing that any misstep could lead to your lynching, result in your cracked skull, the demolishment of your face. Looking at Till meant looking at his mother, Mamie, whose grief and melancholy were matched only by her conviction and resolve, whose love for her son and commitment to justice fueled her lifelong activism. Looking at Till meant looking closely at your mother, your father, your sister, your brother, aunt, uncle, niece, nephew, partner, daughter, son, cousin, grandmother, grandfather; it meant taking stock of your entire family, lavishing them with love and care while acknowledging the capacity of the state and anti-Black vigilantes to harm them and yourself. For the people who attended Till's open-casket funeral, who viewed his corpse close-up, looking at him produced cries of despair and shouts of mercy. Some people passed out; others doubled over in convulsion with tears.

Looking at Till's corpse entailed listening as well, and the photographs, according to the poet and cultural theorist Fred Moten, amplified the senses. Even those who were not at the funeral, even those who were not alive in 1955, could see his dead body and, as Moten asserts, could hear sounds of anguish. Moten argues that Till's photographs bear "a phonic substance," an element that bonds looking with listening and that a central focus on the ocular only obscures; his photographs, particularly the photograph of Till lying in the casket, influence ontology. "How can this photograph challenge ontological questioning?" Moten asks. "*By way of a sound* and by way of what's already there in the decision to display the body, to publish the photograph, to restage death and rehearse mo(ur)nin(g)."[73] Moten claims that when you look at Till's photograph, you can hear the sound of a whistle, which, according to several reports, was the gesture that precipitated Till's death: he was accused of wolf-whistling at Carolyn Bryant Donham. Whistling, however, was a technique Till's mother taught him to help manage his disability, she said. Till contracted polio when he was a child, and it left him with muscle damage that caused him to stutter.[74] And when you look at the photograph, you can hear sonic repercussions of pain and sorrow, an aural fusion of moaning and lament. "These are the complex musics of the photograph," writes Moten. "This is the sound before the photograph: Scream inside and out, out from outside, of the image. Bye, baby. Whistling. Lord, take my soul. Redoubled and reanimating passion, the passion of a seeing that is involuntary and uncontrollable, a seeing that redoubles itself as sound, a passion that is the redoubling of Emmett Till's passion, of whatever passion would redeem, crucifixion, lynching."[75] Thus, the photographs not only reproduce images but reverberate sounds.

For all of the photographs' amplifications, however, they are also an indispensable reminder that, despite our advances and progress, there are realities that technology alone cannot resolve. Although aided by photographs and later DNA analysis, we still do not know pertinent facts that happened in the days immediately before and soon after Emmett Till's lynching. And as Goldsby spotlights, the visual archive of

Till's lynching is incomplete. We do not have photographs of his exchange with Carolyn Bryant Donham inside the store; the archive does not include images of his beating and killing; we have no photographic evidence of J. W. Milam and Roy Bryant tossing Till's body into the Tallahatchie; and there are photographs of Till's corpse that are unavailable for public viewing. "The images that do exist," Goldsby argues, "forestall the hard fact that a missing one points toward, which is that photography's capacities to document the real are not indisputable, and that the medium is more capable of *depicting* (not documenting)."[76] In other words, photography does not have the capacity to tell us *everything*, for something is always left out of the frame. Photographs, then, allow us to be spectators of an event, not witnesses. They are part of the evidentiary pool of information we can use to reconstruct events, and, thus, they should supplement, not substitute, other forms of evidence, such as testimony. Similarly to the DNA analysis performed after Till's autopsy, which produced minimal new substantial evidence and did not result in the arrest, indictment, or conviction of other parties, the photographs of Till's corpse are an example that there are limits to what our techniques and technologies can reveal.

The other harsh reality that neither DNA analysis nor photography could resolve is the conflicting way Till's corpse has been deployed and interpreted in the US cultural imagination. Even as Till's family has imagined that his body could be used as a means of cultivating racial healing, we must also contend with the fact that his injured and violated body has also functioned as a potent embodiment of white supremacy and racial terror. As Priest argues, "Till's torn corpse becomes an embodied site of U.S. racial memory, ripped apart and patched together again, exhumed and reburied, re-membered by conflicting desire: the desire to maintain power in the infliction of racial injury; the desire to forget it ever occurred; the desire to memorialize it, to repair it, and to end it." These opposing forces configure Till's body, Priest asserts, "not as a site for remembering but a battleground, a red record of disjunctures and discontinuities."[77] This battleground is especially fraught, since it emerged out of yet another racial injury: the refusal to believe Till-Mobley's testimony and the attempt to silence her voice.

Notwithstanding these forces, Mamie Till-Mobley and her family used technology for an alternative purpose, and there are important lessons to be learned from their activism. The limits of technology—whether the photograph or DNA testing—should neither diminish our personal capacity to recognize racist violence when we see it nor allow us to disavow the harmful effects such violence can cause if left unchecked. These technologies have the power to reveal evidence that might otherwise remain hidden from public view. They can spotlight the significance of the "disprized dead" and amplify the voices of "disprized mourners" by enabling them to resist interminable power structures.[78] "Emmett Till's murder," says John Edgar Wideman, "was an attempt to slay an entire generation. Push us backward to the bad old days when our lives seemed not to belong to us. When white power and racism seemed unchallengeable forces of nature."[79] Mamie Till-Mobley's decision to open her son's casket and publish his photographs, to "let the world see" what happened to her son, was an attempt to challenge those seemingly incontestable forces—to pry open the public's eyes, condemn indifference, confront Black mourning, and raise the dead. By creating a space in the break "between grief and grievance" and "between the complaint that is audible" and "the extralinguistic mode of black noise that exists outside the parameters of any strategy or plan for remedy," Mamie Till-Mobley created "a public space for black grief," a "sounding [for] our collective plaint."[80] To counter the state's refusal to recognize or identify her son and its refusal to believe her testimony or hear her plea for justice, she cultivated a community of spectators, of mourners, of listeners with whom she could commiserate about her son's death and with whom she could commemorate her son's life even though she could not undo the violence inflicted on him and recognized that a legal remedy would never be achieved as long as the ideology of color blindness disavowed the conditions that led to his death.[81] Her lesson to us all is clear: color blindness cannot conquer antiblackness; color blindness sustains it. That lesson was, miserably, true for her son, and it is true also for all the other Black lives that have been lost to racial violence, including Eric Garner's.

This lesson is also why so many activists have demanded that the public forgo color blindness and engage in a color vision—one that recognizes, listens to, and speaks about racism and shows a concern for Black people. For example, Esaw Garner, Eric's widow, refused to accept the remorse of Officer Daniel Pantaleo, expressing a fervent wish that Pantaleo would have exhibited concern for her husband before placing him in a choke hold until he could no longer breathe. "Hell no!" said Esaw Garner when asked whether she accepted Pantaleo's apology: "The time for remorse would have been when my husband was yelling to breathe. That would have been the time for him to show some type of remorse or some type of care for another human being's life—when [my husband] was screaming eleven times that he can't breathe."[82] Esaw Garner's rejection of Pantaleo's apology reflects a defiance of belated sentiments of remorse and a call for the protection and prioritization of Black life. Pantaleo did not protect or value Eric Garner's life; instead, he choked him to death and witnessed him take his final breath.

"I Can't Breathe": Listening to and Looking at the Killing of Eric Garner

"I can't breathe": the declaration of his respiratory distress. "I can't breathe I can't breathe": the expression of his corporeal vulnerability and harm. "I can't breathe I can't breathe": the plea for mercy and the call for justice. "I can't breathe I can't breathe I can't breathe": the announcement of "*his* experience of the ongoing act of racial animus, antiblack racism, violent policing . . . that structures life in the United States."[83] "I can't breathe I can't breathe": the testimony of the interminable ways Black lives have been susceptible to the disabilities of the color line. "I can't breathe": the complaint that Eric Garner, while under duress, lodged against the police eleven times. It was a complaint he lodged over and over and over again—each time with bated breath, each breath shorter and shallower than the previous one. But the police did not listen—until, that is, he said nothing.

The bare facts of Eric Garner's killing, which are largely gleaned from video recordings, display the disproportionate relationship between crime and punishment, between police protection and racial injury. On July 17, 2014, two NYPD officers (Daniel Pantaleo and Justin Damico) dressed in plain clothes approached Eric Garner on suspicion of selling "loosies" (single cigarettes) from packs that were untaxed. Garner denied that he had sold any single cigarettes, and he expressed frustration at the daily harassment he received from the police and told the officers to leave him alone. After a back-and-forth exchange between Garner and the officers that lasted several minutes, the officers, upon the arrival of additional backup, decided to arrest Garner. As Officer Daniel Pantaleo reached to grab Garner's right wrist and Officer Justin Damico reached to grab his left one, Garner raised his hands, telling the officers not to touch him. Pantaleo then put his right arm underneath Garner's right arm and put his left arm around Garner's neck and clasped both of his hands together (a technique, according to the NYPD Patrol Guide, that fits the description of a choke hold, which the NYPD banned in the early 1990s), forcibly pulling Garner backward toward the store window and then down to the ground. Once Garner was on the ground in a prone position, someone said, "Stop." During Pantaleo's use of the choke hold, several other officers swooped in to help handcuff Garner. After removing his arm from around Garner's neck and while Garner was being handcuffed, Pantaleo kneeled and pushed Garner's face into the ground. During the arrest, Garner stated, "I can't breathe," eleven times. While handcuffed on the sidewalk and almost immediately after being put in a choke hold, Garner apparently lost consciousness. The officers placed Garner on his side, but in the video recordings, he did not seem to move or respond after being placed in this position. His body appeared motionless. Garner remained lying on the sidewalk (still in handcuffs) for several minutes as officers waited for the ambulance to arrive. Neither the police nor the EMTs performed CPR on Garner. Approximately one hour later, Garner was pronounced dead at the Richmond University Medical Center.[84]

To write an account of the facts, I had to watch the videos of Eric Garner's arrest and killing. I watched the videos, because I think the facts are important and wanted to be as precise as possible in my description and analysis of what happened. I also watched the recordings to distinguish what actually happened from what the media and commentators claimed happened. With no arrest, no indictment, and no trial and with the grand jury transcripts sealed, sworn testimony withheld, and additional evidence unavailable, the videos (one of which was recorded by Ramsey Orta, a friend of Eric Garner's) are perhaps the most significant pieces of evidence available to the public. Watching these recordings made me a spectator of Garner's killing—even though I was not there on that street the day that he died and I did not witness his killing in real time. The recordings are a reproduction—an audiovisual

archive—of racial violence that haunts the imagination. To be a spectator of Black death—for many viewers, including myself—is a painful
and traumatic ordeal. It is a terror on the mind, an aural and ocular assault on the senses. I now know more about the substance that may have
led Elizabeth Alexander to ask, in the title of her essay on Rodney King,
slave narratives, and the lynching of Emmett Till, "Can you be BLACK
and look at this?" Alexander's question compels you to consider the relationship between what it means to "be BLACK" and what it means to
"look at" reproductions of anti-Black violence—whether it be footage of
Rodney King's beating, a photograph of Emmett Till's corpse, or video
recordings of violence and police brutality.

If allowed the poetic license to revise Alexander's question, I would
like to pose related questions about the audiovisual recordings of Garner's killing: Can you be Black and look at this without experiencing
some form of transference? Can you be Black and look at anti-Black
violence without feeling like your life or the life of someone you love
is in imminent danger or jeopardy? Or, alternatively, in a nation where
the ideology of color blindness reigns supreme and disavowals of racism and police brutality are prevalent, how does the practice of color
blindness prompt us to watch Black death, and what does such a viewing
cost us? In the aftermath of Garner's death, several commentators saw,
heard, and interpreted the encounter between Garner and the police in
conflicting ways. Racial and disability justice activists have argued that
the video shows evidence of excessive force by the police, the use of a
banned technique called the choke hold, and disregard for the health
and life of Eric Garner—who, despite having asthma and audibly stating
eleven times that he could not breathe, was offered no accommodations
by law enforcement. However, some Republican state representatives
and political commentators have put forth an opposing narrative, arguing that the video shows appropriate police force, that the technique
used during the arrest was either unintended or not a choke hold, that
Garner's ability to speak signaled his ability to breathe, and that his underlying medical conditions caused his death, not excessive police force.
Simultaneously fat shaming Eric Garner and deemphasizing the racial
aspects of his killing, these commentators have engaged in a color-blind
performance of disability, pretending not to see or hear racism and the
infliction of injury on a Black, disabled person. And—insofar as Dan-

iel Pantaleo was not indicted by the grand jury for the killing of Eric Garner—their performances have proved effective within the law. Such opposing narratives are riddled with distortion, and they, as I have discussed in chapter 2, resemble the kind of historical "narratives of dominion" that attempt to "amplify or deny the story an African-American body appears to be telling" and "talk black people out of what their bodies know."[85]

One notorious example of such commentary comes from congressman Peter King, a Republican in the US House of Representatives. In his appearance on *The Situation Room with Wolf Blitzer*, King told CNN host Wolf Blitzer that he did not feel that Officer Daniel Pantaleo should have been indicted for the death of Eric Garner and was thankful the grand jury acquitted him. His comments effectively capture the way a performance of color blindness enables the disabilities of the color line:

> First of all, the, uh, death was tragic, and, uh, our hearts have to go out to the, uh, Garner family. Having said that, I do not believe—I feel strongly—the police officer should not have been indicted. I've been following this case from the start. You had a 350-pound person who was resisting arrest. The police were trying to bring him down as quickly as possible. If he had not had asthma and a heart condition and was so obese, uh, almost definitely he would not have died from this. The police had no reason to know that he was in serious condition. I know people were saying that he said eleven times or seven times "I can't breathe." Well the fact is if you can't breathe, you can't talk. And if you've ever seen anyone, uh, locked up resisting arrest, and I've seen it—and it's been white guys—and they're always saying, "you're breaking my arm," "you're choking me," "you're doing this," so police hear that all the time. They, uh, in this case, uh, a choke hold was not illegal. It is against department regulations. But, uh, as you look carefully, I don't think it was an intent to put him in a choke hold because he does move the baton as he brings him down. Also, people are saying very casually that this was done out of racial motives or violation of civil rights. There's not a hint there that anyone used any racial epithets. And also what's not mentioned is the senior officer on the spot who was there at the location was an African American female sergeant. So I don't know where the racial angle comes in. I have no doubt that if that was a 350-pound white guy, he would have been treated the

same. And the reason the police were there is Tompkinsville is primarily a minority area. The local businesspeople were complaining about Garner, who was constantly selling cigarettes outside their establishments, and he was creating a problem in the neighborhood. It was at the request of the community—the people in that minority community—who went to police headquarters who wanted the police out there to remove him. So this was not any attempt by the cops to harass some guy for selling cigarettes. It was the request of the community that it be done—and this was a minority community—struggling businesspeople trying to make a living.[86]

Peter King's comments are insidious. On the one hand, he expresses sympathy for the Garner family and describes Eric Garner's death as "tragic"; on the other, he claims that Garner's weight and health were ultimately what led to his death and suggests that his race had no bearing on police tactics. This is not how you offer condolences to a grieving family that has lost a loved one. This is how you engage in antiblackness. King's comments are also a gross form of victim blaming, holding Garner responsible for his own death but excusing the behavior of the officers because they were unaware of his health conditions. The officers' ignorance relieved them of their duty to protect and serve Garner, while references to Garner's health aim to shame him. King refers to Garner's weight and disability in two different forms of attack. Because Garner weighed "350-pound[s]," says King, the police were justified in using all resources at their disposal to "bring him down." Simultaneously, King suggests that Garner's death was caused by his asthma, obesity, and heart condition, not by police force. Here King's emphasis on Garner's health and disability deploys ableism to cloak structural racism. As the historian David M. Perry argues, "Ableism doesn't excuse racism. Racism doesn't excuse fat-hatred. Fat-hatred doesn't excuse the class-based discrimination. Rather, they sweep together, enabling us to see patterns of prejudice and their horrific outcomes."[87] One horrific outcome is the commentary of Peter King, who, by focusing on Garner's health and disability, perceives Garner as the problem. The way Peter King tells it, Eric Garner killed himself.

In King's interpretation of the video, he also displays a selective racial vision. Describing Garner as a "350-pound *person*," he renders Garner's race invisible such that Garner's Black male body can be easily exchanged with a white male one. "I have no doubt," he says, "that if that was a 350-pound white guy, he would have been treated the same." King's focus on sameness and racial fungibility is an attempt to prove that Garner's race was not a factor in his arrest. Yet when racial matters could buttress King's claim that racial animus did not exist, race is an essential part of his narrative. Even though the senior officer at the location did not use force on Garner, King informs viewers, apropos of nothing, that she was a Black woman. Although local business owners did not participate in the arrest, King states that the police were responding to complaints from the "minority community—struggling businesspeople trying to make a living." Even while viewers watch Pantaleo put Garner into a choke hold in a split-screen video, King emphasizes the fact that the officers did not use "racial epithets" for the purpose of deemphasizing the fact that they did use excessive force. These details, according to King, show that the officers' actions were not motivated by racism and did not violate Garner's civil rights. In King's disturbing defense of the officers' actions, he manages somehow to translate the killing of Eric Garner into a myth of racial inclusivity and minority protection: the police were supervised by a Black woman, they were responding to the requests of the minority community, and they did not disparage or verbally abuse Garner. The fact that they killed Garner simply goes unmentioned.

In fact, King's account attempts to diminish the violent acts committed against Garner's body altogether, to make the choke hold appear as if it is not a choke hold and to make Garner's claims of suffocation appear as evidence of his ability to breathe. Focusing on the question of intent, King suggests that the choke-hold maneuver was not really intended to operate as a choke hold. The officer's use of the baton, he claims, suggests that a different maneuver was initiated. But the baton was a figment of King's imagination; he saw what he wanted to see. Officer Pantaleo does not have a baton in the video. Both he and Officer Damico are dressed in plainclothes, and they would not have had batons on them. Additionally, King not only sees the video differently but also hears what is said differently from the activists fighting on behalf of Eric Garner. While activists (including Eric Garner's widow and daughter) had been framing Garner's last words as testimony of his inability to breathe, King interprets Garner's statement "I can't breathe" as a sign that he could.

Because Garner could speak, King says, he could also breathe. King even creates an excuse for the officers' failure to pay heed to Garner's last words by depicting Garner as a liar like all the "white guys" who resist arrest and claim that they are being choked or harmed by the police. The key difference between these phantom "white guys" and Eric Garner is that Garner was not lying. He could not breathe. The medical examiner determined that Garner's death was caused by "compression of neck (choke hold), compression of chest and prone positioning during physical restraint by the police."[88] Completely ignoring these facts, King depicts Garner as guilty and Pantaleo as innocent.

King's remarks epitomize an ableist performance of color blindness. In his telling, Garner's race is effectively unseen, his disability warrants no accommodation, his voice is virtually unheard, and the particular gendered and racial violence against his body is nearly erased. King neither recognizes nor perceives what I and others recognize when we watch the videos of Eric Garner's killing. Indeed, he crafts a counternarrative rooted in the premise that we did not see what we saw and that we did not hear what we heard. King could not see Eric Garner's vulnerability as a big, Black man or as a man managing his comorbidities; he could only see him as a threat. He could not hear Eric Garner gasping for air; he could only hear sounds of defiance. He could not recognize the significance and specificity of Eric Garner's blackness and disability; he could only acknowledge the similarities between Garner and, remarkably, white men. At every convenient moment, King, like many color-blind advocates, makes race, racial violence, and racism appear imperceptible. His brand of color blindness represents a remarkable ruse of twenty-first-century racial politics: a technique that both makes race mean so much and also makes it mean so little. This technique is the danger of a color-blind future.

It should come as no surprise, then, that Daniel Pantaleo made similar claims as Peter King in his defense during grand jury proceedings. He, too, thought Eric Garner could breathe, and he also denied intending to use the choke hold on Garner. According to Pantaleo's lawyer, Stuart London, Officer Pantaleo testified to the grand jury that "Mr. Garner's ability to speak . . . suggested that he, in fact, could breathe." London also said that Pantaleo "testified that when he put his hands on Mr. Garner, he was employing a maneuver taught to him at the Police

Academy, hooking an arm underneath one of Mr. Garner's arms while wrapping the other around Mr. Garner's torso." "The move is meant to 'tip the person so they lose their balance and go to the ground,' as seen in wrestling," added London.[89] While Pantaleo's defense is deeply offensive, I am disgusted but unsurprised that it proved successful. Neither Pantaleo nor the other officers were indicted for the death of Eric Garner. Since the grand jury transcripts are sealed, we cannot know for certain how the jury reached its decision. But it appears as if the jurors did not see or hear what many other protestors saw and heard. They saw and heard something else, perhaps something similar to Peter King and Daniel Pantaleo.

These performances of color blindness have the effect of compelling those who resist this ideology to repeatedly encounter racial violence and death, forcing us to confront yet again what many Americans pretend not to see. Therefore, the victims of anti-Black, state-sanctioned violence are not the only ones who are injured. Their families and supporters as well as the Black community writ large suffer racial trauma, too. The stress of viewing and experiencing daily racial violence is injurious. Consider, for example, that the daughter of Eric Garner, Erica, a mere three and half years after her father was killed, died at the age of twenty-seven from a heart attack—probably due both to her enlarged heart and the stress of dealing with her father's death. For these reasons and others, many activists and scholars have rejected the notion of color blindness and have advocated for color consciousness instead. "Seeing race is not the problem," says Michelle Alexander. "Refusing to care for the people we see is the problem."[90] This kind of care work entails being attentive to how race intersects with other identities.

What is so promising about contemporary Black activists, in addition to their calls for color consciousness, is how they care for Black people: how they imagine and create an inclusive space for all Black lives by engaging in an intersectional framework and organizing for those who are most vulnerable, including Black, disabled folks. A crucial part of this care work involves listening to marginalized communities.[91] For example, when the Harriet Tubman Collective, a group of "Black Deaf & Black Disabled organizers," noticed that the initial six-point policy platform for the Movement for Black Lives (M4BL) "did not once mention disability, ableism, audism or the unspeakable violence and Black death found at the intersection of ableism, audism, and anti-Black racism," it insisted on the inclusion of disability: "We demand that 'social justice' coalitions, networks and organizations end the violent erasure of disability from these and all other narrative[s] of the victims of police violence and murder. . . . Our Black Disabled Lives Matter."[92] This call for disability inclusion prompted M4BL to revise its platform. At the urging of the Harriet Tubman Collective, M4BL has a new vision, one that accounts for the lives that were noticeably absent. Its vision statement now reads, "We are intentional about amplifying the particular experiences of racial, economic, and gender-based state and interpersonal violence that Black women, queer, trans, gender nonconforming, intersex, and disabled people face. Cisheteropatriarchy and ableism are central and instrumental to anti-Blackness and racial capitalism, and have been internalized within our communities and movements."[93]

Indeed, from #BlackLivesMatter and BYP100 to the Harriet Tubman Collective and #SayHerName, what we find are demands to recognize, listen to, and speak about Black life differently via the lens of intersectionality, an analytical approach that shows how institutional structural failures make certain identities vulnerable to discrimination and oppression.[94] It is why the #SayHerName campaign, launched by the African American Policy Forum (AAPF) and Center for Intersectionality and Social Policy Studies (CISPS), spotlights Black women's susceptibility to police brutality and state-sanctioned violence by listing their names, lifting up their stories, and requesting the public to confront a pointed question via its tagline: "Can you see them?"[95] It is why Black Lives Matter, in its mission statement, highlights its goal to "affirm the lives of Black queer and trans folks, disabled folks, undocumented folks, folks with records, women, and all Black lives along the gender spectrum."[96] These intersectional frameworks display the kind of interability compassion that every activist must engage in to occasion collective liberation and political action. The family and supporters of Till and Garner offer one model for how to engender compassion by resisting the ideology of color blindness. They have shown how feigning blindness to racism and ableism does not alleviate racial trauma and social injustice; it merely allows it to manifest itself and flourish in harmful and horrific ways.

Emmett Till and Eric Garner are only two names of a litany of Black people who have been killed as a result of anti-Black violence by the state and its unruly citizens. Those of us who have been grieving Black lives recount their stories and remember their names because so many others refuse to. This refusal compels us to catalogue our collective devastation in an effort to tally losses that are ultimately unquantifiable. The leitmotif of cataloguing, according to Dagmawi Woubshet, is infused with "a poetics of compounding loss," a formal characteristic of mourning narratives that emphasizes not only the "overwhelming quantity and scale" of death but also how "the negative aspects—the pain, the confounded psyche, the exhausted body and soul—of each loss are compounded by the memory and experience of the losses just before." The serial aspect of compounding loss denies the bereaved the essential "time, consolation, and closure" needed in order to grieve and "move on."[97] This denial is extremely violent, for each compounding loss reinscribes trauma in exponential ways. Yet, in a world where refusals, disavowals, and denials of racism abound and are protected by the custom of color blindness, public expressions of compounding grief have a place and serve a purpose. Tabulating loss, while by no means sufficient for revolution and "always an incomplete endeavor" (particularly when the loss remains ongoing), is nevertheless a necessary form of redress.[98] A catalogue of those who have been lost is a commemoration of their lives. It is a remembrance of the precious souls stolen by state violence and vigilantism and ignored due to national silence and indifference. It is an archival method, a means of ensuring that the disprized dead do not "go ungrieved" in a nation determined to destroy them.[99] Accordingly, we who know that Black lives matter must continue to tell the stories and say the names of Black lives lost, including the dearly departed lives of Tanisha Anderson, Ahmaud Arbery, Kisha Arrone, India Beaty, Sean Bell, Sandra Bland, Rekia Boyd, Mike Brown, Eleanor Bumpers, Miriam Carey, Philando Castile, Alexia Christian, Decynthia Clements, John Crawford, Michelle Cusseaux, Deborah Danner, Jordan Davis, Shantel Davis, Monique Jenee Deckard, Amadou Diallo, George Floyd, Janisha Fonville, Ezell Ford, Shereese Francis, Shelly Frey, Pearlie Golden, Oscar Grant, Freddie Gray, Akai Gurley, Milton Hall, Mya Hall, Meagan Hockaday, Kendra James, Atatiana Jefferson, Kathryn Johnston, Bettie Jones, Redel Jones, India Kager, Regis Korchinski-Paquet, Quintonio LeGrier, Kyam Livingston, Trayvon Martin, Renisha McBride, Elijah McClain, Tony McDade, Laquan McDonald, Natasha McKenna, Marquesha McMillan,

Tyisha Miller, Margaret Laverne Mitchell, Kayla Moore, Gabriella Nevarez, Frankie Perkins, Nina Pop, Tamir Rice, Walter Scott, Yvette Smith, Alberta Spruill, Aiyana Stanley-Jones, Timothy Stansbury, Laronda Sweatt, Breonna Taylor, Stephon Watts, Darnell Wicker, Tarika Wilson, Mario Woods, and all the other names we do not know . . .

We see you. We hear you. We speak your names.

Epilogue

The Problem of the Color Line in the Age of COVID-19

"This is how Black people get killed!" said Susan Moore, a Black doctor-turned-patient who was being treated for COVID-19 at the IU Health North Hospital in Carmel, Indiana. Lying in her hospital bed with an oxygen tube hooked into her nostrils, Moore turned to social media to express her frustration about the poor treatment she received from the hospital staff in November and December 2020. As a physician herself, who understood her own ethical responsibility to protect the health of her patients, she recognized the extent to which her care was being compromised at this hospital. While Moore took issue with her patient advocate as well as the on-call nurse, she described her doctor's behavior as especially egregious: First, he downplayed her condition when she complained of a sharp pain in her neck. Then, he wanted to prematurely send her home after only issuing her two drug treatments, stating that she did not qualify for more treatment because she did not appear to be out of breath. Finally, when Moore pressed the issue further, her doctor admitted that he felt uncomfortable giving her more narcotics—making her feel, as she put it, like she "was a drug addict." Only after Moore's stat CT scan revealed, as she described it, "new pulmonary infiltrates [and] new lymphadenopathy all throughout [her] neck" was she able to receive the care and drug treatment that she needed to adequately treat her condition. For Moore, the entire ordeal clarified an ugly and painful truth about the discriminatory treatment Black patients too often receive from the medical establishment. As a Black patient, Moore said, "You have to show proof that you have something wrong with you in order for you to get the medicine." "I put forth and I maintain," she asserted, "if I was white I wouldn't have to go through that."[1]

Hers is a prime example of what the journalist and medical ethicist Harriet A. Washington calls the United States' "medical apartheid" system, which has grossly mistreated and frequently withheld care from Black Americans to such an extent that their health profile stands in stark contrast to those of other Americans.[2] Moore's story, in particular, effectively captures the reasons for the health deficit experienced by Black people, who often bear the burden of having to prove their pain, who are accused of misrepresenting their condition or characterized as drug-seeking addicts, and who are typically underdiagnosed or misdiagnosed because practitioners do not take their symptoms seriously. The stress of having to deal with these issues can be overwhelming. It was so overwhelming for Dr. Moore that, despite her voice being strained and her breathing labored, she declared, "This is how Black people get killed, when you send them home and they don't know how to fight for themselves. I had to talk to somebody—maybe the media, somebody—to let people know how I'm being treated up in this place."[3] Although she advocated for herself and demanded better care—a practice that, according to her son, she has always done given her profession and her history of dealing with sarcoidosis, an inflammatory disease that commonly occurs in the lungs and lymph nodes—Dr. Moore did not win her battle against the coronavirus.[4] Just more than a couple of weeks after she posted her video on Facebook about her mistreatment at IU North, she died from complications of COVID-19, on Sunday, December 20, 2020.

She was one of many.

The disproportionate rate at which Black people are being infected with, hospitalized for, or dying from COVID-19 is staggering. According to analysis by the Brookings Institution, the "death rate for Black people is 3.6 times that for whites."[5] The *Washington Post* observed similar disparities, noting that the percentage of Black people dying from the virus is significantly higher than the percentage of the Black population in several states. In Louisiana, Black folks comprise 32 percent of the state's population but have made up 70 percent of the deaths from COVID-19. In Illinois, Black folks are 14 percent of the state population but make up 40 percent of its COVID-19 deaths. In Michigan, a similar phenomenon has been occurring: Black people comprise 14 percent of the population but represent roughly 40 percent of those who have died from COVID-19.[6] These numbers tell an alarming tale of how, to this day, the color line has severely compromised the health of Black Americans, creating racial health disparities that make them vulnerable to a deadly virus.

Yet what is also disturbing is how politicians and commentators have been using these statistics to blame Black people for dying of the coronavirus. As the historian Ibram X. Kendi observes, "To explain the disparities in the mortality rate, too many politicians and commentators are noting that black people have more underlying medical conditions but, critically, they're *not explaining why*. Or they blame the choices made by black people, or poverty, or obesity—but not racism." Significantly, Kendi acknowledges that "African Americans suffer disproportionately from chronic diseases such as hypertension, cardiovascular disease, diabetes, lung disease, obesity, and asthma, which make it harder for them to survive COVID-19."[7] But he questions why more politicians and health officials are not attempting to determine which structural barriers make it more likely for Black people to suffer from such chronic diseases. For example, when the host David Greene asked Republican Senator Bill Cassidy (who is also a US medical physician) on NPR's *Morning Edition* whether Black people's "underlying health conditions" are "rooted in years of systemic racism," Cassidy replied, "Well, you know, that's rhetoric, and it may be. But as a physician, I'm looking at science." And what the science told Senator Cassidy, as he mentioned at the beginning of the interview, was "if you have diabetes, obesity, hypertension— and diabetes and hypertension are *clearly* risk factors for problems from COVID—then African Americans are going to have more of those receptors [that the virus likes to hit] inherent in their having the diabetes, the hypertension, [and] the obesity and inherent in them having an overrepresentation of that. So there's a physiologic reason explaining this."[8] With all the factors that could explain the racial health disparities of Black folks—including inadequate health care, lack of medical insurance, a scarcity of hospitals in majority-Black communities, or the general racism and exploitation of the medical establishment—Senator Cassidy repeatedly chose to diagnose Black people as having "inherent" health issues that make them more susceptible to COVID-19 rather than to discuss the precarious conditions set in motion by centuries of governmental neglect, violence, and indifference.

This is an all-too-familiar narrative of the disabilities of the color line, in which Black people are cast as inherently disabled and diseased and, as such, are deemed at fault for conditions they have been made vulnerable to. This book has demonstrated how that narrative has been frequently repeated from the antebellum period to the present. It has also shown how Black people have responded to such claims not only by reframing racism as a disease but also by detailing their discursive and material disablement as a form of redress. As I watched the "racial pandemic" unfold within the "viral pandemic" and listened to the various commentators discuss the causes of our country's massive health deficit, I realized that the story this book tells is as important to our current historical moment as it is to the nineteenth and twentieth centuries because it encourages others to reconsider the intersections of blackness and disability at a time when harmful narratives about racial health are on the rise.[9] Watching the news and scrolling through social media platforms, I have observed how certain politicians and health officials could benefit from the rich and vibrant work of Black studies and disability studies. They need to read the visionary work of Frederick Douglass, David Walker, Henry Box Brown, William and Ellen Craft, Charles Chesnutt, Frances Harper, Anna Julia Cooper, James Weldon Johnson, Patricia Williams, and Mamie Till-Mobley. They need to hear how Black writers and activists have explored the distinct ways disability has served as a constructed yet naturalized element in the alchemy of US race, rights, and health. They need to know how Black theorists have actively redefined the meanings of blackness and disability in ways that have allowed and could still allow themselves and the nation to imagine an otherwise way of being and becoming. What they need to understand, it turns out, is the central idea presented in this book: how disablement has shaped Black social life since the antebellum period as well as how Black activists and authors have acknowledged the profound role of disability in their lives to emphasize how their bodies, minds, and health have been made vulnerable to harm by the relentless infliction of anti-Black violence.

The actions and resistance of the Black writers and thinkers in this book took many forms and entailed difficult choices. For Douglass, resistance meant framing the color line as a disease that haunts and hunts Black lives to counter the narratives of innate Black degeneracy that he heard throughout the nineteenth century. For David Walker, it meant excoriating slavery and enslavers and crafting a pamphlet that could double as a blueprint for Black liberation and be accessible for literate and illiterate readers alike. For Henry Box Brown, it meant sacrificing his finger and enduring twenty-seven hours of pain in a cramped wooden crate to claim ownership of his body and express his own sense of personhood through criminality and disability. For Ellen Craft, it meant disguising herself as a disabled white male planter while her husband played the role of faithful servant to execute their extraordinary escapes. For Charles Chesnutt, it meant suturing the racial health of white and Black people and presenting disability as something inflicted onto Black people by the perils of slavery, segregation, and white-supremacist discourses. For James Weldon Johnson, it meant anonymously writing a novel about the relationship between racial passing and lynching in addition to leading an antilynching campaign for nearly two decades while refusing to publicly disclose the details of his near-lynching experience lest he might crumble under the weight of remembering his physical assault and psychological trauma. For the family and supporters of Emmett Till and Eric Garner (and countless others), it meant using photographic, scientific, or audiovisual technologies to compel the public to recognize racial violence and antiblackness, to forsake color-blind performances of disability, and to engage in care work that is inclusive and intersectional.

The remarkable stories of all these Black authors and activists stand as evidence of the promising work that has engendered racial and disability justice, work that captures the full complexities of Black life: the times of grief and the times of triumph. The pursuit of racial justice entails, according to the legal and cultural studies scholar Imani Perry, holding the "inescapable" injustice of racism alongside the "immense and defiant joy" of blackness. As Perry asserts, "The trauma" endured by Black Americans "is repetitive. We weep. But we are still, even in our most anguished seasons, not reducible to the fact of our grief. Rather, the capacity to access joy is a testament to the grace of living as a protest."[10] The work of disability justice involves affirming this kind of duality, too. According to Sins Invalid, a performance project on disability and sexuality cofounded by Patty Berne and Leroy Moore, "Disability Justice [is] an honoring of the longstanding legacies of resilience and resistance which are the inheritance of all of us whose bodies or minds will not conform. . . . Disability Justice is a vision and practice of a *yet-to-be*, a map that we create with our ancestors and our great grandchildren onward, in the width and depth of our multiplicities and histories, a movement towards a world in which every body and mind is known as beautiful."[11] This intergenerational, dynamic framework effectively captures the work of the Black folks in this book and their desire for collective liberation and coalition. The ties that bind their stories are their aesthetics of redress: the way they find light through darkness and healing through pain and, ultimately, the way they avow the disabled beauty and abundance of Black life—a life that, though conditioned and constrained by the color line's *longue durée*, is so precious and resilient it cannot be torn asunder.

ACKNOWLEDGMENTS

Whenever my dad saw me laboring excessively at a task, he would always say, "Work work. Don't let work work you." By that remark, he meant that there is usually a more efficient way to complete a job, one that does not require so much time or effort. Having worked quite hard on this book for a long time, I often wished I had taken his advice. This book worked me in every which way and at different stages of my academic life: as a graduate student, a postdoctoral fellow, a tenure-track professor, and a tenured one. The book was so challenging to write in large part because I was adhering to another code, one that both of my parents instilled in me: "Anything worth doing is worth doing well." This principle has long served as my modus operandi and has fueled my writing through difficult times—through professional hurdles, personal obstacles, and doubt and uncertainty. While these challenges slowed my progress, they did not deter me from my ultimate goal of completing this book. I was raised within a tradition of persistence and perseverance—one rooted in Black resilience and excellence, defiance and triumph—and that tradition has been my guiding light even during moments of struggle. I have also been encouraged every step of the way by a formidable network of mentors, colleagues, organizations, friends, and family (biological and chosen), who have advised me, checked in on me, provided resources and support, prepared a home-cooked meal for me, and either read portions of my work or let me vent about it. These acknowledgments are my attempt to thank those who have supported me on the journey of finishing this book, yet I write them with the full knowledge that it is extraordinarily difficult to thank everyone who has shaped my ideas or offered encouragement along the way and that, for some of you, a mere acknowledgment is by no means a sufficient thanks for all that you have done for me.

This book began as an idea in a seminar on disability studies while I was graduate student in the Department of English at the University of

California, Los Angeles. That idea then turned into a dissertation, which was directed by a phenomenal committee—Richard Yarborough, Eric Sundquist, and Helen Deutsch—who all gave me incredible guidance, affirmation, and support. I have said on more than one occasion that Richard Yarborough is the advisor and mentor that everyone deserves, for he approaches the profession with a kind of care, rigor, and precision that is an absolute marvel to witness and that should serve as a model for us all. I would not have finished my dissertation without his incisive feedback, encouragement, and compassion. (It is no surprise, sir, that you have a mentoring award named in your honor.) Eric Sundquist taught me the value and importance of interdisciplinary work within literary studies and has always shown unwavering support for my work throughout my career. The wonderful Helen Deutsch introduced me to the field of disability studies, and I will always be grateful for that introduction as well as for her intellectual generosity.

My cohort, advisors, professors, and friends during my stint in graduate school made my time in Los Angeles an enjoyable and worthwhile experience. I appreciate our many conversations while in seminars or over coffee, lunch, hors d'oeuvres, dinner, and drinks; our late-night dance sessions throughout the city; the Black People's Meeting (BPM) at Roscoe's House of Chicken & Waffles; all of the epic tennis matches we watched (especially the ones in the wee hours of the morning) as well as the tennis we played together; and the numerous house parties and gatherings we attended either to celebrate a special occasion or to enjoy each other's company. Many thanks to Nathan Brown, Devon Carbado, King-Kok Cheung, Abimbola Cole, Kimberlé Crenshaw, Denise Cruz, John Alba Cutler, Dustin Friedman, Yogita Goyal, Georgina Guzmán, Melanie Ho, Birgitta Johnson, Antualisa Johnson, Julian Knox, Joyce Lee, Julia Lee, Arthur Little, Chris Looby, Courtney Marshall, Kate Marshall, Jennifer McMillan, Carrie Meathrell, La'Tonya Rease Miles, Keidra Morris, Harryette Mullen, Thomas O'Donnell, Erica Onugha, Bryan Cooper Owens, Therí Pickens, Val Popp, Leslie Poston (thank you for making my draft supreme!), Kimo Reder, Joseph Rezek, the late Sam See (you are dearly missed, my friend), Karim Shah, Maureen Shay, Caroline Streeter, Erin Suzuki, and Brandy Underwood. I want to give special thanks to my dear Laura Haupt, for being my forever cheerleader and for the countless times you have read, chatted with me about, and provided substantive feedback on my work; to Lynn Itagaki and Leslie Wingard, my writing and accountability buddies, for all of your tremendous feedback during the final push; and to Deirdre Cooper Owens, my sista, for always offering me sage advice and for being a constant well of encouragement and good cheer.

I have received funding for my research from a number of institutions, including the Mellon Foundation; Woodrow Wilson Foundation; Ford Foundation; University of California, Los Angeles; Getty Research Institute; Social Science Research Council; Carter G. Woodson Institute at the University of Virginia; and Fordham University. In particular, the Mellon Mays Undergraduate Fellowship (MMUF), SSRC-Mellon Mays Graduate Initiatives Program, Carter G. Woodson Institute, and Woodrow Wilson Career Enhancement Fellowship have enabled and fostered a sense of community and introduced me to an amazing group of people. I do not think I would have pursued this profession were it not for the support I received from MMUF as an undergraduate at Stanford University. I am grateful to Laura Selznick, my MMUF coordinator, who motivated me to follow this career path; Harry Elam, who recommended me for the Mellon fellowship and who gave me one of my most memorable experiences at Stanford during his sophomore college course Social Protest Drama; Sharon Holland, whose freshman seminar Growing Up in America rocked my world and who served as my introduction to American studies, Black studies, and the life of a Black academic; and Arnold Rampersad, who served as my thesis advisor and provided keen insights on my work that have shaped my writing to this day. I must also thank the SSRC-Mellon Mays Graduate Initiatives Program, particularly Cally Waite and Emma Taati, for all of your generosity and the tremendous work you have done for me and other fellows throughout the years. The rigorous workshops at the Carter G. Woodson Institute greatly improved the quality of my work. I will always be thankful for the remarkable mentorship of Deborah McDowell and Marlon Ross and the insightful comments I received from them as well as from Lawrie Balfour, my invited respondents Katherine Bassard and Jennifer Rae Greeson, and my other Woodson fellows. I am grateful to my two incredible mentors for the Woodrow Wilson Fellowship, Daphne Brooks and Samuel K. Roberts, for their steady encouragement and guidance. I also want to express gratitude to Herman Beavers, who stepped in and served as my mentor during the Woodson Retreat. I truly appreciate the friendship and support I have received from so many people within this beloved community, particularly that of Jan Barker Alexander, Jenifer Barclay, Shanna Greene Benjamin, Barbara Boswell, andré carrington, Jeffrey Coleman, Sonya Donaldson, Erica Edwards, Jonathan Fenderson, Julius Fleming, Tyler Fleming, Miles Grier, Fareeda Griffith, Z'étoile Imma, Kwame Holmes, James Jordan, Janaka Bowman Lewis, Jarvis McInnis, Uri McMillan, Trimiko Melancon, McKinley Melton, Anoop Mirpuri, Jonathan Rosa, Michelle Scott Hillman, Maurice Stevens, Elizabeth Todd-Breland, and Rebecca VanDiver. Alisha Gaines, my collaborator and coconspirator, thank you for being such a wonderful friend and for helping me sharpen my ideas in this book at crucial moments during the writing.

Much of this book was revised while working at Fordham University and living and partaking in the greater New York community, and I have benefited from the support of many friends, colleagues, and interlocutors. For providing useful advice about the book, reading portions of my work, inviting me to give a talk about my research, or offering support or a listening ear at key moments, I give special thanks to Rachel Adams, Andrew Albin, Hugo Benavides, Rezarta Bilali, Liz Bowen, Lenny Cassuto, Aimee Meredith Cox, Diane Detournay, Fabienne Doucet, Shonni Enelow, Anne Fernald, Nicole Fleetwood, Elizabeth Frost, Chris GoGwilt, Susan Greenfield, Christina Greer, Glenn Hendler, Shabnam Javdani, Julie Kim, Oneka LaBennett, Laurie Lambert, Natalie Léger, Natasha Lightfoot, Timothy Lyle, Corey McEleney, Micki McGee, Brandy Monk-Payton, Zein Murib, Fawzia Mustafa, Kinohi Nishikawa, Kameelah Phillips, Scott Poulson-Bryant, Julia Miele Rodas, Lotti Silber, Jordan Stein, Cheryl Sterling, Scott Terrell, Audrey Trainor, Fatima Varner, Vlasta Vranjes, Irma Watkins-Owens, Jenice Wilson, Rafael Zapata, and Sarah Zimmerman. I want to give a special shout-out to Imani Owens, for your clutch feedback and your willingness to chat with me about my work. And a hearty thanks to Rebecca Sanchez, whose intellectual generosity is astounding; thank you for reading several chapters and for giving such helpful advice.

Thank you to the anonymous readers at the University of Minnesota Press and New York University Press. I especially want to thank my editor at NYU Press, Eric Zinner, for his early enthusiasm for this project and for his encouragement as I approached the finish line. It has also been a pleasure to work with Alicia Nadkarni, Furqan Sayeed, and Alexia Traganas at NYU Press. I am excited to have this book as part of the Crip series. Thank you to the series editors: Michael Bérubé, Ellen Samuels, and particularly Robert McRuer, who gave me the most valuable and supportive feedback at the most critical moments and kept reminding me of the book's potential and possibilities. I also want to give special thanks to Therí Pickens and Cynthia Wu, for providing such incisive and encouraging feedback on my manuscript.

Portions of the introduction and chapters 4 and 5 appeared as earlier essays and were published in the following sources: "Race and Disability," in *Oxford Bibliographies Online*; "Losing Limbs in the Republic: Disability, Dismemberment, and Mutilation in Charles Chesnutt's Conjure Stories," in *Journal of Literary & Cultural Disability Studies* 11, no. 1 (2017): 35–51; and "Jim Crow's Disabilities: Racial Injury, Immobility, and the 'Terrible Handicap' in the Literature of James Weldon Johnson," in *African American Review* 50, no. 2 (Summer 2017): 185–201.

I consider myself lucky to have such nurturing and kind friends. For all the ways you have supported me, thank you to Misty Cunningan, Claudine Davillier Davis, Joel De Andrade, Adelso García Rodríguez, Lakesha Glover, Tiffany Thomas, and Erika Thoms. I thank my dear friend Álvaro Arce for his big heart, his generosity, his no-holds-barred critique, and his impeccable shade; ours is an enduring friendship and brotherhood that I am eternally grateful for. Tracy Tyler, you have been my rock, my calm in the storm for nearly three decades. Although we are not biologically related—despite sharing the same last name—I consider you family. Richon May, you are usually the first person I call in moments of crisis and joy. I thank you for every "therapy session," every encouraging word, every discerning piece of advice, every hug, and every laugh. I will always want to cut a rug with you, love.

Thank you to my family—especially my aunts Beverly, Joanie, Pearlie, and Claudia and my cousin Devin—who have doted on me and nourished me while I worked on this book. Your love and support have meant the world to me. I am immensely grateful to my parents, Lydia and Jimmie, to whom I dedicate this book. You have taught me invaluable lessons about persistence and raised me with a love and care that is immeasurable. The extent of this book's virtue is in part attributable to the foundation you laid. I love y'all.

NOTES

PROLOGUE

1. This statement is a riff on W. E. B. Du Bois's famous aphorism: "The problem of the twentieth century is the problem of the color-line" (*Souls*, 17).

2. Douglass, "Color Line," 573.

3. Douglass, 567, 572, 569, 575, 568, 567.

4. This sentiment of white-supremacy-as-impairment has accrued some currency in Black culture. One notable example could be located in Toni Morrison's 1993 interview with Charlie Rose, following the publication of her novel *Jazz*. In an effort to reframe Rose's question about whether she, after winning the Pulitzer Prize and being "honored in the halls of academe," still experiences racism, Morrison explained, "Don't you understand that the people who do this thing, who practice racism, are bereft? There is something distorted about the psyche. . . . It's like it's a profound neurosis that nobody examines for what it is. . . . It has just as much of a deleterious effect on white people and possibly equal that it does [on] Black people." She concluded, "If you can only be tall because somebody's on their knees, then you have a serious problem. And my feeling is white people have a very, very serious problem, and *they* should start thinking about what *they* can do about it. Take me out of it." Morrison's final sentence captures the subtext of Douglass's essay: that white people need to take an active role in resolving white supremacy in a manner that no longer puts the burden on Black folks. Morrison, interview by Charlie Rose, 00:38:10–00:40:56.

5. *Dred Scott v. Sandford*, 60 U.S. 393, 403, 409 (1857).

6. Douglass, "Color Line," 573, 575, 576.

7. Douglass, 568.

8. Douglass's description of how slavery's shadow poisons the atmosphere reminds me of the Black studies scholar Christina Sharpe's work on the weather, in which "the weather is the totality of our environments; the weather is the total climate; and that climate is antiblack." According to Sharpe, "The weather trans*forms Black being. But the shipped, the held, and those in the wake also produce out of the weather their own ecologies. When the only certainty is the weather that produces a pervasive climate of antiblackness, what must we know in order to move through these environments in which the push is always toward Black death?" (*In the Wake*, 104, 106). Douglass's work is one example of how early Black writers produced their own ecologies in the midst of Black death and destruction.

9. Douglass, "Color Line," 572.

10. As Douglass outlined near the conclusion of *Life and Times* (1881), his third and last autobiography, he "lived several lives in one: first, the life of slavery; secondly, the life of a fugitive from slavery; thirdly, the life of comparative freedom; fourthly, the life of conflict and battle; and fifthly, the life of victory, if not complete, at least assured" (chap. 19). This incomplete-yet-assured future of Douglass's imagination is due, in no small part, to his own abolitionism and writing over the course his career. For more biographical details on Douglass, see Blight, *Frederick Douglass*.

11. In the *History of Woman Suffrage*, which provided a detailed account of the Women's Rights Conventions held in 1848 in Seneca Falls and Rochester, New York, it is recorded that, at the convention in Rochester, Frederick Douglass delivered "a long, argumentative, and eloquent appeal" and "thought the true basis of rights was the capacity of individuals." Stanton, Anthony, and Gage, *History of Woman Suffrage*, 86, 87.

12. Because of "the assumption that there is only one side to the question of disability," Alison Kafer states, "contradictions and logical inconsistencies" are an inevitable part of projects that reflect "our convoluted approaches to disability." Kafer adds, "The desire for clear answers, free of contradiction and inconsistency, is understandable, but I want to suggest that accessible futures require such ambiguities." Kafer, *Feminist, Queer, Crip*, 19.

13. "Disability Justice [is] an honoring of the longstanding legacies of resilience and resistance which are the inheritance of all of us whose bodies or minds will not conform," according to Sins Invalid. The tenth principle of disability justice, collective liberation, poses a question that has underpinned the work of Black authors and activists in this book: "How do we move together as people with mixed abilities, multiracial, multi-gendered, mixed class, across the orientation spectrum—where no body/mind is left behind?" (Berne et al., "Ten Principles of Disability Justice," 229). All coalitional work should be searching for and working toward an answer to this question.

14. Cunningham, on *AM Joy*, 01:07:00–01:08:40.

15. Sharpton, "Reverend Al Sharpton Eulogy Transcript," 00:07:42–00:10:22.

16. Ashon Crawley's analysis of the killing of Eric Garner is instructive for thinking about Sharpton's eulogy of George Floyd. Crawley's examination of Garner's final words, "I can't breathe," demonstrates how Garner's individual experience is connected to a history of "modernity's violence": "'I can't breathe' as both the announcement of a particular moment and rupture in the life world of the Garners, and 'I can't breathe' as a rupture, a disruption, an ethical plea regarding the ethical crisis that has been the grounds for producing his moment, our time, this modern world" (*Blackpentecostal Breath*, 1).

17. Douglass, "Future of the Colored Race," 439. The historian David Blight also heralds Douglass as a "prophet of doom and of redemption" and a "disruptive, disturbing prophet of justice" whom many people channel with their words, whether "knowingly or not" (*Frederick Douglass*, 760, 748, xiv).

18. Berne et al., "Ten Principles," 229.

19. The visionary methods to imagine communities "elsewhere," "elsewhen," and "otherwise" emerge from the work of disability studies, queer studies, Black studies, and feminist studies. The feminist-queer-crip scholar Alison Kafer helped me understand how all three methods are essential to "a politics of crip futurity." She writes, "Throughout the course of the book, I hold on to an idea of politics as a framework for thinking through how to get 'elsewhere,' to other ways of being that might be more just and sustainable. In imagining more accessible futures, I am yearning for an elsewhere—and, perhaps, an 'elsewhen'—in which disability is understood otherwise: as political, as valuable, as integral" (*Feminist, Queer, Crip*, 3). Kafer's references to "elsewhere" and "otherwise" are informed by the work of Donna J. Haraway and Robert McRuer. In *Simians, Cyborgs, and Women: The Reinvention of Nature*, Haraway defines "elsewhere" as "brought into being out of feminist movement rooted in specification and articulation, not out of common 'identities' nor assumption of the right or ability of any particular to 'represent' the general. The 'particular' in feminist movement is not about liberal individualism nor a despairing isolation of endless differences, much less about rejecting the hope for collective movement" (239). And Robert McRuer's generative theorizing of crip theory is nothing if not a call to think otherwise. Indeed, as McRuer states at the conclusion of *Crip Theory*, "It's a crip promise that we will always comprehend disability otherwise" (208). The call to imagine "otherwise" is also, of course, rooted in Black studies—particularly in the work of Nahum D. Chandler, Ashon Crawley, and Christina Sharpe. Chandler argues, "Difference named under the heading of such 'world' or 'worldhood,' then, must be elaborated simultaneously as a question of the radical possibility of difference, of the general possibility of the otherwise, and, yet, it should also be understood as remarking the 'fact' that there is difference (maintaining thereby a critical inhabitation of a situation, historical, at once temporal and spatial)" ("Of Exorbitance," 351). Ashon Crawley theorizes that "otherwise bespeaks the ongoingness of possibility, of things existing other than what is given, what is known, what is grasped" (*Blackpentecostal Breath*, 24). And Christina Sharpe asserts, "There is a long history and present of imaging and imagining blackness and Black selves otherwise, in excess of the containment of the long and brutal history of the violent annotations of Black being" (*In the Wake*, 115).

INTRODUCTION

1. For other significant work on the color line, see Kawash, *Dislocating the Color Line*; Somerville, *Queering the Color Line*; Ross, *Manning the Race*; S. Smith, *Photography on the Color Line*; Stoever, *Sonic Color Line*; and Hartman, *Wayward Lives*.

2. Harding, "Responsibilities of the Black Scholar," 280–81.

3. R. Ferguson, "To Catch a Light-Filled Vision," 333–34.

4. Gumbs, *brokenbeautiful press*.

5. The ADA Amendments Act of 2008 (ADAAA) amended the American with Disabilities Act of 1990 (ADA), and it made changes to the definition of the term *disability* in an attempt to clarify and broaden it. It, among other things, clarified what the phrase "major life activities" means in its definition. Although those changes have increased the number and type of persons who are protected under the ADA, the amended definition is still narrower than the historical definition of the word *disability*. ADA Amendments Act of 2008, Pub. L. 110-324, § 12102, www.ada.gov.

6. *The Oxford English Dictionary Online*, s.v. "Disability," www.oed.com.

7. Russell, *Reading Embodied Citizenship*, 1, 3.

8. Some of the ADA's list of exclusions highlight this point. According to the ADA, "homosexuality and bisexuality are not impairments and as such are not disabilities," and neither are "transvestism, transsexualism, pedophilia, exhibitionism, [and] voyeurism," "compulsive gambling, kleptomania," or "psychoactive substance use disorders resulting from current illegal use of drugs" (§ 12211). Even in the lawmakers' clarification of what the definition of disability does not include, there is an exclusive focus on individual identity and behavior, not the system or structures.

9. Baynton, "Disability and the Justification of Inequality," 23.

10. James, *Freedom Bought with Blood*, 15.

11. For example, Samira Kawash writes, "To speak of the color line today is apparently to refer to a particular historical era in U.S. history, the era of Jim Crow and legal segregation. In the late nineteenth and the first half of the twentieth centuries, the color line was a palpable, physical boundary of separation. With a fine enough lens, one could map out the separate zones of blackness and whiteness within the nation's borders" (*Dislocating the Color Line*, 1). Kawash's use of the word "apparently" spotlights a scholarly trend of situating the color line within the Jim Crow era and linking it to racial segregation.

12. Douglass, "Address to the People of the United States," 674.

13. Du Bois, *Souls of Black Folk*, 17.

14. Du Bois, 17.

15. Du Bois, *Philadelphia Negro*, 325, 322.

16. Du Bois, "Strivings of the Negro People."

17. Du Bois, "Conservation of the Races," 46.

18. Douglass, "Color Line," 571. This "race of life" metaphor could also be understood through Liat Ben-Moshe's concept of "race-ability," "the ways race and disability, and racism, sanism, and ableism as intersecting oppressions, are mutually constitutive" (*Decarcerating Disability*, 5).

19. Du Bois, *Souls of Black Folk*, 16.

20. Du Bois, 10.

21. Du Bois, 11.

22. Du Bois, 11.

23. Stepto, *From Behind the Veil*, 113; Quashie, *Sovereignty of Quiet*, 14.

24. Chesnutt, *Marrow*, 61.
25. Chesnutt, 61.
26. Chesnutt, "What Is a White Man?," 38.
27. F. Harper, *Iola Leroy*, 233, 230.
28. F. Harper, 232, 233.
29. Gladwell, *Tipping Point*, 92, 7.
30. Goffman, *Stigma*, 4.
31. My observation is inspired by Eula Biss's examination of Marvin Bell's poem "Replica." Bell writes, "and Vico says all things having been named for the namers, us, / we give a chair arms, legs, a seat and a back, a cup has its lip / and a bottle its neck." Biss, *On Immunity*, 12.
32. Toomer, *Cane*, 57.
33. Geary, *I Is an Other*, 100.
34. Geary, 127.
35. Elizabeth I, qtd. in Doran, "The Queen," 50.
36. Hobbes, *Leviathan*, 80.
37. Schalk, *Bodyminds Reimagined*, 34.
38. Biss, *On Immunity*, 18.
39. Puar, *Right to Maim*, 72, 68–9.
40. R. Wright, "Literature of the Negro," 74, 106, 76–77, 102.
41. See, for example, the scholarship of Brooks, *Bodies in Dissent*; Hartman, *Scenes of Subjection*; McMillan, *Embodied Avatars*; Muhammad, *Condemnation of Blackness*; Nelson, *Body and Soul*; Pickens, *Black Madness*; D. Roberts, *Killing the Black Body*; S. Roberts, *Infectious Fear*; Ross, *Manning the Race*; Samuels, *Fantasies of Identification*; Spillers, "Mama's Baby, Papa's Maybe"; Sundquist, *To Wake the Nations*; and Washington, *Medical Apartheid*.
42. Hartman, *Scenes of Subjection*, 12.
43. Hartman, 13.
44. Brooks, *Bodies in Dissent*, 4.
45. Spillers, "Mama's Baby, Papa's Maybe," 72, 66; Brooks, *Bodies in Dissent*, 5.
46. Hartman, *Scenes of Subjection*, 12.
47. Brooks, *Bodies in Dissent*, 10.
48. Brooks, 5; Hartman, *Scenes of Subjection*, 11, 10.
49. In *The Long Emancipation*, the cultural studies scholar Rinaldo Walcott considers the relationship between deformation and Black social life. The "states of being for Black life-forms," he writes, "are fundamentally premised on practices of what Houston A. Baker Jr. called, in the context of African American literature, 'mastery of form and deformation of mastery.' I turn to Baker to flesh out how Black life-forms survive by both mastering the conditions under which life proceeds and simultaneously deforming those conditions so that they might have access to selves beyond the degrading violence of everyday life. . . . Black people had to master and deform the social relations of white supremacy as a structure of survival" (34).

50. Hartman, *Scenes of Subjection*, 77.
51. Saidiya Hartman's threefold framework of redress within enslaved communities informs my understanding of not only the limits of redress but also its possibilities. She writes,

     If redress does not or cannot restore or remedy loss, redeem the unceremoniously buried, or bridge the transatlantic divide, then what possibilities for relief, restitution, or recovery does it provide? First, redress is a re-membering of the social body that occurs precisely in the recognition and articulation of devastation, captivity, and enslavement. The re-membering of the violated body must be considered in relation to the dis-membered body of the slave—that is, the segmentation and organization of the captive body for purposes of work, reproduction, and punishment. This re-membering takes the form of attending to the body as a site of pleasure, eros, and sociality and articulating its violated condition. Second, redress is a limited form of action aimed at relieving the pained body through alternative configurations of the self and the redemption of the body as human flesh, not beast of burden. Third, redress concerns the articulation of needs and desires and the endeavor to meet them. It is an exercise of agency directed toward the release of the pained body, the reconstitution of violated natality, and the remembrance of breach. (*Scenes of Subjection*, 76–77)

52. Douglas Baynton, whom I have cited earlier, is one scholar who has explicitly articulated this claim. But this sentiment regarding Black folks' disavowal of disability recurs, though in a more moderate way, in the work of other scholars examining disability. That is, Baynton's assertion is usually accepted as the norm rather than as a point of contention.
53. Bell, "Is Disability Studies Actually White Disability Studies?," 374.
54. Puar, *Right to Maim*, xix.
55. Mitchell and Snyder, *Narrative Prosthesis*, 2.
56. Jarman, "Coming Up from Underground," 9.
57. Couser, "Disability Studies."
58. This kind of interdisciplinary work has been challenging for at least two other reasons. First, when examining two categories or identities, one must inevitably confront the issue of analogy, which can create a false separation and opposition between two categories or groups, obscuring the importance of one in favor of another. Analogy can be dangerous, particularly when discussing the intersections of race and disability. "If race and disability are conceived of as discrete categories to be compared, contrasted, or arranged in order of priority," says Anna Mollow, "it becomes impossible to think through complex intersections of racism and ableism in the lives of disabled people of color" ("When *Black* Women Start Going on Prozac," 69). Analogy, of course, can be powerful too, bridging a divide and forging a connection between disparate categories; and analogy so infuses our language that it can be nearly impossible to avoid. Our aim, then, should not be "to attempt to escape from analogy," suggests Ellen Samuels, but rather to "seek

to employ it more critically than in the past" ("My Body, My Closet," 235). Taking heed of these suggestions, I critically employ metaphor and other forms of analogy in this book, and I actively resist the impulse to flatten out different experiences of race and disability. This approach is vital because blackness and disability are neither monolithic nor homogeneous, and attempts to make them so diminish their protean possibilities.

Another reason that this interdisciplinary work has been challenging is that a desire for increased disciplinary visibility has led to a competitive strain between disability studies and other fields. For instance, in an effort to expand the stature and recognition of the field, disability studies scholars have characterized the attention given to matters of race, gender, and sexuality as more extensive than the attention paid to disability issues (Mitchell and Snyder, "Introduction," 1–2). The desire for disability to be included and acknowledged in a manner that is not marginal or cursory is certainly significant, but one effect of this framing is the formation of a competition between fields and competition for resources, with the added potential of eliding the differences between and neglecting the intersectionality of gender, race, sexuality, and disability. Moreover, scholars who, like me, are examining the intersections of two or more of these categories and fields are often put in the difficult position of prioritizing one over another. On more than one occasion, I have been asked whether the intended audience for my project is a disability studies audience or a race studies one. When I have explained that I want my book to speak to both of those audiences and beyond, my response has been met with stern suggestions to choose one, which has given me the impression that I am required to show some kind of disciplinary allegiance regardless of what my research reveals.

59. Puar, *Right to Maim*, xv, xiii–xiv.
60. Ben-Moshe, *Decarcerating Disability*, 30.
61. McRuer, *Crip Theory*, 208. See also Sandahl, "Queering the Crip or Cripping the Queer?," 25–56.
62. Kafer, *Feminist, Queer, Crip*, 15, 12. The disability studies scholar Michael Bérubé makes a similar point in his book *The Secret Life of Stories*. He argues "that disability in the relation between text and reader *need not involve any character with disabilities at all*. It can involve *ideas about* disability, and ideas about the stigma associated with disability, regardless of whether any specific character can be pegged with a specific diagnosis" (19, emphasis in original).
63. Hartman, *Wayward Lives, Beautiful Experiments*, 228.
64. Kendi, "Stop Blaming Black People."
65. Morrison, *Beloved*, 223.

CHAPTER 1. DAVID WALKER'S ACCESSIBLE *APPEAL*

1. In Richmond, Virginia, the mere sight of Walker's *Appeal* in the possession of a Black person was enough to spur a secret session of the General Assembly to fore-

stall the pamphlet's circulation; *Niles' Weekly Register* recorded that the Virginia House of Delegates even narrowly passed a bill eighty-one to eighty, making it illegal to instruct enslaved people to read or write in any venue ("school house, church, or meeting house, or other place") as well as to write, print, or circulate incendiary publications among them—though the Senate rightly rejected that bill eleven to seven (March 27, 1830, 87–88). Walker stated in his *Appeal* that he heard a "wretch in the state of North Carolina" say "that if any man would teach a black person whom he held in slavery, to spell, read or write, he would prosecute him to the very extent of the law." This "ignorant wretch" also said that "a Nigar, ought not to have any more sense than enough to work for his master" (55). While that ignorant wretch remained nameless, the law to which said wretch referred became even more stringent. By November 1830, three months after Walker's death, the General Assembly of North Carolina passed laws to prohibit "any person" (free or enslaved) not only from circulating and publishing "written or printed" materials ("pamphlet or paper") as well as using speech or "words" that "endeavor to excite in any slave or slaves or free negro or person of colour a spirit of insurrection, conspiracy or rebellion" but also from teaching enslaved people to read or write or giving or selling them "any books or pamphlets." The penalty for writing or circulating prohibited publications was twofold: any person convicted "shall for the first offence be imprisoned not less than one year and be put in the pillory and whipped, at the discretion of the court; and for the second offence shall suffer death without benefit of clergy." The penalty for teaching an enslaved person to read or write, however, varied depending on one's status as a "white man or woman," "free person of color," or "slave": a white man or woman shall "be fined not less than one hundred dollars, nor more than two hundred dollars, or imprisoned; and if a free person of color, shall be fined, imprisoned, or whipped, at the discretion of the court, not exceeding thirty nine lashes, nor less than twenty lashes"; and an enslaved person "shall be sentenced to receive thirty nine lashes on his or her bare back." North Carolina General Assembly, *Acts*, chaps. 5 and 6, 10–11. For more information about these laws and other restrictions, see Eaton, "Dangerous Pamphlet"; and Hinks, *To Awaken My Afflicted Brethren*.

2. Walker, *Appeal*, 68, 2.

3. Cornelius, *"When I Can Read My Title Clear,"* 66.

4. Several scholars have noted the challenges and difficulties of using the WPA testimonies. Saidiya Hartman, for instance, has detailed a litany of problems with the interviews, including "the construction of voice, the terms in which agency is identified, the dominance of the pastoral in representing slavery, the political imperatives that informed the construction of national memory, the ability of those interviewed to recall what had happened sixty years earlier, the use of white interviewers who were sometimes the sons and daughters of former owners in gathering the testimony, and so on" (*Scenes of Subjection*, 11). Nonetheless, Hartman agrees with the historian John Blassingame that the WPA narratives "are an important source of information about slavery," and she adds "that there is no

historical document that is not interested, exclusive, or a vehicle of power and domination" (12). I agree with Hartman and Blassingame about the significance of these narratives to the history of enslavement and its afterlife, and I use them with the same level caution outlined by Hartman, "with the awareness that a totalizing history cannot be reconstructed from these interested, selective, and fragmentary accounts and with an acknowledgment of the interventionist role of the interpreter, the equally interested labor of historical revision, and the impossibility of reconstituting the past free from the disfigurements of present concerns" (11).

5. Federal Writers' Project, *Slave Narrative Project*, vol. 13.
6. Hall and Elder, *Samuel Hall*, 18.
7. Walker, *Appeal*, 63, 64, 68, 18, 56.
8. Hinks, "Editor's Note," xlv; Wilentz, introduction to *David Walker's Appeal*, xix.
9. See, for example, Marable and Mullings, *Let Nobody Turn Us Around*, which does not reproduce the pointing index fingers.
10. Dinius, "Look!! Look!!! at This!!!!," 56.
11. Walker, *Appeal*, 2, 75.
12. Walker, 42, 29, 78, 79, 54.
13. Walker's ambiguous use of the pronoun "them" raises a number of questions: Does, as the historian Peter P. Hinks suggests, the pronoun "them" in the final clause and the pronoun "them" in the penultimate clause on the title page verso share the same antecedent: a literate "some one" (*To Awaken My Afflicted Brethren*, 107)? Does "them" in the final clause refer to "them" in the penultimate clause: an illiterate community? Does "them," as the literary scholars Elizabeth McHenry and Gene Jarrett imply, refer to what McHenry dubs "men of sense," a group that Walker also identifies as inspiration for his book design (McHenry, *Forgotten Readers*, 34; Jarrett, *Representing the Race*, 44)? Does "them" in the final clause refer to both "some one" and "them" in the penultimate clause and, hence, to both readers and auditors?
14. Walker, *Appeal*, 30, 74.
15. Walker, 23. I recognize that my reading of Walker's complicated understanding of ignorance is not a common one. It certainly does not help that Walker included in the *Appeal* a harsh criticism of an elderly Black man who boasts that his "son has a good education" because "he can read and write as well as any white man" (33). Taking issue with the way the elder framed good penmanship as equivalent to a good education rather than realizing that the mastery of grammar "in prose and in verse" constitutes an accurate measure of "the substance of learning," Walker replied, "Your son, . . . then, has hardly any learning at all—he is almost as ignorant, and more so, than many of those who never went to school one day in all their lives" (33). Later, Walker said that there are many "school-boys and young men of colour" in Boston, New York, Philadelphia, and Baltimore who are considered to have "an excellent education" because they "can write a good hand" but "may be almost as ignorant, in comparison, as a horse" (35). Gene Jarrett has interpreted Walker's lines as "the highest degree of his intellectual condescen-

sion" and as evidence that while he "was poised to represent the race, he did not see himself as part of it" (*Representing the Race*, 44). Although Walker's harsh comments are certainly difficult to read, I think that Jarrett's assessment of Walker is an overstatement and that we run the risk of misrepresenting Walker's commentary if we fail to consider it in its fuller context. First, the line that compares "young men of colour, *who have been to school*" yet have only attained good penmanship to a horse is repeated almost verbatim in a footnote in the fourth article to describe the violence of white people who have denied literacy to Black people. "It is a fact," Walker wrote, "that in all our Slave-holding States (in the countries) there are thousands of the whites, who are almost as ignorant in comparison as horses, the most they know, is to beat the coloured people, which some of them shall have their hearts full of yet" (*Appeal*, 55). In this example, white people are described as "ignorant" because of their violent and abusive antiliteracy tactics; here ignorance is determined by anti-Black vehemence, not race. Second, Walker's criticisms of the way some Black people equate penmanship with education came on the heels of his exchange with a Boston bootblack, who, after Walker reminded him of the "low" station of Black folks in the antebellum United States, exclaimed, "I am completely happy!!! I never want to live any better or happier than when I can get a plenty of boots and shoes to clean!!!" (31). The bootblack's reaction distressed Walker. But he was careful to explain that his objections to this man's reaction had nothing to do with his occupation: "Understand me, brethren, I do not mean to speak against the occupations by which we acquire enough and sometimes scarcely that, to render ourselves and families comfortable through life. I am subjected to the same inconvenience, as you all.—My objections are, to our *glorying* and being *happy* in such low employments; for if we are men, we ought to be thankful to the Lord for the past, and for the future. Be looking forward with thankful hearts to higher attainments than *wielding the razor* and *cleaning boots and shoes*. The man whose aspirations are not *above*, and even *below* these, is indeed ignorant and wretched enough" (31–32). Ignorance, in this instance, is measured by the bootblack's low aspirations, his contentment with a world that suppresses his will and fosters his complacency.

16. *Pieces I Am*, 00:09:33–00:10:16.
17. *Pieces I Am*, 00:08:12–00:08:17. In *Black Skin, White Masks*, Frantz Fanon describes the white gaze in violent terms: "I arrive slowly in the world; sudden emergences are no longer my habit. I crawl along. The white gaze, the only valid one, is already dissecting me. I am *fixed*. Once their microtomes are sharpened, the Whites objectively cut sections of my reality. I have been betrayed. I sense, I see in this white gaze that it's the arrival not of a new man, but of a new type of man, a new species. A Negro, in fact!" (95).
18. Kazanjian, *Colonizing Trick*, 9–10.
19. Walker, *Appeal*, 78–79.
20. McHenry, *Forgotten Readers*, 36.
21. Walker, *Appeal*, 54.

22. Sheridan, *General Dictionary of the English Language*, 46.

23. Sheridan, 46.

24. Sheridan, 47.

25. Fliegelman, *Declaring Independence*, 10. Fliegelman writes, "The locations of the marks on the rough draft of the Declaration as well as the locations of the 'quotation marks' on the proof copy of the Dunlap broadside represent not breath or punctuational pauses but precisely what Jefferson discusses: rhythmical pauses of emphatical stress that divide the piece into units comparable to musical bars or poetic lines. These marks are identical to the ones suggested by the influential Irish rhetorician Thomas Sheridan in his *Lectures on the Art of Reading* (1775)" (10).

26. Sheridan, *General Dictionary of the English Language*, 47.

27. Foster, "Narrative of the Interesting Origins," 725–26.

28. Foster, 726.

29. Jarrett, *Representing the Race*, 28.

30. PBS Online, "David Walker, 1796–1830."

31. McHenry, *Forgotten Readers*, 42, 23.

32. Minich, *Accessible Citizenships*, 12, 18–19.

33. McRuer, *Crip Theory*, 94.

34. *Dred Scott v. Sandford*, 60 U.S. 393, 407 (1857).

35. Walker, *Appeal*, 3.

36. Walker, 68–69.

37. Dinius, "Look!! Look!!! at This!!!!," 59.

38. Bynum, "Why I Heart David Walker," 15.

39. Backscheider, "Punctuation for the Reader," 874.

40. Brody, *Punctuation*, 150.

41. Adorno, "Punctuation Marks," 300.

42. Lasky, *Proofreading and Copy-Preparation*, 30.

43. Lasky, 30.

44. Adorno, "Punctuation Marks," 304.

45. Walker enclosed racial euphemisms within parentheses in other sections of his *Appeal*. In a revealing footnote that was inserted after a different parenthetical phrase "(Negro Slavery.)*," Walker wrote, "*'Niger,' is a word derived from the Latin, which was used by the old Romans, to designate inanimate beings, which were black: such as soot, pot, wood, house, &c. Also, animals which they considered inferior to the human species, as a black horse, cow, hog, bird, dog, &c. The white Americans have applied this term to Africans, by way of reproach for our colour, to aggravate and heighten our miseries, because they have their feet on our throats" (57). Walker's explanation of the Romans' use of "Niger" drew a connection to the Americans' use of the pejorative *nigger*. Only once did Walker use the word "NIGGER!!!!" in his *Appeal*, and he used it only in the third edition (11). His limited usage of the term suggests that he knew all too well how this expletive has been used to stigmatize Black people.

46. Sherman, *Used Books*, 29, 42.
47. Sherman, 29.
48. I wonder to what extent there might be a connection between the pointing index fingers and American Sign Language (ASL). The history of the pointing index finger predates the formation of ASL (which emerged as a language in 1817 in the American School for the Deaf in West Hartford, Connecticut), but the visual and performative aspects of the pointing index finger (as well as the image of the hand) probably would have been of interest to deaf communities.
49. Sherman, *Used Books*, 33.
50. Sherman argues,

    There are, however, clear benefits in knowing that the word you are using to describe something will be the same word used in the databases you (or your readers) might want to search and that it will be understood by most people without requiring a trip to the dictionary. For my part, I have settled on "manicule" because it is the most general, accurate, and neutral description of the symbol: it derives from the Latin *maniculum*, simply meaning "a little hand" (in any posture). Another thing that "manicule" has going for it is that it applies equally to little hands in all kinds of texts, and to those produced *by* readers as well as *for* them, whereas "fist" has its origins in printers' slang and should probably be restricted to the products of the printing press. The biggest problem with "manicule"—aside from its failure to account for the pointing finger—is that it is not (officially) an English word, and will be easily confused with "manacle" and "manicure." It is apparently the standard term for the symbol in modern romance languages and it is belatedly being imported into English, but it is not yet in the *OED* or any other dictionary of current usage. (34)

51. Federal Writers' Project, *Slave Narrative Project*, vol. 4.
52. Robin Bernstein, *Racial Innocence*, 71–72.
53. Jarrett, *Representing the Race*, 30.
54. Walker, *Appeal*, 18, 17.
55. Onuf, introduction to *Notes on the State of Virginia*, xi. See also Ellis, *American Sphinx*.
56. Jarrett, *Representing the Race*, 31. This connection between the Declaration of Independence and *Notes* and rights and capability has a particular genealogy worth unpacking. Harvey C. Mansfield Jr. suggests reading *Notes* "as Jefferson's own justification for the Declaration of Independence." Mansfield writes, "Now that the *right* of the American people to independence has been established, their *capability* for independence must be demonstrated" ("Thomas Jefferson," 56). Matthew Cordova Frankel, then, invites scholars to "read anew" Mansfield's old proposition ("'Nature's Nation' Revisited," 702). Jarrett does so by thinking about political representation of Black people in Jefferson's *Notes* (*Representing the Race*).
57. Jefferson, *Notes on the State of Virginia*, 133, 129, 130.

58. Jefferson, 133, 129, 131.
59. Jefferson, 128, 129, 132, 133.
60. Brodie, *Thomas Jefferson*, 158.
61. Jefferson, *Notes on the State of Virginia*, 129, 130, 66, 67.
62. Jefferson, 129, 128.
63. Jefferson, 136.
64. Jefferson, 129.
65. Jordan, *White over Black*, 438.
66. Jefferson, *Notes on the State of Virginia*, 125–26.
67. Walker, *Appeal*, 9.
68. Jefferson, *Notes on the State of Virginia*, 131.
69. Walker, *Appeal*, 16.
70. Walker, 17.
71. Jefferson, *Notes on the State of Virginia*, 131.
72. Jefferson, 133.
73. Holland, *Erotic Life of Racism*, 107.
74. Holland, 107.
75. Stanton, *"Those Who Labor for My Happiness,"* 8.
76. State of Virginia, "Act Declaring What Persons Shall Be Deemed Mulattoes."
77. Jefferson, *Notes on the State of Virginia*, 131.
78. M. Wright, *Becoming Black*, 58.
79. According to the historian R. B. Bernstein, Senator Warren G. Harding coined the term "founding fathers" in his 1916 keynote address at the Republican National Convention in Chicago. Bernstein, *Founding Fathers Reconsidered*, 3–5.
80. Gordon-Reed, *Hemingses of Monticello*, 267.
81. Walker, *Appeal*, 17.
82. Walker, 9.
83. Walker, 48, 49, 47–48.
84. Walker, 48.
85. Walker, 48, 68, 67, 65.
86. Walker, 59, 62.
87. Walker, 59, 60.
88. Walker, 60.
89. Walker, 67.
90. Walker, 70.
91. *The Oxford English Dictionary Online*, s.v. "Injury," www.oed.com.
92. Walker, *Appeal*, 28–29.
93. Foucault, *Order of Things*, 386.
94. Wynter, "Unsettling the Coloniality of Being/Power/Truth/Freedom," 266, 277.
95. Walker, *Appeal*, 28.
96. Walker, 30.
97. Walker, 12.
98. Walker, 30.

99. Walker, 41, 42.
100. Walker, 51.
101. Walker, 63–64.
102. Walker, 41.
103. Wheatley, "On Being Brought from Africa to America," 18.
104. Walker, *Appeal*, 78.
105. Dinius, "Look!! Look!!! at This!!!!," 68.
106. Walker, *Appeal*, 2.

CHAPTER 2. FUGITIVES' DISABILITIES

1. Brown, *Narrative of the Life*, 85. There are two versions of Brown's *Narrative*: the 1849 Boston edition (which is titled *Narrative of Henry Box Brown: Who Escaped from Slavery, Enclosed in a Box Three Feet Long, Two Wide, and Two and Half High, Written from a Statement of Facts Made by Himself, with Remarks upon the Remedy for Slavery by Charles Stearns*) and the 1851 British edition (which is titled *Narrative of the Life of Henry Box Brown, Written by Himself*). Charles Stearns, Brown's amanuensis, assumed more narrative control over the 1849 publication of Brown's *Narrative*. The title of the 1849 edition states that the narrative is a "Statement of Facts Made by Himself," and it ambiguously lists Charles Stearns as the author of the "Remarks upon the Remedy for Slavery" (which refers to Stearns's essay titled "Cure for the Evil of Slavery"). Stearns's essay is appended to the *Narrative* but does not conclude it. The 1851 publication of *Narrative*, however, emphasizes Brown's authorial control. The title page lists only Brown's name as author, and the title states that the narrative was "Written by Himself." Unless stated otherwise, my analysis of Brown's *Narrative* relies primarily on the 1851 edition. However, I occasionally move between the two texts to illustrate how disability and other aspects of the narrative are emphasized or deemphasized. For instance, the 1849 edition refers to Brown's finger as "disabled" and "lame," while the 1851 version revises this language, opting instead to focus on the overseer's suggestion to wrap the finger in a poultice. Brown, *Narrative of Henry Box Brown*, 58.

2. Craft and Craft, *Running*, 37, 23–24.

3. "By the turn of the century," Baynton writes, "medical doctors were still arguing that African Americans were disabled by freedom and therefore in need of greater oversight" ("Disability and the Justification of Inequality," 21). One of those doctors was J. F. Miller, who, in the *North Carolina Medical Journal*, claimed that "there are more congenital defects among the negroes as demonstrated by the large number of symmetrically developed crania. . . . In his ignorance of the laws of his being, the functions of citizenship and the responsibilities and duties which freedom imposed, demands were made upon the negro which his intellectual parts were unable to discharge. . . . In the wholesale violation of these laws after the war, as previously stated, was laid the foundation of the degeneration of the physical and mental constitution of the negro" ("Effects of Emancipation," 289, 290).

4. Brown, *Narrative of the Life*, 83, 84.

5. Brown, *Narrative of Henry Box Brown*, 59.

6. Brooks, *Bodies in Dissent*, 11.

7. For accounts of Brown as a magician, scientist, showman, performance artist, or mesmerist, see Brooks, *Bodies in Dissent*; Ernest, "Introduction"; Grover, *Fugitive's Gibraltar*; Ruggles, *Unboxing of Henry Box Brown*; Rusert, *Fugitive Science*; and M. Wood, *Blind Memory*.

8. Brown, *Narrative of the Life*, 84.

9. Douglass, *Narrative*, 75, 74.

10. Brown, *Narrative of the Life*, 66.

11. Northup, *Twelve Years a Slave*, 116.

12. Brown, *Narrative of the Life*, 66.

13. Brown, 87.

14. Brown, 67.

15. Brown, 84–85, 89.

16. Brown, 93, 95.

17. Dayan, *Law Is a White Dog*, 169, 148.

18. Redmond, *Everything Man*, 89.

19. Brown, *Narrative of the Life*, 96.

20. Brown, *Narrative of Henry Box Brown*, 61.

21. Brown, 92.

22. Brown, *Narrative of the Life*, 85.

23. Grover, *Fugitive's Gibraltar*, 201.

24. Brown, *Narrative of the Life*, 85–86.

25. Goodell, *American Slave Code in Theory and Practice*, 105.

26. Robin Bernstein, *Racial Innocence*, 50. Saidiya Hartman also discusses the slander of Black insensateness: "If this pain has been largely unspoken and unrecognized, it is due to the sheer denial of black sentience rather than the inexpressibility of pain. The purported immunity of blacks to pain is absolutely essential to the spectacle of contented subjection or, at the very least, to discrediting the claims of pain" (*Scenes of Subjection*, 51).

27. If Brown's self-inflicted disability and descriptions of disabling pain during his boxed journey combated the libel of Black insensateness, then his restaging of his escape in Britain combated the libel of his unfitness for citizenship. For one of his lectures in Britain, Brown enclosed himself in a box for a ninety-minute train trip between Bradford and Leeds. He made a spectacular entrance, jumping out of the box in front of an audience. This reenactment revealed Brown's remarkable stamina. When he restaged his boxed escape for British audiences, he not only showed them how he executed his escape but also exhibited that he had the stamina—the fitness—to do it all again (if necessary).

28. Schalk, *Bodyminds Reimagined*, 38. Schalk does clarify that there are "two major exceptions to this representational absence" of disability in slave narratives: "one, when disability is represented as an effect of slavery on another person who is

not the author and is then used as an example of the evils of the slave system, and, two, when disability is represented with the narrator, but cured, erased, or overcome in freedom" (38).

29. For more on birthright citizenship, see M. Jones, *Birthright Citizens*.

30. Craft and Craft, *Running*, 16. "Although William is the narrator of *Running a Thousand Miles for Freedom*," Ellen Samuels observes that "there appears to be no critical consensus on the authorship of the narrative." Samuels notes that some scholars, like Barbara McCaskill, Charles Heglar, and Sarah Brusky, credit William and Ellen as collaborators in "the production of the narrative." Other scholars, such as John W. Blassingame and Dawn Keetley, "attribute the narrative to a collaboration between Ellen, William, and a (presumably white) amanuensis." Laura Browder, on the other hand, disputes the possibility that William, because of his illiteracy during slavery, could have written the narrative. I agree with Samuels's take, and I am "treating the narrative as a collaborative effort and referring to both Crafts as the authors." Samuels, *Fantasies of Identification*, 218n2.

31. Craft and Craft, *Running*, 21–22, 19, 20–21, 39, 24, 35, 23–24.

32. Craft and Craft, 37, 24. Ellen's performance of disability was not novel. Some scholars have noted how enslaved people feigned illness and disability as a form of resistance. See Ernest, "Introduction," 11; Fett, *Working Cures*, 169–92; Hartman, *Scenes of Subjection*, 50–52; Savitt, *Medicine and Slavery*, 163; and White, *Ar'n't I a Woman?*, 79–87.

33. Erevelles, "Race," 146.

34. For more on racial uplift, see K. Gaines, *Uplifting the Race*.

35. Samuels, *Fantasies of Identification*, 30.

36. Samuels, 28, 70, 29.

37. McMillan, *Embodied Avatars*, 75, 76.

38. Barrett, "Hand-Writing," 331, 324, 323.

39. Samuels, *Fantasies of Identification*, 32.

40. McMillan, *Embodied Avatars*, 76.

41. Samuels, *Fantasies of Identification*, 37.

42. Samuels notes this dynamic in her examination of the Crafts. Even though the "disability of illiteracy profoundly impacted the lives of formerly enslaved authors like the Crafts and Frederick Douglass," Samuels observes that "to discuss illiteracy as disability resonates with centuries of characterizations of African Americans as flawed or defective, incapable of acquiring the ability that has come to equal personhood in post-Enlightenment Western culture" (36).

43. E. Alexander, "Can You Be BLACK and Look at This?," 94. Elizabeth Alexander discusses how dominant narratives have historically situated African Americans in opposition to citizenship. The primary reason for this oppositional relationship is because "the white-authored national narrative deliberately contradicts the histories our bodies know. There have always been narratives to justify the barbaric practices of slavery and lynching," Alexander argues. "African-Americans have always existed in a counter-citizen relationship to the law; how else to contend

with knowing oneself as a whole human being when the Constitution defines you as 'three-fifths'? The American way with regard to the actual lived experience of African-Americans has been to write a counter-narrative where needed, which erased bodily information as we knew it and substituted a counter-text that has in many cases become a version of national memory" (94–95).

44. This erasure is why Lindon Barrett argues that formerly enslaved authors composing slave narratives face a "central textual dilemma" during the writing process. "Given that African American bodies are understood in terms of a 'fleshliness' that overdetermines all other possible aspects of their identity," Barrett states, "these narrators must not only recover their bodies within their narratives but also, more importantly, remove their bodies from these narratives" ("Hand-Writing," 315). This dual process of both recovery within and removal from narratives of slavery is a formidable task. It requires that ex-slave authors, like the Crafts, "highlight the primary terms by which African American identity is construed . . . as obdurate materiality" yet either revise or reject these "hostile terms of absolute corporeality and also refigure and represent white bodies" (316, 318).

45. Jenkins, *Private Lives*, 5, 4, 6, 8.

46. Craft and Craft, *Running*, 24.

47. Craft and Craft, 22.

48. "The most common disability argument for slavery," states Douglas Baynton, "was simply that African Americans lacked sufficient intelligence to participate or compete on an equal basis in society with white Americans." Medical authorities, for example, explained that "a deficiency of cerebral matter in the cranium, and an excess of nervous matter distributed to the organs of sensation and assimilation . . . [caused] that debasement of mind, which has rendered the people of Africa unable to take care of themselves" ("Disability and the Justification of Inequality," 20).

49. Barrett, "Hand-Writing," 323–24.

50. Craft and Craft, *Running*, 36, 37.

51. Robin Bernstein, *Racial Innocence*, 71, 12.

52. Craft and Craft, *Running*, 37.

53. Craft and Craft, 34.

54. Samuels, *Fantasies of Identification*, 45.

55. Craft and Craft, 45, 46, 47.

56. Craft and Craft, 40. In *Black on Both Sides*, C. Riley Snorton refers to this exchange among William Johnson, William Craft, a white mistress, and a "very respectable looking gentleman" as a "*mise en abyme*, as a smaller copy with the larger portrayal of the context and logics that shaped the Crafts' escape" (79).

57. Craft and Craft, *Running*, 21.

58. Welter, "Cult of True Womanhood," 152.

59. Gilman, *Difference and Pathology*, 101.

60. Jenkins, *Private Lives*, 7. For more on the cult of true womanhood, see Carby, *Reconstructing Womanhood*; and duCille, *Coupling Convention*, 3–12.

61. Summers, *Manliness and Its Discontents*, 100.

62. Craft and Craft, *Running*, 68–69.

63. Craft and Craft, 10–11.

64. Craft and Craft, 10.

65. E. Alexander, "Can You Be BLACK and Look at This?," 108.

66. The phrase "furtive-yet-firm 'fuck you'" is inspired by the commentary of Robin Bernstein, who describes the "trenchant political critique" and bitter "humor" of enslaved female dollmakers as a "demurely murmured fuck you'" (*Racial Innocence*, 89, 90).

67. Kuppers, *Disability and Contemporary Performance*, 1–2.

68. Craft and Craft, *Running*, 54.

69. Rusert, "Science of Freedom," 298.

70. Still, *Underground Rail Road*, 374, 375.

71. McCaskill, "William and Ellen Craft."

72. Still, *Underground Rail Road*, 374.

73. McCaskill, "William and Ellen Craft."

74. McCaskill, "Yours Very Truly," 523, 524.

75. Brooks, "Introduction," xv.

76. Ernest, "Appendix A," 118–21.

77. Ernest, "Appendix A," 108.

78. Craft and Craft, *Running*, 10.

79. Craft and Craft, 24.

80. Bland, *Voices of the Fugitives*, 150.

81. For additional analyses of the engraving, see McCaskill, "Yours Very Truly"; and Weinauer, "Most Respectable Looking Gentleman."

82. Samuels, *Fantasies of Identification*, 34.

83. McMillan, *Embodied Avatars*, 88.

84. Barrett, "Hand-Writing," 328.

CHAPTER 3. THE CURIOUS CASE OF JIM CROW

1. Woodward, *Strange Career of Jim Crow*, v.

2. Woodward, 7.

3. "Old Actor's Memories," 10.

4. In *Scenes of Subjection*, Hartman argues that the "innocent amusements and spectacles of mastery orchestrated by members of the slaveholding class to establish their dominion and regulate the little leisure allowed the enslaved were significant components of slave performance. Consequently, it is difficult, if not impossible, to establish an absolute and definitive division between 'going before the master' and other amusements" (8).

5. Litwack, *Trouble in Mind*, xiv.

6. *Plessy v. Ferguson*, 163 U.S. 537, 542 (1896).

7. *Plessy*, 163 U.S. at 543.

8. *Plessy*, 163 U.S. at 551–52.

9. *Plessy*, 163 U.S. at 557.
10. Hartman, *Scenes of Subjection*, 206.
11. *Dred Scott v. Sandford*, 60 U.S. 393, 410, 416 (1857).
12. *Dred Scott*, 60 U.S. at 407.
13. *Dred Scott*, 60 U.S. at 409.
14. Sundquist, *To Wake the Nations*, 236.
15. Hartman, *Scenes of Subjection*, 201.
16. *Plessy*, 163 U.S. at 559.
17. *Plessy*, 163 U.S. at 540.
18. Irons, *Jim Crow's Children*, 24.
19. My account of *Plessy v. Ferguson* and its background relies primarily on the following sources: Elliott, *Color-Blind Justice*, 262–95; Irons, *Jim Crow's Children*, 24–42; Medley, *We as Freemen*; Olsen, *Thin Disguise*; Sundquist, *To Wake the Nations*, 225–70; Thomas, introduction to *"Plessy v. Ferguson"*; and Tourgée, "Brief for Plaintiff in Error."
20. Referring to the Daniel Desdunes case, Mark Elliott claims that "the choice of male plaintiff probably came from the committee's desire to project an image of 'manly resistance' to the public—as well as its recognition that the plaintiff would be hauled off to jail and put in a position of vulnerability while in police hands" (*Color-Blind Justice*, 265).
21. Roach, *Cities of the Dead*, 235. For more on the Citizens' Committee's objectives, see Elliott, 264; and Best, *Fugitive's Properties*.
22. Tourgée, "Brief for Plaintiff in Error," 32–33.
23. Tourgée, 62–63.
24. Tourgée, 63.

CHAPTER 4. LOSING LIMBS IN THE REPUBLIC

1. Chesnutt, "What Is a White Man?," 38.
2. Cable, "Negro Question," 1; Chesnutt, "What Is a White Man?," 38.
3. In *Reconstruction: America's Unfinished Revolution*, the historian Eric Foner, resisting the narratives of Reconstruction that pit the North against the South and white people against Black people, argues for a more comprehensive understanding of the period, during which the fight for racial equality "arose from a complex series of interactions among blacks and whites, Northerners and Southerners, in which victories were often tentative and outcomes subject to challenge and revision." He asserts that the "ongoing process of social and economic change, moreover, was intimately related to the politics of Reconstruction, for various groups of blacks and whites sought to use state and local government to promote their own interests and define their place in the region's new social order" (xxxiii).
4. Chesnutt, "What Is a White Man?," 37.
5. Chesnutt, 37. Chesnutt wrote, "It is of course perfectly obvious that the writer or speaker who used this expression—perhaps Mr. [Henry] Grady of Georgia— did not say what he meant. It is not probable that he meant to exclude from full

citizenship the Celts and Teutons and Gauls and Slavs who make up so large a proportion of our population; he hardly meant to exclude the Jews" (37). For a book-length examination of the political history of whiteness, see Jacobson, *Whiteness of a Different Color.*

6. Chesnutt, "Future American," pt. 3, 24.
7. Chesnutt, "What Is a White Man?," 38.
8. Chesnutt, "Future American," pt. 3, 24.
9. Ross, *Manning the Race*, 32.
10. S. Ferguson, "Chesnutt's Genuine Blacks," 109–10.
11. Elder, "Future American Race," 122, 123.
12. Chesnutt, "Future American," pt. 2, 15; Chesnutt, "Future American," pt. 1, 20.
13. Ross, *Manning the Race*, 33.
14. Ross, 34.
15. Chesnutt, "What Is a White Man?," 41.
16. Chen, *Animacies*, 218.
17. Chesnutt, "Negro in Books," 180.
18. Chesnutt, 178.
19. While Chesnutt was pursuing his writing career and breaking into the literary scene, he worked as a legal stenographer and court reporter.
20. Cable, *Grandissimes*, 191, 192.
21. Puar, *Right to Maim*, xviii.
22. *The Conjure Stories*, a volume edited by Robert B. Stepto and Jennifer Rae Greeson, includes all fourteen Uncle Julius stories, presented "in the order in which Chesnutt composed them, mainly so that the reader can discern how Chesnutt experimented with his plots and characters and with the *idea* of the conjure story over time" (Stepto, introduction to *The Conjure Stories*, vii). Seven of the stories included in this edition were published together in the 1899 volume *The Conjure Woman*. And all of the stories, with the exception of "The Dumb Witness," were published while Chesnutt was alive.
23. Howells, "Mr. Charles W. Chesnutt's Stories."
24. See Baker, *Modernism and the Harlem Renaissance*; Stepto, "Simple but Intensely Human Inner Life"; Sundquist, *To Wake the Nations*; and Wonham, *Charles W. Chesnutt*.
25. Mollow, "When *Black* Women Start Going on Prozac," 70.
26. Chesnutt, "Post-Bellum," 906.
27. Chesnutt, 906. For more on the structure of Chesnutt's conjure tales, see Stepto, "The Simple but Intensely Human Inner Life of Slavery."
28. Penningroth, *Claims of Kinfolk*, 102.
29. Chesnutt, *Conjure Stories*, 5, 4, 131.
30. Chesnutt, 14.
31. Garland-Thomson, *Extraordinary Bodies*, 105.
32. Chesnutt, *Conjure Stories*, 17.
33. Chesnutt, 17.
34. Chesnutt, 18.

35. Chesnutt, 19.
36. Penningroth, *Claims of Kinfolk*, 101.
37. Douglass, *Narrative*, 71.
38. Chesnutt, *Conjure Stories*, 21, 22.
39. Sklar, "What the Hell Happened to Maggie?," 142.
40. Chesnutt, *Conjure Stories*, 16.
41. Chesnutt, 3.
42. Stepto and Greeson argue that "Annie's 'ailment,' as John describes it, seems related to neurasthenia, a condition thought by turn-of-the-century physicians to afflict elite American women disproportionately. Since the couple is childless, too, the nature of the story Julius concocts in response to her 'ailment' suggests that Annie may have suffered a miscarriage or other problems related to childbearing." Chesnutt, *Conjure Stories*, 102n2. For more on neurasthenia, see also Brodhead, introduction to *The Conjure Woman and Other Conjure Tales*, 6–7; Herndl, *Invalid Women*, 117–18; and Lutz, *American Nervousness*.
43. *Code Noir English Regulations*, 431.
44. Chesnutt, *Conjure Stories*, 21.
45. Chesnutt, 63.
46. Chesnutt, 67n1, 68.
47. Chesnutt, 61.
48. Chesnutt, 66n8.
49. Chesnutt, 66, 67, 62.
50. Chesnutt, 66.
51. Chesnutt, 65.
52. Garrison, "Dumb Witness," 94.
53. Chesnutt, *Conjure Stories*, 66, 68.
54. Chesnutt, 68.
55. Van Evrie, *White Supremacy and Negro Subordination*, 221.
56. Cartwright, "Report on the Diseases," 707.
57. Pickens, *Black Madness*, 8.
58. Chesnutt, *Conjure Stories*, 69.
59. Sundquist, *To Wake the Nations*, 390.
60. Boster, *African American Slavery and Disability*, 2.
61. Chesnutt, *Conjure Stories*, 30–31.
62. Chesnutt, 22.
63. Bennett, *Being Property Once Myself*, 2.
64. Chesnutt, *Conjure Stories*, 28–31.
65. Chesnutt, 24.
66. Jackson, *Becoming Human*, 18, 1.
67. Jackson, 20.
68. Chesnutt, *Conjure Stories*, 24.
69. Chesnutt, 25.
70. Wonham, *Charles W. Chesnutt*, 30–31.

71. Wonham, 32.

72. For more on these racial stereotypes and beliefs of Black inhumanity and innate biological defects, see Fredrickson, *Black Image in the White Mind*; and Cassuto, *Inhuman Race*.

73. Sundquist, *To Wake the Nations*, 360.

74. Chesnutt, *Conjure Stories*, 31.

75. Slote, "Listening to 'The Goophered Grapevine,'" 693. Additionally, in an 1889 letter to Albion W. Tourgée, Chesnutt disclosed a nagging sense that he had exhausted his use of Julius and that he should abandon the familiar features of the plantation legend: "I think I have used up the old Negro who serves as a mouthpiece," he fretted, "and shall drop him in future stories, as well as much of the dialect." Chesnutt to Albion W. Tourgée, September 26, 1889, in *"To Be an Author,"* 44.

76. Howells, "Mr. Charles W. Chesnutt's Stories," 700.

77. Howells, "Psychological Counter-Current," 882. Howells was not alone in his displeasure with Chesnutt's *Marrow*. Other critics, like J. Saunders Redding, expressed disappointment with the novel's interest in "propaganda [and] melodramatic madness" (*To Make a Poet Black*, 74–75). Echoing Redding, Edward Margolies also described Chesnutt's novels as "melodramatic, propagandistic and overwritten" and claimed that "his stories are on a level not much higher than his novels" (*Native Sons*, 24). Though some critics considered propaganda and melodrama as strange bedfellows and conveyed frustration with Chesnutt's use of such elements in his novel, Chesnutt probably included both in *Marrow* on purpose. In a 1901 letter to Houghton Mifflin, he expressed a sincere hope that his work might "become lodged in the popular mind as the legitimate successor to *Uncle Tom's Cabin* and the *Fool's Errand*," two novels that are well known for their political bent and sentimentality. Chesnutt to Houghton, Mifflin and Company, October 26, 1901, in *"To Be an Author,"* 162.

78. Chesnutt to Walter Hines Page, November 11, 1898, in *"To Be an Author,"* 116.

79. Chesnutt, *Marrow*, 33.

80. Chesnutt, 31.

81. Chesnutt, 61.

82. For more information on Procrustes (also spelled Prokroustes), see Gantz, *Early Greek Myth*, 253–55; Hamilton, "Theseus," 211; and Hemenway, "Baxter's Procrustes."

83. Chesnutt, *Marrow*, 251, 304.

84. Gillman, *Blood Talk*, 78.

85. Ianovici, "Living Death," 42–43. Gillman and Ianovici are not the only scholars who evaluate the figure of Procrustes in relation to class. For example, Bryan Wagner argues, "This gruesome image of decapitation naturalizes class distinction through a metaphor of organic growth. It asserts that members of the African American middle class have effectively grown taller than their working-class associates. Moreover, by representing the African American middle class as the

principal target of white animosity, Chesnutt observes the extent to which the African American working class was also victimized by these policies" ("Charles Chesnutt," 336).

86. Wagner, "Charles Chesnutt," 336.
87. Chesnutt, *Marrow*, 53–54.
88. Chesnutt, 54–55.
89. Chesnutt, 80.
90. Chesnutt, 58.
91. Chesnutt, 59.
92. Lee, *Interracial Encounters*, 66.
93. Chesnutt, *Marrow*, 60, 61.
94. Chesnutt, 56.
95. Garland-Thomson, *Staring*, 40, 43.
96. Chesnutt, *Marrow*, 49, 57.
97. Chesnutt, 56.
98. City of Chicago, *Municipal Code of Chicago*, 377. Marcia P. Burgdorf and Robert Burgdorf Jr. describe these codes as "ugly laws" ("History of Unequal Treatment," 863).
99. Schweik, *Ugly Laws*, 184.
100. Schweik, 185.
101. Chesnutt, *Marrow*, 109, 58, 59.
102. Chesnutt, 111, 112.
103. Chesnutt, 251–52, 110.
104. Sundquist, introduction to *Marrow*, xli.
105. Chesnutt, *Marrow*, 109.
106. Yarborough, "Violence, Manhood, and Black Heroism," 232.
107. Chesnutt, *Marrow*, 110.
108. Chesnutt, 112, 111.
109. Chesnutt, 113–14.
110. K. Mitchell, *From Slave Cabins to the White House*, 5, 3.
111. Chesnutt, 284, 59, 309.
112. Chesnutt, 308, 243, 298.
113. Chesnutt, 133, 35, 13, 312.
114. Ianovici, "Living Death," 40–41.
115. Chesnutt, *Marrow*, 295–96.
116. Chesnutt, 287.

CHAPTER 5. THE DISABILITIES OF CASTE

1. For more on theories of racial degeneracy and racial extinction, see Fredrickson, *Black Image in the White Mind*, 228–55.
2. J. Johnson, "Best Methods," 425.
3. J. Johnson, 423.
4. For more on caste, see Dollard, *Caste and Class in a Southern Town*; Davis, Gardner, and Gardner, *Deep South*; and Wilkerson, *Caste*. Wilkerson writes, "Caste

and race are neither synonymous nor mutually exclusive. They can and do coexist in the same culture and serve to reinforce each other. Race, in the United States, is the visible agent of the unseen force of caste. Caste is the bones, race the skin. Race is what we can see, the physical traits that have been given arbitrary meaning and become shorthand for who a person is. Caste is the powerful infrastructure that holds each group in its place" (19).

5. J. Johnson, "Best Methods," 423.

6. See Rachel Adams, Benjamin Reiss, and David Serlin's definition of disability in *Keywords for Disability Studies* ("Disability").

7. Cooper, *Voice from the South*, 218.

8. Cooper, 192, 193. See Frances E. W. Harper's *Iola Leroy* and Jessie Fauset's *Plum Bun* for more examples of Black writers during Johnson's era who were commenting on the intersections of blackness and disability.

9. Erevelles, "Crippin' Jim Crow," 85.

10. Erevelles, 94.

11. Ross, *Manning the Race*, 22.

12. The critical race theorist Cheryl I. Harris outlines the close relationship between race, property, and value in her examination of the four functional criteria of property: the right of possession, use, and disposition; the right to use and enjoyment; the right to protect one's reputation; and the absolute right to exclude. In her discussion of the classical theory of property and its focus on human rights, liberties, and immunities (such as freedom of expression and freedom from bodily harm), Harris also shows how property was described as diametrical to disability ("Whiteness as Property").

13. Best, *Fugitive's Properties*, 15.

14. Alongside other scholars in Black studies, gender studies, US history, and disability, I expand the way we understand the era of Jim Crow. See M. Alexander, *New Jim Crow*; Erevelles, "Crippin' Jim Crow"; Gilmore, *Gender and Jim Crow*; and Ross, *Manning the Race*, 2. Also, for more information about the concept of positional goods, see Brighouse and Swift, "Equality, Priority, and Positional Goods."

15. V. Smith, *Self-Discovery and Authority*, 45.

16. For more details on Johnson's train ride to Atlanta University as well as other biographical details, see J. Johnson, *Along This Way*, 58–66; Fleming, *James Weldon Johnson*, 1–6; and Levy, *James Weldon Johnson*, 3–48.

17. J. Johnson, *Along This Way*, 64, 65.

18. In *Along This Way*, Johnson admitted that he had no prior knowledge of the Florida law: "This was the year in which Florida passed its law separating the races in railroad cars, and it was just being put into operation; a matter that I, at least, was then ignorant of" (64).

19. J. Johnson, *Along This Way*, 64, 65.

20. *Plessy v. Ferguson*, 163 U.S. 537, 542 (1896).

21. Although Johnson claimed that he and Ricardo had no intention of moving from their seats, he also acknowledged that they did not have to put up much of a fight:

"I explained to him [Ricardo] what the conductor was trying to make us do; we decided to stay where we were. But we did not have to enforce the decision. As soon as the conductor heard us speaking a foreign language, his attitude changed." J. Johnson, *Along This Way*, 65.

22. Miller, *Slaves to Fashion*, 194.
23. J. Johnson, *Along This Way*, 65.
24. J. Johnson, 86.
25. J. Johnson, 86.
26. J. Johnson, 86.
27. J. Johnson, 87.
28. Kelley, *Right to Ride*, 39.
29. J. Johnson, *Along This Way*, 87.
30. Mitchell and Snyder, *Cultural Locations of Disability*, 1; Davidson, *Concerto for the Left Hand*, 38.
31. J. Johnson, *Along This Way*, 87.
32. J. Johnson, 164, 165.
33. J. Johnson, 167.
34. J. Johnson, 166.
35. Goldsby, *Spectacular Secret*, 171.
36. J. Johnson, *Along This Way*, 170.
37. J. Johnson, 169–70.
38. Goldsby, *Spectacular Secret*, 166.
39. Goldsby, 166.
40. See Belluscio, *To Be Suddenly White*; Goldsby, *Spectacular Secret*; Griffin, "Who Set You Flowin'?"; P. Harper, *Are We Not Men?*; Kawash, *Dislocating the Color Line*; Miller, *Slaves to Fashion*; Nielsen, *Writing between the Lines*; V. Smith, *Self-Discovery and Authority*; Somerville, *Queering the Color Line*; Stepto, *From Behind the Veil*; Sugimori, "Narrative Order"; Sundquist, *Hammers of Creation*; and Wald, *Crossing the Line*.
41. J. Johnson, *Autobiography*, 92, 13.
42. J. Johnson, 86.
43. J. Johnson, 82.
44. J. Johnson, 110–11.
45. J. Johnson, 111.
46. J. Johnson, 110.
47. A. Wood, *Lynching and Spectacle*, 11.
48. J. Johnson, "Lynching," 71.
49. For more on the various meanings of lynching, see Dray, *At the Hands of Persons Unknown*; Goldsby, *Spectacular Secret*; K. Mitchell, *Living with Lynching*; Waldrep, "Word and Deed"; and A. Wood, *Lynching and Spectacle*.
50. Goldsby, *Spectacular Secret*, 288–89.
51. K. Mitchell, *Living with Lynching*, 174, 165.
52. J. Johnson, *Autobiography*, 112.

53. Carby, *Race Men*, 47.

54. Harper, *Are We Not Men?*, 103, emphasis in original.

55. Jarman, "Dismembering the Lynch Mob," 92.

56. J. Johnson, "Lynching," 75.

57. J. Johnson, *Autobiography*, 102.

58. J. Johnson, 31.

59. J. Johnson, 107.

60. Johnson and Johnson, *Books of American Negro Spirituals*, 11–12, 23.

61. Mackethan, "Black Boy and Ex-Coloured Man," 145–46.

62. J. Johnson, *Autobiography*, 108.

63. Sundquist, *Hammers of Creation*, 9.

64. J. Johnson, *Autobiography*, 113.

65. J. Johnson, 124, 113, 110.

66. J. Johnson, 117.

67. Fredrickson, *Black Image in the White Mind*, 250.

68. Tourgée, *Appeal to Caesar*, 80.

69. Huxley, "Emancipation," 20.

70. Hoffman, "Vital Statistics of the Negro," 542.

71. J. Johnson, *Autobiography*, 45, 46, 70.

72. J. Johnson, 10.

73. J. Johnson, 12.

74. J. Johnson, 11.

75. J. Johnson, 11.

76. Belluscio, *To Be Suddenly White*, 151–52.

77. J. Johnson, *Autobiography*, 121.

78. Garland-Thomson, *Staring*, 44, 45.

79. Gates, "Introduction to the Vintage Edition," xvii–xviii; J. Johnson, *Autobiography*, 13, 14. For another examination of Johnson's use of Du Bois's metaphor of double consciousness, see Sundquist, *Hammers of Creation*.

80. Hobbs, *Chosen Exile*, 6.

81. J. Johnson, *Autobiography*, 125.

82. J. Johnson, *Along This Way*, 239.

CHAPTER 6. THE ABLEISM OF COLOR-BLIND RACISM

1. Patricia J. Williams, "Emperor's New Clothes," 00:01:27–00:01:29, 00:01:05–00:01:12.

2. I. Perry, *More Beautiful and More Terrible*, 16; Bonilla-Silva, *Racism without Racists*, 1; Williams, "Emperor's New Clothes," 00:00:12–00:09:12; M. Alexander, *New Jim Crow*, 240–44; Holland, *Erotic Life of Racism*, 30–32; and Itagaki, *Civil Racism*, 65–101.

3. Williams, "Emperor's New Clothes," 00:01:15–00:01:30.

4. Williams, 00:00:30–40.

5. Bonilla-Silva, *Racism without Racists*, 77, emphasis in original. Style and fashion, it turns out, are embedded within the etymology of *color blindness*. Consider, for instance, the depictions of Lady Justice, the Roman goddess whom Albion Tourgée (Homer Plessy's lawyer) once imagined as the mother of color blindness. She is often pictured blindfolded, not blind, holding a sword in her right hand and scales in her left. Clothing and accessories are fundamental to her representation. Tourgée, "Brief for Plaintiff in Error," 46.

6. Williams, "Emperor's New Clothes," 00:04:37–00:04:43.

7. Williams, 00:03:53–00:04:05. This distinction is also why, as the literary scholar Alisha Gaines asserts, "soul sister" Rachel Dolezal, a white woman who stubbornly self-identifies as Black, could "recoun[t] her self-birth into blackness by recalling how she drew self-portraits with the brown crayon rather than a peach one," repeatedly claiming that the brown crayon made her skin color look better while the peach crayon simply "didn't resonate with [her]" (*Black for a Day*, 158, 165).

8. Murakawa, *First Civil Right*, 7.

9. Itagaki, *Civil Racism*, 95, emphasis in original.

10. Color blindness also makes it difficult to organize collectively against racial inequality. In *The Miner's Canary*, the legal scholars Lani Guinier and Gerald Torres explain the threefold way color blindness can inhibit grassroots organizing: "colorblindness misdiagnoses racial inequality as a residual individual problem; it masks systemic racial injustice; and, perhaps merely the precipitate of the first two, it cripples the capacity for collective organization and democratic mobilization" (55).

11. Andrew Kull marks the 1840s as the starting point of the history of legal color blindness (*Color-Blind Constitution*). And Mark Elliott tracks the use of the term *color-blind* from Robert Green Ingersoll to Albion Tourgée to Justice John Marshall Harlan. At a mass protest in Washington, DC, on October 22, 1883, Ingersoll, "a talented lawyer and renowned orator, delivered a point-by-point rebuttal to the Court's majority opinion [in the *Civil Rights Cases* (1883)] that amounted to one of the most cogent statements of Radical Republican constitutionalism. . . . In reference to the Thirteenth Amendment, in particular, he said, it had 'abolished not only slavery, but every 'badge and brand and stain and mark of slavery.' It abolished forever all distinctions on account of race or color. . . . From the moment of the adoption of the 13th Amendment the law became color blind'" (*Color-Blind Justice*, 269). Elliott claims that Tourgée's argument in *Plessy* echoes that of Ingersoll and that Harlan borrowed his use of "color-blind" from Tourgée's brief (270, 4).

12. *Plessy v. Ferguson*, 163 U.S. 537, 559 (1896).

13. Amar, "*Plessy v. Ferguson* and the Anti-Canon," 77, 76.

14. For example, see *Parents Involved in Community Schools v. Seattle School District No. 1*, 551 U.S. 701 (2007).

15. For example, see Boulware et al., "Brief for Appellants."

16. King, "I Have a Dream," 232. For more information on how liberals and conservatives have deployed color blindness, see M. Alexander, *New Jim Crow*, 236–44; Taylor, *#BlackLivesMatter*; and T. Johnson, "How Conservatives Turned."

17. The term *citizen* was not explicitly defined in the Constitution until the Fourteenth Amendment (1868), which states that "all persons born or naturalized in the United States, and subject to the jurisdiction thereof, are citizens of the United States and of the State wherein they reside." Until the addition of the Citizenship Clause in the Constitution, there were several debates about who could and could not be considered as citizens. In 1857, for example, *Dred Scott v. Sandford* infamously declared that Black people "are not included, and were not intended to be included, under the word 'citizens' in the Constitution, and can therefore claim none of the rights and privileges which that instrument provides for and secures to citizens of the United States." *Dred Scott v. Sandford*, 60 U.S. 393, 404 (1857). Additionally, the Constitution has historically made distinctions among citizens, outlining different rights for natural-born citizens and naturalized citizens, for citizens who have been convicted of crimes and those who have not, and for taxed persons and untaxed Native Americans.

18. E. Alexander, "Can You Be BLACK and Look at This?," 94.

19. Tourgée, "Brief for Plaintiff in Error," 46.

20. Elliott, *Color-Blind Justice*, 4.

21. Elliott, 4.

22. *Plessy*, 163 U.S. at 559.

23. *Plessy*, 163 U.S. at 561.

24. Harlan's discrimination against Chinese people is more evident in his vote in *United States v. Wong Kim Ark*. In that case, Harlan concurred with Chief Justice Melville Fuller's dissent, which argued that Wong Kim Ark, who was born in San Francisco, California, was not a US citizen because his parents were not US citizens and because Chinese people were ineligible for naturalization. It was an outrageous argument that would have had dire consequences, and, thankfully, the Supreme Court majority did not agree with it. Justice Horace Gray argued in his majority opinion of *Wong Kim Ark* that to "hold that the Fourteenth Amendment of the Constitution excludes from citizenship the children, born in the United States, of citizens or subjects of other countries, would be to deny citizenship to thousands of persons of English, Scotch, Irish, German or other European parentage, who have always been considered and treated as citizens of the United States." *United States v. Wong Kim Ark*, 169 U.S. 649, 694 (1898).

25. Chin, "*Plessy* Myth," 182.

26. Harlan argued in his dissent in *Plessy*, "If a State can prescribe, as a rule of civil conduct, that whites and blacks shall not travel as passengers in the same railroad coach, why may it not so regulate the use of the streets of its cities and towns as to compel white citizens to keep on one side of a street and black citizens to keep on the other? Why may it not, upon like grounds, punish whites and blacks who ride

together in street cars or in open vehicles on a public road or street? Why may it not require sheriffs to assign whites to one side of a court-room and blacks to the other? And why may it not also prohibit the commingling of the two races in the galleries of legislative halls or in public assemblages convened for the consider-ations of the political questions of the day? Further, if this statute of Louisiana is consistent with the personal liberty of citizens, why may not the State require the separation in railroad coaches of native and naturalized citizens of the United States, or of Protestants and Roman Catholics?" (*Plessy*, 163 U.S. at 557–58).

27. T. Johnson, "How Conservatives Turned."
28. Boulware et al., "Brief for Appellants," 578.
29. *Parents Involved in Community Schools v. Seattle School District No. 1*, 551 U.S. 701, 748 (2007).
30. M. Alexander, *New Jim Crow*, 240, 243.
31. Nelson, *Social Life of DNA*, 15–16.
32. Nelson writes,

> The word "reconciliation" readily brings to mind the South African Truth and Reconciliation Commission. . . . Less well known is one of the United States' own truth and reconciliation processes, which suggests the intensity with which racial healing is still being sought generations after the cessation of the transatlantic slave trade and decades after the civil rights movement of the mid-twentieth century. . . . Inspired by the South African example, in 1999 the citizens of Greensboro, North Carolina, inaugurated a truth and reconciliation process—the first ever in the United States—in an attempt to confront and dismantle long-standing racial tensions between blacks and whites in that community. (38)

33. The discourse of a postracial United States spread quickly following Obama's elec-tion in 2008. A range of commentators wasted minimal time declaring that racial discrimination had ended. In November 2009, the right-wing conservative radio host Lou Dobbs proclaimed, "We are now in a 21st[-century] post-partisan, post-racial society" ("Dobbs Calls on Listeners"). A mere two months later, immedi-ately following Obama's 2010 State of the Union address, the former MSNBC host Chris Matthews commented, "He is post-racial by all appearances. You know, I forgot he was Black tonight for an hour" (TPM TV, "Chris Matthews on Obama," 00:00:08–00:00:14). That these two men, with divergent political views, could so impulsively and misguidedly proclaim the emergence of a postracial nation a year into Obama's presidency exposes how the idea of a postracial United States could be used for varied political purposes. As the scholar-activist Keeanga-Yamahtta Taylor stated, "Colorblindness and 'postracial' politics are vested in false ideas that the United States is a meritocratic society where hard work makes the difference between those who are successful and those who are not" (*#BlackLivesMatter*, 72). Such false ideas have served as founding democratic principles, infusing color blindness with an ideological sinew that has wreaked havoc on communities of color.

34. Hartman, "Venus in Two Acts," 11, 4.

35. Hartman, 7, 4; Best and Hartman, "Fugitive Justice," 2.

36. Priest, "Nightmare Is Not Cured," 2.

37. Best and Hartman, "Fugitive Justice," 3, 1–2.

38. Till-Mobley and Benson, *Death of Innocence*, 134.

39. For more on the killers' confession, see Huie, "Shocking Story of Approved Killing."

40. Davey and Ruethling, "After 50 Years." For more information on Strider's comments to the press and his trial testimony, see Till-Mobley and Benson, *Death of Innocence*, 145–48; Houck and Grindy, *Emmett Till and the Mississippi Press*, 26–43; and *Murder of Emmett Till*.

41. Till-Mobley and Benson, *Death of Innocence*, 146.

42. Till-Mobley and Benson, 146.

43. C. Johnson, "FBI Releases Emmett Till Autopsy Results."

44. Ruethling, "Kin Disagree on Exhumation of Emmett Till."

45. Ruethling, "FBI Will Exhume the Body of Emmett Till."

46. C. Johnson, "FBI Releases Emmett Till Autopsy Results."

47. Tyson, *Blood of Emmett Till*, 4, 6.

48. Weller, "How Author Timothy Tyson Found the Woman."

49. J. Mitchell, "Bombshell Quote Missing from Emmett Till Tape."

50. Tyson, *Blood of Emmett Till*, 222n14.

51. Nelson, *Social Life of DNA*, 4.

52. Nelson, 8.

53. Nelson, 6.

54. All family members were not initially on board with the idea. For instance, Bertha Thomas, a distant cousin of Till, expressed concern about the necessity of an exhumation. "I personally don't see the point at this time of digging his body up," said Thomas at a news conference at the Rainbow PUSH Coalition headquarters in May 2005. "They don't need his body or remains in order to pursue them if they have solid proof that other people were involved." Simeon Wright, however, thought it was necessary for other reasons. Ultimately, the family came to an agreement on the matter. Ruethling, "Kin Disagree on Exhumation of Emmett Till."

55. Nelkin and Lindee, *DNA Mystique*, 3.

56. Samuels, *Fantasies of Identification*, 186, 2.

57. Till-Mobley wrote in her memoir that "as many as one hundred thousand people would file past Emmett's glass-enclosed casket during the four days he lay there" (Till-Mobley and Benson, *Death of Innocence*, 141). In a photo caption, *Jet* magazine reported that "more than 600,000, in an unending procession, later viewed [his] body" ("Nation Horrified," 8).

58. Woubshet, *Calendar of Loss*, 1.

59. Till-Mobley and Benson, *Death of Innocence*, 139, 142.

60. For information on ammunition data, see FBI, "Emmett Till Part 1."

61. Goldsby, *Spectacular Secret*, 241, 1–11.

62. Houck and Grindy, *Emmett Till and the Mississippi Press*, 23.

63. "Nation Horrified," 6, 7.

64. Till-Mobley and Benson, *Death of Innocence*, 145.

65. Goldsby, *Spectacular Secret*, 295.

66. *Brown v. Board of Education*, 347 U.S. 483, 495 (1954).

67. Robin Bernstein provides an excellent reading of the "brilliant drama" of the Clarks' experiments, including a different perspective of the child subjects. She characterizes them neither "as psychologically damaged dupes" nor as "passive internalizers of racism" but as "agential experts on children's culture" (*Racial Innocence*, 198). Additionally, rather than critiquing the Clarks for their flawed science, Bernstein recuperates them by figuring the Clarks as creative masterminds at eliciting theatrical performances, arguing that they manipulated their data and reordered their eight imperative statements to children in order to produce a desired result: the image of innocent, suffering Black children (235–43).

68. Baldwin, *Evidence of Things Not Seen*, 40–41.

69. Wideman, "Looking at Emmett Till," 24.

70. Baker, *Turning South Again*, 3, 4.

71. Hunter-Gault, *In My Place*, 115.

72. van der Kolk, *Body Keeps the Score*, 21, 88.

73. Moten, *In the Break*, 197, 196. Even though there were several photographs of Till's corpse circulating in the Black press and *Jet* magazine published three photographs of his corpse in the same issue, most writers and scholars, as does Moten in his chapter, tend to refer to the photographs in the singular—as, for example, "the photograph" or as "a picture." The photograph of most interest is the one of Till in his casket. For other examples, see Wideman, "Looking at Emmett Till," 25; Holloway, *Passed On*, 132; E. Alexander, "Can You Be BLACK and Look at This?," 102–6; and Ali, *Greatest*, chap. 1.

74. Till-Mobley and Benson, *Death of Innocence*, 38–40, 65–66.

75. Moten, *In the Break*, 200.

76. Goldsby, *Spectacular Secret*, 303, 304.

77. Priest, "Nightmare Is Not Cured," 4.

78. Woubshet, *Calendar of Loss*, x, 12.

79. Wideman, "Looking at Emmett Till," 31.

80. Best and Hartman, "Fugitive Justice," 3, 2.

81. As Priest argues, Mamie Till-Mobley "created a community of hearers to give ear to her complicated articulation of grief and grievance" ("Nightmare Is Not Cured," 15).

82. NBC News, "Hell No," 00:00:04–00:00:24.

83. Crawley, *Blackpentecostal Breath*, 1.

84. For a full video compilation, see Staks Studios, "I Can't Breathe."

85. E. Alexander, "Can You Be BLACK and Look at This?," 108.

86. P. King, commentator on *Situation Room with Wolf Blitzer*, 0:00:15–00:02:05.

87. D. Perry, "When Disability and Race Intersect."

88. Nathan, "Eric Garner Died from Chokehold."

89. Goodman and Wilson, "Officer Daniel Pantaleo Told Grand Jury."

90. M. Alexander, *New Jim Crow*, 244.

91. The activist and performance artist Leah Lakshmi Piepzna-Samarasinha provides an example of intersectional "care work," which she describes "as a place where disability justice and queer femme emotional labor intersect" (*Care Work*, 24).

92. Harriet Tubman Collective, "Disability Solidarity."

93. Movement for Black Lives (M4BL), "Vision for Black Lives."

94. For a definition of "intersectionality," see Crenshaw, "On Intersectionality."

95. For information about the #SayHerName campaign, see African American Policy Forum, "About #SayHerName."

96. Black Lives Matter, "About Black Lives Matter."

97. Woubshet, *Calendar of Loss*, 3–4. The context in which Woubshet discusses the "poetics of compounding loss" is in works of early AIDS mourning. But his concept applies to the content of my chapter on antiblackness and color blindness as well.

98. Woubshet, 146.

99. Woubshet, 146.

EPILOGUE

1. Moore, "This is how Black people get killed."

2. Washington, *Medical Apartheid*, 20.

3. Moore, "This is how Black people get killed."

4. Eligon, "Black Doctor Dies of Covid-19."

5. Ford, Reber, and Reeves, "Race Gaps in COVID-19 Even Bigger than They Appear."

6. Thebault, Tran, and Williams, "Coronavirus Is Infecting and Killing Black Americans."

7. Kendi, "Stop Blaming Black People."

8. "Sen. Bill Cassidy on His State's Racial Disparities."

9. Kendi, "Stop Blaming Black People."

10. I. Perry, "Racism Is Terrible."

11. Berne et al., "Ten Principles of Disability Justice," 229.

BIBLIOGRAPHY

Adams, Rachel, Benjamin Reiss, and David Serlin. "Disability." In *Keywords for Disability Studies*, edited by Rachel Adams, Benjamin Reiss, and David Serlin, 5–11. New York: New York University Press, 2015.

Adorno, Theodor W. "Punctuation Marks." Translated by Shierry Weber Nicholsen. *Antioch Review* 48, no. 3 (Summer 1999): 300–305.

African American Policy Forum. "About #SayHerName." Accessed April 10, 2020. www.aapf.org.

Alexander, Elizabeth. "'Can You Be BLACK and Look at This?': Reading the Rodney King Video(s)." In *Black Male: Representations of Masculinity in Contemporary American Art*, edited by Thelma Golden, 91–110. New York: Whitney Museum of American Art, 1994.

Alexander, Michelle. *The New Jim Crow: Mass Incarceration in the Age of Colorblindness*. New York: New Press, 2012.

Ali, Muhammad and Richard Durham. *The Greatest: My Own Story*. London: Hart-Davis, MacGibbon, 1976. Kindle.

Allen, Richard. "Letter from Bishop Allen." *Freedom's Journal*, November 2, 1827, 134.

Amar, Akhil Reed. "*Plessy v. Ferguson* and the Anti-Canon." *Pepperdine Law Review* 39 (December 2011): 75–89.

Americans with Disabilities Act Amendments Act of 2008. Pub. L. 110-325. www.ada.gov.

Andrews, William L. *The Literary Career of Charles W. Chesnutt*. Baton Rouge: Louisiana State University Press, 1980.

Asher-Schapiro, Avi. "Should Growing Up in Compton Be Considered a Disability?" *Vice News*, October 20, 2015. http://news.vice.com.

Backscheider, Paula. "Punctuation for the Reader—A Teaching Approach." *English Journal* 61, no. 6 (September 1972): 874–77.

Baker, Al, J. David Goodman, and Benjamin Mueller. "Beyond the Chokehold: The Path to Eric Garner's Death." *New York Times*, June 13, 2015. www.nytimes.com.

Baker, Houston A., Jr. *Modernism and the Harlem Renaissance*. Chicago: University of Chicago Press, 1987.

———. *Turning South Again: Re-Thinking Modernism/Re-Reading Booker T*. Durham, NC: Duke University Press, 2001.

Baldwin, James. *The Evidence of Things Not Seen*. New York: Holt, Rinehart and Winston, 1985.

Barrett, Lindon. *Blackness and Value: Seeing Double*. Cambridge: Cambridge University Press, 1999.

———. "Hand-Writing: Legibility and the White Body in *Running a Thousand Miles for Freedom*." *American Literature* 69, no. 2 (June 1997): 315–36.

Battle-Baptiste, Whitney and Britt Rusert, eds. *W. E. B. Du Bois's Data Portraits: Visualizing Black America: The Color Line at the Turn of the Twentieth Century*. Princeton, NJ: Princeton Architectural Press, 2018.

Baynton, Douglas C. "Disability and the Justification of Inequality in American History." In *The Disability Studies Reader*, 4th ed., edited by Lennard J. Davis, 17–33. New York: Routledge, 2013.

Bell, Christopher M., ed. *Blackness and Disability: Critical Examinations and Cultural Interventions*. East Lansing: Michigan State University Press, 2011.

———. "Is Disability Studies Actually White Disability Studies?" In *The Disability Studies Reader*, 3rd ed., edited by Lennard J. Davis, 374–82. New York: Routledge, 2010.

Bell, Marvin. "Replica." *Nightworks: Poems 1962–2000*. Port Townsend, WA: Copper Canyon, 2000. Poetry Foundation. www.poetryfoundation.org.

Belluscio, Steven J. *To Be Suddenly White: Literary Realism and Racial Passing*. Columbia: University of Missouri Press, 2006.

Ben-Moshe, Liat. *Decarcerating Disability: Deinstitutionalization and Prison Abolition*. Minneapolis: Minnesota University Press, 2020.

Bennett, Joshua. *Being Property Once Myself: Blackness and the End of Man*. Cambridge, MA: Harvard University Press, 2020.

Berne, Patricia, Aurora Levins Morales, David Langstaff, and Sins Invalid. "Ten Principles of Disability Justice." *Woman's Studies Quarterly* 46, nos. 1–2 (Spring–Summer 2018): 227–30.

Bernstein, R. B. *The Founding Fathers Reconsidered*. Oxford: Oxford University Press, 2009.

———. *Thomas Jefferson: The Revolution of Ideas*. 2003. Reprint, Oxford: Oxford University Press, 2005.

Bernstein, Robin. *Racial Innocence: Performing American Childhood from Slavery to Civil Rights*. New York: New York University Press, 2011.

Bérubé, Michael. *The Secret Life of Stories: From Don Quixote to Harry Potter, How Understanding Intellectual Disability Transforms the Way We Read*. New York: New York University Press, 2016.

Best, Stephen M. *Fugitive's Properties: Law and the Poetics of Possession*. Chicago: University of Chicago Press, 2004.

Best, Stephen M., and Saidiya Hartman. "Fugitive Justice." *Representations* 92, no. 1 (Fall 2005): 1–15.

Biss, Eula. *On Immunity: An Inoculation*. Minneapolis, MN: Graywolf, 2014.

Black Lives Matter. "About Black Lives Matter." Accessed June 3, 2020. https://blacklivesmatter.com.

Bland, Sterling Lecater, Jr. *Voices of the Fugitives: Runaway Slave Stories and Their Fictions of Self-Creation*. Westport, CT: Praeger, 2000.

Blight, David W. *Frederick Douglass: Prophet of Freedom*. New York: Simon and Schuster, 2018.

Bonilla-Silva, Eduardo. *Racism without Racists: Color-Blind Racism and the Persistence of Racial Inequality in America*. 5th ed. Lanham, MD: Rowman and Littlefield, 2018.

Boster, Dea H. *African American Slavery and Disability: Bodies, Property, and Power in the Antebellum South, 1800–1860*. New York: Routledge, 2013.

Boulware, Harold, Robert L. Carter, Jack Greenberg, Oliver W. Hill, Thurgood Marshall, Louis L. Redding, Spottswood W. Robinson III, and Charles S. Scott. "Brief for Appellants in Nos. 1, 2, and 4 and for Respondents in No. 10 on Reargument." In *Landmark Briefs and Arguments of the Supreme Court of the United States: Constitutional Law*, vol. 49, edited by Philip B. Kurland and Gerhard Casper, 481–748. Arlington, VA: University Publications of America, 1975.

Brawley, Benjamin. *The Negro Genius: A New Appraisal of the Achievement of the American Negro in Literature and the Fine Arts*. 1937. Reprint, New York: Biblo and Tannen, 1969.

Brighouse, Harry, and Adam Swift. "Equality, Priority, and Positional Goods." *Ethics* 116, no. 3 (April 2006): 471–97.

Brodhead, Richard H. Introduction to *The Conjure Woman and Other Conjure Tales*, by Charles W. Chesnutt, 1–21. Durham, NC: Duke University Press, 1993.

Brodie, Fawn M. *Thomas Jefferson: An Intimate History*. New York: Norton, 1974.

Brody, Jennifer DeVere. *Punctuation: Art, Politics, and Play*. Durham, NC: Duke University Press, 2008.

Brooks, Daphne A. *Bodies in Dissent: Spectacular Performances of Race and Freedom, 1850–1910*. Durham, NC: Duke University Press, 2006.

——. "Introduction: Catch Me If You Can: The Art of Escape and Anti-Slavery Performance in the Narratives of William Wells Brown, Henry Box Brown, and William and Ellen Craft." In *The Great Escapes: Four Slave Narratives*, xv–lxvii. New York: Barnes and Noble, 2007.

Brown, Henry Box. *Narrative of Henry Box Brown: Who Escaped from Slavery, Enclosed in a Box Three Feet Long, Two Wide, and Two and Half High, Written from a Statement of Facts Made by Himself, with Remarks upon the Remedy for Slavery by Charles Stearns*. 1849. Reprint, London: Forgotten Books, 2015.

——. *Narrative of the Life of Henry Box Brown, Written by Himself*. 1851. Edited and introduced by John Ernest. Chapel Hill: University of North Carolina Press, 2008.

Brown v. Board of Education. 347 U.S. 483 (1954). Nexis Uni.

Burgdorf, Marcia Pearce, and Robert Burgdorf Jr. "A History of Unequal Treatment: The Qualifications of Handicapped Persons as a Suspect Class under the Equal Protection Clause." *Santa Clara Law Review* 15, no. 4 (1975): 855–910.

Bynum, Tara. "Why I Heart David Walker." *J19* 4, no. 1 (Spring 2016): 11–17.

Cable, George Washington. "The Freedman's Case in Equity." In *"The Silent South": Together with "The Freedman's Case in Equity," "The Convict Lease System," the Appendix to the 1889 Edition, and Eight Uncollected Essays on Prison and Asylum Reform,*

introduction by Arlin Turner. Patterson Smith Reprint Series in Criminology, Law
Enforcement, and Social Problems 57, 1–39. Montclair, NJ: Patterson Smith, 1969.

———. *The Grandissimes: A Story of Creole Life.* 1880. Reprint, with an introduction by
Michael Kreyling. New York: Penguin, 1988.

———. "The Negro Question." In *The Negro Question: A Selection of Writings on Civil
Rights in the South,* edited by Arlin Turner, 132–69. Garden City, NY: Doubleday
Anchor, 1958.

Carby, Hazel. *Race Men.* Cambridge, MA: Harvard University Press, 1998.

———. *Reconstructing Womanhood: The Emergence of the Afro-American Woman Novelist.* 1987. Reprint, Oxford: Oxford University Press, 1989.

Cartwright, Samuel A. "Report on the Diseases and Physical Peculiarities of the Negro
Race." *New Orleans Medical and Surgical Journal* 7 (May 1851): 691–715. HathiTrust.

Cassuto, Leonard. *The Inhuman Race: The Racial Grotesque in American Literature and
Culture.* New York: Columbia University Press, 1997.

Catanese, Brandi Wilkins. *The Problem of the Color[blind]: Racial Transgression and the
Politics of Black Performance.* Ann Arbor: University of Michigan Press, 2011.

Chandler, Nahum D. "Of Exorbitance: The Problem of the Negro as a Problem for
Thought." *Criticism* 50, no. 3 (Summer 2008): 345–410.

Chen, Mel Y. *Animacies: Biopolitics, Racial Mattering, and Queer Affect.* Durham, NC:
Duke University Press, 2012.

Cheng, Anne Anlin. *The Melancholy of Race: Psychoanalysis, Assimilation, and Hidden
Grief.* Oxford: Oxford University Press, 2001.

Chesnutt, Charles W[addell]. "Baxter's Procrustes." *Atlantic Monthly,* June 1904,
823–30. Reprinted in Chesnutt, *Charles W. Chesnutt,* 781–93. Citations refer to the
Charles W. Chesnutt version.

———. "Charles W. Chesnutt's Own View of His New Story, *The Marrow of Tradition.*"
Cleveland World, Oct. 1901. Reprinted in Chesnutt, *Charles W. Chesnutt,* 872–73.
Citations refer to the *Charles W. Chesnutt* version.

———. *Charles W. Chesnutt: Stories, Novels, and Essays.* Edited by Werner Sollors.
Library of America 131. New York: Library of America, 2002.

———. *The Conjure Stories.* Edited by Robert B. Stepto and Jennifer Rae Greeson. New
York: Norton, 2012.

———. *The Conjure Woman.* 1899. Reprinted in Chesnutt, *The Conjure Woman and
Other Conjure Tales,* edited and introduced by Richard H. Brodhead, 29–120. Durham, NC: Duke University Press, 1993.

———. "The Future American." Part 1, "What the Race Is Likely to Become in the Process of Time." *Boston Evening Transcript,* August 18, 1900, 20.

———. "The Future American." Part 2, "A Stream of Dark Blood in the Veins of the
Southern Whites." *Boston Evening Transcript,* August 25, 1900, 15.

———. "The Future American." Part 3, "A Complete Race-Amalgamation Likely to Occur." *Boston Evening Transcript,* September 1, 1900, 24.

———. "The Goophered Grapevine." *Atlantic Monthly,* August 1887, 254–60. Reprinted
in Chesnutt, *Conjure Stories,* 3–14. Citations refer to *The Conjure Stories* version.

———. *The Marrow of Tradition.* 1901. Edited and introduction by Eric J. Sundquist. New York: Penguin, 1993.

———. "The Negro in Art: How Shall He Be Portrayed." *Crisis*, November 1926, 28–29. Reprinted in Gates and Jarrett, *New Negro*, 190–204. Citations refer to the *New Negro* version.

———. "The Negro in Books." December 5, 1916. Fisk University Library, Nashville, TN. Reprinted in Gates and Jarrett, *New Negro*, 173–82. Citations refer to the *New Negro* version.

———. "Post-Bellum—Pre-Harlem." *Colophon: A Book Collectors' Quarterly* 5 (1931): n.p. Reprinted in Chesnutt, *Charles W. Chesnutt*, 906–12. Citations refer to the *Charles W. Chesnutt* version.

———. *"To Be an Author": Letters of Charles W. Chesnutt, 1889–1905.* Edited by Joseph McElrath and Robert C. Leitz. Princeton, NJ: Princeton University Press, 1997.

———. "What Is a White Man?" *Independent*, 30 May 1889, 5–6. Reprinted in *Interracialism: Black-White Intermarriage in American History, Literature, and Law*, edited by Werner Sollors, 37–42. Oxford: Oxford University Press, 2000. Citations refer to the *Interracialism* version.

Chin, Gabriel J. "The *Plessy* Myth: Justice Harlan and the Chinese Cases." *Iowa Law Review* 82 (October 1996): 151–82.

City of Chicago. *The Municipal Code of Chicago: Comprising the Law of Illinois Relating to the City of Chicago, and the Ordinances of the City Council.* Edited by Egbert Jamieson and Francis Adams. Chicago: Beach, Barnard, 1881.

Code Noir English Regulations, Edicts, Declarations and Decrees Concerning the Commerce, Administration of Justice, and Policing of Louisiana and other French Colonies in America Together with the Black Code. TS. Translated by Olivia Blanchard. Baton Rouge: Survey of Federal Archives in Louisiana, Works Projects Administration, 1940. Louisiana Research Collection, Tulane University.

Cooper, Anna Julia. *A Voice from the South.* 1892. Reprint, New York: Oxford University Press, 1988.

Cornelius, Janet D. *"When I Can Read My Title Clear": Literacy, Slavery, and Religion in the Antebellum South.* Columbia: University of South Carolina Press, 1991.

Couser, Tom. "Disability Studies." In *The Encyclopedia of Literary and Cultural Theory*, edited by Michael Ryan. Hoboken, NJ: Wiley, 2011. Credo Reference.

Craft, William, and Ellen Craft. *Running a Thousand Miles for Freedom; or, The Escape of William and Ellen Craft from Slavery.* 1860. Reprint, with an introduction by Barbara McCaskill. Athens: University of Georgia Press, 1999.

Crawley, Ashon T. *Blackpentecostal Breath: The Aesthetics of Possibility.* New York: Fordham University Press, 2017.

Crenshaw, Kimberlé Williams. "Color Blindness, History, and the Law." In *The House That Race Built: Original Essays by Toni Morrison, Angela Y. Davis, Cornel West, and Others on Black Americans and Politics in America Today*, edited by Wahneema Lubiano, 280–88. New York: Vintage Books, 1998.

———. "On Intersectionality." Keynote, Woman of the World Festival, 2016. YouTube, March 14, 2016. https://youtu.be/-DW4HLgYPlA.

Cunningham, Brittany Packnett. Commentator on *AM Joy*, May 30, 2020.

Davey, Monica, and Gretchen Ruethling. "After 50 Years, Emmett Till's Body Is Exhumed." *New York Times*, June 2, 2005. www.nytimes.com.

Davidson, Michael. *Concerto for the Left Hand: Disability and the Defamiliar Body*. Ann Arbor: University of Michigan Press, 2008.

Davis, Allison, Burleigh B. Gardner, and Mary R. Gardner. *Deep South: A Social Anthropological Study of Caste and Class*. 1941. Reprint, Berkeley: University of California Press, 1988.

Davis, Cynthia J. *Bodily and Narrative Forms: The Influence of Medicine on American Literature, 1845–1915*. Stanford, CA: Stanford University Press, 2000.

Dayan, Colin. *The Law Is a White Dog: How Legal Rituals Make and Unmake Persons*. Princeton, NJ: Princeton University Press, 2011.

Declaration of Independence. The Avalon Project: Documents in Law, History, and Diplomacy, Yale Law School. http://avalon.law.yale.edu.

Dinius, Marcy J. "'Look!! Look!!! at This!!!!': The Radical Typography of David Walker's *Appeal*." *PMLA* 126, no. 1 (January 2011): 55–72.

Dixon, Thomas, Jr. *The Leopard's Spots: A Romance of the White Man's Burden—1865–1900*. New York: Grosset and Dunlap, 1902.

"Dobbs Calls on Listeners to Rise above 'Partisan and Racial Element That Dominates Politics.'" Media Matters for America, November 12, 2009. www.mediamatters.org.

Dollard, John. *Caste and Class in a Southern Town*. New York: Doubleday Anchor, 1937.

Doran, Susan. "The Queen." In *The Elizabethan World*, edited by Susan Doran and Norman Jones, 35–58. New York: Routledge, 2011.

Douglass, Frederick. "An Address to the People of the United States." In *Frederick Douglass: Selected Speeches and Writings*, edited by Philip S. Foner, abridged and adapted by Yuval Taylor, 669–84. Lawrence Hill Books, 1999.

———. "The Color Line." *North American Review* 132, no. 295 (June 1881): 567–77.

———. *Frederick Douglass: Selected Speeches and Writings*. Edited by Philip S. Foner. Abridged and adapted by Yuval Taylor. Lawrence Hill Books, 1999.

———. "The Future of the Colored Race." *North American Review* 142, no. 354 (May 1886): 437–40.

———. *Life and Times of Frederick Douglass: His Early Life as a Slave, His Escape From Bondage and His Complete Life Story*. 1881. Reprint, Prague: Madison and Adams, 2018. Nook.

———. *Narrative of the Life of Frederick Douglass, an American Slave*. 1845. Edited by Ira Dworkin. New York: Penguin, 2014.

Downs, Jim. *Sick from Freedom: African-American Illness and Suffering during the Civil War and Reconstruction*. Oxford: Oxford University Press, 2012.

Dray, Philip. *At the Hands of Persons Unknown: The Lynching of Black America*. New York: Random House, 2002.

Dred Scott v. Sandford. 60 U.S. 393 (1857). Nexis Uni.

Du Bois, W. E. B. "The Conservation of the Races." 1897. In *The Oxford W. E. B. Du Bois Reader*, edited by Eric J. Sundquist, 38–47. Oxford: Oxford University Press, 1996.

———. "The Freedmen's Bureau." *Atlantic Monthly*, March 1901. www.theatlantic.com.

———. *The Philadelphia Negro: A Social Study*. 1899. Reprint, Philadelphia: University of Pennsylvania Press, 1996.

———. *The Souls of Black Folk*. 1903. Edited by Henry Louis Gates Jr. and Terri Hume Oliver. New York: Norton, 1999.

———. "Strivings of the Negro People." *Atlantic Monthly*, August 1897. www.theatlantic.com.

duCille, Ann. *The Coupling Convention: Sex, Text, and Tradition in Black Women's Fiction*. Oxford: Oxford University Press, 1993.

Duncan, Charles. *The Absent Man: The Narrative Craft of Charles W. Chesnutt*. Athens: Ohio University Press, 1998.

Eaton, Clement. "A Dangerous Pamphlet in the Old South." *Journal of Southern History* 2, no. 3 (August 1936): 322–34.

Elder, Arlene A. "'The Future American Race': Charles W. Chesnutt Utopian Illusion." *MELUS* 15, no. 3 (Autumn 1988): 121–29.

Eligon, John. "Black Doctor Dies of Covid-19 after Complaining of Racist Treatment." *New York Times*, December 23, 2020. www.nytimes.com.

Elliott, Mark. *Color-Blind Justice: Albion Tourgée and the Quest for Racial Equality from the Civil War to "Plessy v. Ferguson."* Oxford: Oxford University Press, 2006.

Ellis, Joseph J. *American Sphinx: The Character of Thomas Jefferson*. New York: Knopf, 1997.

Ellison, Ralph. *Invisible Man*. 1952. Reprint, New York: Vintage, 1995.

Eng, David L., and David Kazanjian, eds. *Loss: The Politics of Mourning*. Berkeley: University of California Press, 2003.

Erevelles, Nirmala. "Crippin' Jim Crow: Disability, Dis-Location, and the School-to-Prison Pipeline." In *Disability Incarcerated: Imprisonment and Disability in the United States and Canada*, edited by Liat Ben-Moshe, Chris Chapman, and Allison C. Carey, 81–99. New York: Palgrave, 2014.

———. "Race." In *Keywords for Disability Studies*, edited by Rachel Adams, Benjamin Reiss, and David Serlin, 145–48. New York: New York University Press, 2015.

Ernest, John. "Appendix A: Illustrations." In *Narrative of the Life of Henry Box Brown, Written by Himself*, by Henry Box Brown, 107–21. Chapel Hill: University of North Carolina Press, 2008.

———. "Introduction: The Emergence of Henry 'Box' Brown." In *Narrative of the Life of Henry Box Brown, Written by Himself*, by Henry Box Brown, 1–38. Chapel Hill: University of North Carolina Press, 2008.

Fanon, Franz. *Black Skin, White Masks*. 1952. Reprint, New York: Grove, 2008.

Fauset, Jessie Redmon. *Plum Bun: A Novel without a Moral*. 1929. Reprint, Boston: Beacon, 1990.

FBI. "Emmett Till Part 1." February 9, 2006. https://vault.fbi.gov.

Federal Writers' Project. *Slave Narrative Project.* Vol. 4, *Georgia, Part 3, Kendricks-Styles.* 1936. Manuscript/Mixed Material, Library of Congress. www.loc.gov.

———. *Slave Narrative Project.* Vol. 13, *Oklahoma, Adams–Young.* 1936. Manuscript/Mixed Material, Library of Congress. www.loc.gov.

Ferguson, Roderick A. "To Catch a Light-Filled Vision: American Studies and the Activation of Radical Traditions." *American Quarterly* 71, no. 2 (June 2019): 317–35.

Ferguson, SallyAnn H. "Chesnutt's Genuine Blacks and Future Americans." *MELUS* 15, no. 3 (Autumn 1988): 109–19.

Fett, Sharla M. *Working Cures: Healing, Health, and Power on Southern Slave Plantations.* Chapel Hill: University of North Carolina Press, 2002.

Fleming, Robert E. *James Weldon Johnson.* Boston: Twayne, 1987.

Fliegelman, Jay. *Declaring Independence: Jefferson, Natural Language, and the Culture of Performance.* Stanford, CA: Stanford University Press, 1993.

Foner, Eric. *Reconstruction: America's Unfinished Revolution, 1863–1877.* 1988. Reprint, New York: HarperCollins, 2002.

Ford, Tiffany N., Sarah Reber, and Richard V. Reeves. "Race Gaps in COVID-19 Deaths Are Even Bigger than They Appear." Brookings Institution, June 16, 2020. www.brookings.edu.

Foreman, P. Gabrielle. *Activist Sentiments: Reading Black Women in the Nineteenth Century.* Urbana: University of Illinois Press, 2009.

Foster, Frances Smith. "A Narrative of the Interesting Origins and (Somewhat) Surprising Developments of African-American Print Culture." *ALH* 17, no. 4 (Winter 2005): 714–40.

Foucault, Michel. *The Order of Things: An Archaeology of the Human Sciences.* New York: Pantheon, 1970.

Frankel, Matthew Cordova. "'Nature's Nation' Revisited: Citizenship and the Sublime in Thomas Jefferson's *Notes on the State of Virginia.*" *American Literature* 73, no. 4 (December 2001): 695–726.

Fredrickson, George M. *The Black Image in the White Mind: The Debate on Afro-American Character and Destiny, 1817–1914.* 1971. Reprint, Middletown, CT: Wesleyan University Press, 1987.

Gaines, Alisha. *Black for a Day: White Fantasies of Race and Empathy.* Chapel Hill: University of North Carolina Press, 2017.

Gaines, Kevin K. *Uplifting the Race: Black Leadership, Politics, and Culture in the Twentieth Century.* 2nd ed. Chapel Hill: University of North Carolina Press, 1996.

Gantz, Timothy. *Early Greek Myth: A Guide to Literary and Artistic Sources.* Baltimore: Johns Hopkins University Press, 1993.

Garland-Thomson, Rosemarie. *Extraordinary Bodies: Figuring Physical Disability in American Culture and Literature.* New York: Columbia University Press, 1997.

———. *Staring: How We Look.* Oxford: Oxford University Press, 2009.

Garrison, William Lloyd. "The Dumb Witness." *Liberator,* June 12, 1863.

Gates, Henry Louis, Jr. "Introduction to the Vintage Edition." In *The Autobiography of an Ex-Coloured Man,* by James Weldon Johnson, v–xxiii. New York: Vintage, 1989.

Gates, Henry Louis, Jr., and Gene Andrew Jarrett, eds. *The New Negro: Readings on Race, Representation, and African American Culture, 1892–1938*. Princeton, NJ: Princeton University Press, 2007.

Geary, James. *I Is an Other: The Secret Life of Metaphor and How It Shapes the Way We See the World*. New York: HarperCollins, 2011.

Gillman, Susan. *Blood Talk: American Race Melodrama and the Culture of the Occult*. Chicago: University of Chicago Press, 2003.

Gilman, Sander. *Difference and Pathology: Stereotypes of Sexuality, Race, and Madness*. Ithaca, NY: Cornell University Press, 1985.

Gilmore, Glenda Elizabeth. *Gender and Jim Crow: Women and the Politics of White Supremacy in North Carolina, 1896–1920*. Chapel Hill: University of North Carolina Press, 1996.

Gilroy, Paul. *The Black Atlantic: Modernity and Double Consciousness*. Cambridge, MA: Harvard University Press, 1993.

Gladwell, Malcolm. *The Tipping Point: How Little Things Can Make a Big Difference*. 2000. Reprint, New York: Back Bay, 2002.

Goffman, Erving. *Stigma: Notes on the Management of Spoiled Identity*. 1963. Reprint, New York: Simon and Schuster, 1986.

Goldsby, Jacqueline. *A Spectacular Secret: Lynching in American Life and Literature*. Chicago: University of Chicago Press, 2006.

Goodell, William. *The American Slave Code in Theory and Practice: Its Distinctive Features Shown by Its Statutes, Judicial Decisions, and Illustrative Facts*. New York: American and Foreign Anti-Slavery Society, 1853.

Goodman, J. David, and Michael Wilson. "Officer Daniel Pantaleo Told Grand Jury He Meant No Harm to Eric Garner." *New York Times*, December 3, 2014. www.nytimes.com.

Gordon-Reed, Annette. *The Hemingses of Monticello: An American Family*. New York: Norton, 2008.

Griffin, Farah Jasmine. *"Who Set You Flowin'?": The African-American Migration Narrative*. Oxford: Oxford University Press, 1995.

Grover, Kathryn. *The Fugitive's Gibraltar: Escaping Slaves and Abolitionism in New Bedford, Massachusetts*. Amherst: University of Massachusetts Press, 2001.

Guinier, Lani, and Gerald Torres. *The Miner's Canary: Enlisting Race, Resisting Power, Transforming Democracy*. 2002. Reprint, Cambridge, MA: Harvard University Press, 2003.

Gumbs, Alexis Pauline, ed. *brokenbeautiful press* (blog). http://brokenbeautiful.wordpress.com.

Hall, Samuel, and Orville Elder. *Samuel Hall, 47 Years a Slave: A Brief Story of His Life before and after Freedom Came to Him*. 1912. Reprint, Gloucester, UK: Dodo, 2009.

Hamilton, Edith. "Theseus." In *Mythology: Timeless Tales of Gods and Heroes*, 209–23. 1942. Reprint, Boston: Little, Brown, 1998.

Haraway, Donna J. *Simians, Cyborgs, and Women: The Reinvention of Nature*. 1991. Reprint, New York: Routledge, 2010.

Harding, Vincent. "Responsibilities of the Black Scholar to the Community." In *The State of Afro-American History: Past, Present, and Future*, edited by Darlene Clark Hine, 277–84. Baton Rouge: Louisiana State University Press, 1986.

Harper, Frances E. W. *Iola Leroy, or Shadows Uplifted*. 1892. Reprint, Boston: Beacon, 1987.

Harper, Phillip Brian. *Are We Not Men? Masculine Anxiety and the Problem of African-American Identity*. New York: Oxford University Press, 1996.

Harriet Tubman Collective. "Disability Solidarity: Completing the Vision for Black Lives." Tumblr, September 14, 2016. https://harriettubmancollective.tumblr.com.

Harris, Cheryl I. "Whiteness as Property." *Harvard Law Review* 106, no. 8 (June 1993): 1701–91.

Hartman, Saidiya. *Scenes of Subjection: Terror, Slavery, and Self-Making in Nineteenth-Century America*. Oxford: Oxford University Press, 1997.

———. "Venus in Two Acts." *Small Axe* 12, no. 2 (June 2008): 1–14.

———. *Wayward Lives, Beautiful Experiments: Intimate Histories of Social Upheaval*. New York: Norton, 2019.

Hemenway, Robert. "'Baxter's Procrustes': Irony and Protest." In "Before, During, and After the Harlem Renaissance," edited by Therman B. O'Daniel, Philip Butcher, and Iva G. Jones. Special issue, *CLA Journal* 18, no. 2 (December 1974): 172–85.

Herndl, Diane Price. *Invalid Women: Figuring Feminine Illness in American Fiction and Culture, 1840–1940*. Chapel Hill: University of North Carolina Press, 1993.

Hinks, Peter P. "Editor's Note: The Three Editions of the *Appeal*." In *David Walker's Appeal to the Coloured Citizens of the World*, by David Walker, xlv–li. University Park: Pennsylvania State University Press, 2000.

———. Introduction to *David Walker's Appeal to the Coloured Citizens of the World*, by David Walker, xi–xliv. University Park: Pennsylvania State University Press, 2000.

———. *To Awaken My Afflicted Brethren: David Walker and the Problem of Antebellum Slave Resistance*. University Park: Pennsylvania State University Press, 1997.

Hobbes, Thomas. *Leviathan: Or the Matter, Form and Power of a Commonwealth, Ecclesiastical and Civil*. 1651. Introduction by Henry Morley. 4th ed. London: George Routledge and Sons, 1894.

Hobbs, Allyson. *A Chosen Exile: A History of Racial Passing in American Life*. Cambridge, MA: Harvard University Press, 2014.

Hoffman, Frederick L. "Vital Statistics of the Negro." *Arena* 29 (April 1892): 529–42. Internet Archive.

Holland, Sharon Patricia. *The Erotic Life of Racism*. Durham, NC: Duke University Press, 2012.

Holloway, Karla F. C. *Passed On: African American Mourning Stories, a Memorial*. Durham, NC: Duke University Press, 2003.

Houck, Davis W., and Matthew A. Grindy. *Emmett Till and the Mississippi Press*. Jackson: University Press of Mississippi, 2008.

Howells, William Dean. "Mr. Charles W. Chesnutt's Stories." Review of *The Conjure Woman* and *The Wife of His Youth, and Other Stories of the Color Line*, by Charles W. Chesnutt. *Atlantic Monthly*, May 1900, 699–701. www.theatlantic.com.

———. "A Psychological Counter-Current in Recent Fiction." Review of *The Marrow of Tradition*, by Charles W. Chesnutt. *North American Review*, December 1901, 872–88.

Huie, William Bradford. "The Shocking Story of Approved Killing in Mississippi." *Look*, January 24, 1956. PBS Online. www.pbs.org.

Hunter-Gault, Charlayne. *In My Place*. 1992. Reprint, New York: Vintage, 1993.

Huxley, Thomas Henry. "Emancipation—Black and White." 1865. In *Lay Sermons, Addresses, and Reviews*, 20–26. New York: D. Appleton, 1871.

Ianovici, Gerald. "'A Living Death': Gothic Signification and the Nadir in *The Marrow of Tradition*." *MELUS* 27, no. 4 (Winter 2002): 33–58.

Irons, Peter. *Jim Crow's Children: The Broken Promise of the "Brown" Decision*. New York: Penguin, 2002.

Itagaki, Lynn Mie. *Civil Racism: The 1992 Los Angeles Rebellion and the Crisis of Racial Burnout*. Minneapolis: University of Minnesota Press, 2016.

Jackson, Zakiyyah Iman. *Becoming Human: Matter and Meaning in an Antiblack World*. New York: New York University Press, 2020.

Jacobson, Matthew Frye. *Whiteness of a Different Color: European Immigrants and the Alchemy of Race*. 1998. Reprint, Cambridge, MA: Harvard University Press, 1999.

James, Jennifer C. *A Freedom Bought with Blood: African American War Literature from the Civil War to World War II*. Chapel Hill: University of North Carolina Press, 2007.

Jarman, Michelle. "Coming Up from Underground: Uneasy Dialogues at the Intersections of Race, Mental Illness, and Disability Studies." In *Blackness and Disability: Critical Examinations and Cultural Interventions*, edited by Christopher M. Bell, 9–30. East Lansing: Michigan State University Press, 2011.

———. "Dismembering the Lynch Mob: Intersecting Narratives of Disability, Race, and Sexual Menace." In *Sex and Disability*, edited by Robert McRuer and Anna Mollow, 89–107. Durham, NC: Duke University Press, 2012.

Jarrett, Gene Andrew. *Representing the Race: A New Political History of African American Literature*. New York: New York University Press, 2011.

Jefferson, Thomas. *Notes on the State of Virginia*. 1785. Reprint, New York: Barnes and Noble, 2010.

Jenkins, Candice M. *Private Lives, Proper Relations: Regulating Black Intimacy*. Minneapolis: University of Minnesota Press, 2007.

Johnson, Carla K. "FBI Releases Emmett Till Autopsy Results, Discusses Investigation with Slain Boy's Relatives." *Ocala StarBanner*, April 1, 2007. www.ocala.com.

Johnson, James Weldon. *Along This Way: The Autobiography of James Weldon Johnson*. 1933. Reprint, New York: De Capo, 2000.

———. *The Autobiography of an Ex-Colored Man*. 1912. In *"The Autobiography of an Ex-Colored Man" and Other Writings*, edited by George Stade, introduction by Noelle

Morrissette, notes by Delano Greenidge-Copprue. New York: Barnes and Noble, 2007.

———. "The Best Methods of Removing the Disabilities of Caste from the Negro." 1892. In *The Selected Writings of James Weldon Johnson: Social, Political, and Literary Essays*, edited by Sondra Kathryn Wilson, vol. 2, 423–26. New York: Oxford University Press, 1995.

———. "Lynching—America's National Disgrace." 1924. In *The Selected Writings of James Weldon Johnson: Social, Political, and Literary Essays*, edited by Sondra Kathryn Wilson, vol. 2, 71–78. New York: Oxford University Press, 1995.

———. Preface to *The Book of American Negro Poetry*, edited by James Weldon Johnson. 1922. Reprint, Charleston, SC: BiblioBazaar, 2006.

Johnson, James Weldon, and J. Rosamond Johnson. *The Books of American Negro Spirituals*. 2 vols. in 1. 1925, 1926. Reprint, New York: De Capo, 2002.

Johnson, Theodore R. "How Conservatives Turned the 'Color-Blind Constitution' against Racial Progress." *Atlantic*, November 19, 2019. www.theatlantic.com.

Jones, Gavin. *Strange Talk: The Politics of Dialect Literature in Gilded Age America*. Berkeley: University of California Press, 1999.

Jones, Martha S. *Birthright Citizens: A History of Race and Rights in Antebellum America*. Cambridge: Cambridge University Press, 2018.

Jordan, Winthrop D. *White over Black: American Attitudes toward the Negro, 1550–1812*. Chapel Hill: University of North Carolina Press, 1968.

Kafer, Alison. *Feminist, Queer, Crip*. Bloomington: Indiana University Press, 2013.

Kawash, Samira. *Dislocating the Color Line: Identity, Hybridity, and Singularity in African-American Narrative*. Stanford, CA: Stanford University Press, 1997.

Kazanjian, David. *The Colonizing Trick: National Culture and Imperial Citizenship in Early America*. Minneapolis: University of Minnesota Press, 2003.

Kelley, Blair L. M. *Right to Ride: Streetcar Boycotts and African American Citizenship in the Era of "Plessy v. Ferguson."* Chapel Hill: University of North Carolina Press, 2010.

Kendi, Ibram X. "Stop Blaming Black People for Dying of the Coronavirus." *Atlantic*, April 14, 2020. www.theatlantic.com.

Khadaroo, Stacy Teicher. "First-in-Nation Lawsuit in California: Must Schools Address Student Trauma?" *Christian Science Monitor*, May 18, 2015. www.csmonitor.com.

King, Martin Luther, Jr. "I Have a Dream." Speech, Washington DC, August 28, 1963. In *King's Dream*, by Eric J. Sundquist, 229–34. New Haven, CT: Yale University Press, 2009.

King, Peter. Commentator on *The Situation Room with Wolf Blitzer*, CNN, December 3, 2014. *Mediaite*. www.mediaite.com.

Kull, Andrew. *The Color-Blind Constitution*. Cambridge, MA: Harvard University Press, 1992.

Kuppers, Petra. *Disability and Contemporary Performance: Bodies on Edge*. New York: Routledge, 2003.

Lasky, Joseph. *Proofreading and Copy-Preparation: A Textbook for the Graphic Arts Industry*. New York: Mentor, 1941.

Lee, Julia H. *Interracial Encounters: Reciprocal Representations in African and Asian American Literatures, 1896–1937.* New York: New York University Press, 2011.

Levy, Eugene. *James Weldon Johnson: Black Leader, Black Voice.* Chicago: University of Chicago Press, 1973.

Lincoln, Abraham. "Gettysburg Address." Speech, Gettysburg, Pennsylvania, November 19, 1863. The Avalon Project: Documents in Law, History, and Diplomacy, Yale Law School. http://avalon.law.yale.edu.

Litwack, Leon F. *Trouble in Mind: Black Southerners in the Age of Jim Crow.* New York: Knopf, 1998.

Lutz, Tom. *American Nervousness, 1903: An Anecdotal History.* Ithaca, NY: Cornell University Press, 1991.

Mackethan, Lucinda H. "Black Boy and Ex-Coloured Man: Version and Inversion of the Slave Narrator's Quest for Voice." *CLA Journal* 32, no. 2 (December 1988): 123–47.

Mansfield, Harvey C., Jr. "Thomas Jefferson." In *American Political Thought: The Philosophic Dimension of American Statesmanship*, 3rd ed., edited by Morton J. Frisch and Richard G. Stevens, 49–68. New York: Routledge, 2017. First published in 1971.

Marable, Manning, and Leith Mullings, eds. *Let Nobody Turn Us Around: Voices of Resistance, Reform, and Renewal: An African American Anthology.* 2nd ed. Lanham, MD: Rowman and Littlefield, 2009.

Margolies, Edward. *Native Sons: A Critical Study of Twentieth-Century Negro American Authors.* Philadelphia: Lippincott, 1968.

McCaskill, Barbara. "William and Ellen Craft (1824–1900; 1826–1891)." *New Georgia Encyclopedia*, September 3, 2002. www.georgiaencyclopedia.org.

———. "'Yours Very Truly': Ellen Craft—The Fugitive as Text and Artifact." *African American Review* 28, no. 4 (Winter 1994): 509–29.

McHenry, Elizabeth. *Forgotten Readers: Recovering the Lost History of African American Literary Societies.* Durham, NC: Duke University Press, 2002.

McMillan, Uri. *Embodied Avatars: Genealogies of Black Feminist Art and Performance.* New York: New York University Press, 2015.

McRuer, Robert. *Crip Theory: Cultural Signs of Queerness and Disability.* New York: New York University Press, 2006.

Meacham, Jon. *Thomas Jefferson: The Art of Power.* New York: Random House, 2013.

Medley, Keith Weldon. *We as Freemen: "Plessy v. Ferguson."* Gretna, LA: Pelican, 2003.

Miller, J. F. "The Effects of Emancipation upon the Mental and Physical Health of the Negro of the South." *North Carolina Medical Journal* 38, no. 10 (November 20, 1896): 285–94. HathiTrust.

Miller, Monica L. *Slaves to Fashion: Black Dandyism and the Styling of Black Diasporic Identity.* Durham, NC: Duke University Press, 2009.

Minich, Julie Avril. *Accessible Citizenships: Disability, Nation, and the Cultural Politics of Greater Mexico.* Philadelphia: Temple University Press, 2014.

Mitchell, David T., and Sharon L. Snyder. *Cultural Locations of Disability.* Chicago: University of Chicago Press, 2006.

———. "Introduction: Disability Studies and the Double Bind of Representation." In *The Body and Physical Difference: Discourses of Disability*, edited by David T. Mitchell and Sharon L. Snyder, 1–32. Ann Arbor: University of Michigan Press, 1997.

———. *Narrative Prosthesis: Disability and the Dependencies of Discourse*. Ann Arbor: University of Michigan Press, 2000.

Mitchell, Jerry. "Bombshell Quote Missing from Emmett Till Tape. So Did Carolyn Bryant Donham Really Recant?" *Clarion Ledger*, August 21, 2018. www.clarionledger.com.

Mitchell, Koritha. *From Slave Cabins to the White House: Homemade Citizenship in African American Culture*. Urbana: University of Illinois Press, 2020.

———. *Living with Lynching: African American Lynching Plays, Performance, and Citizenship, 1890–1930*. Urbana: University of Illinois Press, 2011.

Mollow, Anna. "'When *Black* Women Start Going on Prozac': Race, Gender, and Mental Illness in Meri Nana-Ama Danquah's *Willow Weep for Me*." *MELUS* 31, no. 3 (September 2006): 67–99.

Moore, Susan. "This is how Black people get killed." Facebook post, December 4, 2020. www.facebook.com/susan.moore.33671748/posts/3459157600869878.

Morrison, Toni. *Beloved*. 1987. New York: Vintage Books, 2004.

———. Interview by Charlie Rose. *Charlie Rose*, May 7, 1993. www.charlierose.com.

Moten, Fred. *In the Break: The Aesthetics of the Black Radical Tradition*. Minneapolis: University of Minnesota Press, 2003.

Movement for Black Lives (M4BL). "Vision for Black Lives." 2021. https://m4bl.org.

Muhammad, Khalil Gibran. *The Condemnation of Blackness: Race, Crime, and the Making of Modern Urban America*. 2010. Reprint, Cambridge, MA: Harvard University Press, 2011.

Murakawa, Naomi. *The First Civil Right: How Liberals Built Prison America*. Oxford: Oxford University Press, 2014.

Murder of Emmett Till, The. Produced and directed by Stanley Nelson. PBS, 2003. www.pbs.org.

Nathan, Giri. "Eric Garner Died from Chokehold While in Police Custody." *Time*, August 1, 2014. http://time.com.

"Nation Horrified by Murder of Kidnaped Chicago Youth." *Jet*, September 15, 1955, 6–9.

NBC News. "'Hell No': Garner Family Rejects Cop's Condolences after Grand Jury Decision." December 3, 2014. www.nbcnews.com.

Nelkin, Dorothy, and M. Susan Lindee. *The DNA Mystique: The Gene as a Cultural Icon*. Ann Arbor: University of Michigan Press, 2004.

Nelson, Alondra. *Body and Soul: The Black Panther Party and the Fight against Medical Discrimination*. Minneapolis: University of Minnesota Press, 2011.

———. *The Social Life of DNA: Race, Reparations, and Reconciliation after the Genome*. Boston: Beacon, 2016.

New York Daily News. "Eric Garner Video—Unedited Version." Video by Ramsey Orta. YouTube, July 12, 2015. www.youtube.com/watch?v=JpGxagKOkv8.

Nielsen, Aldon Lynn. *Writing between the Lines: Race and Intertextuality*. Athens: University of Georgia Press, 1994.

Niles' Weekly Register, March 27, 1830, 87–88. HathiTrust.

North Carolina General Assembly. *Acts Passed by the General Assembly of the State of North Carolina, at the Session of 1830–31*. North Carolina Digital Collections. https://digital.ncdcr.gov/.

Northup, Solomon. *Twelve Years a Slave*. 1853. Reprint, New York: Penguin, 2012.

"Old Actor's Memories, An; What Mr. Edmon S. Conner Recalls about His Career." *New York Times*, June 5, 1881, 10. www.nytimes.com.

Olsen, Otto H., ed. *The Thin Disguise: Turning Point in Negro History; "Plessy v. Ferguson," A Documentary Presentation, 1864–1896*. New York: Humanities Press, 1967.

Onuf, Peter S. Introduction to *Notes on the State of Virginia*, by Thomas Jefferson, ix–xiv. New York: Barnes and Noble, 2010.

Parents Involved in Community Schools v. Seattle School District No. 1. 551 U.S. 701 (2007).

Patterson, Orlando. *Slavery and Social Death: A Comparative Study*. Cambridge, MA: Harvard University Press, 1982.

PBS Online. "David Walker, 1796–1830." Accessed June 18, 2020. www.pbs.org.

Penningroth, Dylan C. *The Claims of Kinfolk: African American Property and Community in the Nineteenth-Century South*. Chapel Hill: University of North Carolina Press, 2003.

Perry, David M. "When Disability and Race Intersect." CNN, December 4, 2014. www.cnn.com.

Perry, Imani. *More Beautiful and More Terrible: The Embrace and Transcendence of Racial Inequality in the United States*. New York: New York University Press, 2011.

———. "Racism Is Terrible. Blackness Is Not." *Atlantic*, June 15, 2020. www.theatlantic.com.

Petrie, Paul R. "Charles W. Chesnutt and the Limits of Literary Mediation." In *Conscience and Purpose: Fiction and Social Consciousness in Howells, Jewett, Chesnutt, and Cather*, 109–48. Tuscaloosa: University of Alabama Press, 2005.

Pickens, Therí Alyce. *Black Madness :: Mad Blackness*. Durham, NC: Duke University Press, 2019.

———, ed. "Blackness and Disability." Special issue, *African America Review* 50, no. 2 (Summer 2017).

Pieces I Am, The. Directed by Timothy Greenfield-Sanders. Magnolia Pictures, 2019. Amazon Prime Video.

Piepzna-Samarasinha, Leah Lakshmi. *Care Work: Dreaming Disability Justice*. 2018. Reprint, Vancouver: Arsenal Pulp, 2020.

Plessy v. Ferguson. 163 U.S. 537 (1896). Nexis Uni.

Prather, H. Leon, Sr. *We Have Taken a City: Wilmington Racial Massacre and Coup of 1898*. Rutherford, NJ: Fairleigh Dickinson University Press, 1984.

Priest, Myisha. "'The Nightmare Is Not Cured': Emmett Till and American Healing." *American Quarterly* 62, no. 1 (March 2010): 1–24.

Puar, Jasbir K. *The Right to Maim: Debility, Capacity, Disability*. Durham, NC: Duke University Press, 2017.

Quashie, Kevin. *The Sovereignty of Quiet: Beyond Resistance in Black Culture*. New Brunswick, NJ: Rutgers University Press, 2012.

Quayson, Ato. *Aesthetic Nervousness: Disability and the Crisis of Representation*. New York: Columbia University Press, 2007.

Rawick, George P. *The American Slave: A Composite Autobiography*. Vols. 6–7. New York: Greenwood, 1972.

Redding, J. Saunders. *To Make a Poet Black*. Chapel Hill: University of North Carolina Press, 1939.

Redmond, Shana L. *Everything Man: The Form and Function of Paul Robeson*. Durham, NC: Duke University Press, 2020.

Roach, Joseph. *Cities of the Dead: Circum-Atlantic Performance*. New York: Columbia University Press, 1996.

Roberts, Dorothy. *Killing the Black Body: Race, Reproduction, and the Meaning of Liberty*. 1997. Reprint, New York: Vintage, 2017.

Roberts, Samuel Kelton, Jr. *Infectious Fear: Politics, Disease, and the Health Effects of Segregation*. Chapel Hill: University of North Carolina Press, 2009.

Ross, Marlon B. *Manning the Race: Reforming Black Men in the Jim Crow Era*. New York: New York University Press, 2004.

Rowden, Terry. *The Songs of Blind Folk: African American Musicians and the Cultures of Blindness*. Ann Arbor: University of Michigan Press, 2009.

Ruethling, Gretchen. "FBI Will Exhume the Body of Emmett Till for an Autopsy. *New York Times*, May 5, 2005. www.nytimes.com.

———. "Kin Disagree on Exhumation of Emmett Till." *New York Times*, May 6, 2005. www.nytimes.com.

Ruggles, Jeffrey. *The Unboxing of Henry Brown*. Richmond: Library of Virginia, 2003.

Rusert, Britt. *Fugitive Science: Empiricism and Freedom in Early African American Culture*. New York: New York University Press, 2017.

———. "The Science of Freedom: Counterarchives of Racial Science on the Antebellum Stage." *African American Review* 45, no. 3 (Fall 2012): 291–308.

Russell, Emily. *Reading Embodied Citizenship: Disability, Narrative, and the Body Politic*. New Brunswick, NJ: Rutgers University Press, 2011.

Samuels, Ellen. "'A Complication of Complaints': Untangling Disability, Race, and Gender in William and Ellen Craft's *Running a Thousand Miles for Freedom*." *MELUS* 31, no. 3 (Fall 2006): 15–47.

———. *Fantasies of Identification: Disability, Gender, Race*. New York: New York University Press, 2014.

———. "My Body, My Closet: Invisible Disability and the Limits of Coming-Out Discourse." *GLQ: A Journal of Lesbian and Gay Studies* 9, nos. 1–2 (2003): 233–55.

Sandahl, Carrie. "Black Man, Blind Man: Disability Identity Politics and Performance." *Theatre Journal* 56 (December 2004): 579–602.

———. "Queering the Crip or Cripping the Queer? Intersections of Queer and Crip Identities in Solo Autobiographical Performance." *GLQ* 9, nos. 1–2 (April 2003): 25–56.

Savitt, Todd. *Medicine and Slavery: The Diseases and Health Care of Blacks in Antebellum Virginia*. Urbana: University of Illinois Press, 1978.

Schalk, Sami. *Bodyminds Reimagined: (Dis)ability, Race, and Gender in Black Women's Speculative Fiction*. Durham, NC: Duke University Press, 2018.

Schweik, Susan M. "Disability Politics and American Literary History: Some Suggestions." *American Literary History* 20, nos. 1–2 (Spring–Summer 2008): 217–37.

———. *The Ugly Laws: Disability in Public*. New York: New York University Press, 2009.

Scott, Daryl Michael. *Contempt and Pity: Social Policy and the Image of the Damaged Black Psyche, 1880–1996*. Chapel Hill: University of North Carolina Press, 1997.

"Sen. Bill Cassidy on His State's Racial Disparities in Coronavirus Deaths." *Morning Edition*, NPR, April 7, 2020. www.npr.org.

Sharpe, Christina. *In the Wake: On Blackness and Being*. Durham, NC: Duke University Press, 2016.

Sharpton, Al. "Reverend Al Sharpton Eulogy Transcript at George Floyd's Memorial Service." *Rev*, June 4, 2020. www.rev.com.

Sheridan, Thomas. *A General Dictionary of the English Language*. Vol. 1. 1780. Reprint, Menston, UK: Scolar, 1967.

Sherman, William H. *Used Books: Marking Readers in Renaissance England*. Philadelphia: University of Pennsylvania Press, 2008.

Showalter, Elaine. *The Female Malady: Women, Madness, and English Culture, 1830–1980*. New York: Pantheon, 1985.

Siebers, Tobin. *Disability Theory*. 2008. Reprint, Ann Arbor: University of Michigan Press, 2011.

Sklar, Howard. "'What the Hell Happened to Maggie?': Stereotype, Sympathy, and Disability in Toni Morrison's 'Recitatif.'" *Journal of Literary & Cultural Disability Studies* 5, no. 2 (2011): 137–54.

Slote, Ben. "Listening to 'The Goophered Grapevine' and Hearing Raisins Sing." *American Literary History* 6, no. 4 (Winter 1994): 684–94.

Smith, Shawn Michelle. *Photography on the Color Line: W. E. B. Du Bois, Race, and Visual Culture*. Durham, NC: Duke University Press, 2004.

Smith, Valerie. *Self-Discovery and Authority in Afro-American Narrative*. Cambridge, MA: Harvard University Press, 1987.

Snorton, C. Riley. *Black on Both Sides: A Racial History of Trans Identity*. Minneapolis: University of Minnesota Press, 2017.

———. "'Passing for White, Passing for Man': Johnson's *The Autobiography of an Ex Colored Man* as Transgender Narrative." In *Transgender Migrations: The Bodies, Borders, and Politics of Transition*, edited by Trystan T. Cotten, 107–18. New York: Routledge, 2012.

Somerville, Siobhan B. *Queering the Color Line: Race and the Invention of Homosexuality in American Culture*. Durham, NC: Duke University Press, 2000.

Sontag, Susan. "Illness as Metaphor." In *"Illness as Metaphor" and "AIDS and Its Meta-phors."* New York: Picador, 1990. Originally published in *New York Review of Books* 24, nos. 21–22 (1978).

———. *On Photography.* 1977. Reprint, New York: Picador, 1990.

Spillers, Hortense J. "Mama's Baby, Papa's Maybe: An American Grammar Book." *Diacritics* 17, no. 2 (Summer 1987): 65–81.

Staks Studios. "'I Can't Breathe'—Eric Garner Dies after NYPD Chokehold." YouTube, December 3, 2014. www.youtube.com/watch?v=OWoZ4Mj9028&t=2s.

Stanton, Elizabeth Cady, Susan B. Anthony, and Matilda Joslyn Gage, eds. *History of Woman Suffrage.* Vol. 1, *1846–1861.* 1881. Reprint, New York: Arno, 1969.

Stanton, Lucia C. *"Those Who Labor for My Happiness": Slavery at Thomas Jefferson's Monticello.* Charlottesville: University of Virginia Press, 2012.

State of Virginia. "Act Declaring What Persons Shall Be Deemed Mulattoes, An." October 1785. *Encyclopedia Virginia.* www.encyclopediavirginia.org.

Stepto, Robert B. *From Behind the Veil: A Study of Afro-American Narrative.* 1979. 2nd ed. Urbana: University of Illinois Press, 1991.

———. Introduction to *The Conjure Stories*, by Charles W. Chesnutt, vii–xxvii. New York: Norton, 2012.

———. "'The Simple but Intensely Human Inner Life of Slavery': Storytelling, Fiction, and the Revision of History in Charles W. Chesnutt's 'Uncle Julius Stories.'" In *History and Tradition in Afro-American Culture*, edited by Günter H. Lenz, 29–55. Frankfurt: Campus Verlag, 1984.

Still, William. *The Underground Rail Road.* 1872. Reprint, New York: Arno, 1968.

Stoever, Jennifer Lynn. *The Sonic Color Line: Race and the Cultural Politics of Listening.* New York: New York University Press, 2016.

Sugimori, Masami. "Narrative Order, Racial Hierarchy, and 'White' Discourse in James Weldon Johnson's *The Autobiography of an Ex-Colored Man* and *Along This Way.*" *MELUS* 36, no. 3 (September 2011): 37–62.

Summers, Martin. *Manliness and Its Discontents: The Black Middle Class and the Transformation of Masculinity, 1900–1930.* Chapel Hill: University of North Carolina Press, 2004.

Sundquist, Eric J. *The Hammers of Creation: Folk Culture in Modern African-American Fiction.* Athens: University of Georgia Press, 1992.

———. Introduction to *The Marrow of Tradition*, by Charles W. Chesnutt, vii–xliv. New York: Penguin Books, 1993.

———. *King's Dream.* New Haven, CT: Yale University Press, 2009.

———. *To Wake the Nations: Race in the Making of America Literature.* Cambridge, MA: Harvard University Press, 1993.

Taylor, Keeanga-Yamahtta. *From #BlackLivesMatter to Black Liberation.* Chicago: Haymarket, 2016.

Thebault, Reis, Andrew Ba Tran, and Vanessa Williams. "The Coronavirus Is Infecting and Killing Black Americans at an Alarmingly High Rate." *Washington Post*, April 7, 2020. www.washingtonpost.com.

Thomas, Brook. "Introduction: The Legal Background." In *"Plessy v. Ferguson": A Brief History with Documents*, edited by Brook Thomas, 1–38. New York: Bedford, 1997.

Till-Mobley, Mamie, and Christopher Benson. *Death of Innocence: The Story of the Hate Crime That Changed America*. New York: Random House, 2003.

Toomer, Jean. *Cane*. 1923. Reprint edited by Darwin T. Turner. New York: Norton, 1988.

Tourgée, Albion W. *An Appeal to Caesar*. New York: Fords, Howard, and Hulbert, 1884.

———. "Brief for Plaintiff in Error." In *Landmark Briefs and Arguments of the Supreme Court of the United States: Constitutional Law*, vol. 13, edited by Philip B. Kurland and Gerhard Casper, 27–63. Arlington, VA: University Publications of America, 1975.

TPM TV. "Chris Matthews on Obama: 'I Forgot He Was Black.'" YouTube, January 27, 2010. www.youtube.com/watch?v=Oty9yvo3vPE.

Tyson, Timothy B. *The Blood of Emmett Till*. New York: Simon and Schuster, 2017.

United States v. Wong Kim Ark. 169 U.S. 649 (1898). Nexis Uni.

US Constitution. The Avalon Project: Documents in Law, History, and Diplomacy, Yale Law School. http://avalon.law.yale.edu.

van der Kolk, Bessel A. *The Body Keeps the Score: Brain, Mind, and Body in the Healing of Trauma*. New York: Penguin, 2014.

Van Evrie, John H. *White Supremacy and Negro Subordination; or, Negroes a Subordinate Race and (So-Called) Slavery Its Normal Condition*. New York: Van Evrie, Horton, 1868.

Wagner, Bryan. "Charles Chesnutt and the Epistemology of Racial Violence." *American Literature* 73, no. 2 (June 2001): 311–37.

———. "Disarmed and Dangerous: The Strange Career of Bras-Coupé." *Representations* 92, no. 1 (Fall 2005): 117–51.

Waid, Candace J. "Conjuring the Conjugal: Chesnutt's Scenes from a Marriage." In *The Conjure Stories*, by Charles W. Chesnutt, edited by Robert B. Stepto and Jennifer Rae Greeson, 315–29. New York: Norton, 2012.

Walcott, Rinaldo. *The Long Emancipation: Moving toward Black Freedom*. Durham, NC: Duke University Press, 2021.

Wald, Gayle. *Crossing the Line: Racial Passing in Twentieth-Century U.S. Literature and Culture*. Durham, NC: Duke University Press, 2000.

Waldrep, Christopher. "Word and Deed: The Language of Lynching, 1820–1953." In *Lethal Imagination: Violence and Brutality in American History*, edited by Michael A Bellesiles, 229–60. New York: New York University Press, 1999.

Walker, David. *Walker's Appeal, in Four Articles, Together with a Preamble to the Colored Citizens of the World, but in Particular and Very Expressly to Those of the United States of America. Written in Boston, in the State of Massachusetts, Sept. 28th, 1829*. Boston: David Walker, 1829. Library Company of Philadelphia.

———. *Walker's Appeal, in Four Articles, Together with a Preamble, to the Colored Citizens of the World, but in Particular, and Very Expressly to Those of the United States of America. Written in Boston, in the State of Massachusetts, Sept. 28th , 1829*. 2nd ed. Boston: David Walker, 1830.

———. *Walker's Appeal, in Four Articles; Together with a Preamble, to the Coloured Citizens of the World, but in Particular, and Very Expressly, to Those of the United States of America, Written in Boston, State of Massachusetts, September 28, 1829.* 3rd ed. Boston: David Walker, 1830. Reprint edited by Peter P. Hinks. University Park: Pennsylvania State University Press, 2000. Citations to the *Appeal* refer to the reprint of the third edition, edited by Hinks.

Washington, Harriet A. *Medical Apartheid: The Dark History of Medical Experimentation on Black Americans from Colonial Times to the Present.* 2006. Reprint, New York: Anchor, 2008.

Weheliye, Alexander G. *Habeas Viscus: Racializing Assemblages, Biopolitics, and Black Feminist Theories of the Human.* Durham, NC: Duke University Press, 2014.

Weinauer, Ellen M. "'A Most Respectable Looking Gentleman': Passing, Possession, and Transgression in *Running a Thousand Miles for Freedom.*" In *Passing and the Fictions of Identity*, edited by Elaine K. Ginsberg, 37–56. Durham, NC: Duke University Press, 1996.

Weller, Sheila. "How Author Timothy Tyson Found the Woman at the Center of the Emmett Till Case." *Vanity Fair*, January 26, 2017. www.vanityfair.com.

Welter, Barbara. "The Cult of True Womanhood: 1820–1860." *American Quarterly* 18, no. 2, pt. 1 (Summer 1966): 151–74.

Wheatley, Phillis. "On Being Brought from Africa to America." 1773. In *The Collected Works of Phillis Wheatley*, edited by John C. Shields, 18. 1988. Reprint, New York: Oxford University Press, 1989.

White, Deborah Gray. *Ar'n't I a Woman?: Female Slaves in the Plantation South.* Rev. ed. New York: Norton, 1999.

Wideman, John Edgar. "Looking at Emmett Till." In *In Fact: The Best of Creative Nonfiction*, edited by Lee Gutkind, 24–48. New York: Norton, 2005.

Wilentz, Sean. "Introduction: The Mysteries of David Walker." In *David Walker's Appeal, in Four Articles; Together with a Preamble, to the Coloured Citizens of the World, but in Particular, and Very Expressly, to Those of the United States of America*, by David Walker, vii–xxiii. New York: Hill and Wang, 1995.

Wilkerson, Isabel. *Caste: The Origins of Our Discontents.* New York: Random House, 2020.

Williams, Pat Ward. *Accused/Blowtorch/Padlock.* Whitney Museum of American Art, 1986.

Williams, Patricia J. *The Alchemy of Race and Rights: Diary of a Law Professor.* Cambridge, MA: Harvard University Press, 1991.

———. "The Emperor's New Clothes." BBC Reith Lectures: The Genealogy of Race, 1997. Audio. www.bbc.co.uk.

Wilson, Matthew. *Whiteness in the Novels of Charles W. Chesnutt.* Jackson: University Press of Mississippi, 2004.

Wonham, Henry B. *Charles W. Chesnutt: A Study of the Short Fiction.* Edited by Wonham. New York: Twayne-Simon, 1998.

Wood, Amy Louise. *Lynching and Spectacle: Witnessing Racial Violence in America, 1890–1940.* Chapel Hill: University of North Carolina Press, 2009.

Wood, Marcus. *Blind Memory: Visual Representations of Slavery in England and America 1780–1865*. New York: Routledge, 2000.

Woodward, C. Vann. *The Strange Career of Jim Crow*. 1955. Reprint, Oxford: Oxford University Press, 2002.

Woubshet, Dagmawi. *The Calendar of Loss: Race, Sexuality, and Mourning in the Early Era of AIDS*. Baltimore: Johns Hopkins University Press, 2015.

Wright, Michelle M. *Becoming Black: Creating Identity in the African Diaspora*. Durham, NC: Duke University Press, 2004.

Wright, Richard. "The Literature of the Negro in the United States." 1957. In *White Man, Listen! Lectures in Europe, 1950–56*, 71–109. New York: Harper Perennial, 1995.

Wynter, Sylvia. "Unsettling the Coloniality of Being/Power/Truth/Freedom: Towards the Human, after Man, Its Overrepresentation—An Argument." *CR: The New Centennial Review* 3, no. 3 (Fall 2003): 257–337.

Yarborough, Richard. "Violence, Manhood, and Black Heroism: The Wilmington Riot in Two Turn-of-the-Century African American Novels." In *Democracy Betrayed: The Wilmington Riot of 1898 and Its Legacy*, edited by David S. Cecelski and Timothy B. Tyson, 225–51. Chapel Hill: University of North Carolina Press, 1998.

INDEX

ABOUT THE AUTHOR

Dennis Tyler is Associate Professor in the Department of English at Fordham University. He has received grants and fellowships from the Ford Foundation, Andrew W. Mellon Foundation, Woodrow Wilson Foundation, and Social Science Research Council and was a Postdoctoral Fellow at the University of Virginia's Carter G. Woodson Institute for African-American and African Studies.